PARTY POLITICS IN AMERICA

The seventeenth edition of *Party Politics in America* continues the comprehensive and authoritative coverage of political parties for which it is known while expanding and updating the treatment of key related topics including interest groups and elections. Marjorie Hershey builds on the book's three-pronged coverage of party organization, party in the electorate, and party in government and integrates contemporary examples—such as campaign finance reform, party polarization, and social media—to bring to life the fascinating story of how parties shape our political system.

New to the seventeenth edition:

- Fully updated through the 2016 election, including changes in virtually all of the boxed materials, the chapter openings, and the data presented.
- Explores increasing partisan hostility, the status of voter ID laws and other efforts to affect voter turnout, young voters' attitudes and participation, and the role of big givers such as the energy billionaire Koch brothers in the 2016 campaigns.
- Critically examines the idea that super PACs are replacing, or can replace, the party organizations in running campaigns.
- New and expanded online Instructor's Resources, including author-written test banks, essay questions, relevant websites with correlated sample assignments, the book's appendix, and links to a collection of course syllabi.

Marjorie Randon Hershey is Professor of Political Science at Indiana University, USA.

SEVENTEENTH EDITION

Party Politics in America

MARJORIE RANDON HERSHEY

Indiana University

Foreword by

JOHN H. ALDRICH

Duke University

Routledge
Taylor & Francis Group

NEW YORK AND LONDON

Seventeenth edition published 2017
by Routledge
711 Third Avenue, New York, NY 10017

and by Routledge
2 Park Square, Milton Park, Abingdon, Oxon, OX14 4RN

Routledge is an imprint of the Taylor & Francis Group, an informa business

© 2017 Taylor & Francis

The right of Marjorie Randon Hershey to be identified as author of this work has been asserted by her in accordance with sections 77 and 78 of the Copyright, Designs and Patents Act 1988.

Tenth edition published by Pearson Education, Inc., 2002
Sixteenth edition published by Pearson Education, Inc. 2014, and Routledge, 2016

Library of Congress Cataloging in Publication Data
Names: Hershey, Marjorie Randon, author.
Title: Party politics in America / Marjorie Randon Hershey, Indiana University ; foreword by John H. Aldrich, Duke University.
Description: Seventeenth edition. | New York, NY : Routledge, 2017.
Identifiers: LCCN 2016038261| ISBN 9781138683679 (hardback) | ISBN 9781138683686 (pbk.) | ISBN 9781315544427 (ebook)
Subjects: LCSH: Political parties--United States.
Classification: LCC JK2265 .H477 2017 | DDC 324.273--dc23
LC record available at https://lccn.loc.gov/2016038261

ISBN: 978-1-138-68367-9 (hbk)
ISBN: 978-1-138-68368-6 (pbk)
ISBN: 978-1-315-54442-7 (ebk)

Typeset in Sabon
by Saxon Graphics Ltd, Derby

Visit the companion website: www.routledge.com/9781138683686

BRIEF CONTENTS

CONTENTS

PART III THE POLITICAL PARTY IN THE ELECTORATE 123

FIGURES

TABLES

BOXES

FOREWORD

Why should you be interested in studying political parties? The short answer is that virtually everything important in America's "great Experiment" in democracy is rooted in party politics. Political parties are at the core of American politics and make it what it is today—just as they have virtually from the Founding.

A slightly longer answer is that, today as I write this during the 2016 elections, the parties are newsworthy on two major fronts. They are, at one and the same time, the major structuring feature of the elections—indeed more so over this current generation than in generations preceding—and yet they are today as front and center for their own divisions, especially over this year's presidential nominations. The Democratic contest was surprisingly divided over Hillary Clinton, perhaps the central figure in Democratic party politics, and Bernie Sanders, an avowed socialist for much of his long political career. The Republican contest is perhaps best described as "shockingly" divided, as Donald Trump's rise to nomination as a total outsider (never having held office or even been a Republican until recent years) created chaos on the campaign trail and division within the established party leadership.

Why should you use this book to guide you in the search for understanding democratic politics in America? The short answer is that this book is the best guide you can have, and it has been the best guide in this search for quite a long time.

A longer answer for this question is that I first encountered this text at the same stage in my life you are in now: as an undergraduate, although in my case that was back in the 1960s. At that point, the book was authored by an up-and-coming scholar named Frank Sorauf.[1] Following on the heels of his important study of the effect of political parties on the Pennsylvania legislature,[2] *Party Politics in America* established him as arguably the leading scholar of political parties of his generation. In those days—less so today—it was common for a "textbook" (i.e., a book designed to be used in class) to do more than just tell you what others had written about its subject. Rather, books written for undergraduates were also designed to make a coherent argument about its subject matter—to engage you, the reader, intellectually. So it was then, and with this book, so it remains today.

In the sixth edition, published in 1988, Frank brought in Paul Allen Beck as coauthor. Paul took over the authorial duties beginning with that edition, and Marjorie Randon Hershey did so beginning with the ninth edition in 2001, leading to the book that you are about to read today. Each did so with considerable respect for the substance and the perspective that characterized the previous editions. This has brought a high degree of intellectual continuity to *Party Politics in America*. Most of all, Sorauf, Beck, and Hershey very effectively use a three-part division in the discussion of political parties, considering the political party in its electoral, governing, and organizational roles. These three aspects of a party create a coherent system that (sometimes loosely, sometimes more tightly) provides a degree of integration to the diverse workings of any one political party.

When Sorauf first wrote, the three pieces were rather loosely integrated. Partisanship in the public, for example, was nearly as strongly held as today, but the party in government was deeply divided, especially the majority party, the Democrats (into North and South, or pro- and anti-civil rights), but also the minority Republican Party (into "Wall Street" and "Main Street," or urban vs. suburban, small town, and rural). Today, partisanship is as strong as always. Democratic officeholders, however, are much more strongly united than they were then, and so too are the Republicans, even if they are in some ways divided. They are divided not so much on ideology but on how best to defeat the Democrats in government and enact more conservative legislation than now possible. In addition, the party organizations are much stronger than they were then (and vastly better financed) making their ability to conduct highly partisan campaigns ever more effective.

Even with a highly polarized party system (as this great divide between Republicans and Democrats is called), there are serious strains among the various parts. What, for example, would you do if you were an adviser to the Republican Party faced with the following choice? Do you advise the Republican Speaker of the House, Paul Ryan (Wisc.), to follow the lead of many of your members and work with congressional Democrats to find a solution to our problems? Or do you follow the lead of the former Tea Party and currently House Freedom Caucus calls for holding tight to party positions, not compromising on principle to work with Democrats, expecting that a tough stand will yield electoral rewards in the future?

The second continuity is that Sorauf, Beck, and Hershey see the two major political parties together in the United States as a system. The two-party system has long played a central role in the evolution of American politics (see especially Chapter 7). Although this two-party system has important implications for political dynamics, they also see the two-party system as a part of the intermediary groups in society. By this, the authors mean that the parties serve as points of contact between the public and its government (see Figure 1.2, a figure that I believe has graced this book for all of its editions now).

The third continuity is that each author is a terrific scholar of political parties, and although these continuities have allowed this book to keep its unique intellectual stamp, the transition among authors has also allowed each to bring to the work his or her particular strengths. In the end, this has made the seventeenth edition of the book richer and stronger than ever before. As I noted earlier, Frank Sorauf used his expertise to explain the role of the political party in government. Since then, he became one of the nation's leading experts on the role of money in politics and in later editions reflected that increasingly important but perennially controversial subject.[3] Paul Beck brought a distinguished career of scholarship, examining the role of political parties in the electorate and adding nicely to Frank's expertise about the governing role.[4] Paul is, like Frank and Marjorie Hershey, an expert on American politics. However, Paul is also, more than most of us who study American politics, genuinely knowledgeable about comparative politics.

Marjorie Randon Hershey, through her expertise, has made important contributions to one of the most difficult questions to study: How do candidates and their campaigns shape and how are they shaped by electoral forces?[5] This interaction links the two most important components of the party, elections and governance, into a more coherent whole. It has allowed her to bring clarity to what has become an increasingly confused portion of the field. Marjorie has also closely studied the role of gender in politics, a dimension of party politics that not only has been of long-standing importance from at least the granting of women's suffrage but has also become especially critical with the emergence and growth of the "gender gap."[6] Finally, she has made a long series of contributions to help us understand how to bring meaning to complex events.[7] One special feature of this book is the increased use of narratives from well-known and little-known party figures alike, narratives that serve to bring the subject matter to life.

Not only does each author add a unique and innovative understanding to political parties as they join the continuity of leading scholars who have shaped this book, but also each edition adds new life to the text by considering the politics of the time. This seventeenth edition is not an exception. Here, then, are some of the facets of particular relevance to contemporary politics that I find particularly worth considering (by you that is).

One issue that is critical to all who study American politics is the way that an understanding of politics matters in your life. This is your government, and the political parties are ways in which you can help shape what your government and elected officials do. This is one of the most important meanings of American political parties. They, and the government that they create, are the consequences of you and your political actions. So saying allows me to move more directly to the longer answer about the study of political parties themselves.

At the outset, I mentioned that you should want to study political parties because they are so important to virtually everything that happens in American politics and because political parties are so central to the workings of any democracy. Great, but you are probably asking, "So what questions should I keep in mind as I read this book? What questions will help me understand the material better?" Let me propose as guidelines three questions that are neither too specific nor too general. We are looking, that is, for questions somewhere in between "Are parties good?" on the one hand and

"What role did Boehner's violation of the informal 'Hastert Rule' play in his decision to resign as Speaker in late 2015?" on the other hand.

You are well aware that today politicians can appear magnanimous and statesmanlike if they say that they will be nonpartisan and if they call for Congress to "rise above" partisan politics to be bipartisan. Yet essentially every elected official is a partisan, and essentially every elected official chooses to act in a partisan way much of the time. Why do politicians today, you might ask, speak as if they are of two minds about political parties? Perhaps they actually are. Even if you dismiss this rhetoric as just words, it is the case that the public is of two minds about parties, too. This book, like virtually all written about American political parties, includes quotes from the Founding Fathers warning about the dangers of party and faction, often quoting such luminaries as John Adams, Thomas Jefferson, and James Madison. Yet these very same men not only worried about the dangers of party but were the founders and leaders of our first political parties. So the first question is, "Why are people—leaders and followers, founders and contemporary figures alike—both attracted to and repulsed by political parties?"

Let me suggest two books that might give you additional ways to think about this question. One is Richard Hofstadter's *The Idea of a Party System: The Rise of Legitimate Opposition in the United States, 1780–1840* (Berkeley, CA: University of California Press, 1969). This book is a series of public lectures that Hofstadter gave in which he roots political parties deeply in the American democratic tradition, arguing that they represent the outward manifestation of a change in philosophic understanding of the relationship between citizens and leaders in this, the world's first practicing democracy. Another is Thomas E. Mann and Norman J. Ornstein, *It's Even Worse than It Looks: How the American Constitutional System Collided with the New Politics of Extremism* (New York: Basic Books, 2016). Mann and Ornstein are both political scientists who also worked at major think tanks (The Brookings Institution and the American Enterprise Institute, respectively) applying scholarship to practical politics. In this book, they have made one of the strongest cases for the dangers of hyper partisanship in politics in a partisan polarized era, adding a contemporary account of the classic question of the "idea of a party system."

This question of the purpose of parties in our democracy, both theoretical and practical, leads easily to a second major question that should be in your mind as you work through this book and your course: "How does the individual connect to the political party?" There are two aspects to this question. One is fairly direct—what do parties mean to the individual and how, if at all, has this changed over time? The great work that laid out this relationship in the modern era is *The American Voter* by Angus Campbell, Philip E. Converse, Warren E. Miller, and Donald E. Stokes (New York: John Wiley & Sons, 1960). Many argue that this connection has changed fundamentally. At one extreme, Martin P. Wattenberg has written about the declining relevance of political parties to the voter, such as in his *The Decline of American Political Parties, 1952–1996* (Cambridge, MA: Harvard University Press, 1998), using such striking evidence as a dramatic decline in the willingness or ability of citizens to say what they like or dislike about either of our two major political parties. Others disagree with Wattenberg. Larry Bartels, and in a completely different way, Green, Palmquist, and Schickler, for example, have shown that partisanship remains as influential in shaping the vote as ever.[8] It is certainly the case that today we hear people say, "The government, they ...," and not "The government, we ..." I suspect that few of us think that way. It is certainly common to hear politicians call for a tax cut by claiming that doing so will give the people back their money. Such a statement would not make sense if we thought of the government as being composed of us, ourselves, and thus thought of *our* taxes as using our money to work in *our* government, doing *our* bidding by enacting *our* preferences into legislation selected by *our* representatives whom *we* chose. The question can, however, be cast even more broadly, asking whether the people feel removed from social, cultural, economic, and political institutions, generally, with political parties and the government therefore only one more symptom of a larger ill. This is certainly a part of the concerns that motivated Robert D. Putnam in his *Bowling Alone: The Collapse and Revival of American Community* (New York: Simon & Schuster, 2000). Today that sometimes comes out in the sense that the debate among the politicians in Washington seems to be more about scoring points over the partisan opposition and less about working in the public's interest. This sense of remove peaked during the summer of 2011 in the debate over whether to raise the debt ceiling, in which the elected figures in each party appeared to put the country's economic recovery at risk merely to win their side of a policy dispute.[9]

The change from a trusting, supportive, identified public to one apparently dramatically less so is one of the great changes that took place in American politics over the past half century. A second great change is "polarization," a growing distance between the elected officials of the two parties. That is, compared with 50 years ago, today the Democrats are more liberal and consistently more so than Republicans, who in turn are much more conservative. Although this is not to say that there is anything close to an identical set of beliefs by the members of either party, there is a greater coherence of opinion and belief in, say, the congressional delegations of each party than in earlier times. Even more undeniable is a much clearer divergence between the policy interests and choices of the two parties in Washington than, say, 50 years ago. You might refer to *Polarized Politics: Congress and the President in a Partisan Era* (Washington, DC: CQ Press, 2000), edited by Jon R. Bond and Richard Fleisher, for a variety of fairly early indications of this fact. The question, then, is not whether there is greater polarization today; the question is whether this relative clarity of polarization matters. As usual, there are at least two ways to understand the question. One is simply to ask whether a more polarized Congress yields policies very different from a less polarized one. The readings in Bond and Fleisher generally support that position. Others, for example Keith Krehbiel and David W. Brady and Craig Volden, argue that the Founders' creation of checks and balances makes polarization relatively ineffectual in shaping legislation due to vetoes, compromises necessary between the two chambers, and so on.[10] Even more generally, however, David R. Mayhew has argued that our system generates important legislation regardless of which party is in control or whether they share power under divided partisan control of government.[11] As you might expect, there has been considerable interest in the challenge that Mayhew, Krehbiel, and Brady and Volden have raised. One set of responses can be seen in the Bond and Fleisher volume, another can be found in *The Macro Polity*.[12]

However, this returns us to one of the original questions: Just how closely does the party in the electorate align with the party in government? On this, too, there is considerable disagreement. On the one hand, Alan Abramowitz argues that the partisan public follows only at a degree of lag the polarization of the partisan elite in Washington, while on the other hand, Morris Fiorina argues that the public remains primarily, even overwhelmingly, moderate, and sees the polarization in Washington, but does not follow it. There is, in his words, a "disconnect," presumably caused by political parties and their leaders.[13] And this, of course connects to politics today in a vast number of ways, such as those just discussed. But it also shapes many other aspects of politics: Will the new voter identification laws serve to reduce fraudulent voting or reduce, instead, voter turnout by minorities, young people, and the elderly?

More recently, scholarship has tended to focus on the negative consequences of partisan polarization. For example, Danielle Thomsen finds that polarization affects just who will run for Congress, tending to attract more polarized and discourage less polarizing and more moderate candidates from even trying.[14] Jamie Druckman et al. show how political polarization shapes public opinion in a more polarized way.[15] On the other hand, David Jones finds that polarization has led to a degree of increase in collective accountability of its congressional affiliates in elections.[16] And Gary Jacobson extends that line of argument, in a way, by showing how partisan polarization has also generated increasingly partisan polarization in the public in terms of their evaluations of the incumbent president.[17]

As you can see, we have now reached the point of recently published work. That is, we are asking questions that are motivating the work of scholars today and problems that are motivating the public and its leaders today. So, let's get on with it and turn to the book and the study of political parties themselves.

John H. Aldrich

Duke University

Notes

1   Frank Sorauf passed away on September 6, 2013. We miss him.
2   Frank J. Sorauf, *Party and Representation: Legislative Politics in Pennsylvania* (New York: Atherton Press, 1963).
3   See, for example, Frank J. Sorauf, *Money in American Elections* (Glenview, IL: Scott Foresman/Little, Brown College Division, 1988) or *Inside Campaign Finance: Myths and Realities* (New Haven, CT: Yale University Press, 1992).
4   He has written a great deal on this subject. One illustration that has long been one of my favorites is his "A Socialization Theory of Partisan Alignment," which was originally published in *The Politics of Future Citizens,* edited by Richard Niemi (San Francisco, CA: Jossey-Bass, 1974, pp. 199–219) and reprinted in *Classics in Voting Behavior*, edited by Richard Niemi and Herbert Weisberg (Washington, DC: CQ Press, 1992).
5   See especially her books, *Running for Office: The Political Education of Campaigners* (Chatham, NJ: Chatham House, 1984) and *The Making of Campaign Strategy* (Lexington, MA: D.C. Heath-Lexington, 1974).
6   Especially interesting accounts of the ways the political parties reacted to female suffrage can be found in Anna L. Harvey, *Votes Without Leverage: Women in American Electoral Politics 1920–1970* (Cambridge: Cambridge University Press, 1998) and J. Kevin Corder and Christina Wolbrecht, *Counting Women's Ballots: Female Voters from Suffrage through the New Deal* (Cambridge: Cambridge University Press, 2016).
7   See, for example, "Constructing Explanations for the U.S. State Governors' Races: The Abortion Issue and the 1990 Gubernatorial Elections," *Political Communication* 17 (July–September 2000): 239–262; "The Meaning of a Mandate: Interpretations of 'Mandate' in 1984 Presidential Election Coverage," *Polity* (Winter 1995): 225–254; and "Support for Political Women: Sex Roles," in John C. Pierce and John L. Sullivan, eds., *The Electorate Reconsidered* (Beverly Hills, CA: Sage, 1980), pp. 179–198.
8   Larry M. Bartels, "Partisanship and Voting Behavior, 1952–1996," *American Journal of Political Science* 44 (2000): 35–50. Donald Green, Bradley Palmquist, and Eric Schickler, *Partisan Hearts and Minds: Political Parties and the Social Identities of Voters* (New Haven, CT: Yale University Press, 2002).
9   See the discussion of poll reports in the height of the debate over this concern (July 14, 2001) at http://people-press.org/2011/07/14/the-debt-ceiling-show-down-%E2%80%93-where-the-public-stands (accessed November 29, 2011).
10 Keith Krehbiel, *Pivotal Politics: A Theory of U.S. Lawmaking* (Chicago: University of Chicago Press, 1998); David W. Brady and Craig Volden, *Revolving Gridlock: Politics and Policy from Jimmy Carter to George W. Bush* (Boulder, CO: Westview Press, 2006).
11 David R. Mayhew, *Divided We Govern: Party Control, Lawmaking and Investigations, 1946–1990* (New Haven, CT: Yale University Press, 1991) and *Partisan Balance: Why Political Parties Don't Kill the U.S. Constitutional System* (Princeton, NJ: Princeton University Press, 2011).
12 Robert S. Erikson, Michael B. MacKuen, and James A. Stimson, *The Macro Polity* (Cambridge: Cambridge University Press, 2002).
13 Alan I. Abramowitz, *The Disappearing Center: Engaged Citizens, Polarization and American Democracy* (New Haven, CT: Yale University Press, 2010); Morris

P. Fiorina, *Culture War: The Myth of a Polarized America,* 3rd ed., with Samuel J. Abrams and Jeremy C. Pope (New York: Longman, 2011); and *Disconnect: The Breakdown of Representation in American Politics* with Samuel J. Abrams (Norman, OK: University of Oklahoma Press, 2009).

14 Danielle M. Thomsen, "Ideological Moderates Won't Run: How Party Fit Matters for Partisan Polarization in Congress," *The Journal of Politics* 76, 3 (2014): 786–797.

15 James N. Druckman, Erik Peterson, and Rune Slothuus, "How Elite Partisan Polarization Affects Public Opinion Formation," *American Political Science Review* 107, 1 (2013): 57–79.

16 David R. Jones, "Partisan Polarization and Congressional Accountability in House Elections," *American Journal of Political Science* 54, 2 (2010): 323–337.

17 Gary C. Jacobson, "Partisan Polarization in Presidential Support: The Electoral Connection," *Congress & the Presidency: A Journal of Capital Studies* 30, 1 (2003).

PREFACE

Even the most gifted storyteller would have a hard time coming up with a more outlandish tale than that of the 2016 presidential election. The candidate who outraised his rivals by millions of dollars at the beginning of the primaries had quit in defeat three weeks later. The 2012 Republican presidential candidate called his party's 2016 nominee a phony and a fraud. The heartthrob candidate of most young voters was a rumpled, 73-year-old, self-proclaimed socialist from Vermont. And campaign debate focused not only on the economy and terrorism but also on the size of one candidate's hands as well as his aerodynamically implausible hairstyle.

That's why books about political parties produce new editions with every new election. Although geometry workbooks and Spanish texts may not become outdated quickly, books about American politics do. Consider these changes in only a two-year period: In 2012, Democratic president Barack Obama was handily returned to the White House, and an official Republican study committee acknowledged that voters saw the Republican party as narrow minded, out of touch, and full of "stuffy old white men." Yet, in the 2014 congressional elections, Republicans won their biggest majority in the U.S. House of Representatives since 1930. The job of this new edition of *Party Politics in America* is to explain how these rapid changes, and the drama of the 2016 elections, affect American politics and governance.

But the natural focus on the drama and unexpected results of Donald Trump's victory in 2016 should not obscure the important forces that remained constant. The two major parties continue to be closely balanced at the national level; the presidential popular vote divided 50–50. Even though the major-party presidential candidates' approval ratings were historically low, minor parties have not gained ground. The Democratic and Republican coalitions changed only at the margins in 2016, with non-college-educated white males a bit more prominent among Republican supporters and women a slightly bigger portion of the Democratic coalition. Party and ideological polarization reigns. And most worrisome, the harsh rhetoric and barely veiled calls to violence in the presidential race infused party identification with unprecedented hostility.

New to This Edition

Here are some of the new features of the seventeenth edition:

- Every chapter is updated to include material about the 2016 elections, including election results and campaign finance data incorporated immediately after the election.
- I've revamped Chapter 12 on campaign finance to cut through the complexity with diagrams and a chronological account.
- You'll find more discussion of the role of big givers to the 2016 campaigns, such as the Koch brothers and their many affiliated groups.
- How has the Donald Trump candidacy affected Republican Party organizations, its constituency, and its campaign techniques? Chapters 4, 7, and 11 offer answers.
- Chapters 5 (on political activists) and 8 (on party voter turnout activities) say more about young people's political attitudes and participation, including social media use in politics.
- Both parties are facing a rapidly changing population: many more Hispanic and Latino Americans and a growing group of distrustful twenty- and thirty-somethings. How can the Republicans, in particular, respond to this challenge without turning off their white, married, religious base? See Chapters 6–8 and 16.
- Partisanship has become infused with hostility toward the other side, at a fast-growing pace. What does this do to party politics among voters (see Chapters 6 and 15) and public officials (Chapters 13 and 14)?
- A lot of observers asked in 2016 why minor parties don't compete more effectively with the Republicans and Democrats. Chapters 1 and 2 remind us why two-party politics is so well entrenched in the U.S., even though it is not found in most other Western democracies.
- New and updated Instructor's Resources on the book's webpage (www.routledge.com/9781138683686) include test banks for each chapter with multiple-choice, short answer/identification, and essay questions; an annotated list of websites and correlated sample assignments; the book's appendix incorporating the 2016 election results; and links to a collection of syllabi (including my own).

This book, long known as the "gold standard" of political parties texts, has developed and adapted over a long time period, just as the American parties have. Frank J. Sorauf, a pioneer of modern political science, had the vision to create *Party Politics in America* in 1968, and Paul Allen Beck brought the book into the late 1980s and 1990s, with the intellectual mastery and comparative perspective that has marked his research on parties and voting behavior. Their goal for each new edition was to provide students with the clearest, most comprehensive and engaging understanding of political parties and partisanship, which in turn are key to understanding the workings of elections, public opinion, policy making, and leadership.

Features of This Text

This new edition continues that effort by adding new and updated versions of the features that were so well received in recent editions. The boxes titled "A Day in the Life" tell the personal stories of individuals whose experiences help to illustrate recent changes in the parties. Many of my students see political parties as remote, abstract, and a bit underhanded—something that might interest elderly people, but not teens and twenty-somethings. I hope these compelling stories—for instance, that of a Poli Sci major who spent his sophomore year running for a state legislative seat—can show readers why studying party politics is worth their time.

In other chapters, the feature titled "Which Would You Choose?" illustrates major debates about party politics in summary form: for example, whether encouraging greater voter turnout would help or harm American democracy (see Chapter 8). These mini-essays can provoke classroom debate on fundamental concerns about political parties.

Additional special feature boxes portray examples of "real politics" in action and are strategically distributed throughout the text.

As in previous editions, I've tried to make the reader's job easier by putting important terms in boldface and clearly defining them, emphasizing the vital points, and illustrating them with engaging examples. In addition, for instructors, I have written each chapter to stand alone, so that teachers can assign chapters in any order they choose without leaving their students puzzled because relevant concepts were explained elsewhere.

As elected officials know, good representatives need detailed information about what their constituents want. I've really appreciated hearing from instructors and students what they like about *Party Politics in America* and what they'd like to see changed. I'd like to hear from you as well. You can reach me at hershey@indiana.edu; I'll be happy to respond.

ACKNOWLEDGMENTS

It takes a village to create a book. I have received a great deal of help in researching, writing, and revising this volume: from my graduate and undergraduate students; present and former colleagues at Indiana University, particularly Ted Carmines and Bob Huckfeldt, Bill Bianco, Eileen Braman, Chris DeSante, Mike Ensley, Bernard Fraga, Matthew Hayes, Yanna Krupnikov, Elinor Ostrom, Leroy Rieselbach, John Williams, and Jerry Wright; and departmental staff members Amanda Campbell, Steve Flinn, Sharon Hughes, Sharon LaRoche, Chris McCann, Jan Peterson, James Russell, and Jessica Williams.

Austin Ranney, Leon Epstein, Jack Dennis, and Murray Edelman stimulated my interest in party politics and convinced me of the value of political science. Murray Edelman deserves special mention in that group, not only as a mentor and model for so many of us but also as a much-beloved friend. John Aldrich, one of the most insightful and systematic analysts of political parties, has been kind enough to write the Foreword to the book. I've learned so much as well from Bruce Oppenheimer, Paul Beck, Nate Birkhead, Tony Broh, Tom Carsey, Richard Fenno, Paul Herrnson, John Hibbing, Jennifer Hochschild, David Karol, Geoff Layman, Burdett Loomis, Michael Malbin, Seth Masket, Hans Noel, Kyle Saunders, Kay Schlozman, Brian Silver, Jim Stimson, and John Zaller. Many others provided valuable help with this edition, including Alan Abramowitz, Todd Bradley, Matt Fowler, Audrey Haynes, Scott McClurg, Chuck Prysby, Brad Warren, and Richard Winger.

I was very fortunate to receive suggestions on this edition from a large group of talented people: Lawrence Bensky, California State University-East Bay; David Darmofal, University of South Carolina-Columbia; John Davis, University of Arkansas-Monticello; Michael Hagen, Temple University; Adam Lawrence, Millersville University; Geoff Peterson, University of Wisconsin-Eau Claire; Robert Postic, University of Findlay; Charles Prysby, University of North Carolina-Greensboro; Douglas Roscoe, University of Massachusetts-Dartmouth; Priscilla Southwell, University of Oregon. They and reviewers of previous editions have been central to my efforts to keep the book relevant to students' and instructors' changing needs. And it is a great pleasure to work with the people at Routledge: Jennifer Knerr, Ze'ev Sudry, Alison Daltroy, and the members of the production team.

Most of all, I am very grateful to my family: my husband, Howard, and our daughters, Katie, Lissa, Lani, and Hannah, and grandkiddos Chloe, Parker, Dae'yana, Talan, Jade, and Jack. Everything I do has been made possible by their love and support.

Marjorie Randon Hershey

PART ONE

Parties and Party Systems

On a day in June 2016, 49 people were shot dead in a gay nightclub in Orlando, Florida by a gunman who claimed allegiance to the Islamic State. Later that day, the Democratic president condemned easy access to firearms and hate-filled terrorists. His Republican opponent instead raised questions about the president's loyalties and his immigration policy.

Was this "politics as usual" in the face of unspeakable tragedy? Or was it evidence of a working two-party system, offering voters two alternative explanations for a major national challenge? Just as the two major parties have different answers to domestic terrorism, they also put forward contrasting policies on other matters that affect your life every day, from whether the beer or water you drink should be tested for contaminants to whether your housing should be powered by electricity from coal or from wind energy.

National, state, and local governments make decisions that bear on almost everything you do. Because these government decisions have such great impact, large numbers of groups have mobilized to try to influence the men and women in public office who will make them. In a democracy, the political party is one of the oldest and most powerful of these groups. Parties have a lot of competition, however. Organized interests such as the National Rifle Association and the Gay and Lesbian Victory Fund also work to get the government policies they want, as do pro-life groups and the National Organization for the Reform of Marijuana Laws (NORML). Even organizations whose main purpose is nonpolitical, such as universities, Walmart, and Facebook, try to influence government decisions that affect them.

These groups serve as **intermediaries**—links between citizens and the people in government who make the decisions that affect our lives (Figure I.1). They raise issues that they want government to address. They tell people what government is doing. By bringing together people with shared interests, they amplify these people's voices in speaking to government. They keep an eye on one another as well as on the actions of public officials.

1

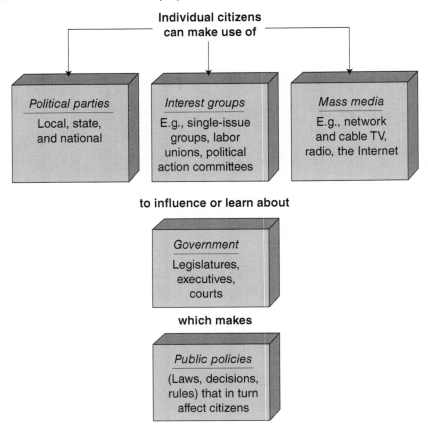

FIGURE I.1 Parties and Other Intermediaries Between Citizens and Government

Different intermediaries specialize in different political activities. Parties focus on nominating candidates, helping to elect them, and organizing those who win. Most organized interests represent narrower groups; they are not likely to win majority support so they try instead to influence the views of candidates who do win office—and of appointed officials, such as bureaucrats and judges. In other democracies, parties may behave differently. The American parties, for example, concentrate on election activities, whereas many parties in Europe have been more committed to keeping their elected officials faithful to the party's program.

Parties compete fiercely with one another. They also vie with interest groups for money, expertise, and volunteer help and then, with those resources in hand, for the support of individual citizens and elected officials. Parties must even fight for a major role in political campaigns; the American parties are not nearly as dominant in the business of campaigning as they were a century ago.

In spite of (or because of) their central role in government, parties provoke very mixed feelings. Large numbers of Americans claim to hate them. Leaders ranging from Washington and Madison to the Progressive movement to the present day have equated parties with "boss rule" and tried to reform or weaken them. This public hostility has led state legislatures to restrict what parties can do and how they can organize. Yet most Americans continue to consider themselves partisans, and parties have coped with these reforms over time by adapting their organizations and activities. The political parties of the 2010s would hardly be recognizable to politicians of a century ago, and the parties that we know today will probably change dramatically in the coming decades.

By the time you finish this book, you'll be able to explain how the American parties developed, the many ways they affect your life, and what they are capable of contributing to a democratic politics. What you read will challenge your ideas about whether political parties are essential to the survival of a democracy, whether they benefit you as a citizen, and how you intend to act as a mover of a representative political system.

CHAPTER 1

What Are Political Parties?

It was a harrowing campaign. During the 2016 election season, presidential candidates referred to one another as "the devil," "stupid," and "unhinged." A Republican Party office in North Carolina was firebombed. Staff members of the *Arizona Republic* were hit with death threats after the paper endorsed a Democratic presidential candidate for the first time in its history.

American politics is more polarized now than it has been in more than a century. On a 0-to-100 scale of favorability, two-thirds of Democrats in 2016 gave Republican presidential candidate Donald Trump a rating of *zero*, and 59 percent of Republicans assigned that dismal rating to Democrat Hillary Clinton. Substantial proportions even view the other party's policies as "so misguided that they threaten the nation's well-being," as you can see in Figure 1.1.[1]

This political polarization does not stem just from bad manners or the influence of "reality TV." It reflects the fact that although most Americans agree on such lofty goals as freedom and national security, we differ greatly on how to reach those goals. "The main reason it is so hard for Democrats and Republicans in Washington to cooperate," one analyst argues, "is ... that they disagree profoundly about the major issues facing the country."[2] Not only in Congress but also in state legislatures and even in courtrooms, Democrats typically hold different views from Republicans about guns, same-sex marriage, taxes, immigration, and other issues. The gulf between the parties in government has grown so dramatically that the U.S. House elected in 2014 was the most polarized in American history, and the picture is not likely to change in 2017 and 2018.

As a result, a shift from Democratic to Republican control of Congress and the White House can now lead to a major change in public policies, as is happening in 2017. In 2008 and 2009, the Democratic-majority House was the most liberal in the past three decades. Yet, just a year later, the Republican swing in the 2010 elections produced the most conservative House in that period.[3] These party conflicts may be painful to watch, and they contribute to the rock-bottom levels of public confidence in Congress.[4]

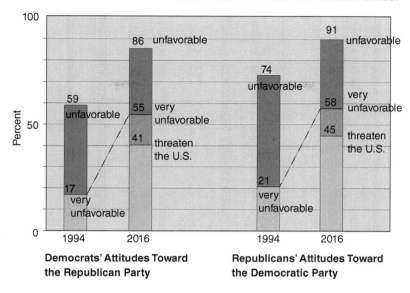

FIGURE 1.1 Partisans' Hostility Toward the Other Party, 1994 and 2016

Note: The question asked in 1994 and 2016 was, "Would you say your overall opinion of the Republican/Democratic Party is very favorable, mostly favorable, mostly unfavorable, or very unfavorable?" In 2016, the survey added, "And [if very unfavorable,] would you say the Republican/Democratic Party's policies are so misguided that they threaten the nation's well-being, or wouldn't you go that far?" Those who answered "mostly" or "very" unfavorable are categorized as "unfavorable."

Source: Adapted from Pew Research Center, "Partisanship and Political Animosity in 2016," June 23, 2016, at www.people-press.org/2016/06/22/partisanship-and-political-animosity-in-2016/ (accessed June 23, 2016).

However, they also help us to clarify our voting choices and hold elected officials accountable to the people. That benefits a democracy.

Hostility between the parties is not new. Nor is hostility toward the parties themselves. George Washington declared in his Farewell Address that "the spirit of party" was the "worst enemy" of popular government. Parties, he feared, would encourage people to pursue their narrow self-interest at other people's expense and cause jealousy, division, and revenge. Without parties, in his view, we'd be more likely to get noble and uncorrupted leaders who could speak for the nation as a whole. Washington's dream of a government "above parties" has long been widely shared. Then, if so many are disgusted by partisan conflict, why is the American political system still driven by partisan conflict? Why do we still have political parties?

The main reason is simply that political parties do necessary things for us that wouldn't get done otherwise. Most people are not very interested in politics, so how would they decide on a candidate without the guidance that party labels provide? Will they spend hours researching the backgrounds and issue stands of dozens of candidates? Would you?

Without parties, how would Americans choose a president? In the absence of party primaries and caucuses, who would have the power to winnow the thousands of presidential wannabes to the very few who will run in the general election? Could members of Congress make that decision? Not in a system designed to separate legislative from executive powers. How about nomination by the nation's mayors and other elected officials, as happens in France? A new version of the television series *Survivor*?

Strong party organizations bring voters to the polls. Without political parties, would voter turnout, already lower in the United States than in most other industrialized democracies, drop even further? How would members of Congress elected as individuals, with no party loyalties to guide them, put together majorities to pass packages of legislation?

Who runs this political organization that is so needed and yet so distrusted? Does "the party" include only the politicians who share a party label when running for and holding public office? Does it also include activists who work on campaigns, citizens who vote for a party's candidates, or interest groups that share a party's aims? Or is a party any group that chooses to call itself a party, whether Democratic or Tea?

The Three Parts of Parties

Most scholars would agree that *a party is a group organized to nominate candidates, to try to win political power through elections, and to promote ideas about public policies.* For many analysts, the central figures in a political party are the candidates and elected officials who share a party's label. Anthony Downs, for example, sees a political party as "a coalition ... seeking to control the governing apparatus by legal means ... [through] duly constituted elections or legitimate influence."[5] Many parties in democratic nations, including the United States, began as groups of political leaders who organized to advance certain policies by winning elections.

Most observers, however, see the American parties as including more than just candidates and officeholders. As John Aldrich points out, parties are organizations—institutions with a life and a set of rules of their own, beyond that of their candidates.[6] Interested individuals can become active in political parties and help set their directions and strategies, just as one would do in a sports team or a student group. These activists and organizations are central parts of the party, too.

Some researchers urge us to define "party" even more broadly, to include other groups that ally with a party's elected officials and organization, such as interest groups and even media organizations. The Republican Party, then, would be seen as encompassing small business lobbies, conservative Christian groups, and media people such as Rush Limbaugh and Glenn Beck, whereas the Democratic Party's umbrella would cover labor unions, environmental and feminist groups, and media outlets with a liberal slant. These groups are "policy demanders" who work in tandem with party organizations to achieve mutual aims.[7]

It is tempting to close our definition at this point and to view the American parties solely as teams of political specialists—elected officials, candidates, party leaders, activists, and organizations—who compete for power and then exercise it. That leaves the rest of the population on the outside of the parties, which many citizens may prefer. Yet this would ignore an important reality: Parties are rooted in the lives and feelings of citizens as well as candidates and political activists. Even though the American parties do not have formal, dues-paying "members," most voters develop such strong and enduring attachments to a particular party that they are willing to tell a pollster, "I'm a Democrat" or "I'm a Republican," and to develop strong negative feelings about the other party. And when writers refer to a "Democratic sweep" or a "Republican area," they see parties that include voters and other supporters as well as officeholders, office seekers, and activists.

The Progressive movement of the late 1800s and early 1900s, which promoted voter registration and the use of primary elections to nominate candidates, strengthened the case for including a citizen base in a definition of American parties. Voters in primary elections make the single most important decision for their party: who its candidates will be. In most other democracies, only the party leaders and activists have the power to make this choice.

Because American voters have the right to nominate the parties' candidates, the line that separates party leaders from followers in most other nations becomes blurred in the United States. American voters are not only consumers who choose among the parties' "products" (candidates) in the political marketplace but also managers who decide which products will be introduced in the first place. Making consumers into managers has transformed political parties, just as it would revolutionize the market economy. So it makes sense to include citizen-supporters as parts of the parties, because they are not just the targets of party activity but also hold the power to tell the party organization who its candidates will be.[8]

In short, the major American parties are composed of three interacting and overlapping parts. These are: the **party organization**, which includes party leaders and the activists who work for party causes and candidates; the **party in government**, composed of the men and women who run for and hold public office on the party's label; and the **party in the electorate**, or those citizens who express an attachment to the party (see Figure 1.2).[9] We explore each of these parts separately, keeping in mind that the character of the American parties is defined by the ways in which they intersect and overlap.[10]

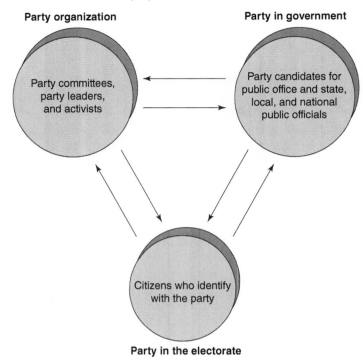

FIGURE 1.2 The Three Parts of American Political Parties

The Party Organization

Party organizations are made up of people who hold party jobs with titles—the national and state party chairs and other officers; the county, city, ward, and precinct leaders and committee people (see Chapters 3 and 4)—and other supporters who are devoted enough to volunteer their time, money, and skills to advancing the party's aims (see Chapter 5). These groups are charged with promoting *all* of the party's candidates and its stands on major issues, not just an individual candidate or two. Some party leaders or activists may be waiting for the right time to run for public office (and thus cross over into the party in government). Others have been pressed into service as candidates for Congress or city clerk when nobody else wanted the job.

The Party in Government

The party in government consists of the candidates for public office and those who hold office, whether elected or appointed, who share a party label (see Chapters 13 and 14). The major figures here are presidents, governors, judges, Congress members, state legislators, bureaucrats, mayors, and other local officials who hold the same party affiliation.

Members of the party in government do not always cooperate smoothly with people in the party organization.[11] They often work together to meet shared goals, but they may have different priorities in reaching those goals. A senator, for example, may be trying to raise as much campaign money as possible, because she believes that a landslide victory will improve her chances of running for president later. At the same time, the party organization's leaders may be hoping that some of her campaign contributors will fund other, more vulnerable party candidates instead, so the party can get or keep a majority in Congress.

These two parts of the parties also contend for leadership of the party as a whole. When reporters want to get a "Republican view" on an issue such as immigration, they will often interview a source in the White House, if the president is a Republican, or a Republican leader in Congress; these members of the party in government are often assumed to speak for the party. Leaders of the party's organization, such as the Florida state Republican Party chair, might want to put a different spin on the issue. But presidents and congressional party leaders do not have to clear their pronouncements with the party organization, nor can they be controlled by it. These tensions and the competition for scarce resources show why it is helpful to treat the party organization and the party in government as separate parts of the party.

The Party in the Electorate

The party in the electorate consists of the women and men who *see themselves* as Democrats or Republicans: citizens who feel some degree of loyalty to the party, even if they have never set foot in the party's headquarters or met its candidates. We call them **partisans** or **party identifiers**. As you'll see in Chapter 6, the great majority of Americans consider themselves partisans. Many of these partisans declared themselves to be a Democrat or Republican when they registered to vote; more than half of the states require citizens to register by party. Others see themselves as partisans even if they never cast a ballot.

Partisans usually support their party's candidates and issue stands, but nothing forces them to do so. In general elections, they may vote for one of their party's candidates and reject another; in primaries, they may decide to saddle the party with a candidate that the organization can't stand. However, they are vitally important as the core of the party's electoral support. Without this reliable base, the party would have to work much harder to win and keep power.

This relationship between the party organization and the party in government, on the one hand, and the electoral party, on the other, is one of the most striking characteristics of the major American parties. Other political organizations—interest groups such as teachers' unions and oil companies—try to attract public support, but these supporters remain outside the group's organization. In contrast, in the American parties, the party in the electorate is not just an external target to be mobilized. In addition to its power to choose the parties' candidates by voting in primaries, in many states the electoral party selects local *party* officials, such as precinct committee leaders. Thus, the major American party is an open, inclusive, permeable organization. The extent to which citizens can affect the choice of its leaders and candidates sets it apart from parties in most other democracies.

What Parties Do

Political parties in every democracy engage in three sets of activities to at least some degree. They select candidates and contest elections; they try to educate citizens about issues important to the party; and they work to influence government to provide certain policies and other benefits.[12] Parties and party systems differ in the degree to which they emphasize each of these activities, but no party can completely ignore any of them.

Elect Candidates

Parties often seem completely absorbed by their efforts to elect candidates. Parties are goal-oriented, and in American politics, achieving goals depends on winning elections. The need to elect candidates links the three parts of the parties. Party leaders and activists committed to a particular elected official join with other members of the party in government and with party identifiers to return that official to office.[13]

Educate (or Propagandize) Citizens

Parties also try to teach or propagandize citizens. (If you like their message, you might call it "voter education." If not, it may sound like propaganda.) They work to focus voter attention on the issues that bind the party together and downplay issues that might split their adherents. The Democrats and Republicans do not promote all-inclusive ideologies like those of a fundamentalist Islamic party. They do, however, represent the beliefs and interests of the groups that identify with and support them. In this sense, the Republicans are usually linked with business and conservatives, and Democrats are often seen as the party of labor and the disadvantaged.

Govern

Almost all American national and state elected officials run for office as either Democrats or Republicans, and their partisanship affects every aspect of the way government works. The legislatures of 49 states[14] and the U.S. Congress are organized along party lines. Although some issues may divide a party, there has been an impressive amount of party discipline in legislative voting in recent decades. In executive branches, presidents and governors usually choose cabinet officers and agency heads of their own party. Even the courts show evidence of the guiding hand of partisanship, though in more subtle ways.

Extended Party Networks

The American parties do not have a monopoly on educating citizens, working to elect candidates, or governing. Interest groups such as the NRA, other organizations such as churches and corporations, and media organizations ranging from networks to bloggers try to affect at least one of these goals. Sometimes parties compete with these groups, as occurred in 2016 when many Republican partisans supported Donald Trump for president but big Republican funders such as the Koch brothers did not. In many local elections, groups backing or opposing a new sports stadium or a referendum on school tax rates try to influence primaries or urge candidates to run. Parties also cooperate with other like-minded political and non-political organizations to achieve particular policy aims, to the point where (as noted on page 6) some observers view these groups as part of the party itself. At the least, parties often maintain long-lasting alliances with non-party groups and some media outlets. Civil rights groups work closely with the Democratic Party and gun rights groups with the Republicans, even though the groups in this "party network" may disagree at times on candidates or preferred tactics.

Because the American parties' activities center on electing candidates, the party in government dominates the party to a degree unusual among Western democracies. In parties more strongly committed to educating citizens about the party's ideology—European Marxist parties, for instance—party organizations are more likely to be able to dictate to the legislative parties, telling them what to emphasize and holding them accountable for their votes.

The Effects of Party Activity

How do these party activities affect American politics? Parties help people make sense of the complexities of politics. Most of us don't pay much attention to government. Parties simplify issues and elections for us; thus, people can make sensible choices in politics even when they don't have a lot of political information, by using their party attachment as a guide for evaluating candidates and issues. By making it easier for citizens to form political judgments, parties ease the way for people to become politically active. They educate Americans by transmitting political information and values to large numbers of current and future voters.

The American parties also help aggregate and organize political power. They put together individuals and groups into blocs that are powerful enough to govern. So in the political world as well as within the individual, parties help to focus political loyalties on a small number of alternatives and then to build support for them. Parties also provide an organized opposition. That is not a popular role to play; the behavior of a constant adversary may seem like that of a sore loser. But an organized opposition is vital to a democracy because it has a natural incentive—its own ambition—to serve as a watchdog on a powerful government. Few of us would be willing to devote the time and effort to play this important role on our own.

Because they are so focused on contesting elections, the parties dominate the recruitment of political leaders. Large numbers of legislators, political executives, and even judges entered public service through party activity. Because they are constants in the election process, parties help to make changes in government leadership more routine and orderly. In nations where parties are not stable from one election to the next, leadership changes can be much more disruptive.

Finally, the parties are capable of bridging the separation of powers in order to get things done (though they may not always choose to do so). The U.S. government was designed to fragment political power, so that no single group could gain enough of it to become a tyrant. The division between the national government and the states, multiplied by the separation of powers at each level, does an impressive job of fragmenting power. The challenge is to make these fragmented units work together to solve problems. Democrats in Congress have a motive to work with a Democratic president—their shared desire for their party to win, in order to achieve their shared goals— to pass legislation their party favors. So do Republicans. Thus, the two major national parties can provide a basis for cooperation within a government marked by decentralization and division.

How Do Parties Differ from Other Political Groups?

We have seen that parties have a lot of competition as intermediaries between citizens and government. *All* political organizations, not just parties, try to educate at least some citizens and mobilize their supporters either to win public office or to influence those who do win. Both parties maintain close working relationships with a variety of organized interests, research groups, and media outlets with shared concerns. How do parties differ from these other political organizations?

Parties Are Paramount in Elections

Above all, a party can be distinguished from other political organizations by its role in structuring elections. In most elections, candidates are listed on the ballot as "Democrat" or "Republican"; they are not listed as "NRA member" or "LGBTQ rights activist." It is the major parties that normally recruit the election clerks and the poll watchers, not the AARP. The parties are paramount among political groups in contesting elections.

They Have a Full-Time Commitment to Political Activity

The major American parties are fully committed to political activity; it is their sole reason for existing. Interest groups and other political organizations, in contrast, move frequently from political to nonpolitical activities and back again. A teachers' union, for example, exists mainly for the purpose of collective bargaining for better pay and working conditions. It may turn to political action to oppose unfriendly candidates or to lobby Congress against antiunion legislation, but its interests are rooted in the workplace. Parties live entirely in the political world.

They Mobilize Large Numbers

An interest group, such as an organization that wants to legalize the carrying of concealed weapons on college campuses, does not need millions of supporters to persuade Congress to pass a bill; it may be able to succeed with only a few strategists and a well-mobilized clientele. However, because winning elections is so vital to parties' goals, parties must mobilize an enormous range of supporters to win large numbers of races. The result is that in a system such as that of the United States, a major party cannot afford to represent only a narrow range of concerns.

They Endure

The American parties are unusually stable and long-lived. Most business, environmental, and single-issue groups are mere juveniles by comparison. Both major American parties can trace their histories for more than 150 years, and many of the major parties in other Western democracies also have impressive life spans. This remarkable endurance adds to their value for voters. The parties are there as points of reference election after election and candidate after candidate, giving continuity to the choices Americans face and the issues they debate.

They Serve as Political Symbols

Finally, political parties differ from other political organizations in the extent to which they operate as symbols, or emotion-laden objects of loyalty. For tens of millions of Americans, the party label is a social identity, like that of an ethnic or religious group. It is the chief cue for their decisions

Is the Tea Party a Party?

During the Great Recession in 2009, President Obama proposed to help homeowners who were about to default on their mortgage payments. CNBC correspondent Rick Santelli protested that this would force responsible people to pay their "loser" neighbors' mortgages. He called for a new "tea party," similar to the American colonists' protest against British rule by throwing highly taxed British tea into Boston Harbor. Conservative talk radio hosts urged their listeners to call Congress members demanding a repeal of the Affordable Care Act (so-called "Obamacare"). By 2011, polls showed that about one in five Americans—mainly older, white, Republican conservatives—supported the Tea Party movement. Prominent Republicans such as Marco Rubio championed its cause. Tea Partyers focused much of their anger on President Obama and government-funded social services to people they defined as "undeserving," including younger people and undocumented immigrants, though they didn't object to Social Security and Medicare, programs that benefited older people including many Tea Partyers. Tea Party-backed conservatives defeated several mainstream Republican incumbents in 2010 Republican primaries. By 2016, however, the tea was growing cold. Obama's reelection astonished and dismayed many Tea Party activists, and public approval of the Tea Party had dropped.

If the Tea Party has some national leaders, local supporters, and a deeply felt issue, then is it a political party? Not yet. Most Tea Partyers continue to identify as Republicans, though many have criticized Republican congressional leaders for not doing enough to shrink government. Political parties differ from other political organizations in that only the party has the power to nominate candidates. In 2016, the "Tea Party" label was rarely on the ballot; the two major parties have long made it difficult for any group except Democrats and Republicans to get ballot access for their party labels and candidates. Thus, Tea Party activists had to educate their followers as to which Republican candidates favored the group's principles. So, although the Tea Party's colorful and angry protests have grabbed a lot of media attention, the group has functioned more as a movement within the Republican Party—distinctive mainly by its refusal to compromise—than as a party in its own right. To grow into a political party, the movement's adherents would need to do the intensive work of achieving ballot access and running candidates from the local to the national level, developing more of an organizational structure, and agreeing on a platform.

Sources: See Juraj Medzihorsky, Levente Littvay, and Erin K. Jenne, "Has the Tea Party Era Radicalized the Republican Party?" *PS: Political Science and Politics* 47 (2014): 806–812, and Amy Fried and Douglas B. Harris, "The Strategic Promotion of Distrust in Government in the Tea Party Age," *The Forum* 13 (2015): 417–443.

about candidates or issues; it relates their values to the real choices made in American politics.

Remember that the differences between parties and other political organizations are differences of degree. Interest groups do become involved in elections, and the larger organized interests serve as political symbols, too. Groups such as the Sierra Club can recruit candidates, promote their endorsed candidates to their members and friends, and get their supporters to the polls on Election Day. Other groups may do the same (see box "Is the Tea Party a Party?" on page 14). Interest groups also promote issue positions, try to influence officeholders, and give money to campaigns. But candidates are listed on the ballot as representatives of a party, not of an interest group.

In some respects, the major parties have more in common with some of the larger interest groups, such as the NRA and the AARP, than they do with minor or third parties. Most minor parties are electoral organizations in name only. Most of their candidates are in no danger of needing a victory speech on election night. They may have few or no local organizations. Their membership base may be just as narrow as that of most interest groups. However, minor parties may qualify to be listed on the ballot, and their candidates can receive public funding where it is available and where they can meet the criteria for it. In these ways (and sometimes *only* in these ways), they can be more like the major parties than the large interest groups.

How the American Parties Developed

The world's first political parties were created in the United States. For more than 200 years, the development of the American parties has been closely interrelated with the expansion of popular democracy. At times during their history, the party in government, then the party organizations, and then both the parties in government and in the electorate have taken the dominant role within the parties.[15]

The Founding of American Parties

Although the founders of the American government hated the thought of factions, they nevertheless began taking sides soon after the new government was formed, because they disagreed on big issues. The dominant group, led by the ambitious young treasury secretary Alexander Hamilton, believed that the nation's economic survival required centralized (federal government) control over the economy, especially by the executive branch. These **Federalists** pushed for a central banking system and high tariffs (taxes on imported goods) to protect newly developing American industries and to help fund the federal government (see box "The American Major Parties" on page 17).

Thomas Jefferson, James Madison, and others objected. They felt that Hamilton's proposals made the federal government too powerful and threatened states' rights. Each group gathered in meetings, called "caucuses," to plan how to get their ideas adopted. During the 1790s, these alignments took a more enduring form. Their differences, as is the case now, were both principled and personal; as historian David McCullough reports, the animosity between Hamilton and Jefferson "had reached the point where they could hardly bear to be in the same room. Each was certain the other was a dangerous man intent on dominating the government."[16]

These early parties, then, were formed largely "from the top" by people in government. They focused at first on issues that concerned the national leaders who formed them—not surprisingly at a time when most Americans played only an indirect role in politics. At this time, in almost every state the vote was restricted to free men who could meet property-owning or taxpaying requirements. Even these relatively small numbers of voters had limited power, as the writers of the Constitution intended. The president was chosen not directly by the voters, but indirectly by the Electoral College. U.S. Senators were selected not by the voters but by the state legislatures. Only members of the House of Representatives were selected by direct popular vote. This cautious start for democratic self-government produced very limited political parties.

Because Jefferson's supporters were in the minority in Congress, their main hope of passing legislation was to elect more Jeffersonians. They collaborated with like-minded "discussion clubs" formed in local communities to oppose Federalist officeholders. Sympathizers at the grassroots level joined in "committees of correspondence" between national and local leaders. Each side established one or more newspapers to propagandize for its cause. As early as the middle of the 1790s, less than ten years after the Constitution was adopted, almost all national politicians had aligned with either the Jeffersonian **Democratic-Republicans** (often called just Republicans) or Hamilton's Federalists, and these incipient parties had taken sides on the major issues facing the new government.[17]

The more elitist Federalists could not keep up, however, either in grassroots organizing or in winning elections. The Federalist candidate for president, John Adams, was defeated by Jefferson in 1800, and the Federalists faded into history during the next two decades. In short, the pressures for democratization were already powerful enough by the early 1800s to cripple an infant party whose leaders in the government could not adapt to the need to organize a mass electorate. Yet the Federalists gave a historic gift to American democracy. They accepted Adams's defeat in 1800 and handed control of the presidency to their Jeffersonian rivals.[18]

The Democratic-Republicans, who were the party of farming interests, the less-privileged, the South (including its wealthy landowners), and the frontier, then held a one-party monopoly for almost 20 years. They dominated American politics so thoroughly by the time of James Monroe's election in 1816 that the absence of party conflict was called the "Era of Good Feelings." Despite the decline of one party and the rise of another,

The American Major Parties

There have been only five major political parties in more than two centuries of American history:

1. **The Federalist Party, 1788–1816.** The champion of the new Constitution and strong national (federal) government, it was the first American political institution to resemble a political party, although it was not a full-fledged party. Its strength was rooted in New England and the Atlantic Seaboard, where it attracted the support of bankers, shopkeepers, manufacturers, landowners, and other established families of wealth and status. Limited by its narrow electoral base, compared with that of the Democratic-Republicans, it soon faded.

2. **The Democratic-Republican (Jeffersonian) Party, 1800–1832.** Many of its leaders had been strong proponents of the Constitution but opposed the extreme nationalism of the Federalists. It was a party of small farmers, workers, and less-privileged citizens, plus southern planters, who preferred the authority of the state governments to that of the national government. Like its leader, Thomas Jefferson, it shared many of the ideals of the French Revolution, especially the extension of the right to vote and the notion of direct popular self-government.

3. **The Democratic Party, 1832–Present.** Growing out of the Andrew Jackson wing of the Democratic-Republicans, it was the first really broad-based, popular party in the United States. On behalf of a coalition of less-privileged voters, it opposed such business-friendly policies as national banking and high tariffs. It also welcomed new immigrants (and sought their votes) and opposed nativist (anti-immigrant) sentiment.

4. **The Whig Party, 1834–1856.** This party, too, had roots in the old Democratic-Republican Party, but in a faction that opposed the Jacksonians. Its greatest leaders, Henry Clay and Daniel Webster, stood for legislative supremacy and protested the strong presidency of Andrew Jackson. For its short life, the Whig Party was an unstable coalition of many interests, among them nativism, property, and business and commerce.

5. **The Republican Party, 1854–Present.** The Republicans first formed to oppose slavery. As the Civil War approached, the new party came to stand for the Union, the North, Lincoln, the freeing of slaves, victory in the Civil War, and the imposition of Reconstruction on the South. From the Whigs it also inherited a concern for business and industrial expansion.

however, the nature of party politics did not change much during this period. It was a time when government and politics were the business of an elite group of well-known, well-established men, and the parties reflected the politics of the time. Without party competition, leaders felt no need to organize more fully at the grassroots, so the parties' further development was stalled.

American politics began to change markedly in the 1820s. By then, most states had eliminated the requirement that only landowners could vote. The suffrage was extended to all white males, at least in state and federal elections. The growing push for democratization also led state and local governments to make more and more public officials popularly elected rather than appointed.[19]

Another big change at this time affected the election of a president. The framers of the Constitution had crafted an unusual selection process; they specified that each state, in a manner selected by its legislature, would choose a number of presidential voters (electors) equal to the size of its congressional delegation. Collectively called the Electoral College, these electors would meet in the state to cast their votes for president. The candidate who received a majority of the states' electoral votes became president. If no candidate won a majority, the president was to be selected by the House of Representatives, with each state casting one vote.

This Electoral College was an ingenious invention. By leaving the choice of electors to the state legislatures, the framers avoided having to set uniform election methods and voting requirements. Even if the framers themselves had agreed on these rules, some states might have objected to federal control over them. (The most explosive question was, of course, whether and how to count slaves in a state's population.) Requiring electors to meet simultaneously in their respective states helped prevent a conspiracy among electors from different states to put forward their own choice for president. At first, states used a variety of methods for choosing presidential electors. By the 1820s, popular election had become the most common method.[20]

This growing enthusiasm for popular control also raised doubts about whether the party's congressional caucus should have the power to *nominate* presidential candidates for the Electoral College to consider. Some criticized caucus nominations as the actions of a small and self-appointed elite. The congressional party caucus was losing its role as the major force within the parties as the nation entered a new phase of party politics.

A National Two-Party System Emerges

The Era of Good Feelings gave way to a two-party system that has prevailed ever since. The Democratic-Republicans had developed factions that chose divorce rather than reconciliation. Andrew Jackson led the frontier and agrarian wing of the Democratic-Republicans, the inheritors of the Jeffersonian tradition, into what is now called the **Democratic Party**.

Another faction of the old Democratic-Republicans who had promoted Adams for president in 1824 and 1828 later merged with the **Whigs** (an old English term referring to those who opposed the dominance of the king, by whom they meant Jackson). That created two-party politics in the United States.

Just as important, the parties developed a much bigger nationwide grassroots (citizen) base. Larger numbers of citizens were now eligible to vote, so the presidential campaigns became more concerned with reaching out to the public. New campaign organizations and tactics brought the contest to many more people. As the opposition to the Jacksonians formed, presidential elections became more competitive, and voter turnout increased. Party organization in the states and localities also expanded, with the help of improved roads and communications. Candidates for state and local office were increasingly nominated by conventions of state and local leaders, rather than by the narrower legislative caucuses. By 1840, the Whigs and the Democrats were established in the first truly national party system and were competitive in all the states.

During the 1840s and 1850s, both parties worked to keep the bitter issue of slavery off the political agenda because it threatened to break apart both parties' supporting coalitions. Finally, the Whigs fractured on the issue and then collapsed. Antislavery activists created the **Republican Party** to demand that slavery be abolished. The Republicans then adopted the Whigs' commitment to protect American businesses with high tariffs and taxes to subsidize industrial development: roads, railroads, and settlement of the frontier. The party organized widely, except in the South and the Border States, which were Democratic strongholds, and won the presidency in 1860. To a great extent, the party system and the nation broke into North and South.

In short, modern political parties similar to those we know today, with their characteristic organizational structures, bases of loyal voters, and lasting alliances among governmental leaders, had developed by the mid-1800s.[21] The American parties grew hand in hand with the early expansion of voting rights in the United States. Comparable parties did not develop in Great Britain until the 1870s, after laws were passed to give more adult males the right to vote.

The Golden Age of the Parties

As the parties were developing, they received another massive infusion of voters from a new source: European immigrants. Hundreds of thousands of Europeans immigrated to the United States before the Civil War. The newcomers were welcomed by the Democratic Party, which sought their votes. However, their large numbers worried others. An anti-immigrant minor party, the American Party (the so-called Know-Nothing Party), sprang up in response in the 1850s.

The tide of immigration was halted only temporarily by the Civil War. After the war ended, new nationalities came in an almost constant flow from 1870 until Congress closed the door to mass immigration in the 1920s. More than five million immigrants arrived in the 1880s (equal to one-tenth of the 1880 resident population). Ten million more came between 1905 and 1914 (one-eighth of the 1900 resident population).

The political parties played an important role in assimilating these huge waves of immigrants. The newcomers gravitated toward the big cities where industrial jobs were available. A new kind of party organization developed in these cities, called the urban "machine," to respond to the immigrants' needs. These party machines were like social service systems that helped the new arrivals cope with the challenges of an urban industrial society. They softened the hard edge of poverty by helping needy families with food and funds, smoothed the way with government and the police, and taught immigrants the customs of their new home—all in exchange for the immigrants' votes for the party's candidates at election time. With those votes, a party machine could gain and keep control over the city's government. The machines were the means by which the new urban working class won control of the cities from the largely Anglo-Saxon, Protestant elites who had governed for so long.

The period of the late 1800s and the early 1900s was the "golden age" of the American parties: the high point of their power. Party organizations, now the dominant segment of the party, existed in all the states and localities and flourished in the industrial cities. Party discipline reached a record high in Congress and most state legislatures. Parties ran the candidates' campaigns for public office; they held rallies and torchlight parades, canvassed door to door, and brought voters to the polls. They controlled access to many government jobs ranging from sewer inspectors to members of the U.S. Senate. They were an important source of information and guidance for a largely uneducated and often illiterate electorate. As a result, the highest voter turnouts in American presidential history were recorded during the latter half of the 1800s. The parties suited the needs and limitations of the new voters and met the need for creating majorities in the rapidly industrializing nation.[22]

The Progressive Reforms and Beyond

The drive to democratize American politics continued into the 1900s. Passage of the Seventeenth Amendment gave voters, rather than state legislatures, the right to elect U.S. senators. Women and then blacks finally gained the right to vote. As popular democracy expanded, a movement arose that would impose major changes on the parties.

The period that parties saw as their "golden age" did not seem so golden to groups of reformers. To Progressive crusaders, party control of politics had led to rampant corruption and inefficient government. Because many

Progressives saw party power as the culprit, they tried to weaken the control that the parties, and especially the party organizations, had achieved by the late 1800s. The reformers attacked party "boss rule" by pressing for primary elections (see Chapters 9 and 10), which gave party voters rather than party leaders the power to choose the parties' candidates. Presidential nominations were made more open to the public by establishing presidential primaries in many states. State legislatures wrote laws to regulate party organizations.

The reforms did weaken the party organizations and their power in elections. When the party in the electorate gained the right to nominate the parties' candidates, the party organizations and leaders lost their most important function. Candidates could now appeal directly to primary voters rather than having to depend on the party organizations. The effect of the Progressive reforms, then, was to undercut the dominance of the party organization within the party as a whole. Therefore, the expectations of a democratic society, which first made the parties more public and more active at the grassroots level, later turned on the party organization, leaving it less capable of the important role that it once played in American politics.[23]

More recently, however, the party organizations and their leaders have created new sources of power for themselves. Beginning in the 1970s, first the Republicans and then the Democrats expanded the fund-raising capacity of their national party organizations. They used this new money to provide more services to candidates and to increase the capabilities of state party organizations. In the past four decades, the Democratic Party, through its national committee and convention, has created rules for state Democratic Parties to follow in nominating a presidential candidate. Both of these changes have strengthened the national party organizations. In fact, the national organizations probably have more of a presence now within the two major parties, relative to the state and local party organizations, than at any other time in American history. (Chapters 3 and 4 say more about these changes.)

In short, the parties have changed dramatically and continue to change. Yet they remain the leading organizations of popular democracy. They grew with the expansion of the right to vote and the increasing role of citizens in electoral politics. They are the channel through which voters come together to choose representatives and ambitious people gain positions of power. They help to clarify the alternatives on such challenging issues as abortion, taxes, and terrorism. They amplify the voices of some groups in making demands on public policy and dampen the voices of others.

What Do the Parties Stand For?

The parties have changed their stands on many issues over time, even major issues.[24] The national Democratic and Republican parties, for example, have shifted their positions dramatically over the years on the question of civil rights for black Americans and equal rights for women. The traditional decentralization of the American parties (discussed in Chapter 2) has meant that party organizations in some states or local communities have taken stands different from organizations of the same party in other areas.

Yet there have been times when the major parties differed clearly on big policy questions. The current period is one of those times. Although some would argue that the parties' issue stands are simply a means to attract votes, the ongoing competition between the Democrats and Republicans has always been more than just a story of raw ambition. Ever since the parties began, they have organized to gain power in order to achieve particular policy goals. Changes in the electorate and the growing strength of the national party organizations in the past four decades have encouraged **party polarization**: greater agreement on policy stands *within* each party and sharper policy differences *between* the Democrats and Republicans.

If you explore the Republican National Committee's website, the party platform, or the votes of Republicans in Congress, you will find that the Republican Party has long believed in a strong business sector. It warns that a government powerful enough to remedy individual inequalities, by creating welfare programs or guaranteeing civil rights to minorities, is a government that can take away other people's rights and property. The party's platform has long criticized a Washington "governing elite" that prevents individuals from building up their own wealth. Especially since the 1980s, it has heavily emphasized the value of religion and faith in public life.

These principles can be seen in the party's stands on many current issues (see Table 1.1). Tax cuts for individuals and businesses rank high on the party's agenda. Lower taxes shrink the government's revenue and, therefore, its ability to create new programs—a strategy that some conservatives call "starving the beast" (government).[25] The tax cuts should favor those who are wealthy, Republicans argue, because that helps them create jobs. The party stresses the importance of protecting property rights, which also limits government's ability to interfere in citizens' economic decisions.

Republican positions on other issues also demonstrate these commitments to private rather than governmental solutions to problems and to state and local rather than national and international authority. On the environment, for example, the party feels that many environmental laws keep business from growing. The Republican tradition defines a strong national defense as requiring a powerful military, with equipment built by private contractors, rather than as giving priority to international arms control agreements.

Over time, Republicans have been more likely than Democrats to draw their party leaders and candidates from the business community. The party has long favored restricting labor unions' power because unions, they feel, interfere with the working of the free market. The relationship between labor unions and the Republican Party is somewhere between strained and nonexistent, as could be seen in state legislative battles over the rights of public employee unions in the 2010s. Recent polls report that only 28 percent of Republicans hold a favorable view of unions, compared with

TABLE 1.1 Party Differences in the 2010s: Issues and Core Supporters

Democrats	Republicans
Core belief	
A strong government provides needed services and remedies inequalities.	A strong government interferes with business and threatens freedom.
Biggest exception	
Government should stay out of people's decisions on such issues as abortion and gay rights.	Government should regulate people's behavior in such matters as abortion and gay rights.
Issue agenda	
Social services, health, education Taxes on high incomes permit government to provide services to the needy. International negotiations Environmental protection	Less government spending Tax cuts for the wealthy to grow the economy Strong military Property rights
Emphasizes	
Fairness, especially for disadvantaged groups	Individual success, not group rights
Relations with labor unions	
Close and supportive	Distant and hostile
Core supporters	
Northeast, West Coast Minority groups Secular individuals Teachers, trial lawyers	South Caucasians Conservative Christians Business people

Source: Compiled by the author from materials including the 2016 party platforms.

65 percent of Democratic identifiers.[26] Core groups of Republican supporters include conservatives (conservative Christians in particular), white southerners, and people living in rural and exurban areas.

The Democratic Party represents a different tradition. To Democratic activists, government is a valuable means of redressing the inequalities that the marketplace can cause. These activists believe that needed social services should be provided by government rather than be privatized. Tax cuts limit the ability of government to provide these services. Any tax cuts, they say, should be directed toward helping the needy rather than those who are more affluent. Whereas Republicans believe that the purpose of government is to promote greater individual economic achievement, even at the cost of economic inequality, Democrats feel that fairness requires reducing economic inequality, and that it is government's job to offer a safety net to those who need it.

During the past half-century, the national Democratic Party has favored using government to enforce civil rights for black Americans. In the past 30 years, it has been the party of abortion rights, LGBTQ rights, and environmental action. If property rights get in the way of environmental protection, Democratic activists contend, then property rights must usually give way. The party's stand on education, similarly, stresses the need to invest in public schools and aim for equality of opportunity. That is one reason why the Democrats are more likely to draw their candidates and activists from among teachers and trial lawyers. The core of Democratic support comes from liberals, lower-income people, those living in the Northeast and West Coasts, minorities, and labor unions.

These party differences were crystal clear in the 2015–16 Congress. Characteristically, the House Republican majority proposed reducing the federal deficit by cutting government social services, such as aid to lower-income people, and environmental regulations. House Democratic leaders, just as characteristically, opposed the cuts and demanded greater regulation of business. And during the 2016 election, 70 percent of Clinton supporters said that government regulation of business is necessary to protect the public interest, whereas only 17 percent of Trump supporters agreed.[27]

Yet, even today, neither party is perfectly consistent on issues. As Table 1.1 shows, the parties seem to switch core beliefs on some "values" issues. The Republican Party, which usually opposes government interference, asks for government action to ban abortions and same-sex marriage and to support conservative family values. And the Democrats, the party that sees government as an ally for the needy, want government to stay out of individuals' lives on issues such as abortion and homosexuality. Perhaps because "values" issues affect people differently from economic issues, individuals' attitudes toward abortion and homosexuality do not always correlate with their preferences for a strong or a weak government.[28]

These inconsistencies often reflect the parties' strategic efforts to reach out for support from new groups. In the case of traditional values, for example, conservative Republicans in the 1970s realized that the pro-life and antigay rights stands of the Christian Right were much more engaging to groups of swing voters (including, at that time, many conservative white southerners) than were many of the party's economic stances. Republican candidates increasingly began to appeal to conservative Christians' values. And as more Christian conservatives became enthusiastic Republican activists, their concerns rose to the top of the party's agenda.

Donald Trump's candidacy in 2016 could develop into another coalitional shift. Trump's nativist, anti-immigrant stance appealed to the fears of many non-college-educated whites. That appeal, in turn, repelled many big business leaders who depended on international trade (and, occasionally, on undocumented immigrant labor). Trump's long-term impact on the Republican coalition is unclear, but it would not be surprising to see the current party coalition survive this fracture. Just as the Democratic New Deal coalition included both conservative southern whites and liberal northern blacks for decades, a Republican coalition that combined nativist appeals with business tax cuts could hold for some time.

These changes also grew out of the powerful impact of their environment on the parties' development. The Republican Party could begin life as a party of both business interests *and* big government because the expanding businesses of the 1800s needed government help. Building roads and other means of transporting products, large-scale communications networks, and high tariffs to protect American-made goods could be done much more efficiently by the national government than by the states or by businesses themselves. Once American business became well established and the needed infrastructure was in place, however, a strong national government could become a threat to businesses—as it did in responding to the Depression of the 1930s—because it could regulate their operations, raise their taxes to help fund social programs, and make it easier to unionize their workers.

Parties Are Shaped by Their Environment

Throughout their history, then, the parties' activities, their issue positions, and their organizations have been influenced by forces in their environment, and they have affected their environment in return. A major task of this book is to explain those impacts. One of the most important of these forces has been the nature of the electorate: Who has the right to vote?

Voters and Elections

As we have seen, the expansion of the right to vote has helped shape the parties' development. Each new group of voters entering the electorate challenges the parties to readjust their appeals as they vie for the group's support. Now, for instance, both parties are working hard to appeal to the increasing numbers of Latino-American voters. Republicans, in particular, debate whether to change their strong opposition to letting illegal immigrants gain a path to citizenship, or whether simply running more Latino candidates will be enough.

The parties' fortunes are also bound up with the *nature* of American elections. If you were thinking about running for office in a state that had just adopted primary elections, attracting party leaders' support would become less vital than raising money for TV ads to persuade large numbers of primary voters or earning free media coverage. These electoral institutions set the rules within which the parties compete for votes and thus affect parties' efforts and organization.

Political Institutions

The two main "rules" of American politics, federalism and the separation of powers, profoundly affect the parties. Because of the separation of powers, American legislators and executives are elected independently of one another. That makes it possible and, in recent decades likely, for the legislature and the governorship or presidency to be controlled by different parties. Many other democracies, in contrast, have parliamentary systems in which the legislative majority chooses the officials of the executive branch from among its own members. When that parliamentary majority can no longer hold, a new government must be formed. In contrast, in the American system, legislators can vote against a president or governor of their party on key issues without fearing that they will bring down the government and force new elections. As a result, American legislative parties only rarely achieve the degree of party discipline that is common in parliamentary systems.

The federal system, in which states have a number of independent powers (rather than being "branch offices" of the national government), has also left an imprint on the American parties. It has permitted the survival of local political loyalties and traditions. It has spawned a tremendous range of public offices to fill, creating a system of elections dwarfing that of all other democracies in size and diversity. These local traditions and loyalties have nurtured a large set of semi-independent local parties within the two national parties.

Laws Governing Parties

No other parties among the world's democracies are as regulated by laws as are the American parties. It was not always this way. Before the Progressive reforms a century ago, American parties were self-governing organizations, almost unrestrained by state or federal law. For most of the 1800s, for example, the parties made their own rules for nominating candidates and also printed, distributed, and often—with a wary eye on one another—even counted the ballots. Since then, the "Australian" (secret) ballot gave government the responsibility for running elections. The arrival of the direct primary in the early 1900s and more recent reforms of the presidential nominating process have also severely limited the parties' freedom to govern themselves.

The existence of 50 different sets of state laws governing the parties has produced 50 different varieties of political parties. Most states try to govern their party organizations by regulating their fund-raising. State laws even define which groups will be considered parties in the sense of having the right to place candidates on the ballot. The federal government has a more limited set of rules for party fund-raising.

Political Culture

A nation's political culture is the set of political values and expectations held by its people. This chapter began by noting that the American political culture has long regarded party politics as underhanded and corrupt. Recent public opinion polls show near-record-low public approval ratings of the Democratic and Republican parties; in fact, one memorable recent poll found that a sample of Americans held higher opinions of cockroaches, head lice, and Brussels sprouts than of the U.S. Congress.[29]

These and other elements of the political culture help shape the parties' behavior. Public distrust of parties leads many candidates to downplay mentions of party when they campaign. Cultural values affect people's judgment as to whether a method of fund-raising is acceptable or improper. Whether a strongly worded campaign ad—for instance, "Congressman X has taken thousands in pay raises for himself while refusing to support our veterans"—is seen as "mudslinging" or as "hard-hitting and informative" depends on the political values held by large numbers of Americans at a particular time, not on some set of universal standards.

The Broader Environment

Parties are conditioned by other forces as well. Dramatic changes in media technology have greatly influenced the parties' behavior.[30] A few decades ago, the media world was dominated by network television, which required party and candidate ads to appeal to a broad, undifferentiated national audience. Today, candidates and parties can use Twitter, Facebook, YouTube, and a wide range of other platforms to reach particular types of voters. Huge databases of political and consumer information allow parties to micro-target their communications to rural, conservative Christians who favor gun rights or to high-income, agnostic professionals with an interest in alternative energy. Strong liberals tend to rely on different news sources from strong conservatives, in which they hear their own views consistently reinforced.

Economic trends in the nation as a whole can greatly affect the parties. Income inequality—the gap in income between the wealthy and the poor—has increased in recent decades.[31] That increases the ability of wealthy people to contribute to parties and campaigns. Income inequality is also affected by the core beliefs of the two major parties. When the Democrats hold power, the party is likely to respond to this inequality with government-funded social services for needy people. When power moves to the Republicans, we are more likely to see tax cuts for the wealthy, with the intention of putting more money into the hands of people who can create jobs.

In this chapter, we have explored the nature of parties, what they do, and how they have developed in and been shaped by their environment. These themes will continue to guide us throughout the book. The next chapter tackles one of the biggest puzzles that students of parties face when comparing the American parties with those in other nations: Why does the United States have two major parties, rather than several, or only one?

Notes

1 Data from Pew Research Center, "Partisanship and Political Animosity in 2016," June 23, 2016, at www.people-press.org/2016/06/22/partisanship-and-political-animosity-in-2016/ (accessed June 23, 2016). See also Shanto Iyengar, Gaurav Sood, and Yphtach Lelkes, "Affect, Not Ideology," *Public Opinion Quarterly* 76 (2012): 405–431.

2 Alan I. Abramowitz, *The Disappearing Center* (New Haven, CT: Yale University Press, 2010), p. 112.

3 Jacob Hacker and Paul Pierson, "No Cost for Extremism," *American Prospect*, Spring 2015, at http:/prospect.org/article/no-cost-extremism (accessed June 15, 2016).

4 In June 2016, only 9 percent of respondents expressed "quite a lot" or "a great deal" of confidence in Congress; see Jim Norman, "Americans' Confidence in Institutions Remains Low," Gallup poll, June 13, 2016, at www.gallup.com/poll/192581/americans-confidence-institutions-stays-low.aspx? (accessed June 15, 2016).

5 Anthony Downs, *An Economic Theory of Democracy* (New York: Harper & Row, 1957), p. 24.

6 John H. Aldrich, *Why Parties? A Second Look* (Chicago: University of Chicago Press, 2011), p. 297.

7 See Marty Cohen, David Karol, Hans Noel, and John Zaller, *The Party Decides* (Chicago: University of Chicago Press, 2008).

8 Among those who regard the party in the electorate as central to the political parties are William Nisbet Chambers, "Party Development and the American Mainstream," in Chambers and Walter Dean Burnham, eds., *The American Party Systems* (New York: Oxford University Press, 1967), p. 5; and V. O. Key, Jr., *Politics, Parties, and Pressure Groups* (New York: Crowell, 1958), pp. 180–182.

9 V. O. Key, Jr., used this "tripartite" conception to organize his classic text, *Politics, Parties, and Pressure Groups.* Key attributed the concept of party in the electorate to Ralph M. Goldman, *Party Chairmen and Party Factions, 1789–1900* (Ph.D. diss., University of Chicago, 1951).

10 See Denise L. Baer and David A. Bositis, *Elite Cadres and Party Coalitions* (Westport, CT: Greenwood Press, 1988), pp. 21–50.

11 See, for example, Bruce E. Altschuler, *Running in Place* (Chicago: Nelson-Hall, 1996), p. 107.

12 See Joseph A. Schlesinger, "The Primary Goals of Political Parties," *American Political Science Review* 69 (1975): 840–849.

13 See Joseph A. Schlesinger, "The New American Political Party," *American Political Science Review* 79 (1985): 1152–1169.

14 State legislative elections in Nebraska are nonpartisan, although the candidates' partisan ties are obvious to many voters, and statewide officials (such as the governor and attorney general) are elected on a partisan ballot.

15 See William N. Chambers, *Political Parties in a New Nation* (New York: Oxford University Press, 1963).

16 David McCullough, *John Adams* (New York: Simon & Schuster, 2001), p. 436.

17 Kathleen Bawn, Martin Cohen, David Karol, Seth Masket, Hans Noel, and John Zaller, "A Theory of Political Parties," *Perspectives on Politics* 10 (2012): 591–597.

18 See John H. Aldrich and Ruth W. Grant, "The Antifederalists, the First Congress, and the First Parties," *Journal of Politics* 55 (1993): 295–326.

19 Chilton Williamson, *American Suffrage* (Princeton, NJ: Princeton University Press, 1960).

20 Neal R. Peirce and Lawrence D. Longley, *The People's President* (New Haven, CT: Yale University Press, 1981).

21 See Aldrich, *Why Parties?*, Chapter 4; and A. James Reichley, *The Life of the Parties* (Lanham, MD: Rowman & Littlefield, 1992), Chapter 5.

22 See Reichley, *The Life of the Parties*, Chapters 6–11.

23 On party reform, see Austin Ranney, *Curing the Mischiefs of Faction* (Berkeley: University of California Press, 1975).

24 See David Karol, *Party Position Change in American Politics* (Cambridge: Cambridge University Press, 2009).

25 See Mark A. Smith, *The Right Talk* (Princeton, NJ: Princeton University Press, 2000).

26 Pew Research Center, "Mixed Views of Impact of Long-Term Decline in Union Membership," April 27, 2015, at www.people-press.org/2015/04/27/mixed-views-of-impact-of-long-term-decline-in-union-membership/.

27 Pew Research Center, "Clinton, Trump Supporters Have Starkly Different Views of a Changing Nation," August 18, 2016, at www.people-press.org/2016/08/18/clinton-trump-supporters-have-starkly-different-views-of-a-changing-nation (accessed September 15, 2016).

28 Thanks to Charles Prysby for emphasizing this point.

29 Public Policy Polling, "Congress Less Popular than Cockroaches, Traffic Jams," January 8, 2013, at www.publicpolicypolling.com/main/2013/01/congress-less-popular-than-cockroaches-traffic-jams.html (accessed June 15, 2016). Distrust of parties is common in other nations as well; see Ingrid van Biezen and Michael Saward, "Democratic Theorists and Party Scholars," *Perspectives on Politics* 6 (2008): 21–35.

30 See Markus Prior, *Post-Broadcast Democracy* (Cambridge: Cambridge University Press, 2007).

31 See Larry M. Bartels, *Unequal Democracy* (Princeton, NJ: Princeton University Press, 2008).

CHAPTER 2

The American
Two-Party System

In most Americans' experience, party politics comes in twos, like the animals in Noah's Ark. Voters see two parties, two candidates running for each office, and two sides of every issue. A two-party system has dominated American politics for most of two centuries. So it seems logical that all democracies work this way.

Except that they don't. Most democracies have more than two parties—or fewer. Some democratic nations, such as Mexico and Japan, have had extended periods of one-party rule. Many more democracies, including most European nations, support multiparty systems with three, four, or even more parties. The Netherlands had 11 competitive political parties in 2016, plus an assortment of local and regional parties. Eleven parties hold seats in Israel's Congress (the Knesset), and more than two dozen other parties wish they did. In these multiparty systems, when one single party fails to win a majority of the votes, then two or more parties come together in a coalition in order to govern.[1]

In the United States as well, some states and cities have a long tradition of one-party rule. In other areas, several parties have flourished at times. Minor ("third") parties and independent candidates occasionally affect elections. Green Party candidate Ralph Nader took just enough votes in key states from the Democrats in 2000 to tip the presidential election to Republican George W. Bush.[2] As an independent presidential candidate in 1992, Ross Perot actually ran ahead of both major parties' candidates in polls early in the race. At the state level, comic country singer Kinky Friedman ran for governor of Texas as an independent candidate in 2006 with the campaign slogan "Kinky: Why the Hell Not?" (He got a lot of media coverage but only 13 percent of the vote. In 2014 he actually got into the primary runoff for agriculture commissioner running as a Democrat who advocated legalizing marijuana.)

These campaigns are fun to watch; Friedman, for instance, may have been the only candidate to support both school prayer and same-sex marriage and had written a book titled *Kill Two Birds and Get Stoned*. Minor party and independent candidacies are rarely successful, however. For most of

American history, since the Era of Good Feelings ended in the 1820s, only two parties have had a realistic chance of winning any given national election. Even the rapid rise of the most successful third party in American history, the Republican Party, shows the power of two-party politics in the United States. The party was founded in 1854, but instead of competing with the existing Democrats and Whigs, it replaced the Whig Party within two short years.

What protects a two-party system in American politics, when most other democracies have more than two competitive national parties? In this chapter, we look at the level of competition between the parties, the major theories as to what sustains two-party politics, and the efforts by minor parties and independent candidates to break the two-party pattern.

The National Party System

Over this remarkably long period of two-party politics, the two major American parties have been close competitors, at least at the national level. Since 1868, the great majority of presidential elections have been decided by less than 10 percent of the vote. It has been decades since a presidential candidate—Ronald Reagan in 1984—won the popular vote by more than 10 percentage points. Some of the closest presidential contests in American history have taken place in the past 20 years.

Congress was a different story from 1932 to 1980, when Democrats dominated both houses most of the time. But since 1980, the parties have exchanged control frequently. In the Senate alone, party control has switched seven times since then—a pace unprecedented in U.S. history.[3] If we average election results by decade during the past 70 years, we find that the percentage of the two-party vote cast for all Democratic candidates has not differed much from the percentage cast for Republicans (see Table 2.1).

Even though Republicans gained control of a number of state legislatures in the 2014 elections, Democrats hold majorities in a number of state legislative houses as well. As of early 2016, 20 states had divided party control (in which the governor's party did not control at least one house of the state legislature), 7 were fully Democratic controlled, and 22 were Republican controlled. (The remaining state, Nebraska, has a nonpartisan legislature.) The 2016 elections added to the Republican dominance.

Both major parties, then, have shown a great deal of resilience over time. Media coverage may suggest otherwise because it focuses on the events of the moment. But whenever one party has had a string of big wins, the other party has been able to restore the balance. For example, big Democratic gains in the House and Senate in 2006 and 2008 led one expert analyst to title a blog post, "Are the Republicans Still a National Party?" Only two years later, however, in the 2010 midterm elections, Republicans won a remarkable net gain of 63 House seats, bringing the party totals in Congress nearly back to what they were in 2004. Democrats recovered in 2012, only

TABLE 2.1 Percentage of the Two-Party Vote Won by Republican Candidates for President and House of Representatives, 1940–2016

Decade Average	Presidential Elections		House Elections	
	Republican Share of Two-Party Vote (%)	Difference Between Republican and Democratic Vote (%)	Republican Share of Two-Party Vote (%)	Difference Between Republican and Democratic Vote (%)
1940s	46.3	7.5	49.8	5.9
1950s	56.6	13.0	48.1	3.9
1960s	46.3	7.9	46.6	6.7
1970s	55.4	12.8	44.6	10.9
1980s	56.1	12.3	46.3	6.7
1990s	45.9	8.1	49.5	4.4
2000s	49.1	3.4	49.0	5.2
2010s	49.0	2.0	51.8	3.8

Sources: Calculated and updated from Norman J. Ornstein, Thomas E. Mann, Michael J. Malbin, Andrew Rugg, and Raffaela Wakeman, *Vital Statistics on Congress* (Washington, DC: Brookings Institution, 2014), Table 2.2, for House elections; and calculated from Dave Leip's "Atlas of U.S. Presidential Elections," at www.uselectionatlas.org for presidential elections (accessed November 16, 2016).

to face decisive congressional losses in 2014, when Republicans increased their House majority to nearly a hundred-year high.

The 50 State Party Systems

Yet close party competition is limited to the national level. Increasingly, we find one-party dominance within states and localities. Most states have voted for the same party's presidential candidate in almost every election since 2000. Only about 10 states are true battlegrounds between the parties. The election remains competitive nationally because the remaining states are fairly balanced by party: A little less than half have consistently supported Democratic presidential candidates, and a little more than half have consistently been safe for Republicans. Even though governors' races can still supply a lot of drama due to changing economic conditions and other short-term events, most states and local governments have become relatively safe for one party or the other.

Measuring State Party Competition

How can we measure the competitiveness of the 50 state party systems? Political scientists often use an index originated by Austin Ranney.[4] This index averages three indicators of party success during a particular time period: the percentage of the popular vote for the parties' gubernatorial candidates, the percentage of seats held by the parties in each house of the legislature, and the length of time plus the percentage of the time that the parties held both the governorship and a majority in the state legislature. Like any other summary measure, the Ranney index picks up some trends more fully than others, but it gives us useful information about states' partisan lean.

As you can see in Figure 2.1, showing the Ranney index for 2012–2016, states vary a lot in their competitiveness and their partisan lean. In comparison with previous four-year periods, two trends are clear. First, a number of states took a sharp right turn after Republican victories in the 2010 elections and the subsequent round of redistricting; the Ranney index leans much more Republican now than it did in 2007–2011. And second, the states have become more politically polarized: There has been an ongoing movement from one pattern of regional party strength to a different, but just as noncompetitive, pattern. Party change in the South and New England has driven this transition. For years a solid Democratic region, southern states have become dominantly Republican in recent decades. The tipping point occurred in 1994 (see Chapter 7). Since then, states such as Alabama

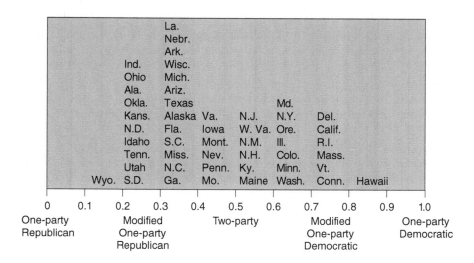

FIGURE 2.1 Interparty Competition in the States, 2012–2016

Source: Thomas M. Holbrook and Raymond J. La Raja, "Parties and Elections," in Virginia Gray, Russell L. Hanson, and Thad Kousser, eds., *Politics in the American States*, 11th. ed. (Washington, DC: CQ Press, 2017), Chapter 3.

have moved from "competitive" to "modified one-party Republican." The New England region has shifted dramatically in the opposite direction. Although moderate Republicans won most congressional elections in these states until fairly recently, not a single Republican was elected to the U.S. House from a New England state in 2012.

Races below the statewide level, such as U.S. House races, are even less competitive. In the 2016 elections, the great majority of U.S. House seats were regarded as safe for one party; fewer than 10 percent of House races were seen as competitive. Even in the Republican sweeps of 2010 and 2014, the great majority of House seats remained safe for the incumbent (or the incumbent's party). Competition at the *state* legislative level is so rare that in recent years only about 60 percent of the races had both a Democratic and a Republican candidate. In the remaining races (43 percent in 2014), nothing but an occasional (and usually poorly funded) minor party contender stood between the sole major party candidate and victory.[5] Very recently, the tide in state legislative elections has been heavily Republican; as of 2017, more than two-thirds of state legislative houses had a Republican majority.

Limits on Competitiveness: Incumbency

What keeps the relatively close party competition at the presidential level from infiltrating congressional districts to a greater extent? One brake on competition in these districts has been the electoral value of incumbency. Although there was a lot of party turnover during the 1800s, members of Congress gained much greater electoral security between the 1960s and the early 1980s. During that time, well over 90 percent of U.S. House incumbents seeking reelection were returned to office, along with more than 80 percent of U.S. Senators. These rates were somewhat inflated by the fact that incumbents who think they might lose the next election may choose not to run again, but they are impressive indeed. Incumbents in most state legislatures were just as likely to keep their jobs.[6] In fact, the incumbency advantage increased in elections for all types of legislative and executive offices.[7]

Why were incumbents so safe? The temporary weakening of party identification during that time led some voters to look for other signals to guide their choices.[8] Incumbents' advantage in name recognition filled that void, along with other advantages of incumbency: the attention they receive in media coverage, the services they can provide to constituents, the greater ease with which they can raise campaign money, as well as their experience in having run previous successful campaigns.

The result was that between the 1960s and the early 1980s, even those incumbents who represented districts favoring the other party were able to keep their jobs. But as levels of party identification rebounded, and straight-ticket voting returned, these incumbents have had greater reason to watch their backs. The greater nationalization of voting behavior means that in an election year when national conditions heavily favor one party, the "wave" will carry into office candidates who win in districts that normally support the other party. These "exposed" candidates will then be at risk in the next election. Most of the elections since 2006 have been wave elections. The Republican sweep in the 2010 midterms cut the House reelection rate to a 40-year low of 85 percent. The losing incumbents were disproportionately those from districts where the opposite party was dominant. Many of these losers were the moderate voices in both parties. So the incumbency advantage now—in 2016, 97 percent of House incumbents running for reelection were returned to office, as were 90 percent of Senate incumbents—is more conditioned by party.

... And Other Reasons for Limited Competitiveness

Gerrymandering also helps to limit party competition at the state level. In most states, the legislature redraws congressional and state legislative districts after the decennial Census. The big increase in single-party control of state government has permitted the dominant party—in most states, the Republicans—to reduce the number of competitive legislative districts and increase those likely to elect a representative of the dominant party. Republican victories in the 2010 midterm elections permitted Republican state legislative majorities to control redistricting after the 2010 Census. The result was that in 2016, Democrats held fewer state legislative seats than they had since the 1920s.

Redistricting can't be the only reason why competition has declined, because that is true of offices that are not redistricted as well, such as local and statewide offices. But it helps explain why a party's proportion of the total vote often differs from the proportion of seats it holds in Congress; in 2017, for instance, Republicans held 55 percent of all House seats though the party got only 50 percent of all the votes cast in 2016.

Bruce Oppenheimer has suggested another alternative: New patterns of residential mobility can reduce party competition. As people have become more mobile, they are more able, and more inclined, to move to areas where like-minded people live. They may be motivated mainly by qualities such as an area's hip vibe or its concentration of churches, but these qualities, of course, have partisan relevance. As a result, areas become more homogeneous—and, thus, congressional districts are more likely to be dominated by one party.[9] This ideological "sorting" has added to the growing geographic divergence in party loyalties. An analyst found that although the 2000 and 1976 presidential elections were both won by narrow margins, almost twice as many of the voters in 2000 lived in counties where one candidate or the other won by a landslide. This suggests, he argues, that there has been a "voluntary political segregation" in the United States.[10]

Figure 2.2 demonstrates the extent of this decline in party competition in House elections. Two decades ago, almost a quarter of all House members were elected from "swing" districts—those in which both parties commanded enough voter support to stand a realistic chance of winning the presidency. Since then, competition has declined so dramatically that only 35 House members—about 8 percent of all members—were elected from swing districts in 2012. More than half of the members were elected in "landslide" districts—those where the presidential vote was at least 20 percent more Democratic or Republican than the national vote as a whole. So in recent decades, when we have seen lively party competition in the nation as a whole, it has not been built on a lot of highly competitive House districts. Instead, it reflects a very large proportion of districts that vote consistently Democratic or consistently Republican, but in which the large number of fairly safe Democratic districts has been closely matched by the number of fairly safe Republican districts.

What difference does this make? Political competition is vital in a democracy. When an officeholder expects to win reelection easily, he or she has less incentive to pay close attention to voters' needs. In particular, the needs of disadvantaged citizens are more likely to be ignored (because advantaged citizens have other means to make their voices heard in government, in addition to voting). Further, the decline of swing districts is linked to the polarization of American political life. Because swing districts are closely divided by party, they tend to be diverse in population, so they are often inclined to elect moderate officeholders, who can appeal to both

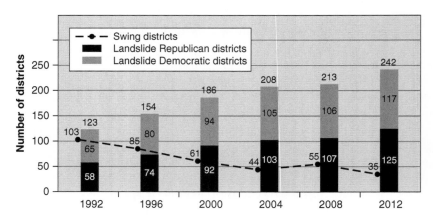

FIGURE 2.2 The Declining Number of "Swing" Districts in the U.S. House, 1992–2012

Note: A swing district is defined as a U.S. House district in which the presidential vote is within 5 percentage points of the national popular vote margin. In a landslide district, the presidential vote is at least 20 percent more Democratic or Republican than the national vote as a whole.

Source: Data compiled by Nate Silver, "So Few Swing Districts, So Little Compromise," *New York Times*, December 28, 2012, p. A16.

parties. The steady disappearance of these districts has eliminated most of the moderate Congress members who used to be elected in them—southern "Blue Dog" Democrats and moderate northeastern Republicans. Most House members now represent districts in which their party wins by a comfortable margin. These members are more likely to worry about a threat in their party's primary, where those who donate the most time and money are more likely to hold extreme views, than they are about a challenge from the other party. Republican candidates and elected officials have been pulled toward the right wing of their party and Democrats to the left, and Congress has become increasingly polarized.[11]

Another result of the increase in one-party control of state government is that the party in control then is in a position to accomplish major changes in state policy. Single-party Republican control in Wisconsin, Indiana, and other states since 2010 has led to laws seriously undercutting the power of labor unions, especially those representing government employees. The much smaller number of Democratic-controlled states have advanced liberal policies, such as California's expansion of abortion rights. A variety of big donors and political action committees (see Chapter 12) have helped to make this one-party dominance possible in two-thirds of the states, the most in decades; this pattern can then be maintained through partisan redistricting of state legislative seats. At a time when Washington is frequently deadlocked, parties and organized interests see states as the opportunity to enact their wish lists for major policy change.

Keep in mind, however, that because of the more competitive presidential contests, as well as frequent elections and long ballots, most Americans do experience at least one close race regularly.[12] That provides one clue as to why the United States has sustained a two-party system.

What Causes a Two-Party System?

We have seen that the American parties are durable and that, at least at the presidential level, when one party has had a run of dominance, the other party has been able to bounce back. Why have we had a two-party system for so long, when most other democracies do not? There are several possible explanations.

Institutional Forces

The most frequent explanation of the two-party system ties it to the nature of American electoral institutions. Called **Duverger's law**,[13] it argues that plurality elections in single-member districts (with no runoff elections) tend to produce two-party systems. A **single-member district** means simply that one candidate is elected to each office, and a **plurality election** is one in which the candidate with the largest number of votes wins, even if not a majority. Finishing a close second, or third or fourth, brings no rewards.

The American election system is, for most offices, a plurality election system with single-member districts; it offers the reward of winning an office only to the single candidate who gets the most votes. Thus, the theory suggests that minor parties will see no point in running candidates if they don't have a shot at winning.

The flip side of Duverger's law is that proportional representation in multimember constituencies results in multiparty systems. A system with multimember constituencies is one in which a particular legislative district will be represented by, say, three or four elected legislators rather than one.[14] In proportional representation (PR), each party prepares a slate of candidates for these positions, and the number of party candidates who win is proportional to the overall percentage of the vote won by the party slate (see box "Plurality versus Proportional Representation: How It Works in Practice" on page 39). Because a party may be able to elect a candidate with only 15 or 20 percent of the votes, depending on the system's rules, smaller parties have reason to keep competing.

However, a puzzle remains. Single-member district systems with plurality elections exist in some other democracies that support more than two parties. Shouldn't the United States, with its great diversity, do the same? To some analysts, the nature of the American presidency helps to sustain Duverger's law. The presidency is the most visible single-member district in the United States. It is the main prize of American politics, and only one person is elected to that office at a time. Many other democracies, which use a parliamentary system, have a governing "cabinet" as the executive authority. This cabinet is made up of a number of officeholders, so it can be a coalition that includes representatives of several parties, including smaller parties.

In a system with a single executive, minor parties will be weakened because they do not have a realistic chance of competing for the presidency. That denies a minor party the national attention that major parties get. Add to that the uniquely American institution of the Electoral College. To win, a presidential candidate must get an absolute majority of electoral votes—so far, at least, an impossible task for a minor-party candidate. Because the presidency is so prominent in American politics, the argument goes, it shapes the politics of the system as a whole. Because minor parties have no chance of winning the presidency, they may survive for a time, but they will not thrive.[15]

Some minor parties try for the presidency anyway. In 1996, the Reform Party focused primarily on the presidential race. But its leader, Ross Perot, a billionaire willing to spend tens of millions on his presidential campaign, was clearly not typical of most minor parties' candidates, who can only dream of such an opportunity. In 2016, some Republican leaders and activists opposed to their party's nominee, Donald Trump, tried to recruit a conservative candidate to run in the general election against both Trump and Democratic nominee Hillary Clinton. They failed, largely because the

Plurality Versus Proportional Representation:
How It Works in Practice

Does it matter whether an election uses plurality or proportional representation (PR) rules to count the votes? To find out, let us compare the results of one type of American election in which both rules are used. In presidential primaries—the elections in which party voters choose delegates to the national parties' presidential conventions—the Democrats use PR to select delegates (with at least 15 percent of the vote needed for a candidate to win delegates) and the Republicans can use some form of plurality election (also called winner-take-all).

Imagine a congressional district that will send four delegates to the national convention, in which candidates A, B, C, and D get the following percentages of the vote. The candidates would win the following numbers of delegates, depending on whether the plurality or PR rule was used:

		Delegates Won	
	Vote %	Plurality	PR
Candidate A	40	4	2
Candidate B	30	0	1
Candidate C	20	0	1
Candidate D	10	0	0

With the **plurality** (winner-take-all) rule, candidate A, who received the most votes, wins all the delegates at stake in that district. So in a typical Republican primary using the plurality rule, only the leading candidate will emerge with delegates; the other candidates win nothing. Under most circumstances, the less successful candidates will find it hard to stay in the race very long when they are not winning any delegates in return for their efforts. Under **PR** rules, in contrast, three candidates win delegates in rough proportion to their popular support. Therefore, in a typical Democratic primary, the less successful candidates are encouraged to stay in the race longer because the PR rules permit them to keep winning at least a few delegates.

The contrast is even clearer when we compare British elections with the multimember district systems of most European legislative elections. The use of PR in the European elections promotes multiparty politics and coalition governments in which two or more different parties often share control of the executive. In the British parliamentary system, on the other hand, single-member districts operating under plurality rules typically produce a parliamentary majority for one party, giving it sole control of the executive, even if it does not win a majority of the popular vote. In the 2015 British parliamentary elections, the Conservative Party took only 37 percent of the overall vote, but because its supporters were distributed well enough to win a plurality in most parliamentary districts, it won a majority (331) of the seats in Parliament. In contrast, the anti-European Union UK Independence Party (UKIP) got 13 percent of the vote, but its votes were so evenly distributed across the nation that there was only one district where the party earned a plurality, and therefore elected a Member of Parliament. (In some PR systems, UKIP would have won more than 80 seats with the same overall vote totals.)

presence of a third alternative would have divided Republican votes and assured Clinton's election. Thus, the importance of the single, indivisible executive office in the American system strengthens the tendency toward two-party politics.

Political scientist Leon Epstein has identified another institutional factor, the direct primary, as a force that prevented the development of minor parties in areas dominated by one party.[16] Primaries, which allow voters to choose the parties' nominees, have become the main method of selecting party candidates in the United States (see Chapter 9). When disgruntled groups have the opportunity to make their voices heard within the dominant party through a primary and may even succeed in getting a candidate nominated, the resulting taste of power will probably discourage them from breaking away to form a third party. Thus, in the one-party Democratic South of an earlier era, where age-old hatreds kept most people from voting Republican, factional disputes that otherwise would have produced one or more minor parties were contained within the Democratic Party by the use of primary elections.

Manipulating the Rules

Once a two-party system has developed, the two dominant parties will do their best to protect it. The major parties will support election systems (such as plurality elections and single-member districts) that make it hard for minor parties to do well. Through their control of Congress and state legislatures, the Democrats and Republicans have manipulated the rules to keep minor parties from qualifying for the ballot. The major parties have no interest in leveling the playing field so that their minor-party competitors can take a shot at replacing them.[17] Further, after the two-party system was launched, it created loyalties within the American public to one party or the other (see Chapter 6).

Another challenge to the development of strong minor parties is that the major parties have been very open to absorbing new groups and adapting to changing conditions. Just when a minor party rides the crest of a new issue to the point where it can challenge the two-party monopoly, one or both of the major parties is likely to try to absorb the new movement.[18] Since the Tea Party movement began in 2009, for instance, Republicans have worked hard to keep its supporters within Republican ranks rather than breaking away to form another party.

The most important of these explanations for a two-party system is the institutional arrangement of American electoral politics. Without plurality elections, single-member districts, the Electoral College, and an indivisible executive, it would have been much easier for minor parties to break the duopoly enjoyed by the Republicans and Democrats. Other Anglo-American democracies such as Britain and Canada, which share many of the American institutional arrangements, also tend to be dominated by two parties, although minor parties are more successful in these nations than in the United States.

Exceptions to the Two-Party Pattern

As we have seen, the American two-party system contains many states and localities where one party dominates. Some areas have even developed a uniquely American brand of no-party (nonpartisan) politics. Minor parties or independent candidates have occasionally made their presence felt. Where do we find these exceptions to two-party politics? Have they made a difference?

Nonpartisan Elections

One of the Progressive movement's most treasured achievements was to restrict the role of parties by removing party labels from many ballots, mostly in local elections. About three-quarters of American cities and towns, including Los Angeles, Chicago, Miami, and Atlanta, run their local elections on a nonpartisan basis. Many states elect judges using a nonpartisan ballot. Nonpartisanship adds to the parties' burdens; even the strongest local parties have to work much harder to let voters know which candidates are affiliated with their party.

Removing party labels from the ballot has not usually removed partisan influences where parties are already strong. A resourceful party organization can still select its candidates and persuade voters when party labels are not on the ballot. Even where local elections are nonpartisan, local voters are still affected by the partisan content of state and national elections. Typically, however, the reform took root in cities and towns that already had weak parties and for offices, such as judgeships and school boards, where the traditional American dislike of party politics is most deeply felt. Most northeastern cities, where strong party machines were the main targets of the Progressives, were able to resist the reforms and to continue holding partisan local elections.

Beyond adding to the difficulties faced by party organizations, what difference does it make if an election is nonpartisan? Researchers had long believed that nonpartisan elections gave an advantage to Republican candidates, who were more likely to have the financial resources to attract voter attention in the absence of party labels. More recent research suggests, however, that it is the minority party in an area that benefits, because the nonpartisan ballot takes away the party cue that would remind the majority's voters to choose the majority party's candidates.[19] Nonpartisan elections also reduce voter turnout. Most voters use the party label as a helpful shortcut for making choices in elections. When this shortcut is not listed on the ballot, fewer people make the effort to vote.[20]

In an ingenious experiment, one group of researchers compared the behavior of state legislators in Nebraska, who are selected in nonpartisan elections, with those in partisan Kansas. The legislators in both states took clear stands on major policy issues. But legislators' votes on bills were not as clearly structured in Nebraska as they were in Kansas. That made it harder for Nebraskans to predict how their representatives would behave and to hold them accountable.[21] Therefore, nonpartisan elections can weaken the policy links between voters and their legislators—a result that would have greatly disappointed the Progressives.

Areas of One-Party Monopoly

In thousands of counties, cities, and towns, one party dominates public life so thoroughly that the other party might not even be able to field candidates. Where do we find these one-party areas? For most of their history, the major parties, especially in national elections, have divided the American voters roughly along social-demographic lines. (More about this can be found in Chapter 7.) A local constituency may be too small to contain the social diversity that supports both Democratic and Republican politics. Thus, we can find "safe" Democratic congressional districts in the poorer, older, and black neighborhoods of large cities and "safe" Republican districts in small town and rural, heavily white, Christian and southern areas. The less diverse its people are, at least in terms of the demographic characteristics that typically divide Republican from Democratic voters, the more likely the district is to foster one-party politics.

Alternatively, some forces may be so powerful in an area that they override the relationship between socioeconomic status and partisanship. In the classic one-party politics of the American South for many decades, racial fears, white hatred of Republicans as the party of abolition and Reconstruction, and laws and practices preventing blacks from voting long outweighed the factors that were dividing Americans into two parties in most of the rest of the country.

Once one party has established dominance in an area, the weaker party will face an uphill climb. The winning party is likely to have the loyalty of most voters in the district. Voters do not easily change their partisan attachments, even when the reasons for the original attachment have faded. A party trying to become competitive may find itself caught in a vicious circle. Its inability to win elections limits its ability to raise money and recruit attractive candidates because, as a chronic loser, it offers so little chance of achieving political goals. For much of the 1900s, for example, the Republican Party in the South found that the Democrats had recruited the region's most promising politicians and claimed its most powerful appeals. Now, in many parts of the South, it is the Democrats who face this same disadvantage.

The weaker party's ability to attract voters locally is also affected by media coverage of its national party's stands. If the Democratic Party is identified nationally with the hopes of the poor and minority groups, its appeal in an affluent suburb may be limited, no matter how attractive its candidates are. Thus, a nationalized politics may rob the local party organization of the chance to develop strength based on its own issues and candidates. To the extent that party loyalties grow out of national politics, as Democrats in the South have learned, competitiveness may be beyond the reach of some local party organizations.

And as noted earlier in this chapter, redistricting can make it harder for the weaker party to bounce back. Majority parties have found effective ways to redraw legislative district lines that preserve their advantage, so the minority party in an area must compete in districts drawn by the stronger party. This is why parties are especially concerned with winning state legislative majorities in years ending in zero, when district lines must be redrawn. The 2020 state legislative elections, then, will be a do-or-die time for both major parties.

Minor Parties

In one of the many ironies of American politics, most people claim that we need a third major party,[22] but few people ever vote for candidates other than Democrats or Republicans. Only seven minor parties in all of American history have carried even a single state in a presidential election. The recent high point of minor-party strength was Ross Perot's run as the Reform Party candidate for president in 1996, when he won just over 8 million votes. Analysts speculated in 2016 that the Libertarian Party's candidate, Gary Johnson, might have a real shot in 2016 with Republican voters who couldn't stomach Republican nominee Donald Trump, but Johnson got only 4 percent of the general election vote and failed to win a single Electoral College vote.

Minor parties rarely succeed at the state and local level either. Of more than a thousand governors elected since 1875, fewer than 20 ran solely on a minor-party ticket and another handful ran as independents.[23] One of the best known was former professional wrestler Jesse "The Body" Ventura's election as governor of Minnesota in 1998. Ventura's Reform Party candidacy got enormous media attention precisely because it was so unusual, but Ventura stepped down from the governorship in 2002 after having been largely ignored by the state legislature, and the next candidate of his party attracted only 16 percent of the vote.[24] Nationally, minor-party and independent candidates for governor rarely win more than 5 percent of the vote; since 2010, only two such candidates have won governorships, and one of them became a Democrat before running again.

The Libertarian Party has been the strongest vote getter of any minor party in the past quarter century. Libertarian candidates won 1.5 million votes in top of the ticket state races (governor, U.S. Senate, or U.S. House) and ran 122 candidates for the U.S. House in 2014, though not enough in any district or state to elect anyone. Eight minor party candidates were

A DAY IN THE LIFE

Competing Against the "Big Guys"

The Democrats and the Republicans, Brad Warren says, have a "death grip" on the American political process. Warren, a tax attorney in Indianapolis, is a Libertarian Party activist who ran for the U.S. Senate under that party's banner. "If I need a new pair of socks," he points out, "I can go to dozens of stores and pick from several different brands and dozens of colors—for something as insignificant as socks. But when it comes to politics, which has a monopoly on the lawful use of force in our society, we have only two choices. That is tremendously scary! How do you hold them accountable? If you get angry with the incumbents, you can throw them out, only to reelect the nasty incumbents you had thrown out in the previous election. Four years from now, you'll be throwing out the incumbents you elected today. There's no choice."

Minor-party activists such as Warren must compete against the "big guys"—the two major parties—on an uneven playing field. A major problem for a minor party is simply to get its candidates' names on the ballot. The Arkansas state legislature used to permit any organized party to list its candidates on the state ballot. The American Party candidate for governor of Arkansas won 6 percent of the vote in 1970. The result? The legislature raised the hurdle the following year— to 7 percent. Ballot access requirements differ from state to state, making it difficult for a minor party to appear on the ballot in all 50 states.

"Even once you have ballot access," Warren argues, "you will still be excluded from any meaningful participation in the election. In practice, we run elections on money, not on votes, and in presidential elections, the Republicans and Democrats divide up hundreds of millions of federal dollars among themselves."

The worst problem for minor parties, Warren feels, is getting noticed after the major parties hold primary elections. "I got pretty good media coverage up to the primary election. After the primary, I was nobody. Even though the primary doesn't elect anybody to any office, it seems to. Primaries are a government-funded means of anointing the two major parties' candidates as the 'real' candidates and delegitimizing all the others. The media say we have no chance to win, so they won't cover any candidates except the [major] party-anointed ones. The debates typically don't include third-party candidates. Why? Because the commissions that decide who's going to be allowed to participate in debates are 'bipartisan' commissions, made up entirely of Republicans and Democrats, just like the legislatures that write the ballot access laws and the judges who interpret them. A party that has gotten on the ballot in all 50 states, like the Libertarians, deserves to be heard."

"The two major parties won't give you any choice," Warren contends, and "if you continually vote for the lesser of two evils, what you get is evil." So what is the role of a minor party? To Warren, "It's like that of a bee: You rise up, you sting, and then you die."

elected to the Vermont state legislature in 2014 (under the Progressive label), in addition to 15 independent state legislators and about a dozen local officials in partisan races.

More significantly, a minor party has sometimes shifted the balance in an important race. In 2008, the Minnesota Senate race was so close that a lengthy recount was required. The Democrat, Al Franken, finally won. The stakes were high: Franken's win gave the Senate Democrats 60 seats—in theory, enough to quash a Republican filibuster. An Independence Party candidate took 15 percent of the vote in the Minnesota Senate election; if only a tiny proportion of minor-party voters had chosen the Republican candidate instead, the Minnesota seat would have gone to Franken's Republican opponent, and the Senate Republicans would then have been assured of enough votes to block almost any Democratic legislation. However, for every example of minor-party success, there are thousands of races with no minor-party candidate. The two major parties have monopolized elections even more fully in the states and cities than at the national level. (See box "A Day in the Life: Competing Against the "Big Guys" on page 44.)

Minor parties in the United States vary greatly in their purposes, origins, and levels of activity:[25]

Differences in Ideology Most minor parties are driven by issues and ideologies, but they differ in the nature and scope of that commitment. The American Freedom Party and the Christian Liberty Party are very specific and targeted: the former in promoting white supremacy and the latter in favoring Christian principles in politics. At the other extreme are socialist parties whose programs demand sweeping changes, including an end to capitalism and class privilege. The Libertarian Party wants government to involve itself only in national defense and criminal law and to turn over all other programs, from Social Security to education, to private efforts.[26] In sharp contrast, Green Parties argue for extensive government programs on behalf of the environment, peace, and social justice.

Difference of Origins Minor parties differ in their origin. Some were literally imported into the United States. Much of the early Socialist Party strength in the United States came from the freethinkers and radicals who fled Europe after the failed revolutions of 1848. Socialist candidates did well in cities such as Milwaukee, New York, and Cincinnati because of the concentrations of liberal German immigrants there. Other parties, especially the Granger and Populist Parties, were homegrown channels of social protest, born of social inequality and economic hardship in the marginal farmlands of America.

Some minor parties began as splinters or factions of one of the major parties. For example, the Progressives (the Bull Moose Party) of 1912 and the Dixiecrats of 1948 objected so strenuously to the platforms and candidates of their parent parties that they ran their own slates and presented their own programs in presidential elections. In fact, the Dixiecrats, an anti-civil rights faction within the Democratic Party, substituted their own candidate for the one chosen by the party's national convention as the official Democratic presidential candidate in several southern states. If Tea Party activists were to nominate their own candidates for office, rather than try to influence Republican primaries, then they, too, could become a minor party.

Differing Purposes Finally, minor parties differ in their intentions. Some of these parties aim to educate citizens about their issues; getting votes is merely a sideline. They run candidates because their presence on the ballot brings media attention that they could not otherwise hope to get. Many of these parties serenely accept their election losses because they have chosen not to compromise their principles to win office. The Prohibition Party, for example, has run candidates in most presidential elections since 1872 with unflagging devotion to the cause of banning the sale of alcoholic beverages even though its highest proportion of the popular vote was 2 percent, and that came in 1892. Other minor parties are serious about trying to win office. Often, their goal is local, although today they find it difficult to control an American city, as the Socialists once did, or an entire state, like the Progressives.

What Difference Do They Make? Some argue that minor parties deserve the credit for a number of public policies—programs that were first suggested by a minor party and then adopted by a major party when they became politically popular. The minimum wage, for example, was advocated by the Socialist Party for more than two decades before a Democratic Congress passed the minimum wage law in the 1930s. Did the Democrats steal the Socialist Party's idea, or would they have proposed a minimum wage for workers even if there had been no Socialist Party? There is no way to be sure. Major parties usually propose a new policy once a lot of Americans have accepted the idea, so the party can gain votes. However, the major party might have picked up the new proposal from any of a number of sources in addition to the Socialists.

If minor parties have such limited impact, then how do they survive? To Steven Rosenstone and colleagues, minor parties result from the failure of major parties "to do what the electorate expects of them—reflect the issue preferences of voters, manage the economy, select attractive and acceptable candidates, and build voter loyalty to the parties and the political system."[27] Thus, minor parties gain support when they promote attractive ideas that the major parties have ignored, or because of public dissatisfaction with the major party candidates, rather than because many voters believe in a multiparty system as a matter of principle.

The Rise of Independent Candidates

In recent elections, dissatisfaction with the major parties has led several candidates to run as independents, unconnected with any party organization. The most successful was Ross Perot, who mounted a well-funded independent candidacy for president in 1992 before running as the Reform Party candidate in 1996. The story of Perot's two candidacies, one as an independent and the other as a minor-party candidate, helps us understand some of the advantages and disadvantages of each choice.

In his independent candidacy in 1992, Perot and his supporters built a remarkably strong national organization. Through its efforts, Perot got on the ballot in all 50 states. He ended the race with 19.7 million votes—a larger share of the popular vote than any "third" candidate in history who was not a former president. In fact, he outdrew the combined total of all his minor-party opponents in that race by more than 19 million ballots. The key ingredient in his success was money; Perot invested more than $65 million of his own funds in his campaign. That financed organizational efforts at the grassroots level and bought large blocks of expensive television time. Even so, Perot failed to win a single state, and much of his support came from voters who were more dissatisfied with the major-party candidates than they were attracted to a long-lasting commitment to another party or candidate.[28]

Three years later, Perot organized the new Reform Party and sought to qualify it for the ballot in all 50 states. That was harder than qualifying to run as an independent. In California, his toughest challenge, Perot had to get at least 890,000 signatures on a petition by October 1995 to win a place on the state's ballot 13 months later. He failed. Using a different mechanism, Perot finally qualified in California and in all other states but found it difficult to recruit acceptable Reform candidates for other offices. On Election Day, Perot got less than half as many votes as a Reform Party candidate than he had four years earlier as an independent.

Why was his minor-party effort less successful? Many factors were at work. One reason may have been simple familiarity; some candidates do not benefit from letting voters get to know them better. Perot spent much less of his own money in 1996 than he had four years earlier. In addition, it is harder for an organization to support many candidates rather than just one. In 2000, for example, conflicts among Reform Party activists became so intense that the party's national convention disintegrated into a fistfight and the party split. (See box "Want to Run for Office as an Independent? Good Luck!" on page 48.)

Ralph Nader's experience as a presidential candidate in 2000 and 2004 was very different from Perot's. In 2000, Nader won access to 14 state ballots fairly easily because he ran as the Green Party candidate, which had already qualified for ballot access in those states. In 2004, Nader struggled to get on those same ballots as an independent candidate. Democratic activists filed lawsuits to try to keep Nader off state ballots, because his

Want to Run for Office as an Independent? Good Luck!

If you want to run for the U.S. House of Representatives as an independent (nonparty) candidate in Georgia, Montana, or North or South Carolina, you will have to get more than 10,000 people to sign a petition for you. (As a result, no independent candidate for the House has ever appeared on a government-printed ballot in either North or South Carolina.)

If you'd prefer to run as an independent candidate for president, then you must get a total of almost a million valid signatures on petitions. Each state has its own requirements, which you will have to research and follow. In Texas alone, you'd need to get about 80,000 signatures from registered voters during a 75-day period, which ends in May of an election year, and none of the signers can have voted in the most recent party primaries. In Florida, you must have almost 120,000 signatures from registered voters by September 1 of the election year. (You'll actually need about twice as many signatures, because Democratic and Republican election clerks can disallow any signatures they don't regard as valid.) And you'll need to counter major party efforts to thwart you; in 2014, for instance, the Ohio Republican Party's records show that it paid a law firm $300,000 to help keep the Libertarian gubernatorial candidate off the ballot.

Paid signature gatherers usually earn about $2 for each signature collected, so unless you are able to recruit a small army of volunteers, you'd pay several million dollars just to get the petitions signed and much more for the lawyers in each state who will be needed to defend your petitions against legal challenges from other candidates or parties. These are examples of ways in which state legislatures, made up almost entirely of Democrats and Republicans, have protected the two major parties by passing laws making it much tougher for minor party and independent candidates to get on the ballot.

Sources: Richard L. Winger, *Ballot Access News*, September 1, 2016, p. 3 (on presidential candidates), Winger, personal communication (on House candidates), and Winger, *Ballot Access News*, June 1, 2015, p. 3.

candidacy was expected to hurt Democrat John Kerry more than Republican George W. Bush. And in 2016, the effort by anti-Trump Republicans to run a "true conservative" in the general election began too late to assure ballot access for the candidate as an independent.

Even when a minor party meets the difficult challenge of getting and keeping its line on the ballot, it will still face the enormous hurdle of recruiting candidates for thousands of state legislative seats and county offices as well as for president. The Greens and the Libertarians have made real efforts since 2000 to establish themselves as organizations that contest offices from the top to the bottom of the ballot. If history is any guide, however, that is a battle they will lose. The result is that when voters consider alternatives to the major parties, independent candidates (especially if they happen to be billionaires, such as New York mayor Michael Bloomberg, who considered running for president as an independent in 2016) will continue to have advantages over those who try to form fully elaborated minor parties.

Will the Two-Party System Continue?

We can draw two main conclusions from this look at two-party politics and its alternatives. First, the two-party system is secure in the United States. Minor parties are not gaining ground. Third-party members of Congress, common in the early decades of the two-party system, have been rare in the past century and especially in recent years. Since 1952, only three members of Congress have been elected on a minor-party ticket. And even though the major-party presidential nominees in 2016 had record-high unfavorability ratings, minor-party and independent presidential candidates still failed to attract a big following.

Some of the barriers to ballot access for minor-party and independent candidates have been lowered. And quirks in some states' election laws continue to support a few minor parties. New York is a good example; several minor parties, notably the Conservatives and the Working Families Party, survive because state law allows them to nominate candidates of a major party to run under their own parties' labels as well.[29] But in most cases, candidates other than Republicans and Democrats must still jump substantial hurdles to get on state ballots and satisfy a patchwork of differing state laws to qualify for the ballot nationwide. Even when courts have overturned laws that discriminate against these candidates, the decisions have been limited, requiring petitioners to mount a challenge in each state.[30]

In addition, independent and minor-party candidates still face huge financial disadvantages. Although candidates don't need to be Democrats or Republicans in order to reach voters throughout the United States with television and the Internet, the enormous cost of modern campaigns probably restricts this opportunity to only a few highly visible or personally wealthy individuals. Minor-party presidential candidates can receive public funding for their campaign (as they do in other democracies, such as Canada and Australia) if they win at least 5 percent of the popular vote. However, in 30 years, the only campaign to qualify was that of Perot's Reform Party in 1996. That assured the Reform Party's 2000 presidential candidate of receiving $12 million in federal funds for his campaign. The money no doubt increased the attractiveness of the party's presidential nomination. Yet the eventual nominee, Patrick Buchanan, earned less than half of 1 percent of the popular vote.

Independent candidates for president and governor have made some elections less predictable. But running by themselves, with no other candidates on their "tickets," they are not likely to create a lasting challenge to the Democrats and Republicans. To make a sustained challenge that could fundamentally transform the American parties, these independents would need to organize to confront the major parties from the top to the bottom of the ballot. Those who try soon realize that the two-party system may not be greatly beloved, but it is very well entrenched.

How would a multiparty system change American politics? Proponents could cite a number of benefits. Voters would have more choices. A greater variety of views would be able to find expression through a party platform. Smaller parties, speaking for identifiable segments of society, might give citizens in these groups more confidence that their voices are being heard.

On the other hand, when the threshold for ballot access is lowered, extremist parties are better able to compete. In a system where the government will probably be a coalition of several parties, voters need to anticipate the compromises that their preferred party will make in order to form a government. To influence that compromise, voters may cast their ballot strategically for a party whose views are more extreme than their own.[31] In contrast, votes are more directly translated into leadership in a majoritarian two-party system, though American politics, with its separation of powers, limits that direct translation now. Coalition governments can be unstable. And a multiparty system would likely require major changes in American electoral institutions, such as the single-member presidency and plurality elections. But these advantages and disadvantages are a moot point because American two-party politics remains durable.

The second major trend we have seen in this chapter is an especially intriguing one. The Democratic and Republican Parties are highly competitive at the national level. Presidential elections are won by relatively small margins, and both parties have had recent runs of dominance in Congress. When we look beneath this level at individual House and state legislative districts, however, much of the close competition disappears. The intense party competition at the national level reflects the existence of fairly equal numbers of safe Democratic and safe Republican congressional and lower-level seats.[32]

Officeholders elected in districts that are relatively safe for their party may not feel as great a need to appeal to independents and voters of the other party as they would if the district were more competitive. Incumbents in safe districts face more of a threat from within their own party, in the primary election, than from the other party. These primary threats usually come from the ideological extremes of their party. As Chapter 13 shows, then, safe incumbents can take more partisan stands in order to ward off a primary challenger, knowing that they are not likely to suffer for it in the general election. Party polarization in Congress, state legislatures, and among politically involved citizens has accompanied this process. Even in a relatively stable two-party system such as that in the United States, moderation in political debate can be in short supply.

Notes

1 Arend Lijphart, *Electoral Systems and Party Systems* (New York: Oxford University Press, 1994).

2 See John F. Bibby and L. Sandy Maisel, *Two Parties—Or More?* 2nd. ed. (Boulder, CO: Westview, 2003), p. 46. Final election results may show this to be true of 2016 as well.

3 My thanks to Frances Lee for this point.

4 *Inter*party competition refers to competition between the parties, as opposed to competition within a particular party ("*intra*party"). The index was first presented in Austin Ranney, "Parties in State Politics," in Herbert Jacob and Kenneth Vines, eds., *Politics in the American States* (Boston: Little, Brown, 1965), p. 65. For alternative indices, see Thomas M. Holbrook and Emily Van Dunk, "Electoral Competition in the American States," *American Political Science Review* 87 (1993): 955–962 and James W. Ceaser and Robert P. Saldin, "A New Measure of Party Strength," *Political Research Quarterly* 58 (2005): 245–256.

5 See Steven Rogers, "Strategic Challenger Entry in a Federal System," *Legislative Studies Quarterly* 40 (2015): 539–570.

6 John M. Carey, Richard G. Niemi, and Lynda W. Powell, "Incumbency and the Probability of Reelection in State Legislative Elections," *Journal of Politics* 62 (2000): 671–700.

7 Stephen Ansolabehere and James M. Snyder Jr., "The Incumbency Advantage in U.S. Elections," *Election Law Journal* 1 (2002): 315–338. See also David W. Romero, "What They Do Does Matter," *Political Behavior* 28 (2006): 241–258.

8 Gary C. Jacobson, "It's Nothing Personal: The Decline of the Incumbency Advantage in US House Elections," *Journal of Politics* 77 (2015): 861–873.

9 Bruce I. Oppenheimer, "Deep Red and Blue Congressional Districts," in Lawrence C. Dodd and Bruce I. Oppenheimer, eds., *Congress Reconsidered*, 8th ed. (Washington, DC: CQ Press, 2005), pp. 135–157.

10 Bill Bishop with Robert G. Cushing, *The Big Sort* (New York: Houghton Mifflin, 2008). See also Torben Lutjen and Robert Matschoss, "Ideological Migration in Partisan Strongholds," *The Forum* 13 (2015): 311–346 and Jesse Sussell and James A. Thomson, "Are Changing Constituencies Driving Rising Polarization in the U.S. House of Representatives?" Rand Research Report, 2015, at www.rand.org/pubs/research_reports/RR896.html (accessed September 7, 2016).

11 Marjorie Randon Hershey, Nathaniel Birkhead, and Beth C. Easter, "Party Activists, Ideological Extremism, and Party Polarization," in Mark D. Brewer and L. Sandy Maisel, eds., *The Parties Respond*, 5th ed. (Boulder, CO: Westview Press, 2013), pp. 75–102.

12 Bernard L. Fraga and Eitan D. Hersh, "Why Is There So Much Competition in U.S. Elections?" undated, at www.eitanhersh.com/uploads/7/9/7/5/7975685/fraga_hersh_compet_v2_8_1.pdf (accessed September 7, 2016).

13 Maurice Duverger, *Political Parties* (New York: Wiley, 1954). See also Octavio Amorim Neto and Gary W. Cox, "Electoral Institutions, Cleavage Structures, and the Number of Parties," *American Journal of Political Science* 41 (1997): 149–174.

14 In 1955, 58 percent of all American state legislative districts were multimember; this number had declined to 10 percent by the 1980s. See Richard Niemi, Simon

Jackman, and Laura Winsky, "Candidates and Competitiveness in Multimember Districts," *Legislative Studies Quarterly* 16 (1991): 91–109.

15 See A. James Reichley, *The Life of the Parties* (Lanham, MD: Rowman & Littlefield, 2002), p. 4.

16 Leon Epstein, *Political Parties in the American Mold* (Madison, WI: University of Wisconsin Press, 1986), pp. 129–132.

17 Marjorie Randon Hershey, "How American Election Law and Institutions Cripple Third Parties," in Matthew J. Streb, ed., *Law and Election Politics* (New York: Routledge, 2012).

18 See Ronald B. Rapoport and Walter J. Stone, *Three's a Crowd* (Ann Arbor, MI: University of Michigan Press, 2005) on Republican successes in appealing to Ross Perot supporters in 1994 and 1996; and Shigeo Hirano and James M. Snyder, Jr., "The Decline of Third Party Voting in the U.S.," *Journal of Politics* 69 (2007): 1–16.

19 Brian Schaffner, Matthew J. Streb, and Gerald C. Wright, "A New Look at the Republican Advantage in Nonpartisan Elections," *Political Research Quarterly* 60 (2007): 240–249.

20 Brian F. Schaffner, Matthew J. Streb, and Gerald C. Wright, "Teams without Uniforms," *Political Research Quarterly* 54 (2001): 7–30.

21 Gerald C. Wright and Brian F. Schaffner, "The Influence of Party," *American Political Science Review* 96 (2002): 367–379.

22 In a 2015 Gallup Poll, for instance, 60 percent said a third major party is needed because the Republicans and Democrats "do such a poor job" of representing the American people. See Justin McCarthy, "Majority in U.S. Maintain Need for Third Party," Gallup Poll, September 15, 2015, at www.gallup.com/poll/185891/majority-maintain-need-third-major-party.aspx (accessed September 7, 2016).

23 J. David Gillespie, *Politics at the Periphery* (Columbia: University of South Carolina Press, 1993).

24 Holly A. Heyser, "Minnesota Governor," in Larry J. Sabato, ed., *Midterm Madness* (Lanham, MD: Rowman & Littlefield, 2003), pp. 233–245.

25 Among the best books on American third parties are Steven J. Rosenstone, Roy L. Behr, and Edward H. Lazarus, *Third Parties in America*, 2nd. ed. (Princeton, NJ: Princeton University Press, 1996); Paul S. Herrnson and John C. Green, *Multiparty Politics in America*, 2nd. ed. (Lanham, MD: Rowman & Littlefield, 2002); Bibby and Maisel, *Two Parties—Or More?*; Scot Schraufnagel, *Third Party Blues* (New York: Routledge, 2011); and Rapoport and Stone, *Three's a Crowd*.

26 Minor parties' websites can be found at www.politics1.com/parties.htm.

27 Rosenstone, Behr, and Lazarus, *Third Parties in America*, p. 162.

28 See Paul R. Abramson, John H. Aldrich, and David W. Rohde, *Change and Continuity in the 1992 Elections* (Washington, DC: CQ Press, 1994).

29 This is called "fusion." See Howard A. Scarrow, *Parties, Elections, and Representation in the State of New York* (New York: New York University Press, 1983).

30 See *Ballot Access News* at www.ballot-access.org, and issues of the *Election Law Journal*.

31 Orit Kedar, "When Moderate Voters Prefer Extreme Parties," *American Political Science Review* 99 (2005): 185–199.

32 James E. Campbell, "The 2002 Midterm Election," *PS* 36 (2003): 203–207.

PART TWO

The Political Party as an Organization

The next three chapters will examine the formal **party organization**—the set of party committees and volunteers who work at all the levels at which Americans elect public officials: precincts, townships, wards, cities, counties, congressional districts, states, and the federal government—and the informal groups of activists who give life to these organizations. How do the party organizations work, and how have they changed over time? What kinds of people become party activists? The nature of its organization influences the party's ability to act effectively in the larger political system.

American party organizations vary tremendously, from powerful and elaborate structures to empty shells. Compared with those of other Western democracies, however, most American party organizations would be considered fairly weak. Constrained by state laws, the party organizations have rarely been able to exercise much influence over the party's candidates and officeholders (the party in government) and the party in the electorate.

The three parts of a party differ in their goals. In an election, for instance, the party organization and party activists hope to support as many of the party's candidates as possible. In contrast, each individual candidate wants as much of the party's money as he or she can get, while party voters are concerned instead with taxes or same-sex marriage or cheaper college tuition. Each seeks control of the party to achieve its own ends. In the American system, the party organizations find it difficult to hold their own in this competition and to get the resources they need to affect elections and promote policies. American party organizations can't translate their platform planks into law. They must depend on the members of their party in government to do that. Party organizations must work hard to court and mobilize the party electorate, who may support some party candidates but not others.

This lack of integration among the party's component parts is typical of **cadre parties**—one of two terms often used to describe the nature of party organizations. Imagine that party organizations are arranged along a continuum. At one end is the cadre party, in which the organization is run by a few leaders and activists with little or no broader public participation. These officials and activists make the organization's decisions, choose its candidates, and select the strategies they think will appeal to voters. They focus largely on electing party candidates rather than on issues. Thus the party becomes active mainly during campaigns, when candidates need their party organization's help the most. The cadre party, then, is a coalition of people and interests brought together temporarily to win elections, only to shrink to a smaller core once the election is over.

At the other end of this scale is the **mass-membership party**, a highly participatory organization in which all three parts of the party are closely linked. In this type of party, large numbers of voters become dues-paying members of the party organization and participate in its activities year-round, not just during campaigns. A mass-membership party concentrates on promoting an ideology and educating the public as well as on winning elections. Its members decide what the party's policies should be and choose its organizational leaders. Members of the party in the electorate are so essential to the party organization that the party may even provide them with such nonpolitical benefits as insurance and leisure-time activities. Because the membership-based party organization has great power over candidate selection—it does not need to give less involved voters the right to choose party candidates in a primary election—it can also exercise much greater control over the party in government.

In important ways, the major American parties are cadre parties. The great majority of local and state party leaders and activists are not paid professionals but volunteers, whose party activities increase at election time. These organization leaders do not try hard to control the party's candidates and elected officials, nor are they likely to succeed. Most party identifiers in the United States have no involvement in the party organization.

They do not fit the cadre mold perfectly; in practice, parties have a tendency to slip out of precise definitions.[1] For example, party leaders contact their supporters in the electorate more often now than they did a few decades ago, and the state and national party organizations are active year-round. Nevertheless, these changes have not made the major American parties into mass-membership organizations. The major parties concentrate on electing candidates more than on educating voters on issues.

Why does it matter whether party organizations are strong or weak, cadre or mass membership? Because party organizations are the backbone of the political parties. They are the sector of the parties that provides continuity, while the party's candidates, elected officials, and identifiers come and go. A strong party organization can hunt for the resources needed for long-term election success. It can provide voters with choices and candidates with expertise. When the organization is weak, a power vacuum develops that may be filled by interest groups, ambitious individuals, or unending conflict.

As the American party organizations have become more robust in recent years, they have altered our politics in ways ranging from campaign fundraising to the nature of political debate. Chapter 3 begins by exploring the party organizations closest to home: state and local parties.

Note

1   See Alan Ware, ed., *Political Parties* (New York: Basil Blackwell, 1987).

CHAPTER 3

The State and Local Party Organizations

If you ever get so involved in an issue—or so irritated at government—that you might think about running for office, you have lots of options. There are more than 500,000 elective offices in the United States, and all but 537 are in state and local governments. State and local party organizations, then, are vital to American campaigning. Even candidates for national office, such as Hillary Clinton and Donald Trump in 2016, must pay special attention to the health of the state and local parties' field organizations. Why? These are the organizations where much of the voter mobilization takes place. The stronger these party organizations, the more effectively they can mobilize support.

Yet in recent decades, battles between mainstream groups and insurgents have riddled many of these party organizations. In particular, Tea Party activists, evangelical groups, and business-oriented factions have struggled for control over many state Republican parties. These splits worry national Republican leaders and presidential candidates, whose hopes for the future direction of their party are at stake. They also suggest that the state and local parties are important enough to party activists to be worth fighting for.

State and local party organizational power has shifted markedly over time. In the late 1800s, many urban party organizations functioned as political "machines," which controlled city governments by bringing lots of new immigrants to the polls to vote for their party. Just a few decades later, a variety of forces had drained the strength of these party machines, and most party organizations had become weak or inactive. Since that time, and coinciding with the national parties' polarization, party organizations have revived at all levels and moved into the Internet age. State and local parties, in short, have been on a wild ride during the past century—demonstrating their ability to adapt even to major changes in the American political environment.

In turn, these changes in party strength have profoundly affected American politics. As the introduction to Part II noted, the party organization is the foundation of a political party. It gives the party a way to endure, despite a changing cast of candidates and elected officeholders. More than the party in government or the party identifiers, the party organizations are the keepers of the parties' brands—the unifying labels and ideas that give candidates a shortcut in identifying themselves to voters and that give voters a means to choose among candidates. Without this organization, a party becomes only an unstable alliance of convenience among candidates, and between candidates and groups of voters—too changeable to accomplish the important work that parties can perform in a democracy.

This chapter will trace these tumultuous changes in the state and local party organizations. After considering how to measure "party strength," we will begin by exploring the evolution of local party organizations from the fabled political machines that dominated a number of eastern and Midwestern cities beginning in the late 1800s and early 1900s to the fall and rise of local parties more recently. Finally, we will see how the state parties grew from weakness to greater strength in the past four decades.

What Is a "Strong" Party?

How can a "strong" party be defined? Many researchers measure a party's vigor by examining its organizational features. Stronger parties would have larger budgets and more full-time, paid staff members. That can be termed **party organizational strength**.

There are other ways to measure party strength. A strong party would work effectively to register voters, tell them about party candidates, and get them to the polls on Election Day. It would be successful in filling its ticket with attractive candidates. Its candidates would win more races than they lose. We could even measure whether the party is able to get its platform enacted into law (as we will in Chapter 15). But in order for a party to do these things—and especially to register voters, canvass, and get out the vote—it needs money, staff, and other forms of organizational strength. We will look at most of these measures of party strength in this chapter but focus mainly on party organizational strength.

How States Regulate the Parties

Consistent with the traditional American suspicion of political parties, most states extensively regulate their party organizations. State laws often tell parties how they must choose their candidates, who can sign a party's petition to get on the ballot, even the types of public buildings in which parties must hold their conventions. Party committees are regulated "lightly" in only about a third of the states, most of them in the South, Plains states, and upper Midwest.[1] At the other extreme, in 15 states—including California, New Jersey, and Ohio—lawmakers have chosen to control almost every detail of the parties' activities.

Even the most picky state restrictions have not necessarily weakened the parties. Some of the strongest party organizations in the nation are also the most tightly regulated. In fact, all these state laws help protect the Democratic and Republican Parties against competition from minor parties. However, they do give state governments a set of tools for keeping an eye on their parties. They indicate as well that state law does not view the parties simply as private groups. As Leon Epstein argued, the parties are seen as public utilities that can be subject to a great deal of state direction.[2] Congress, too, has passed several laws since the 1970s regulating national party organizations' campaign fund-raising.

States don't have complete freedom to make rules for their party organizations. Federal courts have frequently stepped in to protect citizens' voting rights (see Chapter 8), to keep the states from unreasonably limiting minor-party and independent candidates' ballot access (see Chapter 2), and to acknowledge the parties' right to control their internal affairs. In the 1980s, for example, the Supreme Court ruled that the state of Connecticut could not prevent the Republican Party from opening up its primary to independents if it wanted to. Soon after, the Court threw out a California law saying, among other things, that parties could not endorse candidates in primary elections. A 2000 Supreme Court decision overturned a California state initiative setting up a "blanket primary" on the ground that it violated the party organization's First Amendment right to decide who votes in its primaries.[3] Nevertheless, American party organizations are more heavily regulated than are parties in other democracies.

Levels of Party Organization

Americans elect officeholders at different levels: county, state, national. The party organizations follow the same pattern. This structure is often pictured as a pyramid based in the grassroots and stretching up to the statewide organization. A pyramid, however, gives the misleading impression that the layer at the top can give orders to the layers below. So picture these party organizations, instead, as they fit into a geographic map (Figure 3.1).

Local Party Committees

The county is the main unit of local party organization in most states, because so many important local officials are elected at the county level, and usually in partisan elections: sheriffs, prosecutors, clerks, judges, council members, treasurers, assessors, surveyors, coroners, and more. These officials control vital functions ranging from policing the area to assessing and collecting property taxes. The party organizations at the county level, which support candidates for these offices, are the parties' "grassroots," where most of the activity of party volunteers takes place. In a few states, local parties are organized at the town, state legislative, or congressional district level.

In most areas, counties are divided into smaller units called precincts. Each precinct (or town, township, or ward, in some areas) in theory has a party leader—a committeeman and/or committeewoman—to conduct the

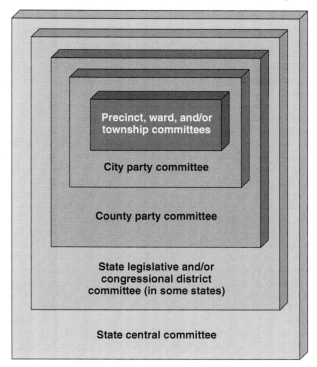

FIGURE 3.1 The Party Organizations in a Typical State

party's activities in that area. Because there are about 193,000 precincts in the United States, it would be easy to imagine a vibrant party base made up of at least 200,000 committed men and women. However, this exists only in the dreams of party leaders; in reality, up to half of these (unpaid) local committee positions are vacant because nobody volunteers to serve in them.

Most precinct committeemen and women are chosen at local party caucuses or in primary elections. Party caucuses are meetings in the precincts and wards that are open to any voters in the area who consider themselves affiliated with the party. These local party supporters elect the precinct committee leaders and often elect delegates to county and/or state conventions as well. In states that choose precinct committeemen and women in primaries, any voter may nominate him- or herself for the job by filing a petition signed by a handful of local voters. If, as often happens, there are no nominees, the committeeman or woman may be elected by an even smaller handful of write-in votes. These local committee positions, in short, are not normally in great demand, especially in the weaker party in an area. So the local parties are far from being exclusive clubs; their "front doors" are open to anyone who chooses to walk in.

What do these precinct and county party leaders do? Their three most important jobs are registering new voters, going door-to-door (called "canvassing" or "D2D") to talk to potential supporters about the party's candidates, and getting voters to the polls (known as "GOTV," or "get out the vote"). They need to recruit volunteers to help with these labor-intensive tasks. County party leaders may also try to raise money to support local candidates. And when there are vacancies on the party ticket—offices for which nobody chose to run in the primary election—then the local party committees may be responsible for appointing someone to run. In the less active local parties, these tasks may not get done. The precinct committeemen and women usually come together to make up the next level of local party organization, or they elect the delegates who do.

State Central Committees

At the state level, the party organization is usually called the state central committee. The state parties typically help to recruit candidates for statewide offices (for instance, state treasurer and attorney general) and state legislative seats, assist in training them, and raise money to support their campaigns. They may also work with local parties on the crucial tasks of voter registration, canvassing, and GOTV.

State law usually gives party central committees a number of other important powers: the responsibility for organizing party conventions, drafting party platforms, supervising the spending of party campaign funds, and selecting the party's presidential electors, representatives to the national committee, and some of the national convention delegates. In some states, the party's statewide convention has these powers instead. In a few states, such as Indiana, the party's state convention actually nominates candidates for some statewide offices, a reminder of the power that party conventions held in the days before primary elections.

We can draw four important conclusions from these organizational patterns. First, the levels of party organization have been set up to correspond to the voting districts in which citizens choose public officials in that state (for example, county and congressional districts), and the main responsibility of these organizations under state law is to contest elections. State laws, then, see the party organizations as helpers in the state's task of holding nominations and elections—tasks that before the turn of the twentieth century belonged almost entirely to the parties alone.

Second, the laws indicate that state legislators are ambivalent about what constitutes a party organization. Many of these laws treat the parties as cadre organizations (see page 53) run by a small number of party officials. Yet when they specify that the party's own officials, including local committeemen and women, must be chosen in a primary election, this gives party voters—and potentially, any voters—a vital, quasi-membership role in the party organization. So state laws help to create a party that is semipublic, rather than a genuinely private group whose active members choose its leaders and set its direction.

Third, party organizations in one state or locality can behave differently from party organizations in another area. One state's Democratic Party may use a primary election to choose a presidential nominee; another state's Democratic organization might choose a caucus instead. One state Republican Party may use a winner-take-all system (see Chapter 2) to make that choice; another state's Republican organization might use a more proportional system.

Finally, one reason for these differences among state parties is that the American party organizations are not a hierarchy, in which the lower levels take their orders from the higher levels. Instead, through much of their history, the parties were best described as "a system of layers of organization,"[4] or as a "stratarchy,"[5] in which each level has some independent power. In fact, power traditionally flowed from bottom to top in the local and state parties.[6] Thus, the party organizations remain fairly decentralized and rooted in local politics, even in the face of recent trends toward stronger state and national committees.

The Legendary Party Machines

Local party organizational strength in the United States peaked in the late 1800s and early 1900s, when the urban political "machine" reached the height of its power. By some accounts, most American cities were governed by machines at this time.[7] The party machine was a disciplined organization that controlled the nominations to elective office. It had the hierarchical structure that today's local parties lack. It relied on material incentives—giving out jobs and favors—to build support among voters. Above all, it controlled the government in a city or county.

Yet, for all their power in shaping how we think of party organizations, the great urban machines were not found in all cities, and they gradually disappeared. The decline began in the 1930s, and almost all were gone by the 1960s and 1970s. These "traditional party organizations"[8] were brought down by a number of forces. Some party machines, such as those in Pittsburgh and New York, never recovered from election upsets by middle-class reformers. Others, including those in Philadelphia and Gary, Indiana, lost power when racial tensions overshadowed the old ethnic politics.[9]

How the Party Machines Developed

In the late 1800s, large numbers of the immigrants arriving in major American cities had urgent economic and social needs. These newcomers were poor, often spoke no English, and faced a difficult adjustment to their new urban environment. Party leaders in many of these cities—usually Democrats, reflecting that party's history of openness to immigrants—saw the opportunity for a mutually profitable exchange. The immigrants needed jobs, social services, and other benefits that a city government could provide.

The party leaders needed large numbers of votes in order to gain control of city government. If the party could register these new arrivals to vote, their votes could put the party in power. In return, the party would then control the many resources that the government had available and could give the new voters the help they needed so desperately.

Jobs ranked high among the newcomers' needs. So the most visible benefits offered by party machines were **patronage** jobs in the city government—those awarded on the basis of party loyalty rather than other qualifications. During the glory days of the machine, thousands of these patronage positions were at the machines' disposal. By giving patronage jobs to party supporters, the party's leaders could be assured that city workers would remain loyal to the machine and work to help it win elections by delivering not only their own votes but those of their family, friends, and neighbors as well. After all, if the party lost the election, then these patronage workers would lose their jobs.

In its prime, many decades ago, the Chicago Democratic machine controlled an estimated 35,000 patronage jobs in government and influenced hiring for another 10,000 jobs in the private economy. Adding the families and friends of these jobholders, the party machine could deliver 350,000 motivated voters at election time. Local party workers also won voter loyalties by finding social welfare agencies for the troubled or providing deliveries of coal to the poor. Machine leaders, called "bosses," attended weddings and wakes, listened to job seekers and business executives, bailed out drunks, and helped the hungry and homeless.

The machine had favors to offer local businesses as well. Governments purchase many goods and services from the private sector. If a bank wanted to win the city's deposits, it could expect to compete more effectively for the city's business if it were willing to contribute to the party machine. Insurance agents and lawyers who wanted city contracts, newspapers that printed city notices, even suppliers of soap to city bathrooms were motivated to donate money or services to the party machine. In addition, city governments regularly make decisions that affect individuals' and businesses' economic standing, such as issuing building permits and conducting health inspections. If you were helped by one of these decisions, you could expect the machine to ask for your thanks in the form of contributions. These so-called **preferments** could be used effectively to build political power.

How Machines Held on to Power

The classic urban machine, then, was not just a party organization but also an "informal government," a social service agency, and a ladder for upward social and economic mobility. In some ways, it looked like the local organization of a European mass-membership party, except that the American machine had little or no concern with ideology. Its world was the city; it focused on the immediate needs of its constituents, and its politics were almost completely divorced from the issues that animated national politics.

An important source of the machines' strength was their ability to appeal to ethnic loyalties. Although there were party machines in cities without large immigrant populations, the rise and fall of the American political machine is closely linked to changes in ethnic-group migration to the big cities. The machine was a method by which ethnic groups, especially the Irish, gained a foothold in American politics.[10]

Machines could create a "designer electorate" by using force and intimidation to keep their opponents from voting. Because the party machines controlled the election process, it was possible, in a pinch, to change the election rules and even to count the votes in a creative manner. One of the indispensable tools of rival party workers in Indianapolis, for example, was a flashlight—to locate ballots that did not support the dominant party's candidates and happened to fly out of the window at vote-counting headquarters in the dark of night.

Machine politics was most likely to flourish in the big cities, but American party machines took root in other areas as well. The conditions that led to the development of machines, especially a large, parochially oriented population with immediate economic needs, were also found in small southern and one-company towns. Even some well-to-do suburbs have spawned strong machine-style party organizations. In the affluent Long Island suburbs of New York City, for example, a Republican Nassau County political machine dominated by Italian Americans controlled local government for generations before losing its power in the 1990s.[11] In nearby Queens, the local Democratic organization rebounded from scandal and continues to control primaries and elect candidates.

We cannot be certain how powerful the party machines really were, even at their strongest. A Chicago study found, for example, that the party machine distributed public services mainly on the basis of historical traditions and bureaucratic decision rules rather than to reward its political supporters.[12] In New Haven, researchers reported that the party machine was more concerned about ethnic loyalties than its own survival. The machine, led by Italian Americans, distributed summer jobs disproportionately to Italian kids from nonmachine wards, who rarely took part in later political work, and not to kids from strong machine areas.[13]

During the 1900s, however, the conditions that helped sustain party machines waned. Political reforms took away most of the patronage jobs that used to reward the party faithful. People get government jobs now by scoring well on civil service exams, not by supporting party candidates. Federal entitlement programs, such as food stamps and Social Security, reduced the need for the favors that party machines could provide. Economic growth has boosted many Americans' income levels and reduced the attractiveness of the remaining patronage jobs; the chance to work as a sewer inspector just doesn't hold the allure that it once may have had.

Higher education levels have increased people's ability to fend for themselves in a complex bureaucratic society. And in many areas, racial divisions have overwhelmed the machine's ability to balance competing ethnic groups.

Local Party Organizations Declined and Then Rebuilt

After the machines failed, local party organizations weakened. By the mid-1900s, many city and county parties were starved for leadership, money, and volunteers. Then the local organizations began to rebuild. But the new local parties were no longer as capable of *running* campaigns as the traditional machines had been. Instead, they focused on providing services to candidates.

Local Parties in the 1970s

We got the first comprehensive look at the nature of local party organizations in a 1979–1980 survey of several thousand county leaders (see Table 3.1).[14] The results showed the distinctive fingerprints of cadre parties, and fairly weak ones at that. The researchers found that most county organizations were headed by a volunteer party chair and executive committee; almost none were paid for their efforts. Not many of these local party leaders had even the most basic forms of organizational support, such as a regular budget, a paid staff, a year-round office, or a listed telephone number. Most did meet regularly and tried to recruit and raise money for candidates. Their activity peaked during campaigns and then dropped off.

Democratic local parties didn't differ much from Republican local parties in the overall strength of their organizations during the 1970s. But states differed a great deal in the organizational strength of their local parties. Some states in the East and Midwest had relatively strong local organizations in both parties, while others—Louisiana, Georgia, Alabama, Kentucky, Texas, and Nebraska—had weak parties at the county level. In a few states, such as Arizona and Florida, one party was much stronger than the other party at the local level. But most often, strong organizations of one party were matched with strong organizations in the other party.[15]

There is persuasive evidence, however, that county party organizations in 1980 were in the middle of a growth spurt. In a 1984 survey, researchers found that most local parties had become much more involved in the nuts-and-bolts activities of registering voters, raising money, and publicizing candidates. A national survey in 1988 indicated even higher levels of local party activity.[16] This was happening as national party politics was becoming more polarized (see Chapter 7), which may have motivated local activists to re-energize their party organizations.

TABLE 3.1 Changes in Local Parties' Organizational Strength

The local party organization has (in percent)	Democrats		Republicans	
	1980	2008	1980	2008
A complete or nearly complete set of officers	90	89	81	92
A year-round office	12	25	14	23
A telephone listing	11	33	16	28
A website	–	70	–	70
Some paid staff members				
Full-time	3	6	4	5
Part-time	5	8	6	6
A regular annual budget	20	34	31	34
A campaign headquarters	55	54	60	63
Campaign activities				
Door-to-door canvassing	49	73	48	60
Organized campaign events	68	79	65	77
Arranged fund-raising events	71	75	68	72
Contributed money to candidates	62	57	70	59
Distributed posters or lawn signs	59	84	62	82
Used public opinion polls	11	11	16	13

Note: 1979–1980 figures are based on responses from 2,021 Democratic and 1,980 Republican organizations to a mail survey; 2008 data are from an Internet survey of local party chairs in 49 states, with responses from 511 Republicans and 676 Democrats. The 2008 survey is the most recent available.

Sources: John Frendreis and Alan R. Gitelson, "Local Parties in the 1990s," in John C. Green and Daniel M. Shea, *The State of the Parties*, 3rd ed. (Lanham, MD: Rowman & Littlefield, 1999), pp. 138–139 (for 1980), and Douglas D. Roscoe and Shannon Jenkins, *Local Party Organizations in the Twenty-First Century* (Albany, NY: SUNY Press, 2016), pp. 52 and 55.

Local Parties Today: More Active, More Structured

Local parties have continued to develop as structured organizations, though they are still not very institutionalized. Typically, they function only during the campaign season, and they rely on unpaid volunteers; paid staff members are rare. But their organizational effort has increased in the past three decades. Especially in urban areas, more county parties in the 2010s had the basic ingredients for a viable party organization (a permanent office, a budget, a phone listing, a staff) than in 1980.[17]

What do they do? Most county parties report that they concentrate on labor-intensive grassroots activities: organizing campaign events, voter registration, canvassing, and get out the vote drives, voter contact by phone and email, and distributing lawn signs and literature; and again, more local parties report conducting these activities now than they did in 1980. In particular, county parties are increasing their use of the Internet, including social media such as Twitter and Facebook. Websites, which can be more accessible to prospective volunteers than are local headquarters, are a boon to local parties.

Recently, many county party leaders have stepped up their efforts to promote absentee and early voting. By 2008, most states had relaxed their requirements for casting an absentee ballot. Large numbers of people can now vote by mail or in person before Election Day (see Chapter 8). To take advantage of these changes, many local parties now mail absentee ballot requests to all known party voters. By working to "bank" as many loyalists' votes as possible, the party organization can protect itself against last-minute shocks or Election Day thunderstorms that might depress the party vote. Local parties can spread their GOTV efforts over several weeks and then focus their Election Day activities on mobilizing less involved voters. The downside is that because absentee voting is much harder to monitor than voting at the polls, parties need to find ways to keep the other party from delivering absentee ballots that were filled out with "help" from overzealous party workers.

Local parties have also expanded their efforts to recruit candidates.[18] One study found that more than a third of people regarded as potentially strong candidates for Congress had in fact been contacted by local party leaders and that those contacted were more likely to run.[19] In another study, almost half of all state legislative candidates reported that local party leaders had encouraged them to run.[20]

Not many local party organizations put a priority on mobilizing young voters,[21] in part because people under 30 have such low voter turnout rates. And some local party activities have declined in recent decades. The main decline has been in activities that require funding; local parties often have limited success in raising money on their own, and since BCRA (see Chapter 12), national and state party organizations find it much harder to transfer money to local parties. State parties are more likely to provide assistance such as campaign training and legal advice than cash.[22] But more local parties have been energized and communicate with voters.

Michigan's Democratic Party provides an example of this increase in party organizational strength. Michigan Democrats, long the minority party, were in sorry shape for the first half of the 1900s, after machine politics had faded. By the end of the 1940s, more than half of the state's counties had no Democratic county committees. Then, labor unions, led by the United Auto Workers, stepped in to bring volunteer and financial support to the Democrats. Within two years, there was a Democratic Party organization in almost every county in the state. After internal conflicts took their toll in both parties during the 1960s and 1970s, organized labor moved again to rebuild the Democratic organization. By the late 1990s, the great majority of local Democratic Parties were raising money and contributing to candidates, buying ads, and distributing literature.[23]

In sum, we have good evidence that county party organizations are stronger and more active now than they were a generation ago, though their activity tends to ramp up mainly around elections. Local parties are especially active in more competitive and urban areas. It is harder to determine whether county parties today are as effective organizationally as were the old city machines, because there are so few reliable records prior to the 1960s. But it is possible that many counties now have more robust party organizations than they have ever had.

At the same time, however, the nature of the local parties has changed. From organizations that once were at the very center of election activity, county parties have become service providers to candidates who often have several other sources of help. Parties provide labor in the form of volunteers, but they are no longer a major source of campaign funds. So the challenge for the local parties is this: In an age of largely candidate-centered campaigns, does this growing county organizational presence matter as much as it would have a few decades ago?[24]

The State Parties: Gaining Money and Services

Throughout the parties' history, the state committees rarely had significant power within the party organizations. There have been exceptions; some powerful, patronage-rich state party organizations developed in the industrial heartland in the late 1800s.[25] But in most states, most of the time, the state committee was the weak link in the party organization. Yet in recent years, state parties have grown in importance. They are richer, more professional, and more active now, though they face major challenges from non-party groups and restrictive campaign finance laws. Let us start the story in the years before these changes began.

Traditional Weakness

State party organizations were traditionally weak for several reasons. They began as loose federations of semi-independent local party chairs. If one of these factions gained control over the state party organization, the others would be seriously threatened. So this threat was often avoided in the past by keeping most of the party's resources out of the hands of the state organization. Power was decentralized, collecting in the most effective of the local organizations.

Progressive reforms in the early 1900s kept the state party organizations weak. In particular, the introduction of the direct primary (see Chapters 9 and 10) limited the influence of state parties on campaigns for state offices. Candidates could win party nominations in primary elections, raise money for their own campaigns, and run them without party organizational help. Even today, relatively weak state party organizations are still found in the states where the Progressives and Populists had greatest strength—the more rural, western states.[26]

Beginning in the late 1960s, the national Democratic Party adopted reforms that greatly increased the number of primaries in the presidential nominating process. That reduced the state party's role in selecting a presidential candidate. The voters, rather than the state party organization, choose most convention delegates now, and state party leaders no longer control the delegates' votes. Extensions of civil service protections and unionization eroded the patronage base for many state parties. In fact, some courts have even prevented the firing of patronage workers when the governing party changes.

To add to the state party organizations' burden, one-party dominance in several states during the first half of the 1900s left several state parties weak and conflict-ridden. Southern Democratic Parties were a notable example. When a single party dominates a state's politics, the diverse forces within the state are likely to compete as factions within that party. The state party organization lacks the incentive and the ability to unify, as it would be inclined to do if it faced a viable opposition party. For all these reasons, many state party organizations had become "empty shells" in the 1940s and 1950s.[27]

Increasing Strength in Recent Decades

Since the 1960s, however, state party organizations have become more active and organizationally complex. Between the early 1960s and 2015, for example, the number of state parties with a permanent headquarters and a full-time, paid executive director, perhaps the most crucial position in a state party organization, has greatly increased; now, almost every state party has both. These resources—full-time leaders and a stable location—are vital to the development of parties as organizations.[28] In addition to their field staff members, many state parties have created internship programs for college students.

The problem is that the state party organizations face much stronger competition now from outside groups—super PACs and other non-party groups that can raise and spend unlimited sums, whereas party spending and receiving are tightly regulated by law.

Fund-raising In the 1990s, the national party committees played a vital role in building the state parties' fund-raising by transferring increasing amounts to the state parties and candidates. The transfers peaked in 2000, when the national party organizations gave a whopping $430 million to parties and candidates at the state level, many times the amounts that the national parties had infused into the state organizations just a few years earlier.[29]

But the 2000s have not been kind to the state parties. Beginning in 2002, the Bipartisan Campaign Reform Act (BCRA, discussed in Chapter 12) took away the national parties' ability to transfer soft money to the state parties. That was a blow to the state parties' finances. BCRA did allow state parties to spend federally regulated money (which the national parties could transfer to states without limits) on *federal* campaign activities and to raise a certain amount of soft money themselves (up to $10,000 per donor) for grassroots mobilization and party-building. States worked to become more efficient fund-raisers, spurred by the high stakes of polarized politics. Now, candidates for governor and state legislature receive at least some contributions from the majority of state party organizations. Most state parties recruit candidates for the state legislature, and almost half try to recruit congressional and gubernatorial candidates as well.[30]

Nevertheless, state parties' fund-raising has not been able to make up for the loss of the national parties' subsidy. And at the same time, other groups have far surpassed the state parties in raising money. Changes in national campaign finance law, such as the SpeechNow.org ruling in 2010, permitted some political action committees that spend money only on independent advertising, not on contributions to candidates—the so-called "super PACs" —to raise unlimited sums from individuals, corporations, and unions, as well as to spend unlimited sums on their independent ads. (These and other recent changes in campaign finance are discussed in Chapter 12.) With more dollars than volunteers, these super PACs have focused on costly broadcast and cable advertising. Their fund-raising has skyrocketed, allowing them to dominate the airwaves in some campaigns. State party organizations' advertising is minimal by comparison.

Congress has shown little interest in state party-building; although in 2014 it greatly increased the amount that national party organizations could accept from a single donor, the provision did not apply to the state parties. As a result, state parties, like their local brethren, focus on providing labor to candidates rather than money.

Campaign Services State parties have used their volunteer labor to focus on grassroots mobilization and targeting. To run a competitive campaign, state legislative and statewide candidates need field workers and voter lists, and they often turn to the state party organizations to provide these services. The state parties, whose budgets are better suited to field activity than to big media buys, have been able to comply. About 90 percent of the state parties in 2015 ran GOTV drives, and a similar percentage used online communications to spread the word.[31]

Parity in Organizational Strength As late as 2000, state Republican parties had bigger budgets and larger and more specialized staffs than did their Democratic counterparts. Because they were bigger and richer, they could provide more services to their candidates, such as polling, field staff, and researchers.[32]

But Democratic state parties have now caught up. Howard Dean was elected Democratic National Chairman in 2005 by promising state party chairs that he would give every state, not just the closely fought "battleground states," enough resources to hire at least three or four field organizers and access to a party database of voters. The effort was costly and controversial, but after Democrats made major gains in the 2006 and 2008 elections, Dean's work to build strong state parties was termed "visionary."[33] (For more on this program, see Chapter 4.)

Allied Groups A variety of groups such as labor unions, especially teachers' and government employees' unions, have worked closely with their state Democratic Party organizations to provide money, volunteers, and other services to party candidates. On the Republican side, small business groups, manufacturing associations, pro-life groups, and Christian conservative organizations often provide services to Republican candidates. As the state parties gain strength, these constituency groups often try to increase their influence on, or even take over, state party organizations. Christian Right and Tea Party groups, in particular, have come to dominate or substantially influence a majority of state Republican Parties (see box "What's the Matter with Kansas Republicans?" on page 71).[34]

Because of the close association between parties and activists from these allied groups, it is possible to think of the parties as networks of organizations, which include the interest groups, consulting firms, and "think tanks" (research groups) that offer their resources and expertise to a party.[35] For party leaders, these allied groups can be a mixed blessing, of course; super PACs, labor unions and religious groups have their own agendas, and they can be as likely to try to push the party into locally unpopular stands as to help elect party candidates.

It is not easy to build a powerful state party organization. It requires having to overcome the localism of American politics, widespread hostility toward party discipline, and conflicts among party supporters. Strong and skillful personal leadership by a governor, a senator, or a state chairman helps. So does a state tradition that accepts the notion of a unified and effective party. State law makes a difference as well. More centralized party organization has flourished in states that make less use of primary elections, so the party organization has more control over who the statewide and congressional candidates will be.

What's the Matter with Kansas Republicans?

Conflicts between more moderate and very conservative activists have plagued the Kansas Republican Party for decades. The conservatives won in 2010; Sam Brownback, a very conservative former U.S. Senator, was elected governor with an impressive 63 percent of the vote. He then pushed a highly conservative agenda through the state legislature: deep tax cuts (intended to produce economic growth), and cuts in social programs and education so severe that several Kansas schools eventually had to end their school year early for lack of funds. To seal their victory, Brownback supporters tried to purge the state party of Republican moderates; they challenged and defeated several moderate officeholders in the 2012 party primary.

But the conservative Brownback program didn't produce the results his backers hoped for. The big tax cuts created a drop in revenue so severe that the state's bond rating took a hit. Brownback's approval ratings tanked. When he ran for reelection in 2014, the long-standing internal party dispute erupted again; more than 100 moderate Republicans declared their intention to vote Democratic for governor.

Brownback was trailing in pre-election polls until he got an eleventh-hour boost from outside groups. In an extraordinarily well-funded race, supported by funds from the highly conservative Koch brothers as well as almost $5 million from the Republican Governors Association, Brownback eked out a narrow victory. Then the tide turned yet again in 2016 when moderate candidates beat several Brownback allies in Republican state legislative primaries.

These events demonstrate that the state and local party organizations are *permeable*. Party organization officials are usually elected by party activists and the volunteers they recruit. So groups within (or even outside of) the party structure can take over the party organization if they can gather sufficient numbers to win party elections. Tea Party, pro-life, and other groups have made serious efforts to do this in recent years, just as labor unions have been a vital part of many state Democratic Parties' revival and vibrancy. The result is that the direction and even the policies of a state party organization can change, depending on which group(s) control or influence its leadership at the time.

Sources: Manu Raju, "GOP Moderates Revolt in Kansas," *Politico*, July 16, 2014, at www. politico.com/story/2014/07/kansas-2014-election-sam-brownback-108952.html (accessed June 17, 2016) and Dan Balz, "Will Conservative Kansas Vote Out its Conservative Governor, Sam Brownback?" *Washington Post*, October 28, 2014, p. A1.

The Special Case of the South The most dramatic growth in party organization has occurred in the formerly one-party Democratic South. As the national Democratic Party showed greater concern for the rights of African Americans in the 1960s and 1970s, and particularly as the Voting Rights Acts increased the proportion of African American voters in southern states, conservative southern Democrats became increasingly estranged from their national party. Southern whites' support for Republican candidates grew, first in presidential elections and later in statewide and U.S. Senate races (as you will see in Chapter 7).

In the 1980s, state legislative candidates could sense the opportunity to run and win as Republicans. By 1994, Republicans were contesting as many as one-third of the state legislative seats in the South and winning two-thirds of the seats they contested. Since 1994, Republicans have overwhelmed Democratic candidates in state elections—this in a region where, just a few decades before, it was often more socially acceptable to admit to having an alcoholic than a Republican in the family.[36]

Along with these electoral gains, southern Republican Parties strengthened their organizations. North Carolina's state Republican Party, for example, was only minimally organized in the early 1970s. It started in earnest to recruit state legislative candidates during the mid-1980s. By the 1990s, with a much expanded budget and staff, the party focused on attracting experienced candidates for targeted districts, producing direct mail and radio ads, and helping candidates with training and research.[37] Democrats have had to respond, so both parties' organizations have grown stronger since the 1990s.[38] Southern parties, long among the weakest and most faction-ridden, have become some of the strongest state party organizations in the past two decades.[39]

Summing Up: How the State and Local Party Organizations Have Been Transformed

Party organizational strength has changed dramatically over time at the state and local levels. The high point of *local* party organizations may have been reached a hundred years ago, when some parties could be described as "armies drawn up for combat" with an "elaborate, well-staffed, and strongly motivated organizational structure."[40] Although this description did not apply to all local parties even then, it would be hard to find a local party organization that could be described in these terms today.

Local parties have been buffeted by a variety of forces since then. Progressive reforms adopted in the early 1900s undermined party organizations by limiting their control over nominations and general elections as well as their patronage resources. Federal social service programs, economic growth, a more educated electorate, and even racial conflict also undercut the effectiveness of the local parties.[41]

Yet local parties have come a long way toward adapting to these changes. County parties have moved to fill at least some of the void created by the decline of the urban machines. New technologies such as websites and social networking are enabling county parties to expand their activities. Local party organizations, in short, are demonstrating again their ability to meet the new challenges posed by a changing environment—a resilience that has kept them alive throughout most of American history.

The state party organizations have followed a different route. Traditionally weak in all but a handful of states, the state parties have grown much more robust and professional in recent years. They are providing campaign and organizational services to candidates who, in earlier years, would not have dreamed of looking to their state headquarters for help. In fact, the recent flow of money, resources, and leadership from the national party to the state party, and in turn from the state to the local parties, helped to modify the traditional flow of party power. Through most of their lives, the American parties have been highly decentralized, with power and influence lodged at the grassroots. The parties were hollow at the top, depending on the base for whatever influence and resources they had. Because of the death of urban machines and the birth of vigorous state and national party organizations, we no longer see this extreme decentralization. The nationalization of American society and politics has affected the party organizations, leading to a greater balance of power among party organizations at different levels.

Ironically, although they are stronger now, the state and local party organizations probably have less impact on politics than they once did. They have much more competition for the attention of voters, candidates, and the media. The campaign communications from the parties merge into a flood of Internet, television, and direct mail fund-raising and advertising by super PACs and nonprofit groups, who all try to influence voters' choices. These non-party groups can raise money much more easily than state party organizations can, because contributions to the state parties are limited by law, whereas super PACs and nonprofits can raise and spend unlimited funds. This unlimited spending can drown out the voices of the party organizations, and at times even those of the candidates themselves.

The challenge is that many of these super PACs are funded by a handful of wealthy contributors whose commitment to politics may vary from year to year. They might advertise heavily in one election but not in the next. The party organizations, in contrast, are the "repeat players"—the stewards of the party's brand, who can serve as stable cues for voters over time. The parties must try to win majorities, so they may be more wary of extremist candidates and ideas than are the wealthy donors who drop in and out of elections. As repeat players, the state and local party organizations can more easily be held responsible by voters than can a super PAC that jumps into a race with a massive ad buy and then disappears.[42]

The increasing organizational strength of the state and local parties has helped them adopt modern campaign skills and recapture a role in candidates' campaigns. But it is not a *dominant* role—not in the way it could have been if party organizations, rather than voters in primaries, selected party candidates. Party organizations rarely *run* the campaigns; instead, their new resources give them more of a chance to compete for the attention of those who do—the candidates—at a time when other competitors (organized interests, consultants) have become more effective as well.

Does this mean that the increases in party organizational strength are unimportant? Not at all. In a very competitive political environment, there is little doubt that it is better to have a stronger organization than a weaker one and to have more resources rather than fewer. In the end, however, despite all the changes in party organization during the past few decades, their basic structural features have not changed. The American state and local parties remain cadre organizations run by a small number of activists; they involve the bulk of their supporters mainly at election time. By the standards of parties in other democratic nations, American state and local party organizations are relatively weak—more limited in their activities and authority and more easily dominated by a handful of activists and elected officials. But by the standards of American politics, the state and local organizations are more visible and active than they have been in some time.

Notes

1 Andrew M. Appleton and Daniel S. Ward, *State Party Profiles* (Washington, DC: CQ Press, 1997), Appendix. See also the National Conference of State Legislatures at www.ncsl.org.
2 A public utility is a government-regulated provider of services, such as a gas or a water company. Leon Epstein, *Political Parties in the American Mold* (Madison, WI: University of Wisconsin Press, 1986), pp. 155–199.
3 The cases are *Tashjian v. Republican Party of Connecticut* (1986), *Eu v. San Francisco County Democratic Central Committee et al.* (1989), and *California Democratic Party v. Jones* (2000).
4 V. O. Key, Jr., *Politics, Parties and Pressure Groups* (New York: Crowell, 1964), p. 316.
5 Samuel J. Eldersveld, *Political Parties: A Behavioral Analysis* (Chicago: Rand McNally, 1964).
6 The organization of American political parties differs from what Robert Michels calls the "iron law of oligarchy"—that organizations are inevitably controlled from the top. See Robert Michels, *Political Parties* (Glencoe, IL: Free Press, 1949).
7 M. Craig Brown and Charles N. Halaby, "Machine Politics in America, 1870–1945," *Journal of Interdisciplinary History* 17 (1987): 587–612.
8 See David Mayhew, *Placing Parties in American Politics* (Princeton, NJ: Princeton University Press, 1986), pp. 19–21.
9 See Kenneth Finegold, *Experts and Politicians* (Princeton, NJ: Princeton University Press, 1995).

10 Steven P. Erie, *Rainbow's End* (Berkeley, CA: University of California Press, 1988); but see John F. Bibby, "Party Organizations 1946–1996," in Byron E. Shafer, ed., *Partisan Approaches to Postwar American Politics* (New York: Chatham House, 1998), pp. 142–185.

11 Anne Freedman, *Patronage: An American Tradition* (Chicago: Nelson-Hall, 1994), Chapter 5.

12 Kenneth R. Mladenka, "The Urban Bureaucracy and the Chicago Political Machine," *American Political Science Review* 74 (1980): 991–998.

13 Michael Johnston, "Patrons and Clients, Jobs and Machines," *American Political Science Review* 73 (1979): 385–398. On the impact of patronage on party success, see Olle Folke, Shigeo Hirano, and James M. Snyder, Jr., "Patronage and Elections in U.S. States," *American Political Science Review* 105 (2011): 567–585.

14 James L. Gibson, Cornelius P. Cotter, John F. Bibby, and Robert J. Huckshorn, "Whither the Local Parties?" *American Journal of Political Science* 29 (1985): 139–160.

15 Cornelius P. Cotter, James L. Gibson, John F. Bibby, and Robert J. Huckshorn, *Party Organization in American Politics* (New York: Praeger, 1984), pp. 49–53.

16 See ibid., p. 54, for 1964–1980, and Charles E. Smith, Jr., "Changes in Party Organizational Strength and Activity 1979–1988," unpublished manuscript, Ohio State University, 1989.

17 Douglas D. Roscoe and Shannon Jenkins, *Local Party Organizations in the Twenty-First Century* (Albany, NY: SUNY Press, 2016), pp. 50–61.

18 Melody Crowder-Meyer, "The Party's Still Going," in John H. Green and Daniel J. Coffey, *The State of the Parties*, 6th ed. (Lanham, MD: Rowman & Littlefield, 2010), p. 120.

19 L. Sandy Maisel, "American Political Parties." in Jeffrey E. Cohen, Richard Fleisher, and Paul Kantor, eds., *American Political Parties: Decline or Resurgence?* (Washington, DC: CQ Press, 2001), pp. 112–114.

20 Gary F. Moncrief, Peverill Squire, and Malcolm E. Jewell, *Who Runs for the Legislature?* (Upper Saddle River, NJ: Prentice Hall, 2001).

21 Daniel M. Shea and John C. Green, "Local Parties and Mobilizing the Vote," in John C. Green and Daniel J. Coffey, *The State of the Parties,* 5th ed. (Lanham, MD: Rowman & Littlefield, 2007), pp. 222 and 224.

22 Roscoe and Jenkins, *Local Party Organizations*, pp. 29–37.

23 Carol S. Weissert, "Michigan," in Appleton and Ward, *State Party Profiles*, pp. 153–160.

24 John J. Coleman, "The Resurgence of Party Organization?" in Daniel M. Shea and John C. Green, eds., *The State of the Parties* (Lanham, MD: Rowman & Littlefield, 1994), pp. 282–298.

25 A. James Reichley, *The Life of the Parties* (Lanham, MD: Rowman & Littlefield, 2000), pp. 129–130.

26 Malcolm E. Jewell and Sarah M. Morehouse, *Political Parties and Elections in American States*, 4th ed. (Washington, DC: CQ Press, 2001), p. 4.

27 Ibid., p. 1.

28 See James L. Gibson, Cornelius P. Cotter, John F. Bibby, and Robert J. Huckshorn, "Assessing Party Organizational Strength," *American Journal of Political Science* 27 (1983): 193–222.

29 Raymond J. La Raja, "State Parties and Soft Money," in John C. Green and Rick Farmer, eds., *The State of the Parties*, 4th ed. (Lanham, MD: Rowman & Littlefield, 2003), pp. 132–150.

30 Raymond J. La Raja and Jonathan Rauch, "The State of State Parties," Brookings Institution, 2016, at www.brookings.edu/~/media/research/files/papers/2016/03/08-state-parties-la-raja-rauch/states.pdf (accessed June 17, 2016).

31 See ibid., p. 7.

32 John H. Aldrich, "Southern Parties in State and Nation," *Journal of Politics* 62 (2000): 656–657, Table 7.

33 See Ari Berman, "The Prophet," *The Nation*, January 5, 2009, at www.thenation.com/article/prophet (accessed June 17, 2016).

34 Kimberly H. Conger, *The Christian Right and Republican State Politics* (New York: Palgrave Macmillan, 2009).

35 See Marty Cohen, David Karol, Hans Noel, and John Zaller, *The Party Decides* (Chicago: University of Chicago Press, 2008), and Seth Masket, *No Middle Ground* (Ann Arbor, MI: University of Michigan Press, 2011).

36 See Edward G. Carmines and James A. Stimson, *Issue Evolution* (Princeton, NJ: Princeton University Press, 1989).

37 Charles Prysby, "North Carolina," in Appleton and Ward, *State Party Profiles*, pp. 234–243.

38 See the articles in John A. Clark and Charles Prysby, eds., "Grassroots Party Activists in Southern Politics, 1991–2001," *American Review of Politics* 24 (Spring and Summer, 2001), pp. 1–223.

39 Aldrich, "Southern Parties," p. 655.

40 Walter Dean Burnham, *Critical Elections and the Mainsprings of American Politics* (New York: Norton, 1970), p. 72.

41 Alan Ware, *The Breakdown of the Democratic Party Organization 1940–80* (Oxford: Oxford University Press, 1985).

42 LaRaja and Rauch, "The State of State Parties," p. 3.

CHAPTER 4

The Parties' National Organizations

The Democratic and Republican national party organizations are probably more powerful now than they have ever been. Today's Democratic National Committee (DNC) and Republican National Committee (RNC) are multimillion-dollar fund-raising and candidate-support operations. As a result, even with the explosive growth of non-party super PACs and other big spenders, the parties' national committees have a larger profile in federal candidates' campaigns and in state parties' activities than they once did.

Surprisingly, this was not true during most of American history. Before the 1970s, the two major parties were relatively *decentralized*: the bulk of party organizational strength collected in the local parties. As you saw in Chapter 3, almost all American public officials are chosen in local and state elections. In years past, most of the incentives parties had to offer, such as patronage jobs, were available at the local and state levels. Because the population of Orlando is not the same as the population of Salt Lake City, it made sense for different local organizations of, say, the Republican Party to emphasize different issues and choose different candidates depending on the preferences of their local voters. Till recent decades, then, the local and state party organizations were largely independent of the national party committees, which had little power.[1] The national parties lived like many college students: chronically short of cash and frequently searching for new housing.

So what changed? Both parties reacted to a series of challenges in the 1970s—Watergate for the Republicans and internal battles over civil rights and the war in Vietnam for the Democrats—by moving toward more energized national committees. Although the local pull remains strong, the distribution of power among the national, state, and local parties is now more balanced than ever before.

The National Parties

What is the national party? Officially, each major party's supreme national authority is the **national convention** it holds every four years to nominate a presidential candidate. However, the convention rarely does more than select the presidential and vice-presidential nominees and approve the party's platform and rules. Between conventions, the two parties' main governing bodies are their national committees.

The National Committees

Each party's **national committee** is a gathering of representatives from all its state parties; its leaders run the national party on a daily basis. Their main focus is to help elect the party's presidential candidate. They also distribute polls and policy information, work with state parties, and assist in other races by recruiting and training candidates and helping them raise money. Both national committees have a long history: the Democrats created theirs in 1848 and the Republicans in 1856. For years, every state was represented equally on both national committees, regardless of the size of its population or the extent of its party support. California and Wyoming, then, had equal-sized delegations to the national party committees, just as they do in the U.S. Senate, even though Wyoming's population is only 1/66th that of California's. That system overrepresented the smaller states and also gave roughly equal weight in the national committees to the winning and the losing parts of the party. In practice, this strengthened the southern and western segments of each party, which tended to be more conservative.

Since 1972, when the Democrats revised the makeup of their national committee, the parties have structured their committees differently. After briefly experimenting with unequal state representation in the 1950s, the Republicans give each of the state and territorial parties three seats on the RNC. In contrast, the DNC, now almost triple the size of its Republican counterpart, gives weight to party support as well as to population in representing the states. California, for example, has 19 seats on the DNC, and Wyoming has 4. This change reduced the influence of conservatives and moderates within the DNC.

The two national committees also differ in that the Democrats give national committee seats to representatives of groups especially likely to support Democratic candidates, such as blacks, women, and labor unions—a decision that shows the importance of these groups to the party—as well as to associations of elected officials, such as the National Conference of Democratic Mayors. National committee members in both parties are chosen by the state parties and, for the Democrats, by these other groups as well.

National Party Chairs

The national committee's chair and the staff he or she chooses are the heart of the national party organization. Members of the full national committees come together only two or three times a year, mainly to call media attention to the party and its candidates. The national committees have the power to

Money Is the Mother's Milk of Parties

The Republican National Committee was $24 million in debt in 2011, when it chose Reince Priebus as its new chair. His mandate was to raise lots of money fast and to rebuild the committee's strained relationships with its biggest donors. Priebus hit the ground running; he raised $3.5 million in his first two weeks on the job, and after pulling in almost $400 million, he was re-elected RNC chair in 2013 and 2015.

Then came another big challenge: Donald Trump. Although Trump ran for president in 2016 as a Republican, he often lambasted the Republican Party and hinted that if he didn't win the party's nomination, he would run as an independent, which would split the party's vote. The 2012 Republican presidential nominee, Mitt Romney, called Trump "a phony and a fraud." After winning the nomination, Trump denounced the Ohio Republican state chair three weeks before Election Day because of a dispute over campaign mailings. And about a quarter of all Republican Congress members and governors withdrew or hedged their support of Trump after the release of a tape in which Trump described his efforts at sexual assault—an unprecedented series of events.

Priebus's difficult job was to keep Republicans united and to prevent the controversy from interfering with the RNC's fund-raising. He was only partially successful, but his experience at linking Trump with Washington Republicans later led to his appointment as Trump's White House Chief of Staff.

The Republicans' internal struggle proved to be an unexpected blessing for Democratic National Committee chair Debbie Wasserman Schultz. She, too, had won her post because of her skill at fund-raising and kept it in the wake of the Democratic presidential and congressional gains in the 2012 elections. She was known as a champion of women's issues, an important part of the party's appeal. But even the gift handed to the party by the Republicans' conflicts wasn't enough to silence criticism from within her own party. Several pro-Democratic groups disagreed with Wasserman Schultz's decisions about the number and scheduling of presidential debates in 2016, and supporters of Clinton's Democratic rival, Senator Bernie Sanders, blamed her for giving unfair advantage to Clinton's candidacy.

In the end, even her fund-raising prowess wasn't enough. Leaked emails proving her favoritism toward Clinton caused her to resign just before the 2016 national convention. She was replaced as interim chair by Donna Brazile, a longtime party leader and former DNC vice chair, who is African-American.

Sources: See, for example, Josh Mitchell and Byron Tau, "GOP Chairman Reince Priebus Sees Long Fight Over Donald Trump," *Wall Street Journal*, March 21, 2016, at www.wsj.com/articles/gop-chairman-reince-priebus-sees-long-fight-over-donald-trump-1458517799; and Callum Borchers, "Liberal Pundits Blame Debbie Wasserman Schultz, Not Bernie Sanders, for Democrats' Division," *Washington Post*, May 19, 2016, at www.washingtonpost.com/news/the-fix/wp/2016/05/19/liberal-pundits-blame-debbie-wasserman-schultz-not-bernie-sanders-for-democrats-division/ (both accessed June 18, 2016).

select their own leaders. By tradition, however, the incumbent president normally chooses the national chair of his or her party. Thus, in practice, only the "out" party's national committee actually selects its own chair.[2] In both parties, the chair's most important job is to raise money for the party (see box "Money Is the Mother's Milk of Parties" on page 79).

Serving as the party's national chair does not guarantee great power. Reince Priebus, the Republican National Chair, demonstrated this in 2016 when he unsuccessfully tried to persuade Republican presidential candidate Donald Trump to tone down his rhetoric. Trump paid no attention to Priebus's request, and still won the Republican nomination. National party chairs gain strength through their fund-raising and persuasive skills, not because their institutional positions have many formal powers.

Presidents and Their National Parties

Presidents came to dominate their national committees early in the twentieth century and especially since the 1960s. Thus, in the president's party, the national committee's role is whatever the president wants it to be. James W. Ceaser cites the classic example of Robert Dole, RNC chair from 1971 to 1973, who was quickly fired by the president when Dole tried to put a little distance between the party and the president's involvement in the Watergate scandal: "I had a nice chat with the President ... while the other fellows went out to get the rope."[3] Some presidents have turned their national committees into little more than managers of the president's campaigns and builders of the president's political support between elections. Other presidents, such as George W. Bush, worked to build up the national committee to achieve party, not just presidential, goals.

When their party does not hold the presidency, the national party chair and committee can play a more independent role in national politics. At these times, the "out" party's national chair becomes one of several people (including congressional leaders and past presidential nominees) who may speak for the party and its policies. He or she will also need to energize the party organization around the country and offer a vision for regaining the White House. After the 2012 losses of the GOP ("Grand Old Party," a long-standing nickname for the Republicans), for instance, RNC Chair Priebus appointed a self-study task force (Democrats referred to it instead as an "autopsy"), which produced recommendations to "grow the party and improve Republican campaigns."[4] Above all, the chair must help repay any debts from the losing presidential campaign and raise new money for the party.

Because of changes in campaign finance rules (see Chapter 12), the national committee must work separately from the presidential candidate's own campaign organization in presidential elections. To play this more autonomous role, national chairs have recruited staffers with extensive experience in raising money, dealing with databases, and mobilizing organizers and grassroots supporters.

Other National Party Groups

Several other party organizations are normally included in the term "the national party," even though they work independently of one another and often compete for donors and resources.

Congressional Campaign ("Hill") Committees

The most important of these related groups are each party's **House and Senate campaign committees,** called the **Hill committees** (because Congress is located on Capitol Hill) or the CCCs (Congressional Campaign Committees). The House committees were founded in the immediate aftermath of the Civil War; the Senate committees came into being when senators began to be popularly elected in 1913. The Democratic Congressional Campaign Committee (DCCC) and the National Republican Congressional Committee (NRCC) are concerned entirely with House elections, and the Democratic Senatorial Campaign Committee (DSCC) and the National Republican Senatorial Committee (NRSC) put money into Senate races.

Although incumbent House and Senate members control these committees, they have resisted pressures to work only on behalf of incumbents' campaigns. They also support their party's candidates for open seats and challengers with a good chance of winning. In short, they concentrate their money where they think they can get the biggest payoff in increasing their party's representation in Congress. During the past four decades, the Hill committees have developed major fund-raising and service functions, independent of the DNC and RNC. They provide party candidates with a wide range of campaign help, from get-out-the-vote (GOTV) efforts to hard cash (see box "How the Hill Committees Help Targeted Campaigns" on page 82). For House and Senate candidates, the Hill committees are more influential than their parties' national committees; their help is highly valued, especially by the campaigns they target for special attention, even in comparison with that provided by interest groups and super PACs.[5]

Governors' Associations and Other Groups

Because of recent gridlock in Congress, organized interests have increasingly turned to state governments to achieve their aims. This is feasible especially in the large number of state governments controlled by one single party. Several associations have formed to take advantage of this opportunity by targeting state-level campaigns. For instance, the two parties' governors' associations have become major-league fund-raisers since they were separated from their parties' national committees after campaign finance reforms in the early 2000s (see Chapter 12). Chris Christie, then governor of New Jersey, raised a reported $106 million for the Republican Governors

How the Hill Committees Help Targeted Campaigns

The parties' Hill committees try to maximize their impact by targeting races they think they have a chance of winning and, in lean years, protecting their vulnerable incumbents. The most important criteria for choosing which campaigns to target are the competitiveness of the district and candidate quality, as measured mainly by the candidate's own fund-raising. Candidates, then, raise money not only to run their campaigns but also to leverage even more money by impressing party operatives. In giving money directly to candidates, Hill committee targeters also ask: Is the candidate's organization capable of spending the money effectively? Has he or she effectively generated media coverage? In making independent expenditures, they ask: How expensive are the district's media? Are other groups funding ads in the race? Targeting decisions can change daily as the election approaches, depending on movement in the candidates' poll numbers and on the parties' finances.

The Hill committees can offer these services to targeted campaigns:

- efforts to recruit attractive candidates

- research and "talking points" on issues
- training sessions and advice (including from party-related private consultants) on strategy, polling, advertising, fund-raising, staff, and consultants
- monitoring or video tracking of opponents' campaigns
- help with voter contact, using micro-targeting and huge databases
- participating in coordinated grassroots activities with the state and local party organizations
- collecting contributions from party members in Congress, holding fund-raising events, and party leaders' visits to candidate events
- "hard-money" direct contributions to campaigns*
- "coordinated spending" to buy polls, media ads, or other services for a candidate*
- independent spending by the party's IE (independent expenditure) group on ads in the candidate's district*
- help, contributor lists, and facilities for raising money from individuals, political action committees (PACs), and other groups

Sources: Paul S. Herrnson, *Congressional Elections*, 7th ed. (Los Angeles: Sage/CQ Press, 2016), pp. 93–130; Marian Currinder, *Money in the House* (Boulder, CO: Westview Press, 2009).

Note: * Explained in Chapter 12.

Association during his term as chair in 2013–2014, to help Republican gubernatorial candidates as well as his own prospects as a presidential candidate.[6] Another set of major fund-raisers are the new Republican Attorneys General Association and the Democratic Attorneys General

Association. The Democratic association raises its funds mainly from labor unions, and both groups seek contributions from corporations. Their donors want a voice in state actions that benefit or regulate their corporations or unions, and state attorneys general play a vital role in these actions.[7] Party leaders have formed the Republican State Leadership Committee (RSLC) and the Democratic Legislative Campaign Committee (DLCC), which are now big contributors of money and field organizers to state legislative and statewide campaigns.

Women's and Youth Groups

For a long time, both the Democrats and Republicans have had women's divisions associated with their national committees.[8] These women's groups play different roles now that women have entered regular leadership positions in both parties.

On campuses, the College Republican National Committee (the CRs) and the College Democrats (whose weblog or "blog" is named Smart Ass, in honor of the party's donkey mascot) have grown substantially in the 2000s. Both groups train field representatives to recruit volunteers for campaigns at all levels. The CRs have been closely associated with a number of conservative nonparty groups. The Young Democrats of America and the Young Republican National Federation also work actively among students and other young adults.

Party Networks

The national party committees work closely with a network of allied groups, just as state and local parties do. For the Democrats, these include labor unions, environmental, women's rights, civil rights, and other liberal organizations. Organized labor in particular has supplied many of the volunteer canvassers so vital to Democratic campaigns. The national Republican network includes small business groups, the National Rifle Association, and groups of conservative Christians. Although these groups are not formally a part of the party organizations, they communicate extensively with party organization leaders and play a big role in party campaigns. Hundreds of these groups typically run campaign ads attacking the candidates of the other party. In competitive races, allied groups often run parallel campaigns to those of the candidates—as do the parties themselves—featuring canvassing and other forms of electioneering.[9] Among the biggest advertisers are Americans for Prosperity, supporting conservative Republican candidates, and NextGen Climate Action, supporting Democrats. More rarely, they advertise in the opposition party's primaries to weaken that party's strongest candidate.

Several other groups outside of the formal party structure act as "idea factories" for the party in government. For the Democrats, the leftist Center for American Progress and the more moderate Progressive Policy Institute serve this function. On the Republican side, groups such as the conservative Heritage Foundation and the more libertarian Republican Liberty Caucus try to affect party policy.

Two Paths to Power

The national parties have traveled two different roads to reach these new levels of effectiveness. The Republicans followed a service path by building a muscular fund-raising operation that pays for needed services to their candidates and state parties. The Democrats, in contrast, first followed a procedural path, strengthening their national party's authority over the state parties in nominating a presidential candidate.

The central element in both national parties' continued development, at least until recently, was their ability to attract thousands of small contributions through mass mailings to likely party supporters. This gave the national parties, which formerly depended on funding from the state parties, an independent financial base. Ironically, then, at a time when some were warning that the parties were in decline, the national party organizations were reaching levels of strength that were unprecedented in American politics.

The Service Party Path

A party organization that supports candidates' campaigns with money and other resources, as opposed to running the campaigns itself, can be termed a **service party**. The Republicans pioneered the notion of a service party in response to their electoral defeats during the New Deal. Then, during the 1960s, RNC Chair Ray Bliss expanded the committee's efforts to improve state and local parties' organizational capacity. Chair William Brock continued this work in the mid- to late 1970s to revive the party's election prospects after the devastating losses caused by the Watergate scandals. Under Brock, the RNC helped provide salaries for the executive directors of all 50 state Republican Parties; offered expert assistance to the state parties in organizing, strategizing, and fund-raising; and contributed to more than 4,000 state legislative candidates. Bliss and Brock fashioned a new role for the RNC by making it an exceptionally effective service organization for the state and local parties.[10]

Money and campaign technologies were the key elements in performing this service role. Using a marketing innovation of that time, computer-generated mailing lists, the Republicans began a program of direct-mail appeals that brought in ever-higher levels of income. The RNC's fund-raising jumped from $29 million in 1975–1976 to $106 million in "hard money" (contributions regulated by federal law)[11] in 1983–1984 (see Table A.1 in the online Appendix). The RNC used the money, as Bliss and Brock had, to offer a broad array of services to candidates and state and local party organizations. These services included candidate recruitment and training, research, public opinion polling, data processing, computer networking and software development, production of radio and television ads, direct mailing, and legal advice. State party leaders were glad to accept the help; as the party more closely identified with the business community, Republicans felt comfortable with these marketing techniques.

The Democrats' Procedural-Reform Path

At about the same time, Democrats expanded the power of their national party organization for other reasons. Reformers supporting the civil rights movement and opposing American involvement in the Vietnam War pressed for change in the Democratic Party's positions on these issues. The reformers focused on the rules for selecting presidential candidates. Their aim was to make the nominating process more open and democratic and, in particular, more representative of the concerns of people like themselves: young people, blacks, and women.

The reforms started in the mid-1960s with efforts to tell southern Democratic Parties that they could no longer exclude blacks from party participation and send all-white delegations to the national convention. After the 1968 election, the first of a series of reform commissions, the McGovern–Fraser Commission, overhauled the party's presidential nominating process. (This story is told in more detail in Chapter 10.) The Democrats limited the autonomy of the state parties and the authority of state law in determining how convention delegates were to be selected. That gave the national party the authority over the rules for nominating a presidential candidate.[12] Key court decisions upheld these actions, further solidifying the newfound power of the national party.

This change was limited to the Democrats, however. Republican leaders, consistent with their party's commitment to states' rights, did not want to centralize power in their own party organization.[13] Yet the GOP was still affected by the tide of Democratic Party reform because the bills passed by state legislatures to implement the reforms, including a big increase in the use of primary elections to select a party's presidential candidate, usually applied to both parties.

In the early 1980s, the Democrats took stock of the reforms and did not like what they saw. The newly centralized authority for nominating a presidential candidate and increased grassroots participation in the nominating process had done little to win elections. Further, it had divided the party and alienated much of the Democratic Party in government, many of whom stayed home from party conventions in the 1970s. Therefore, the national Democrats decided to soft-pedal procedural reforms and move toward the Republican service model. Long dependent on the organizational help provided by labor unions, the DNC responded to big Democratic defeats in 1980 by working seriously to broaden its fund-raising base, help recruit candidates, and revitalize state and local party organizations. When the dust from all this effort settled, authority over party rules had become more nationalized, and what had been two models for strengthening the national party were rapidly converging into one.[14]

Both Parties Take the Service Path

The good news for the Democrats in the 1980s was that they were dramatically improving their fund-raising, reducing their long-standing debt, and increasing their activities in the states and localities. The bad news was that the Republicans were far ahead of them and continuing to break new ground. The national Democrats made no secret of their effort to imitate the Republican success in raising money and using it to buy services. Slowly, they began to catch up; what began as a three-to-one and even five-to-one financial advantage for the Republicans was reduced over time (see Figure 4.1).

One reason was the Democratic Party's increasing reliance on "soft money" (see Chapter 12)—funds donated to party organizations in unlimited amounts, most often by labor unions, businesses, and wealthy individuals,

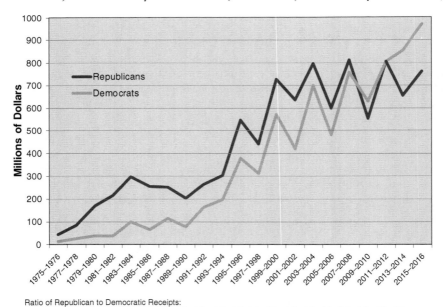

Ratio of Republican to Democratic Receipts:
2.9   3.2   4.6   5.5   3.0   3.9   2.2   2.6   1.6   1.5   1.4   1.4   1.3   1.5   1.1   1.3   1.1   0.9   1.0   .08   .08

FIGURE 4.1 Democratic and Republican Fund-Raising, 1975–1976 to 2015–2016

Note: The data points are total party receipts (including state/local, House, Senate, and national committees) in millions of dollars. Soft money is not included, nor is money (after 1987) transferred among committees. Table A.1 in the Online Appendix provides a breakdown of these totals by type of party committee within each party.

Source: Federal Election Commission data at www.opensecrets.org/parties/index.php?cmte =&cycle=2016 (accessed December 6, 2016). Data for 2016 are as of November 2, 2016.

and exempted from federal campaign finance rules. Big contributions from labor unions made it easier for the Democrats to compete with Republicans in soft money than they could in raising federally regulated donations. Both national parties' committees began major efforts to solicit soft money in the early 1990s. By 2000, almost half of the national parties' fund-raising came in the form of soft money.

Some of the money went into building up the state and even the local parties. A much larger portion of the national parties' money was devoted to races for the U.S. House and Senate. Since the mid-1980s, both parties provided increasing amounts of aid to selected candidates. The Republican committees opened an early lead; the stunning success of GOP candidates in the 1994 congressional elections, for example, was due in part to aggressive fund-raising as well as candidate recruitment by their Hill committees.

Campaign finance reform adopted in 2002 (the Bipartisan Campaign Reform Act, or BCRA, discussed in Chapter 12) barred the national committees from collecting soft money after the 2002 elections. The Democrats saw the coming ban on national party soft money as a particular threat because their soft-money collections had been flourishing—the Democratic Hill committees outdid their Republican counterparts in raising soft money by $151 million to $136 million in 2002—but their federally regulated contributions had expanded only gradually.

Rising to the Challenge of New Campaign Finance Rules

Once the BCRA rules came into effect in 2004, many observers felt that the loss of soft money would seriously weaken the national parties. Transfers of money from national party committees to state and local parties dropped markedly in most states, because BCRA allowed the transfer of federally regulated money only. But as they have so often in their history, the parties adapted to the new rules.

Both national parties tried to make up for the lost soft money by striving to attract hard-money donations from individuals. The DNC greatly expanded its direct mail fund-raising program, which had been minimal during the 1990s, and reaped millions of new donors. In all, the DNC collected more than four times as much federally regulated money in 2004 as it had in 2002—$404 million compared with $93 million—and raised more than 40 percent of its total fund-raising in small contributions of less than $200. The DCCC and the RNC both doubled their hard-money fund-raising in 2004. BCRA made it easier for the party committees to raise hard money by setting the cap on an individual's aggregate donations to party and political action committees higher than the aggregate cap on donations to candidates.

Later action by Congress and the Supreme Court (see *McCutcheon v. FEC* in Chapter 12) permitted individuals in 2016 to give up to about $800,000 in total to all of a party's national committees combined—much more than individual donors had been allowed to give to a national party just four years earlier ($30,800). Using joint fund-raising committees that married candidates and party organizations, the RNC asked donors for $1.34 million per couple in the 2016 election cycle, and the DNC requested about $1.6 million. The givers get a variety of perks in return. And both parties encouraged big hard-money donors to solicit similar contributions from their friends and colleagues and to "bundle" these donations, in return for recognition from the party.

Thus, even after the 2010 *Citizens United* decision (see Chapter 12), which was expected to cut into the parties' appeal as fund-raisers, the two parties' committees came up with an eye-popping total of $1.6 billion during 2011–2012—money raised by party committees at all levels that could be spent on federal elections, and over $1.7 billion in 2015–2016. Remarkably, the Democrats surpassed the Republican Party's fund-raising during the 2010 election cycle for the first time in at least 30 years, and did so again in 2016.

Party Money and Activism in the 2010s

Although the biggest portion of party fund-raising comes from individual citizens, an increasing proportion of party committees' money comes from members of Congress. In the early 1990s, some Republican House leaders, fed up with their long-time minority status, pressed party colleagues to donate some of their campaign war chests to Republicans in more competitive races. The aim was to redirect campaign money from those who could most easily raise it to those who most needed it, to increase the number of House Republicans. Winning a majority of seats would give all House Republicans the power to achieve their policy goals, because the majority party controls the flow of legislation in the House. Republicans did capture control of both the House and Senate in 1994, and soon after, the newly minority Democrats also saw the value of spreading the wealth to help vulnerable incumbents and promising challengers.

Since then, both parties' Hill committees have urged—and House committees have required—their members to channel money to the party committee, not just to particular candidates. This gives the party the opportunity to target the races it considers the most winnable, rather than leaving the decisions to individual incumbent donors. House members can donate funds from their personal campaign committees and their "leadership PACs" (see Chapter 12), set up joint fund-raising operations with party committees, and also ask their own contributors to give to the party's Hill committee. In the mid-2010s, both House Hill committees asked their top party leaders for about $1 million each. Those who want to get or keep these leadership positions find this fund-raising vital to their success; then-Speaker John Boehner gave almost $8 million to the NRCC in 2014 to ward off threats to his leadership (which later proved successful) from Tea Party-aligned House members. Lesser amounts were required from key committee chairs and lower-level party leaders, and rank-and-file members were each assessed "only" $125,000. The DCCC raised $35.2 million from these requests in 2014, and the NRCC raised $37.6 million.[15] Each member's contributions were tracked by party leaders, just as party whips track legislative votes.[16] The Senate committees follow a less formal system of raising funds from their party colleagues. The parties' success in getting incumbents to hand over impressive sums and to put their fund-raising skill in the service of other party candidates demonstrates the extent to which the congressional parties have become important instruments of collective power for their members.

The Hill committees doled out the money carefully. Before an incumbent or a targeted challenger could get funds from the NRCC or DCCC, he or she had to meet a series of benchmarks for fund-raising, media visibility, and numbers of voter contacts. Incumbents were advised to start raising money for their 2016 campaigns immediately after they won in 2014. In fact, the DCCC welcomed newly elected Democratic House members to Washington after the 2012 elections with a slide show recommending that in a typical ten-hour workday, they should spend four hours on the phone with potential donors and another hour on "strategic outreach," which includes fund-raisers. Even on home visits to their district, they were told, they should devote three hours to donor "call time" and an hour to outreach—a schedule that cuts deeply into their legislative work and constituent service. An observer commented, "It is considered poor form in Congress—borderline self-indulgent—for a freshman to sit at length in congressional hearings when the time could instead be spent raising money." One member responded, "You might as well be putting bamboo shoots under my fingernails."[17]

The increased fund-raising from Congress members and other sources gave the Democratic committees the money to take a page or two from the Republicans' playbook. Starting in 2000, the national GOP had created a massive databank of voter information gleaned from party canvassers and commercial databases—individuals' past voting records and their opinions and consumer preferences—so that, just as corporate market researchers do, party strategists could make predictions as to how particular types of people were likely to behave. This "micro-targeting" helped the Republicans focus their persuasive efforts and get-out-the-vote activities on the individuals most likely to support Republican candidates. The resulting database, called Voter Vault, required funding and computer facilities on a scale that the national Republicans could afford. It was widely heralded as a major reason for the Republican victories in 2002 and 2004.

Democrats were slow to respond but later created two separate national databases. VoteBuilder, the DNC's 50-state voter file, is managed by the data systems vendor NGP VAN. The master list is rented to national and state campaigns and some super PACs, which then add the data they've gathered from their own field work. The other, a huge dataset with information on 240 million voting-age Americans, managed by the group Catalist with funds from unions, nonprofits, and individuals, was used extensively by the Barack Obama campaign and liberal groups supporting Obama. Voter contact programs based on these datasets were field-tested in some congressional special elections in 2008, all of which resulted in Democratic wins. The DCCC and DSCC applied these programs nationally in the 2012 elections. (This story is told more fully in Chapter 11.) By then, it was the Republicans who were lagging technologically. They outsourced their list-building to a party-related group called Data Trust in 2011 and, in 2013, added an open platform for data-sharing by national and state parties, candidates, and other groups. In 2014, oil billionaires Charles and David Koch agreed to share the voter files gathered by their political groups, such as Freedom Partners, with Data Trust. Other Republican-leaning groups began their own data-collection efforts.

In addition to campaign contributions, the Hill committees have also used their increased fund-raising to mount lavish independent spending drives in targeted races. As you'll see in Chapter 12, court cases have allowed party organizations to run unlimited amounts of advertising in House and Senate campaigns as long as the party spends its money independently of the candidate it intends to help ("independent spending"). This produces the odd picture of two groups of partisans from the same party—those helping the candidate and those doing independent spending—working to elect the same candidate but officially ignorant of one another's activities. The great majority of party funds in recent House and Senate races now take the form of independent spending (see Figure 4.2 and Figure 4.3), because it is not limited by law, whereas party direct contributions to candidates and coordinated spending are limited. The two parties spent a total of $252 million on independent expenditures in 2012 and about as much in 2016—an impressive increase over earlier election cycles.

So since the mid-1980s, both national parties have become institutionalized as active, well-staffed service parties working to support party candidates and state and local party organizations.[18] Their focus has changed from prospecting for soft money to soliciting federally regulated contributions. They have shifted from investing in computerized direct mail to integrating fund-raising databases with e-mail databases, social media, and other data—a skill at which the Democrats excelled beginning in 2012. And they coordinate their activities quietly with non-party spenders such as super PACs, as we will see in Chapter 12. As campaign finance rules change and new technologies develop, the committees adapt.

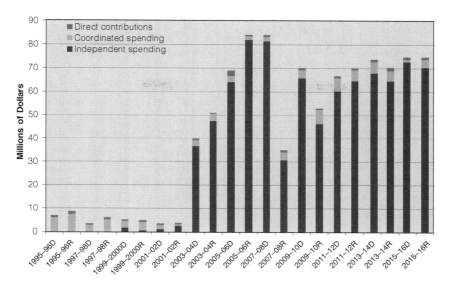

FIGURE 4.2 National Party Money in House Races, 1995–1996 to 2015–2016

Source: Federal Election Commission data at www.opensecrets.org/parties/indexp.php?cyc
le=2016&cmte=DCCC(and=NRCC) (accessed December 6, 2016). Data are as of November
28, 2016.

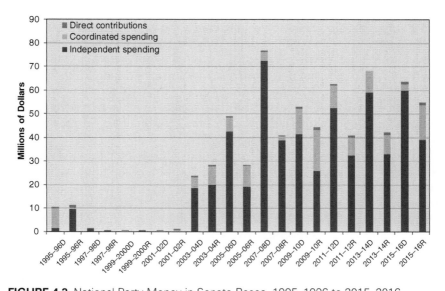

FIGURE 4.3 National Party Money in Senate Races, 1995–1996 to 2015–2016

Source: Federal Election Commission data at www.opensecrets.org/parties/indexp.php?cyc
le=2016&cmte=DSCC(and=NRSC) (accessed December 6, 2016). Data for 2016 as of
November 28, 2016.

What Is the Impact of These Stronger National Parties?

These dramatic changes in the national party organizations have beefed up the parties' roles in nominating and electing candidates, roles that had been seriously undercut a century ago with the advent of the direct primary. To an important degree, the national and state parties are now actively involved in the campaign support functions that private campaign consultants and other political groups had monopolized until recently. The money and services provided by the national parties have helped to raise their profiles in the eyes of candidates. The increasing strength of the national parties has also altered their relationships with state and local party organizations.

Effects on Candidates' Campaigns

The strengthened national parties perform a number of vital functions in presidential campaigns. As we have seen, both national committees research issues, study the opponent's record and background, and search for their own candidate's weak points and ways to thwart attacks. They train state party staff and field directors and maintain relationships with important groups in the party's network.

In Senate and House campaigns, however, there have been some marked changes in the national parties' decisions as to where to deploy their newfound strength. In the 1980s and 1990s, the national party committees had supported a wide range of viable candidates. The committees tended to protect their incumbents when they expected a lean election year and to invest in challengers and open seats when a big victory looked likely. But by the early 2000s, the House and Senate were so closely divided by party and the number of truly competitive seats had shrunk so much that both parties' congressional committees were pouring the great majority of their money and help into those competitive races.[19]

So much party money and field staff flooded these competitive campaigns that at least in those targeted races, party money at times outweighed candidate spending. The national party committees' money and other resources have given them real power over the targeted campaigns. For instance, early in the 2000s, the national parties spent more in a closely fought Colorado congressional race than the candidates' own campaigns did, and the national party committees specified exactly what the campaigns had to do with the party money. The Democratic candidate's campaign manager probably spoke for both candidates in his exasperation at the national party's micromanaging: "They crawl up our ass on a daily basis."[20] The party committee normally agrees to provide funding only if the campaign accepts certain party mandates: that the campaign hire or fire particular staffers, use a particular consultant, or adopt a given campaign technique. Sometimes, party influence on targeted campaigns can backfire.

For instance, party-funded ads are much more likely to attack the opposition than are the candidates' own ads. Because most voters do not distinguish between candidate and party ads, a candidate can be tarred with a negative image that he or she has worked hard to avoid. Thus, conflicts can develop between the party committee and the campaign.

In some recent "wave" elections such as 2008 and 2010, the playing field of targeted campaigns has expanded. But because most congressional races are not competitive, their candidates do not have the luxury of worrying about the strings attached to the party money. In elections where the outcome is predictable, there is no reason for national party committees to invest much of their scarce resources. The lack of party investment can become a self-fulfilling prophecy, because non-party donors often use the party's targeting decisions to guide their own contributions. As one campaign staffer noted, "That is such a death blow to a campaign, when the national party pulls out their money."[21] But the party committee's goal is to place its resources strategically and win enough campaigns to gain control of the House or Senate, so party staffers must make hard choices based on analytics, not compassion.

Effects on State and Local Parties

More generally, have the increasing visibility and resources of the national parties led to a transfer of power from the state and local to the national party organizations—to centralization rather than decentralization of the parties? Probably not. The forces that encourage a state and local party focus remain strong. But it is clear that the national parties' new strength has lessened the *de*centralization of the party organizations. When the national parties have a lot of money and services to give, their power and influence grow. The result can be more of a national imprint on the nature of state and even local campaigns, the kinds of candidates recruited, and the ways in which the parties are organized. Is this a good thing for American politics? Box "Could a Stronger National Party Benefit You?" on page 94 offers both sides of this question.

At times, state parties have welcomed this national involvement. One of the more successful examples of national and state party cooperation was former DNC Chair Howard Dean's **50-state strategy** in the 2006 and 2008 elections. As Chapter 3 mentioned, Dean used DNC money to pay field organizers to work with each of the state parties. Colorado, for instance, had been a Republican state for several decades but had experienced an influx of younger, more liberal voters in the early 2000s. So starting in 2005, the DNC provided money for the state party to fund field directors in rural areas and to purchase a new database of voter information. The DNC investment invigorated several other state parties in areas that the national Democrats had previously written off as Republican-dominated. One study found that these DNC staffers improved the candidates' vote totals in these

■■■■■■■■ WHICH WOULD YOU CHOOSE? ■■■■■■■■

Could a Stronger National Party Benefit You?

YES! Political parties offer you a valuable shortcut. Government decisions affect almost everything you do, but you may not have time to research dozens of complicated issues (health care, energy prices) and candidates in order to vote for those who will act in your interest. A party can do the research for you. If you generally agree with, say, the Republican Party, it can offer you a set of recommended candidates with no effort on your part. But if each state and local Republican organization can act independently, and if some of these organizations are moderate and others are conservative, then how can you be sure that your state and local Republican candidates will support the positions that drew you to the party? A strong national party could help recruit candidates whose views are consistent with the party's philosophy and help them get elected. Besides, who would you rather have raising campaign money: the national party or the individual candidates who will soon be

voting on bills affecting the donors' interests?

NO! The United States is very diverse; the concerns of Democrats in Omaha may well be different from those in San Francisco, New Hampshire, and the Florida Panhandle. If a national party is strong enough to promote a clear set of ideas on what government should be doing, then whose ideas should it promote: those of the Omaha Democrats or the San Francisco Democrats? If a national party is strong enough to elect its candidates, wouldn't it be capable of telling them how to vote in Congress, whether or not their constituents agree? Even if a national party organization confines itself to raising money and giving it to candidates, doesn't that give the national organization a great deal of influence over state and even local candidates? In a nation with a tradition of hostility to "boss rule," couldn't a strong national party raise those fears again?

---

races, even beyond the other advantages that Democrats had in 2006.[22] Dean and his supporters argued that this was the foundation for the Obama campaign's successful national strategy in 2008.[23] The Obama campaign felt differently, noting that it had relied almost entirely on its own staff and money in these "red" states; it contended that the candidate's own strengths and the Bush administration's weaknesses were at least as important.[24] This tension between the state parties and the Obama organization continued beyond the 2012 election, when the Obama campaign renamed itself Organizing for Action (OFA) and used its e-mail list and grassroots organization to promote the president's agenda. Although OFA claimed strong ties to the Democratic Party, it remained independent of the party organization, even competing with the DNC and state parties in raising money.[25]

At times, then, the increased national influence can strain the relationships among party organizations at different levels, just as it has produced strains between the parties and some candidates. One of the areas of greatest conflict between the national parties and their state and local brethren centers on national party involvement in primaries. It is always a temptation for national party officials to try to select and groom the candidate they think will have the best odds of winning in a district. The House and Senate campaign committees, whose chance for a majority in Congress depends on the effectiveness of candidates in competitive races, dread the possibility that a less-capable candidate will win their party's primary and go on to run a lackluster campaign for the seat. But the risk of becoming involved is that if the national party backs a candidate who later loses the primary, then the party might alienate the winning candidate, make itself look weak, and even split the state party and lose the election.

Republican national leaders took the risk in 2010, anticipating a Republican wave election. National Republican campaign committees endorsed several Republican primary candidates who seemed very electable. In some cases, Tea Party supporters and other strongly conservative voters ignored the party establishment's advice. One notable example was the Delaware Senate race, where Republican primary voters rejected the national and state parties' preferred candidate in favor of a colorful, Tea Party-endorsed challenger. Unfortunately, her first general election campaign ad had to explain her earlier admission that she had dabbled in witchcraft, and she was soundly defeated by a Democrat who was previously seen as the underdog in the race.

In reaction, the NRSC chair vowed to stay out of Republican primaries in 2012. But when some far-right candidates who won their party's nomination stumbled in the general election campaign, state and national party leaders were drawn in anyway. The NRSC and other Republican groups felt the need to step in again prior to the state primaries in 2014, at least to the extent of encouraging more electable Republican primary candidates and helping them deal with missteps in their campaigns (see box "When the National Party Tries to Pick a Winner" on page 96). In Colorado, for instance, the NRSC talked right-wing candidates out of challenging a more mainstream Republican before the Senate primary. And in the general election that year, Senate Republican leader Mitch McConnell intervened in a Kansas Senate race where the Republican incumbent was running a sleepy, under-funded campaign. McConnell insisted that the incumbent replace his campaign manager with a national Republican operative who brought in new staff. Both parties' campaign committees were actively involved in recruiting candidates for 2016 races, though their success varied; Democrats were better able to recruit strong candidates for the Senate, where they had a chance of retaking control, than for the Republican-controlled House.

In short, when national party committees use their money to affect the choice of candidates or the direction of a campaign, there will probably be

When the National Party Tries to Pick a Winner

Some Republican candidates have been beloved by Democrats. Take U.S. Rep. Todd Akin, a pro-lifer who won the Missouri Republican primary for a U.S. Senate seat in 2012. Akin was running ahead of his Democratic opponent until he opined in a TV interview that it was not necessary to allow abortions in cases of rape because rape rarely resulted in pregnancy. In a "legitimate rape, the female body has ways to try to shut the whole thing down," Akin said. He was roundly criticized. Despite pleas from the National Republican Senatorial Committee (NRSC) that he step down because his likely defeat would threaten the prospects for GOP control of the Senate, Akin stood firm, continued his candidacy—and lost. Democrats retained control of the Senate.

That's the dilemma that primary elections pose for a party organization: especially in multi-candidate primaries, a candidate can win the party nomination who is too extreme to win the general election. Leaders of the party organization often wish that they could step in and influence nomination races. But party leaders can't rescind the nomination because the power to nominate belongs to the primary voters. And party leaders' efforts to affect the primary may cause voter resentment on Election Day. Take Donald Trump in 2016. When many well-known Republican Party leaders tried to stop Trump from getting the party's presidential nomination, in the words of one member of the Republican grassroots, "The harder they [the party establishment] try to stop Trump, the more likely he is to succeed."

Nevertheless, Republican-oriented groups in 2014 and 2016 decided to take the risk in order to keep some far-right candidates from winning the party's primaries and then losing the general election. In Mississippi, for instance, the U.S. Chamber of Commerce, the American Hospital Association, and the National Association of Realtors joined the NRSC in a massive barrage of ads, spending almost $4 million to help an incumbent Republican Senator, Thad Cochran, defeat a Tea Party candidate for the Republican Senate nomination in 2014. Republican allies even urged Democratic voters to cross over and support Cochran in the primary. This national party involvement caused substantial grassroots resentment. Even so, in 2016, Senate Republican Majority Leader Mitch McConnell insisted that there would be no more Todd Akins winning Republican nominations for Senate: "We will not nominate anybody for the United States Senate on the Republican side who's not appealing to a general-election audience."

Sources: Rick Hampson, "Pa. Voters Rebel Against 'Stop Trump'," *USA Today*, March 29, 2016, p. 1 (from which Trump quote is drawn); Alexander Bolton, "Leader McConnell Warns GOP Voters: We Need Candidates 'Who Can Win'," *The Hill*, December 18, 2015, at http://thehill.com/homenews/senate/263742-mcconnell-warns-gop-voters-we-need-candidates-who-can-win (from which McConnell's quote is drawn; accessed June 18, 2016).

ruffled feathers within the state party and the campaign, who feel that they are better judges of what works in the district. Yet it is difficult for national party committees to stay on the sidelines. As long as primaries can be dominated by activists more extreme in their views than the average voter (see Chapter 5), party organizations will miss chances to capitalize on winnable races.

Effects on the Presidency

Is a stronger national party likely to compete with the president's power or to add to it? Clearly, the national committees' increasing resources enable them to take a more independent political role. Federal funding of presidential campaigns, which strictly limited party spending for presidential races, freed the national committees from their traditional concentration on presidential elections and allowed them to dedicate some of their resources to state and local party-building. At the same time, the party committees carved out new roles in raising money for federal campaigns.

On the other hand, these new capabilities make the national committee an even more attractive resource for presidents. Naturally, presidents want the new party power to be at their service, and every president in recent memory has kept his party's national committee on a short leash. Presidents certainly expect the party committees to mobilize all those members of Congress whom they recruited, trained, and financed to support the president's program. Presidents in their first term will want to draw on the national party's assets for their reelection campaigns, as much as campaign finance rules permit. Thus, there is considerable pressure on these stronger national parties to put their capabilities at the service of presidential goals.

Effects on Congress

At around the time that the Hill committees have become much more active in recruiting and supporting party candidates, Congress members have been more likely to cast legislative votes with the majority of their party (as Chapter 13 shows). Did these new campaign resources help convince Congress members to vote for their party's positions on bills? To this point, the party committees have not made their allocations of campaign money and services contingent on candidates' support for the party's program. The Hill committees want as many as possible of their party's candidates to win, so that their party gains or keeps a majority in Congress. So they put money into close races, even when their candidate has bucked the party leadership, rather than to candidates who are ideologically "pure."[26]

But some members of the party in Congress have used their own campaign funds to try to influence the ideological complexion of Congress. From 2010 through 2014, for instance, then-Senator Jim DeMint (R-SC) used his campaign committee and leadership PAC to funnel campaign money to strong conservative candidates in their Republican primaries. DeMint's aim was to make the Senate Republican contingent more deeply conservative, even though doing so meant that he squared off against the NRSC and business-oriented Republican groups who wanted to pick winners, not ideological purists.

Yet the committees have not been bashful in reminding members, especially newly elected members, that the party played a role in their election success. Party campaign help is only one part of the story of party support in Congress, but the remarkable cohesion of the House Republicans since 1995 was surely bolstered by the party leadership's financial and other support for Republican candidates. Constituency pressures will always come first in Congress. However, the more that senators and representatives can count on campaign help from the congressional party, the more open they will be to party-based appeals.

Relationships Within the National Party

The three national committees of each party—the DNC or RNC and the party's Hill committees—have many shared goals. When the party's presidential candidate does well, most of the voters he or she attracts will also vote for the party's Senate and House candidates. Similarly, an effectively run Senate campaign can bring out voters for party colleagues running for president and House seats.

But the party's resources are limited, and each of the party's national committees wants the biggest share. In 2016, DNC efforts to raise money from wealthy donors for Hillary Clinton's campaign threatened the Democratic Hill committees' ability to get big donations from the same sources. The party committees have long competed with one another in raising money from the same contributors (and jealously guard their contributor lists), and they recruit political talent from the same limited pool.

The Limits of Party Organization

The national party organizations have recently generated remarkable amounts of new money and other resources. They have used these resources and expertise to become major players relative to the state and local parties and major influences on the lives of many federal and even state-level candidates. Organizations capable of raising and spending a billion dollars during a two-year period are not easily ignored. The rise of super PACs (see Chapter 12) probably cut into the parties' fund-raising capability in 2016 and beyond, but the national party organizations are stronger now than they have been through most of their history.

This impressive increase in strength has not come at the expense of the state and local parties. In fact, the national parties have used at least some of their resources to build the capabilities of these party organizations. Nor has the national parties' new strength made the local and state party organizations into branch offices of their national parties, following their orders in developing campaign strategy and taking stands on issues. Too many forces in American politics encourage independence, especially in the local parties, to permit the two major parties to centralize their organization and power. The federal system, in which most public officials are elected at the local level, the separation of powers, variations among states and local areas in public attitudes and regulation of the parties, and the BCRA rules that discourage cooperative campaigns between federal and nonfederal candidates all work against a centralized party system.

Thus, as resource rich as they have become, the American party organizations remain fairly decentralized by international standards. At a time when Americans can be assured of getting the same Big Mac in Cincinnati as they can in San Diego, the American parties lack the top-down control and efficiency, the unified setting of priorities, and the central responsibility that we often find in other nations' parties. Where the party organizations of many other Western democracies have had highly professional leadership and large party bureaucracies, most American party organizations, especially at the local level, are still in the hands of part-time activists.[27]

The parties have increased their emphasis on grassroots campaigning through canvassing and phone banks and have used the information to develop micro-targeting, aiming specific messages at individuals known to be receptive to those messages. Yet even this greater reach into the grassroots may not be enough to make the party organizations more prominent in the public's mind. The parties' messages focus on the candidates rather than on the party itself. Service-oriented parties may be better at helping candidates run for office than in expanding the role of the party organization in citizens' political thinking.[28] American political values do not welcome stronger and more centralized party organizations with more power in American political life. And the results of the 2016 election called into question even the impact of stronger party organizations on candidates' election chances. Democratic state and national party organizations raised money hand over fist in 2016 and built an impressive grassroots campaign, but that wasn't enough to pull Hillary Clinton to victory or Democrats to a majority in the U.S. Senate or House.

The American party organizations are fundamentally flexible and election oriented. Their purpose is to support candidates for office and to make the adjustments needed to do well in a pragmatic political system. As a result, they have long been led by candidates and officeholders, not by career party bureaucrats. As the political system grows more polarized, the party organizations have taken the opportunity to expand their roles and add to the polarization. But at least to this point, even though the national party committees now have unprecedented levels of funding and activity, their impact is felt mainly through the candidates they support.

Notes

1 Cornelius P. Cotter and Bernard C. Hennessy, *Politics without Power: The National Party Committees* (New York: Atherton, 1964).

2 See Philip A. Klinkner, *The Losing Parties* (New Haven, CT: Yale University Press, 1994).

3 James W. Ceaser, "Political Parties—Declining, Stabilizing, or Resurging," in Anthony King, ed., *The New American Political System* (Washington, DC: American Enterprise Institute, 1990), p. 115. See also Sidney M. Milkis, *The President and the Parties* (New York: Oxford University Press, 1993).

4 See the RNC's "Growth and Opportunity Program," March 18, 2013, at goproject.gop.com (accessed June 18, 2016).

5 Paul S. Herrnson, *Congressional Elections*, 7th ed. (Los Angeles: Sage/CQ Press, 2016), pp. 123–129.

6 Michael Barbaro, "By Lending a Hand, Christie Gets a Leg Up for 2016," *New York Times*, November 6, 2014, p. P9.

7 Jonathan Weisman, "G.O.P. Error Reveals Donors and the Price of Access," *New York Times*, September 24, 2014, p. A13.

8 These now include the (Democratic) Women's Leadership Forum, the Democratic Women's Alliance, the DNC Women's Caucus, and RNC Women.

9 David B. Magleby, "Electoral Politics as Team Sport," in John C. Green and Daniel J. Coffey, eds., *The State of the Parties*, 6th ed. (Lanham, MD: Rowman & Littlefield, 2010), pp. 81–100.

10 See Daniel J. Galvin, "The Transformation of the National Party Committees," in Marjorie Randon Hershey, ed., *Guide to U.S. Political Parties* (Los Angeles: Sage, 2014), Chapter 15.

11 The terms *hard money* and *soft money* are explained in Chapter 12.

12 See Austin Ranney, *Curing the Mischiefs of Faction* (Berkeley, CA: University of California Press, 1975); William J. Crotty, *Decisions for the Democrats* (Baltimore, MD: Johns Hopkins University Press, 1978); and John S. Jackson, *The American Political Party System* (Washington, DC: Brookings Institution, 2015), Chapters 3 and 4.

13 John F. Bibby, "Party Renewal in the Republican National Party," in Gerald M. Pomper, ed., *Party Renewal in America* (New York: Praeger, 1981), pp. 102–115.

14 See Paul S. Herrnson, "The Revitalization of National Party Organizations," in L. Sandy Maisel, ed., *The Parties Respond*, 2nd ed. (Boulder, CO: Westview, 1994), pp. 45–68.

15 Herrnson, *Congressional Elections*, p. 95.

16 See Marian Currinder, *Money in the House* (Boulder, CO: Westview, 2009), pp. 34–39.

17 Ryan Grim and Sabrina Siddiqui, "Call Time for Congress Shows How Fundraising Dominates Bleak Work Life," *Huffington Post*, January 8, 2013, at www.huffingtonpost.com/2013/01/08/call-time-congressional-fundraising _n_2427291.html (accessed June 18, 2016).

18 See Paul S. Herrnson, *Party Campaigning in the 1980s* (Cambridge, MA: Harvard University Press, 1988), p. 47.

19 See David B. Magleby and J. Quin Monson, eds., *The Last Hurrah?* (Provo, UT: Center for the Study of Elections and Democracy, 2003).

20 Daniel A. Smith, "Strings Attached," in Magleby and Monson, eds., *The Last Hurrah?*, p. 194.

21 Quoted in Jonathan Weisman, "Democrats' Hopes to Gain in House Fade," *New York Times*, October 15, 2014, p. A25.

22 Elaine C. Kamarck, "Assessing Howard Dean's Fifty State Strategy and the 2006 Midterm Elections," *The Forum* 4 (2006), issue 3, article 5.

23 Ari Berman, "The Prophet," *The Nation*, January 5, 2009, at www.thenation.com/article/prophet (accessed June 18, 2016).

24 Adam Nagourney, "Dean Seeks Some Respect (and Credit) for Obama's Victory," *New York Times*, November 11, 2008, at www.nytimes.com/2008/11/12/us/politics/12web-nagourney.html?_r=0 (accessed June 18, 2016).

25 See Sidney M. Milkis and John W. York, "If the Obama Presidency Is Winding Down, Why Is His Group Organizing for Action Ramping Up?" "The Monkey Cage," *Washington Post*, July 29, 2015, at www.washingtonpost.com/blogs/monkey-cage/wp/2015/07/29/if-the-obama-presidency-is-winding-down-why-is-his-group-organizing-for-action-ramping-up/ (accessed June 18, 2016).

26 Timothy P. Nokken, "Ideological Congruence Versus Electoral Success," *American Politics Research* 31 (2003): 3–26.

27 Leon D. Epstein, *Political Parties in the American Mold* (Madison, WI: University of Wisconsin Press, 1986), p. 200.

28 John J. Coleman, "The Resurgence of Party Organization?" in Daniel M. Shea and John C. Green, eds., *The State of the Parties* (Lanham, MD: Rowman & Littlefield, 1994), pp. 311–328.

CHAPTER 5

Party Activists

They are billion-dollar organizations, but the American parties rely heavily on unpaid help. Volunteers, including a lot of college students, register people to vote, go door-to-door, bring voters to the polls, and maintain a party organization's Facebook page and Twitter feed. But the parties pay a price for all that free labor. People who volunteer time and money to a party organization or candidate are often motivated by strong political views. These party activists tend to be more extreme in their attitudes toward issues than most other voters are; Democratic activists are more consistently liberal, and Republican activists more conservative, than their own party's less-active supporters. And they would like their party's candidates to share their intensity. During President Obama's second term, liberal Democratic activists sharply criticized the president and congressional Democrats for not pressing hard enough for gun control, immigration reform, and taxing the rich, and conservative Republican activists called for the scalps of Republicans who compromised with Democrats on gun control, immigration reform, or taxes.

Party organizations must keep their volunteer activists engaged and enthusiastic. At the same time, the parties want to avoid sounding extreme; that could turn off less-partisan voters. How party organizations achieve this difficult balance, and whether they do, is determined by the ways they attract and keep volunteers.

What Draws People into Party Activity?

People become involved in organizations of all kinds, from party organizations to dance marathons, for three types of reasons. **Purposive incentives** refer to the sense of satisfaction people feel when promoting an issue or cause that matters to them. **Solidary incentives** are intangible as well: the social benefits that people can gain from associating with others, networking, and being part of a group. **Material incentives** are tangible rewards for activity—cash payments or other concrete rewards for one's work.[1]

Purposive (Issue-Based) Incentives

To an increasing extent, people are led to party activism by their commitment to particular issues. Someone dedicated to abortion rights, for example, might begin by working for a pro-choice Democratic candidate and then come to view the candidate's party as a vehicle for keeping abortion legal. A highly observant Christian who believes that life begins at conception might be drawn to the Republican Party as a means of stopping abortion. Since the parties have polarized on many issues in recent years, most of those who volunteer for party work have been motivated by a desire to use the party to achieve policy goals.[2] Although we do not have comparable data on earlier times, there is reason to believe that this was less true of party workers in other periods of the nation's history.[3] The energy and passion in party organizations come increasingly from issue-driven activists—those on the right in the Republican Party and those on the left for the Democrats.

Issue-driven party activism has played a vital role in shaping politics at all levels. In many 2010 and 2014 House races, the activism of Tea Party supporters helped elect dozens of new Republican Congress members, many of them highly conservative on taxes, government spending, and illegal immigration. Some issues have had enough power to lead activists to switch parties. The abortion and race issues, for example, induced many formerly Democratic pro-lifers and southern conservatives to join the Republican Party beginning in the 1970s, and they soon cemented a set of favored issue positions into the platform of their new party.[4]

A large proportion of these issue-based activists are convinced that their activity has made a difference. In one survey, three-quarters of campaign volunteers believed that their involvement had affected at least some votes.[5] So although it might seem irrational to spend a lot of time on party activity in support of an issue that could be termed a "collective good"—one that, if achieved, will benefit the whole society rather than only the activists who worked hard to achieve it—many people become active in a party to do just that. Others become party activists out of a more general sense that citizen participation is essential in a democracy (see box "A Day in the Life: What Did You Do Sophomore Year? I Ran for the State Legislature" on page 104).

Solidary (Social) Incentives

Many more people are drawn to party work by the social contact that it provides. In an age when some people's closest relationship is with their tablet or their smartphone, the face-to-face contact at a party headquarters or in a campaign provides a chance to meet like-minded people and to be part of an active group. Family traditions may lead some young adults to go to party activities looking for social life, just as others may look to a softball league or a bar. Party activism is a form of networking—a standard means of looking for a job. Some find it exciting to meet local officials or others

▆▆▆▆▆▆▆▆▆▆ **A DAY IN THE LIFE** ▆▆▆▆▆▆▆

What Did You Do Sophomore Year?
I Ran for the State Legislature

Patrick Lockhart, a freshman at Indiana University, opened the annual mailer listing the amount of his student loans and worried. Could he finish his education with so much debt? In researching his options, he decided to write to his representative in the Indiana State House of Representatives, who chaired the Education Committee in the legislature. He got no response. That surprised him; why wasn't the democratic process working here?

Lockhart became interested in politics during high school. Although he came from a very conservative family, the Obama campaign caught his attention, as did his high school government class. When he started college, he met many others who shared those interests; "the atmosphere was like political heaven." He became an organizer for Democratic governor and Senate candidates in 2012, knocking on doors, calling prospective voters, and recruiting volunteers, and loved it.

So when Lockhart didn't hear back from his state rep about his student loan concerns, he got motivated. He called the State Democratic Party hoping to hear about internship opportunities. They connected him instead with someone who encouraged him to run for office against his state legislator. The party staffer gave him the basics: what a state rep does, what a campaign looks like, what it costs to run, and then connected him with local political activists. "My learning curve was straight up," he said.

It was an extremely demanding time. As a sophomore, running in the Democratic primary, he made the hour-long commute back to his district three or four times a week while taking 12 credits of coursework *and* holding a part-time job to defray his college costs. It was routine for him to race from his last class at 4 p.m. to a political event in Indianapolis that started at 5. But through trial and error he learned time-management skills: how to set up meetings, host fund-raisers, and go door-to-door even when getting doors slammed in his face in his conservative district, which had most recently voted Democratic for president in the 1960s.

He found the experience "fascinating. For the first time, I really felt like an active member of the community. I loved listening to people's stories, and I got an overwhelmingly positive response to being a college-age candidate. People *want* young people to have a say; we're the ones, after all, who will inherit all the problems!" Lockhart won his primary but lost the general election in the 2014 Republican sweep. Although he doesn't plan another run for office soon, his experience taught him that "politics affects everything in our lives: roads, how much we pay for school, basically everything that's important to us."

who appear on the news and to feel that they are helping to create a small part of history. Researchers find that a large number of party activists cite the social life of party politics as a valuable reward for their efforts.[6]

Material Incentives

The American parties once offered a lot of material incentives for party work. Even before the age of the party "machine," people got involved in party activity mainly to share in the "spoils" gained when a party controlled the government. These "spoils" came in the form of patronage and preferments. **Patronage** means appointing an individual to a government job as a reward for party work. Although patronage is very limited today, the party can still provide loyal workers with a base of support if they seek elected office. **Preferments** are other favors a governing party can grant to party supporters, such as contracts or preferred treatment in enforcing laws. Patronage, access to elected office, and preferments have all played important roles in building and sustaining the American party organizations.

Patronage Early in the life of the American republic and for more than a century afterward, people were attracted to party work by the prospect of being rewarded with government jobs if the party won. Patronage has been used in other nations as well, but no other party system relied on patronage as much and as long as the American system. When party machines controlled many cities, city governments were staffed almost entirely by loyalists of the party in power.[7] In return for their jobs, patronage appointees traditionally "volunteered" their time, energy, and often even a part of their salary to the party organization. They were especially active during campaigns; American party politics is rich with tales of the entire staff of certain government departments being put to work in support of their boss's reelection. Even now, when such practices are usually frowned on and sometimes illegal, some types of government employees can still face pressure to contribute time or money to their party.

As the number of government jobs grew, however, the number of patronage jobs available to the parties dropped dramatically. Most government employees are now hired under civil service and merit systems, in which applicants get jobs based on their scores on competitive exams. The number of full-time federal positions filled by political appointees has dwindled over the years to a few thousand today, many of them high-level policy-making positions. States and cities have followed the same path, though more slowly.

The Supreme Court has helped to dismantle patronage at the state and local levels. In 1976 and 1980, the Court ruled that some county political employees could not be fired simply because the party in power changed. The Court went further in a 1990 Illinois case, determining that politically based hiring and promotion violated the First Amendment freedoms of speech and association. In each case, the Court agreed that party affiliation might be a relevant qualification in filling policy-making positions but not in lower level offices.[8] Even where patronage jobs remain, they are usually under the control of elected executives—mayors, governors, and others—who want to use patronage to build their own political followings rather than to reward loyal service to the party organization.

Some patronage jobs still exist. Mayors, governors, and presidents continue to reserve top policy-making positions for their trusted supporters. Legislatures often resist bringing their staff members under the protection of civil service systems. In 2013, the governor of Kansas convinced the state legislature to limit the coverage of civil service hiring for state jobs. Civil service rules for governmental employees can be bypassed by hiring politically loyal, "temporary" workers outside of the civil service system or by channeling party loyalists into jobs in private firms that depend on government contracts. A few big campaign contributors will continue to be named ambassadors to small and peaceful nations. Whenever political leaders have some discretion in hiring people, in short, they will find a way to award jobs to their supporters, who usually share their party affiliation, so these opportunities will attract at least some people to party activity.

Keep in mind that some observers are sorry to lose the practice of patronage. President Andrew Jackson promoted its use as a way of encouraging a more democratic and less elitist government.[9] When government jobs are filled (and then protected) only by civil service procedures, it becomes almost impossible for reform-minded leaders to replace a sluggish or ineffective bureaucrat with a more efficient worker. Patronage was also thought to keep party organizations strong as instruments of democracy. Material incentives can be very effective in attracting workers. Patronage employees usually share the party organization's main goal: winning elections. That gave the party organization the flexibility to take the issue stands and appeal to the groups that would produce a victory. Patronage, then, helped the American parties behave pragmatically and inclusively.

Patronage jobs in government are not the only employment opportunities a party can offer. State and national party organizations now hire thousands of professional campaign workers, as do consulting firms associated with the parties. To provide services to their candidates, party organizations need pollsters, field organizers, researchers, fund-raisers, strategists, webmasters, database managers, and others. Some activists are drawn to party work by the chance of landing these jobs, but in general, patronage is no longer an important force in motivating activists.

Elected Office Some women and men become party activists because they see party work as a first step toward running for office. This has been true for a long time; about 40 percent of the county chairs interviewed in a 1979–1980 national survey hoped to hold public office, and an earlier study found that one-third of all state party chairs became candidates for elective office after serving the party.[10] Because of primary elections, of course, very few party organizations can just "give" nominations to public office to loyal party activists. It is far more common for candidates to see the party as one of the bases of support for winning votes and, in some areas, as the most important one. Candidates need money, advice, and people (staff and volunteers), and the party remains a likely source of all of these. So the lure of party support in a later campaign for elected office may bring some people into party work.

Preferments Party activity can bring tangible rewards for some people, other than elective or appointive office. Because public officials can use some discretion in distributing government services and granting government contracts, there is the potential for political favoritism. Some people contribute money or time to their party in the hope of attracting these favors. The head of a construction company might give a big campaign contribution in order to win a government contract to build a new school or highway. It is no accident that leaders of the construction industry are so active politically in states and cities that spend millions every year on roads and public buildings.

There are other forms of preference as well. People may hope that in return for activism on behalf of the party, they will get special treatment such as tolerant inspection of their pizzeria by the health department or prompt snow removal in front of their place of business. Or they may provide political support in the expectation of receiving a scarce resource, such as a liquor license for a local restaurant.

Reformers have promoted a number of safeguards to limit government's discretion in giving out benefits and buying goods and services from private firms. Examples are competitive and sealed bidding, conflict of interest statutes, and even affirmative action. Yet, because the potential benefits are so great for both sides, there always seem to be ways of evading even the tightest controls. In addition, many reformers don't want to eliminate *all* government discretion in the awarding of contracts just in order to stamp out *partisan* discretion. The result is that preferments may have taken the place of patronage as the main material incentive for political activity. Unfortunately for party leaders, however, they don't grant the preferments now; it is the elected officials who do.

Mixed Incentives

Most party organizations rely on a variety of incentives to attract activists. Those hoping to build support for a later run for office work together with those motivated by a particular issue and with those who come to party activities for social contact. That can produce strains among party volunteers who are motivated by different incentives. Someone who became a Democratic activist to work for abortion rights, for instance, is not likely to be satisfied with a party that supports a pro-life Democratic candidate, whereas others who participate in the party for social reasons may feel that the party ought to be a "big tent," including people who differ in their attitudes toward abortion.

The incentive that attracts people to party work may not be the incentive that keeps them there. Several studies suggest that those who become active in the party to fight for certain issues are more likely to remain in the party if they come to value the social contact it gives them. The motive that sustains their party work, in short, often shifts to solidary incentives: friendships, identification with the party itself, and other social rewards.[11] It may be that committed issue activists simply burn out, or that the American parties, which try to remain flexible enough to win elections, do not always provide the level of ideological dedication needed to sustain party workers whose lives are devoted to a set of uncompromising ideals.

Pragmatists (Professionals) and Purists (Amateurs)

Drawing on research on these incentives, scholars have classified party activists into two types, based on their beliefs about the purpose of parties in political life. One type of party activist is the **pragmatist** (sometimes known as "professional")—the party worker whose first loyalty is to the party itself. These are the party "regulars" who support their party in good times and bad, when it nominates candidates they approve of and even when it doesn't. A different type is the **purist** (or "amateur")—the issue-oriented activist, motivated by purposive incentives, who sees party activity as only one means of achieving important political goals.[12] (On the differences between these two types, see Table 5.1.)

A party organization populated by purists may behave very differently from a party dominated by pragmatists. Above all, purists are drawn into the party to further some issues or principles; their goal is the issue, and the party is a means of achieving it. If the party or its candidates pull back on its commitment to their issue, they may pull back on their commitment to the party. So they tend to be less willing to compromise their positions in order to win elections. Policy-driven activists want a candidate "they can trust to safeguard their most intense concerns."[13] When they lead party organizations, they often bring a strong push for reform in both the party's internal business and the larger political system, as Bernie Sanders Democrats did in 2016.

For pragmatists, on the other hand, the goal is the party's success in elections. Issues and candidates are the means of achieving that goal. If they believe that their party is most likely to win by downplaying an issue, moderating a position, or nominating a candidate who is popular but not in lockstep with their views, then that is the course they are likely to favor. Party leaders, then, must find a balance between the demands of the growing

TABLE 5.1 Comparing Pragmatists and Purists

	Pragmatists	Purists
Political style	Practical	Ideological
What do they want?	Success for the party	Success for particular issues, candidates
Their loyalty is to	Party organization	Officeholders, other political groups
They want the party to focus on	Candidates, elections	Issues, ideology
The party should choose candidates on the basis of	Their electability	Their principles
Their support of party candidates is	Automatic	Conditional on candidates' principles
They were recruited into politics through	Party work	Issue or candidate organizations
Their socio-economic status level is	Average to above average	Well above average

numbers of issue-oriented, purist activists and those of their more pragmatic colleagues. It is a common dilemma: whether to remain loyal to the group (or the nation) in order to keep it strong and vibrant or to give priority to the principles for which the group was formed.

Note that many activists fall between these two extremes. In practice, even most dedicated purists often come to realize that they can't achieve their policy goals unless their candidates win office. Among county party chairs in 1972, a time when purists were thought to hold the upper hand in the Democratic Party, the purists did not differ from pragmatists in their effort to run effective campaigns, maintain party morale, or communicate within the party.[14] And in 2016, after the defeats of several Tea Party-backed Republican candidates in 2010 and 2012, some very conservative Republican activists urged their party to pay more attention to electability than ideology when recruiting candidates.

Yet the increase in purist activists, and the accompanying increase in party polarization on issues, can cause rifts that damage a party's chances in particular races. In Minnesota, for instance, Republican primary voters in 2010 nominated a conservative state representative, Tom Emmer, as their candidate for governor over moderate Tom Horner. Horner then filed to run as a minor-party candidate instead and split the Republican vote in the general election, leading to a razor-thin Democratic victory. Infuriated, the Minnesota Republican Party State Central Committee decided to punish

Horner's supporters by banning 18 moderate Republicans from participating in party activities for two years and barring them from the 2012 Republican national convention. The banned partisans included two former governors and a former U.S. Senator. Conservative purists argued that the party was better off without these moderates. Some of the moderates replied that the purists were engaging in a "purge" that would reduce the party's appeal to voters. Pragmatists from both parties could well understand that fear.

Where Do Activists Come From?

Like almost all other community groups, party organizations have a hard time attracting volunteers. Except at the national level and in some states where there has been an increase in paid positions and exciting professional opportunities, parties often have few effective means of enlisting new activists. To add to the challenge, state laws often take at least part of the recruitment process out of the party's hands. Rules requiring open party caucuses and the election of party officials in primaries limit the party's control over its personnel. This can lead to the takeover of a local (or even a state) party organization by an intense group of issue activists. At the least, it leaves a party vulnerable to shifts in its direction as some leaders and activists move on and new, self-recruited leaders take their place, as Chapter 3 showed.

Finding Volunteers: Is Anybody Home?

In a much discussed set of writings, political scientist Robert Putnam showed that Americans' participation in community activities has declined in recent years. Groups ranging from churches to bowling leagues have been starved of participants. Many culprits have been identified, from the number of hours Americans spend surfing the Internet and watching television to the increasing numbers of dual-career families. The consequences, Putnam argues, are profound: a reduction in "social capital"—the social connections, values, and trust that enable communities to solve their problems more easily.[15]

The party organizations have not been spared. Fewer people are involving themselves in the face-to-face activities of politics—attending a political speech or a meeting—while the long-distance activities of Internet surfing and tweeting are on the increase. One well-designed survey found that only 8 percent of its national sample reported working on a campaign and just 5 percent said they were involved in a party organization, among the smallest percentages reporting activity in any type of civic organization.[16] Similarly grim conclusions come from the American National Election Studies, in which, in each year since 1994, only about 5 percent have reported going to any political meetings and only about 3 percent said they worked for a party[17]—even in elections when candidates such as Bernie Sanders seemed to have attracted a wealth of volunteers. Granted, even these small percentages represent a lot of people; 3 percent of the adult population would be about 6 million party and campaign activists. But although some of these activists spend a lot of time on political work, mainly at the local level, others are "checkbook participants" who mail in their contributions but do not volunteer their time and energy.

Party organizations need a constant supply of activists of all kinds, so when volunteers are in short supply, the parties are glad to accept whatever help is available. The nature of that help often varies from one political period to another, depending on events in the political world at that time. Thus, activists' political outlooks may differ considerably, depending on the time when they became active.[18] The nature and direction of the Democratic Party were heavily influenced by the influx of liberals activated by the Vietnam War and the civil rights movement in the 1960s and 1970s. Tax revolts and the appeal of Ronald Reagan in the 1980s brought new blood into Republican Party organizations. In recent years, activists from evangelical Christian groups and Tea Party supporters have brought their issues and styles of partisanship into state and local Republican Parties. Because this recruitment process often depends on the presence of magnetic personalities and powerful issues, it usually takes place in spurts rather than continuously.

The parties' recruitment system, then, is not very systematic, and it is closely linked to the movements and passions in the larger society at the time. Yet, although the parties have only limited control over their own recruitment, it clearly affects the parties' ability to achieve their goals. A local Democratic Party whose activists come mainly from labor unions will have different concerns from a local Democratic Party dominated by environmental activists, and a Republican organization run by local business leaders can differ from one controlled by conservative Christians. Depending on the nature of the community that these parties are trying to persuade, these local parties may have different levels of election success as well.

What Kinds of People Become Party Activists?

People are most likely to become involved in party politics if they have the resources to take part, the attitudes that support involvement, and if somebody has encouraged them to do so.[19] The resources needed to become a party activist include time, money, and civic skills such as the ability to organize and communicate. It takes free time to help plan a party's activities, canvass or call people, and attend other party events. People need money if they plan to contribute to the party organization or its candidates or go to party conventions. Their educational level helps to determine how much money and time they have available to spend.

Their attitudes toward politics also propel them toward party activism or steer them away from it. People are more likely to take part if they are interested in what happens in campaigns and concerned about the workings

How Social Media Are Changing Political Activism

Twitter, Instagram, YouTube, Pinterest, Facebook, and other social media have given party organizations and their activists new ways to mobilize and inform prospective supporters. Donald Trump's campaign for the Republican Party's nomination for president is a good example; while some rival candidates were investing heavily in television ads, Trump could reach an audience of more than 13 million people through his Twitter account, and many more through re-tweets, without spending a penny. Here's Trump on Twitter at a critical point in his nomination campaign: "How do you fight millions of dollars of fraudulent commercials pushing for crooked politicians? I will be using Facebook & Twitter. Watch!" Previous presidential candidates might have sold their souls to the devil to achieve that kind of exposure for free.

Of course, very few candidates can attract 13 million followers on social media. But the national parties, many state party organizations and even a lot of local parties now use social media to energize volunteers, ask for contributions, and post photos and other images for supporters to use as their profile pictures. Facebook likers or Twitter followers can be directed to a party or campaign website, asked to sign a petition, or provided with information that the party feels is being ignored or distorted by the traditional media. In 2012, Democratic campaigns used a Facebook application called Social Organizing, which connected their Facebook friends to voting records and let them know which friends had already voted or donated and which ones might still be open to persuasion. In 2016, activating supporters by using highly targeted ads on social media became standard procedure for any campaign that could afford the necessary research (see Chapter 11).

The ability to spread a message almost instantly to widely dispersed populations has affected much more than American campaigns. Social media have let new social movements, from Black Lives Matter to the Arab Spring, take form and gain recruits. They can give a voice to the underdog (if the underdog knows how to tweet) and help elected leaders learn more about public sentiment. But social media can also be used to enable governments to market their appeals more effectively to citizens and to monitor protest movements. As with most technologies, they can enhance and also threaten a democratic system.

Sources: Ludwig Siegele, "The Signal and the Noise," *The Economist*, March 26, 2016, at www.economist.com/news/special-report/21695198-ever-easier-communications-and-ever-growing-data-mountains-are-transforming-politics and Pew Research Center, "Politics Fact Sheet," under frequent revision, at www.pewinternet.org/fact-sheets/politics-fact-sheet/ (both accessed June 20, 2016).

of government, if they feel attached to a party, and if they believe that their involvement could make a difference. Most of these attitudes are related to one's income and education levels and thus add to their impact.

The third important question is simply: Has anybody asked them? The parties now have a whole arsenal of tools to contact potential activists: e-mail, regular mail, Facebook, websites, text messaging, Twitter, phone calls, and in-person canvassing (see box "How Social Media Are Changing Political Activism" on page 112). However, most appeals to take part in campaign work—and especially most *successful* appeals—come from friends or acquaintances of the potential activist. Over the years, most activists have reported that they first became involved with the party as a result of these informal, personal requests for help.[20] Being urged to participate is a powerful motivator; in a major study, almost half of those who were asked to do campaign work said yes. Most people are never asked, however; only about 12 percent of the respondents in that study reported that anyone had ever invited them to work on a campaign.[21] This helps to explain why the proportion of party activists is so small.

Who are these people who are active in party affairs? How representative are they of the rest of the American population?

Better Educated and Wealthier Than Average

American party activists have several characteristics in common that set them apart from the general population. One of the most distinctive characteristic of party activists—and one of the most concerning—is that they tend to have higher incomes, more years of formal education, and higher-status occupations than does the average American. People with higher incomes are much more likely to contribute to campaigns and to do campaign work than are those with lower incomes. Those who are politically active online tend to be wealthier and more educated as well (see Figure 5.1). The only way that the Internet reduces inequalities in participation is that younger people are less underrepresented in online political activity than they are offline.[22]

This tendency for party activists to be better educated and wealthier than the average citizen may seem perfectly natural; people with more money and higher education are more likely to have the means to participate in politics, the interest in political affairs, and the expectation that they would be successful at it. As a result, we might expect this pattern to hold in other democratic nations as well. But that is not the case. Most other democracies have a viable socialist party that recruits many of its activists from within labor unions. That dampens the relationship between party activism and higher education and wealth.

In fact, it was not always true of American politics either. The urban political machines of the 1800s and early 1900s recruited party activists who were more representative of the populations with which they worked.

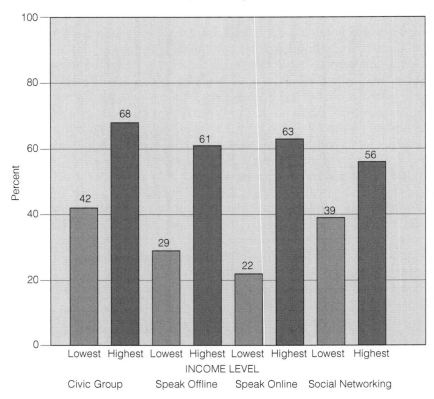

FIGURE 5.1 Wealthy People Are More Politically Active Online and Offline

Note: Bars show the percentage of respondents in each income group who took part in each political activity. *Lowest annual household income*: less than $10,000; *Highest household income*: $150,000 and above. *Civic group*: directly involved with a civic group; *Speak offline*: Communicate publicly about political issues offline. *Speak online*: Communicate publicly about political issues online. *Social Networking*: Politically active on social networking sites.

Source: Data from Aaron Smith, "Civic Engagement in the Digital Age," Pew Research Center Pew Internet and American Life Survey, April 25, 2013, at www.pewinternet.org/2013/04/25/civic-engagement-in-the-digital-age/ (accessed June 19, 2016).

The machines' jobs and favors were the main reasons for political activism at this time. When patronage and other material incentives dwindled, the social character of these parties changed. A comparison of county committee members from both Pittsburgh parties in 1971, 1976, and 1983 shows that as machine control declined, the education levels of party workers increased.[23] As issue-based incentives become more common in the American parties, party activists become even better educated and wealthier than the average citizen.

The social characteristics of Democratic activists differ from those of Republicans, just as the social bases of the parties' voters do. Democratic activists are more likely than their Republican counterparts to be female, black, unmarried, and union members. But differences in education, income, and occupation between the two parties' activists have declined in recent years. Although they may come from different backgrounds and certainly hold different political views, the leaders of both parties are drawn especially from higher-status groups in American society, even more now than in decades past.[24] As a result, party activism and other forms of political participation amplify the voices of privileged groups even more in the United States than in many other democracies.

People from "Political Families"

Party activists often come from families with a history of party activity. Many party activists had an adult party activist in their immediate family when they were growing up. Consider the case of former president George W. Bush. His grandfather was a long-time Republican Party official and U.S. senator from Connecticut. His dad, a former Republican National Committee chair, had served his party in many other posts as well before being elected president. Some of his siblings have been involved in Republican politics, including his brother Jeb, who served as governor of Florida and ran for president in 2016. Jeb's son, George P., won statewide office in Texas in 2014. With such a background, politics becomes the family business.

Different Agendas

In addition to these differences in income, education, and family background, party activists also differ from other Americans in the types of issues that they regard as important. A large study of political activists found that their participation was motivated especially by the issues of education, abortion, the economy, and human needs (including Social Security and Medicare, jobs, health care, and housing). In particular, abortion mattered more to party activists—it was mentioned by almost one in five activists—than to citizens as a whole, as did education.[25]

The activists' issue agendas varied according to their levels of income and education. Higher-income activists expressed greater concern about abortion and the environment, whereas lower-income activists' involvement was more likely to be prompted by a concern about basic human needs.[26] To the extent that higher-income activists are better represented in the parties, issues such as abortion may get more attention in party politics, even though health care, housing, and other types of human needs are obviously critical to lower-income Americans.

The types of issues that most clearly divide Democratic from Republican activists have changed over time. In the early 1970s, one of the primary distinctions between the two major parties' activists was the question of social welfare—how big a role government should play in issues such as welfare and other social services. At that time, there was a lot of variation among both parties' activists in their views about abortion. Today, in contrast, Democratic activists differ greatly from Republican activists on abortion, though the issue is more important to Republican activists than it has been to Democrats.[27]

More Consistent (and Intense) Views

Most significantly, party activists (and people who take active roles in other areas of politics as well) tend to hold more consistent views on issues than does the average American, and those views have come more closely in line with their party's positions. During the past 20 years, consistent liberals have become a larger proportion of Democratic activists, and consistent, strong conservatives have dominated the ranks of Republican activists. This polarization is especially pronounced on health-care reform and other redistributionist economic policies as well as on social issues.[28] Activists are more likely to hold deeply negative views of the other party and its leaders; in fact, these activists are often driven more by their hostility toward the other party than by their attachment to their own. This "negative partisanship" has become much more common during the past two decades.[29] These polarized liberals and conservatives are more likely to talk with others who share their strong views, contact politically like-minded people on social media, and, among the strong and consistent conservatives, restrict their news sources to a few that share their views, such as Fox News.[30] Their greater political activity can give them greater influence over elected officials; as Figure 5.2 shows, consistent conservatives and consistent liberals are much more likely to vote in primaries and to give money to campaigns than are other people. Because party activists are so important a presence in campaigns, party candidates and elected officials are likely to listen when activists urge them to take more consistent and intense stands on issues. That produces increasingly bitter political debate and gridlock.[31]

The main reason for this widening gap has been the increasing conservatism of Republican activists.[32] The trends shown in Figure 5.2 hold more strongly among Republicans than among Democrats, which helps us understand the strong rightward trend of the Republican Party in recent years. Especially since 1994, when Republicans won a majority in both houses of Congress, Republican activists have been motivated by issues and principles to an even greater extent than Democratic activists have, and their dedication to conservative principles has become more intense. So now, on most issues, those active in the Republican Party stand even further to the right of the average voter than Democratic activists are to the left of the average voter.

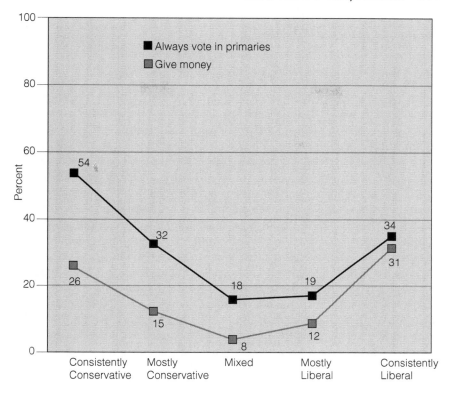

FIGURE 5.2 Consistent Conservatives and Liberals Vote More in Primaries and Give More to Campaigns

Note: Data points are the percentage of each group who report that they always vote in primaries and have contributed to a political candidate or group in the past two years.

Source: Data from Pew Research Center, "Political Polarization in the American Public," June 12, 2014, at www.people-press.org/2014/06/12/political-polarization-in-the-american-public/ (accessed June 19, 2016).

Party Activists and Democracy

In short, as we have seen, American party activists differ a lot from other citizens—the very people these activists aim to persuade—and the gulf has been growing.[33] Research tells us that the major parties attract men and women with the time and financial resources to afford political activity, the attitudes that make politics a priority to them, and the connections with others who are similarly engaged. These activists also tend to be motivated by controversial issues, hold more extreme attitudes than other citizens do, and are more polarized by party than was the case in the mid-1900s. These findings raise some important questions: Does it matter if party activists are not very representative of other Americans? What has been the impact of the increase in issue-oriented, "purist" activists? More generally, how do the characteristics of Republican and Democratic activists affect the workings of party organizations?

The Problem of Representation

When party activists give the appearance of being "true believers" on contentious issues and don't seem to share the concerns of less involved voters, then it is not surprising that many Americans think of the party organizations as alien places. There is a delicate balance to be achieved in party politics. When the two parties sound too much alike on issues, citizens may not feel that they have clear choices in politics. Democracy can be well served when the major parties take clear and distinctive stands on major policy questions. However, when Republican and Democratic activists take polarized, "us vs. them" positions, especially on questions that are not central to most Americans' daily lives, and try to marginalize anyone who disagrees, then the parties expose themselves to public distrust, an old problem in American politics. The impact increases when these activists recruit and support extremists as party candidates for public office.

Further, when both parties' activists come from more privileged backgrounds than most citizens do, we have to ask whether they are truly able to understand the forces that affect most Americans' lives. It is possible, of course, for wealthy and educated individuals to speak for others who are disadvantaged. But we have seen indications that party activists' issue *priorities* differ from those of many other citizens in ways consistent with the economic differences that separate them.[34]

Purists and Pressure for Internal Party Democracy

The increase in issue-oriented, purist activists often increases the demands on the party organization itself. In the past four decades, these activists have insisted on a much louder voice in the party's organization, and their demands have been met. Because volunteer activists are so essential to the party's success, party leaders are often willing to tolerate greater levels of internal party democracy in order to retain their volunteers' loyalty.

An internally democratic party organization might result in a stronger party, better able to fulfill its responsibilities in a democracy, under some circumstances. Rank-and-file activists who are contributing their time and effort in the service of a strongly held principle and who feel sure that their views are taken seriously by party leaders may work even harder on the party's behalf. They might also press the party to remain consistent in its issue stands and strive to hold the party's leaders accountable, at least to the activists themselves.

On the other hand, pragmatic parties, dedicated to the party's success above all else, have a long tradition in American politics. Much of the discipline in the classic party machine resulted from the willingness and ability of party leaders to give or withhold material rewards. A disobedient or inefficient party worker sacrificed a patronage job or the hope of one. The newer incentives cannot be given or taken away so easily. A local Republican organization is not likely to punish an errant, ideologically motivated activist by ending the party's opposition to same-sex marriage. Besides, the activist could find many other organizations that may be more effective at pursuing that goal, such as religious lobbies or other organized interests.

Activists, Party Strength, and Democracy

Strong party organizations have often been considered a threat to American politics. Since the beginning, American political culture has been dominated by a fear that a few "bosses," responsible to no one but themselves, control the selection of public officials and the choice of policies. Supporters of candidates as diverse as Donald Trump and Bernie Sanders made this claim in 2016. The result has been a series of efforts to keep the parties from playing too powerful a role in the lives of candidates, elected officials, and voters.

Several characteristics of party activists help to keep the parties decentralized and limited in power. The shortage of volunteers means that party organizations have to pay attention to their activists' concerns. This prevents a centralization of party power (unless, of course, the party activists push for greater centralization, as they sometimes have). The demand by many activists for internally democratic parties restrains the authority of party leaders at the top. And, in turn, because power in the American parties is diffused through the various levels of party organization, precinct committee members, city leaders, county officials, and activists at all levels are free to define their own political roles and to nourish their separate bases of party power.

The traditional worry about the excesses of party power, then, is probably misplaced. There have been few occasions in American history when the parties have been able to corral the kinds of incentives and resources that they would need to develop a fully staffed, vibrant organization at all levels of government. Although the national, state, and local party organizations have all raised more money and mastered new campaign skills in the past two decades (as Chapters 3 and 4 show), the continuing challenge of putting "boots on the ground"—attracting volunteers—remains one of the biggest challenges faced by the American parties.

Notes

1 For the original formulation, see Peter B. Clark and James Q. Wilson, "Incentive Systems: A Theory of Organizations," *Administrative Science Quarterly* 6 (1961): 129–166.

2 John H. Aldrich, *Why Parties? A Second Look* (Chicago; University of Chicago Press, 2011), p. 188.

3 Samuel J. Eldersveld, "The Party Activist in Detroit and Los Angeles," in William Crotty, ed., *Political Parties in Local Areas* (Knoxville, TN: University of Tennessee Press, 1986), Chapter 4.

4 John A. Clark, John M. Bruce, John H. Kessel, and William Jacoby, "I'd Rather Switch than Fight," *American Journal of Political Science* 35 (1991): 577–597; and Dorothy Davidson Nesbit, "Changing Partisanship among Southern Party Activists," *Journal of Politics* 50 (1988): 322–334.

5 Sidney Verba, Kay Lehman Schlozman, and Henry E. Brady, *Voice and Equality* (Cambridge, MA: Harvard University Press, 1995), p. 121.

6 See ibid., pp. 112–121.

7 See Martin Shefter, *Political Parties and the State* (Princeton, NJ: Princeton University Press, 1994).

8 The 1976 case is *Elrod v. Burns*; the 1980 case is *Branti v. Finkel*, and the 1990 case is *Rutan v. Republican Party of Illinois*.

9 On the case for patronage, see the dissenting opinions to the Supreme Court's *Elrod, Branti,* and *Rutan* decisions. The case against patronage is well put in Anne Freedman, *Patronage: An American Tradition* (Chicago: Nelson-Hall, 1994), Chapter 5.

10 Cornelius P. Cotter, James L. Gibson, John F. Bibby, and Robert J. Huckshorn, *Party Organizations in American Politics* (New York: Praeger, 1984), p. 42; and Robert J. Huckshorn, *Party Leadership in the States* (Amherst, MA: University of Massachusetts Press, 1976), p. 37.

11 See M. Margaret Conway, *Political Participation in the United States*, 3rd ed. (Washington, DC: CQ Press, 2000).

12 See Clark and Wilson, "Incentive Systems." Note that the term "professional," as used here, does not necessarily refer to someone who is paid for party work, and the term "amateur" is not meant to be derogatory.

13 See Marty Cohen, David Karol, Hans Noel, and John Zaller, *The Party Decides* (Chicago: University of Chicago Press, 2008), pp. 88–91, 178 (quote on p. 89).

14 Michael A. Maggiotto and Ronald E. Weber, "The Impact of Organizational Incentives on County Party Chairpersons," *American Politics Quarterly* 14 (1986): 201–218.

15 Robert D. Putnam, *Bowling Alone* (New York: Simon & Schuster, 2000).

16 Verba et al., *Voice and Equality*, Chapter 3. This seems to be true in other democracies as well; see Paul F. Whiteley, "Is the Party Over?" *Party Politics* 17 (2011): 21–44.

17 American National Election Studies, University of Michigan; data made available by the Inter-University Consortium for Political and Social Research.

18 See Paul Allen Beck and M. Kent Jennings, "Updating Political Periods and Political Participation," *American Political Science Review* 78 (1984): 198–201; and Steven E. Finkel and Gregory Trevor, "Reassessing Ideological Bias in Campaign Participation," *Political Behavior* 8 (1986): 374–390.

19 See Verba, Schlozman, and Brady, *Voice and Equality*, pp. 15–16 and Chapters 9–14.

20 Henry E. Brady, Kay Lehman Schlozman, and Sidney Verba, "Prospecting for Participants," *American Political Science Review* 93 (1999): 153–168.

21 Verba et al., *Voice and Equality*, pp. 135 and 139–144.

22 See Kay Lehman Schlozman, Sidney Verba, and Henry E. Brady, *The Unheavenly Chorus* (Princeton, NJ: Princeton University Press, 2012), especially Chapter 16.

23 See Michael Margolis and Raymond E. Owen, "From Organization to Personalism," *Polity* 18 (1985): 313–328.

24 Marjorie Randon Hershey, Nathaniel Birkhead, and Beth C. Easter, "Party Activists and Political Polarization," in Mark D. Brewer and L. Sandy Maisel, eds., *The Parties Respond*, 5th ed. (Boulder, CO: Westview Press, 2012).

25 Verba et al., *Voice and Equality*, pp. 84–91.

26 *Ibid.*, pp. 220–225.

27 Edward G. Carmines and James Woods, "The Role of Party Activists in the Evolution of the Abortion Issue," *Political Behavior* 24 (2002): 361–377.

28 Alan I. Abramowitz, *The Disappearing Center* (New Haven, CT: Yale University Press, 2010), pp. 47–48; Alan I. Abramowitz, *The Polarized Public?* (Boston: Pearson, 2013), pp. 10 and 73.

29 Pew Center for the People and the Press, "Political Polarization in the American Public," June 12, 2014, at www.people-press.org/2014/06/12/political-polarization-in-the-american-public (accessed June 19, 2016).

30 Amy Mitchell, Jeffrey Gottfried, Jocelyn Kiley, and Katerina Eva Matsa, "Political Polarization and Media Habits," Pew Research Journalism Project, October 21, 2014, at www.journalism.org/2014/10/21/political-polarization-media-habits/ (accessed June 19, 2016).

31 Geoffrey C. Layman, Thomas M. Carsey, John C. Green, Richard Herrera, and Rosalyn Cooperman, "Activists and Conflict Extension in American Party Politics," *American Political Science Review* 104 (2010): 324–346. See also Schlozman et al., *The Unheavenly Chorus*, Chapter 9.

32 Kyle L. Saunders and Alan I. Abramowitz, "Ideological Realignment and Active Partisans in the American Electorate," *American Politics Research* 32 (2004): 285–309.

33 Ryan D. Enos and Eitan D. Hersh find that in the 2012 Obama campaign, canvassers tended to be more extreme in views than were the voters they were trying to persuade. See their "Party Activists as Campaign Advertisers," *American Political Science Review* 109 (2015): 252–278.

34 See Schlozman et al., *The Unheavenly Chorus*, especially Chapter 9.

PART III

The Political Party in the Electorate

If there were a Pollsters' Hall of Fame, surely the first question in it would be: Generally speaking, do you usually think of yourself as a Republican, a Democrat, an independent, or what? The question is meant to classify **party identifiers**—people who feel a sense of psychological attachment to a particular party. If you respond that you do usually think of yourself as a Democrat or a Republican, then you are categorized as belonging to the **party in the electorate**—the third major sector of the American parties. Party identifiers (also called **partisans**) make up the core of the party's support: the people who normally vote for a party's candidates and who see politics through a partisan's eyes. They are more apt to vote in their party's primary elections and to volunteer for party candidates than are other citizens. In short, they are the party organization's, and its candidates', closest friends in the public.

Survey researchers have measured Americans' partisanship since the 1940s. The dominant measure, just cited, has been used in polls conducted by the University of Michigan, now under the auspices of the American National Election Studies (ANES). After asking whether you consider yourself a Republican or a Democrat, the question continues:

> [If Republican or Democrat] Would you call yourself a strong [Republican or Democrat] or a not very strong [Republican or Democrat]? [If independent, no preference, or other party] Do you think of yourself as closer to the Republican Party or to the Democratic Party?

Using these answers, researchers classify people into seven categories of party identification: strong party identifiers (Democrats or Republicans), weak identifiers (Democrats or Republicans), independent "leaners" (toward the Democrats or Republicans), and pure independents.[1]

Note that this definition is based on people's attitudes, not on their actual voting choices. Strong party identifiers usually vote for their party's candidates, but the essence of a party identification is an attachment to the

123

idea of the party itself, distinct from feelings about particular candidates. Someone can remain a committed Republican, for example, while choosing to vote for the Democratic candidate in a specific race, as did a number of anti-Trump Republicans in 2016. Because there are so many elective offices in the United States, and given the value American culture places on independence, party identifiers sometimes vote for a candidate or two of the other party. In the same sense, we do not define the party electorate by the official act of registering with a party. Almost half of the states do not require voters to register their party affiliation, and in states that do, some voters change their party attachments long before they change their official registration.[2]

The party electorate's relationship with the other two party sectors, the party organization and the party in government, is not necessarily close and cooperative. Party organizations and candidates ask their party identifiers for contributions and votes during campaigns but often don't keep in touch with partisans at other times. Party identifiers, in turn, seldom feel any obligation to the party organization other than to vote for its candidates, if they choose. Party identifiers are not party "members" in any real sense. In these ways, the American parties resemble cadre parties (see pages 53–4): top heavy in leaders and activists without any real membership, in contrast to the mass-membership parties that have been an important part of the European democratic experience.

Even so, party identifiers give the party organization and its candidates a continuing base of voter support. The parties, then, don't have to start from scratch in each campaign. The party in the electorate also determines most of the party's nominees for office by voting in primaries. It is a potential source of activists for the organization. Partisans help keep the party alive by transmitting party loyalties to their children. A party identification is usually the most significant landmark in an individual's mental map of the political world.

A party in the electorate is not just a collection of individuals; it is a coalition of social groups. Our images of the two parties often spring from the types of people the parties have attracted as identifiers. When people speak of the Democrats as the party of minorities or of the Republicans as the party of business, they are probably referring, at least in part, to the party in the electorate. The groups in a party's coalition help shape its choice of nominees and stands on issues, and in turn, those candidates and appeals help to structure elections and political debate.

The three chapters in Part III explore the nature and importance of these parties in the electorate. Chapter 6 looks at the development of party identification and its impact on individuals' political behavior. Chapter 7 examines the parties as coalitions of social groups and traces the meaning of changes in those coalitions over time. Chapter 8 focuses on the parties' efforts to affect voter turnout, not only by mobilizing their supporters but also by trying to change the rules that govern who can vote.

Notes

1   See Angus Campbell, Philip E. Converse, Warren E. Miller, and Donald E. Stokes, *The American Voter* (New York: Wiley, 1960), Chapter 6.
2   Steven E. Finkel and Howard A. Scarrow, "Party Identification and Party Enrollment," *Journal of Politics* 47 (1985): 620–642.

CHAPTER 6

Party Identification

If you are typical, you probably started thinking of yourself as a Democrat, a Republican, or an independent in childhood, even before you knew what the words meant.[1] The psychological attachment that most Americans develop toward a political party is called a **party identification**, or **party ID**.[2] By the time they get to be young adults, about one-third call themselves "strong" partisans, and almost as many express some party attachment, though not a strong one. Even most of those who at first claim to be independents admit to feeling "closer to" one party and favor that party in their voting.

To most researchers, party attachment is a kind of lasting "team loyalty" that helps people find their place in the group conflicts that characterize the political world.[3] It is an emotional as well as a social tie, which often grows out of other deeply rooted loyalties, such as family, religious, or ethnic identities. A college student might see herself as a Republican because her parents and relatives are Republicans or because she is an evangelical Christian. Many of these researchers view party ID as a perceptual screen—a filter that screens out any conflicting information the student may receive.

Other researchers think party identification is more changeable. To them, it is a running tally of an individual's positive or negative experiences with the party's stands or its performance in office.[4] But no matter how we characterize it,[5] party identification is a vital link between citizens and the party organization as well as the party in government. People's party ID tells us more about their political attitudes and behavior than does any other single piece of information. For citizens, it is also a valuable decision-making shortcut. Politics is complicated, even for political junkies. Americans cope with more elections and longer ballots than do citizens of any other democracy. A party ID offers a useful means of cutting through the complexity. It can help people make efficient voting decisions without taking time to learn much about specific candidates.

How, then, do people—you, for example—develop a party ID?

How People Develop Party Identifications

Families are the most common source of our first party ID, as they are of so much else in our early lives. As children become aware of politics, they absorb their family's judgments about political parties and usually come to think of themselves as sharing their family's partisanship.

Childhood Influences

Most parents do not consciously indoctrinate their children into partisanship, but they are nevertheless the main teachers of political attitudes. Their casual conversations about political events are enough to convey their party loyalties to their children, just as children learn where their family "belongs" in relation to other social groups. In fact, in these polarized times, you can even find children's books titled *Why Mommy Is a Democrat* (in which the narrator explains, "Democrats make sure we all share our toys") and *The Liberal Clause* (Christmas is threatened when elves unionize and make the North Pole into a socialist disaster).[6] Family and other early influences are often powerful enough to last into adulthood, even when young adults are pulled toward independence in other aspects of their lives.

This early party ID usually takes hold before children have much information as to what the parties stand for. Only in the middle-school and high-school years do many students begin to associate the parties with economic interests—business or labor, the rich or the poor—and thus have some reasoning to support the party ID they have already developed. Note the importance of the sequence here. Party loyalty comes first, so it can have a long-lasting impact on political orientations. Only later do people learn about political issues and events, which may then be seen, at least to a degree, through a partisan lens.[7]

Once developed, people's party loyalties are often sustained because we gravitate toward people like ourselves. People's friends, relatives, and coworkers typically share the same partisanship.[8] Some people do leave the party of their parents. Those whose early party loyalty is weak are more likely to change. So are people whose mother and father identified with different parties or who live in a community or work in a setting where the dominant party ID differs from their own. But when parents share the same party ID, they are more likely to produce strong party identifiers among their children.

Other sources of political learning tend to support a person's inherited party loyalty or at least do not challenge the family's influence. Schools typically avoid partisan politics; they are more inclined to teach political independence than partisanship. Many churches and other religious groups have become very engaged in politics recently, but they are not likely to lead young people away from their parents' partisan influence. And the American party organizations do much less outreach than do some European parties, which maintain party youth groups, social, and recreational activities.

Influences in Adulthood

The party ID most people develop in childhood and adolescence is more likely to be challenged in young adulthood, when we move into new environments: college, work, marriage, a new community, and the unexpected honor of paying taxes. At this time, young adults can test their childhood party loyalties against their own personal experience with government. They can get to know others with different party preferences. Their adult experiences may reinforce their early-learned loyalties or may undermine those loyalties.[9] Or the old loyalties may exist peacefully alongside contradictory new information. People can learn more about candidates and issues, and even change their attitudes toward those political objects, without necessarily changing their party ID.[10]

The longer an individual holds a particular party ID, the more stable it normally becomes.[11] Although about 15 percent of people aged 18 to 34 report that they identified with the other party at some point within the past decade, this is true of only about 5 percent of older adults.[12] Party ID tends to become a habit. Partisanship may grow stronger across the life cycle because it is so useful a shortcut for simplifying the political decision making of older voters,[13] or because they surround themselves increasingly with others who share their party loyalties. In fact, researchers find that marriage partners and other mates are more likely to share a party ID than they are to share other social traits, perhaps because these similarities are especially important to us.[14]

At times, however, even the strongest partisans may rethink their attachments. During periods of major party change, when the issue bases of partisanship and the party coalitions themselves are being transformed, some voters drop or switch party loyalties. (We look more fully at the idea of party coalitional change or realignment in Chapter 7.) This happened in the South in the closing decades of the 1900s as conservative whites moved from Democratic partisanship to independence and then to Republican Party ID. Economic calamities and debates about strongly felt issues such as same-sex marriage can make someone rethink her partisanship, especially when party leaders' stands attract a lot of media coverage.[15] Older adults may be caught up in the excitement of the moment as well, but their partisanship, often reinforced by years of consistent partisan behavior, resists change more effectively. Thus, when partisan turmoil begins, young adults are more likely than older adults to embrace the change.[16]

Patterns of Partisanship over Time

Large-scale change in party identifications is the exception, however, and not the rule. Most Americans, once they have developed party loyalties, tend to keep them. People who do change their party ID often change only its intensity (e.g., from strong to weak identification) rather than convert to the other party.

At the national level, we can see this stability in Americans' responses to the poll question measuring party ID that has been asked in every presidential election year since 1952 by researchers for the American National Election Studies. The data are summarized by decade in Figure 6.1; the full data set can be found in Table A.2 in the Online Appendix.[17] There has been some change in the overall partisanship of Americans: although most Americans have identified as Democrats throughout these years, the gap narrowed in each decade, and especially beginning in the 1980s. The increase in Republican support since that time, as we will see in Chapter 7, was propelled largely by the gradual movement of white southerners from Democratic to Republican identification.

Changes in overall partisanship usually happen slowly. In Figure 6.1, look, for example, at the percentage who call themselves *strong* Republicans (represented by the dark segment at the bottom of each Republican column). When summarized by decade, this proportion never rises above 14 percent nor drops below 9 percent. The full dataset in the Online Appendix shows

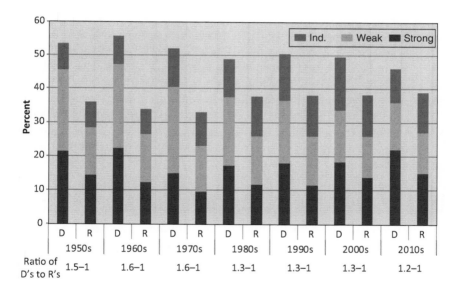

FIGURE 6.1 Party Identification by Decade, 1950s–2010s

Note: Based on surveys of the national electorate conducted immediately before each presidential and most congressional elections as part of the American National Election Studies program. For each party grouping in each decade, the dark segment at the base of the bar is the percentage of respondents calling themselves strong Democrats or Republicans; in the middle are weak Democrats or Republicans, and at the top is the percentage calling themselves independents who lean toward the Democratic or the Republican Party. For the full presentation of data for presidential election years, including the "pure" independents, see Table A.2 in the Appendix.

Source: American National Election Studies, University of Michigan; data made available by the Inter-University Consortium for Political and Social Research.

that during 60 years of history, from years when the Republican Party was triumphant to years when it seemed almost dead, the proportion of strong Republicans has stayed within a 7-percentage–point range, between 9 and 16 percent of those surveyed. Overall, the percentage of respondents in each category of partisanship tends to change very little from one election year to the next; the usual difference is just 2 percent. Election campaigns and other events can produce "bumps" in the pattern, but these are often short lived.[18]

Only a few episodes have disrupted this story of fairly stable partisanship. During an especially turbulent period—1972 through 1976, spanning President Richard Nixon's landslide reelection, the Watergate scandals that caused Nixon to resign, his subsequent pardon by President Gerald Ford, and Ford's own 1976 defeat—researchers interviewed the same set of individuals in three successive surveys. Almost two-thirds of the respondents remained in the same broad category of party ID (44 percent were stable strong/weak Democrats or Republicans, 20 percent stable independents) throughout all three surveys. Only 3 percent changed parties. Party identification was remarkably stable during these agitated times.[19]

Yet a third of the respondents did change from a party ID to independence during these three waves of surveys. At the national level (see Figure 6.2), there was also a drop in the proportion of respondents calling themselves *strong* partisans (Democrats or Republicans) during the 1960s and an increase in the percentage of independent "leaners," especially among younger voters. Combined with other major changes at that time—the civil rights movement, protests against American involvement in the Vietnam War, the women's movement, environmental activism—the growing number of independents suggested to many observers that partisanship was fading in the United States.

Was There a Decline in Partisanship?

Research in other democracies bolstered the argument that partisanship was declining in the 1960s and 1970s. Across the Western industrialized world, analysts found an increase in self-reported independents, a drop in public confidence in political parties, and more **split-ticket voting** (supporting candidates of more than one party).[20] The effects of this "party decline" would have been profound.[21] What could have caused it? Education levels were rising in democracies; perhaps the better educated voters had so much other information available that they didn't need parties as a decision shortcut any more. Maybe media coverage of politics stressed nonpartisanship or ignored parties.

These explanations provoked even more questions, however. If Americans have more information available than ever before, wouldn't they need a device, like a party ID, to help them sift through it? Even though education levels are rising, we know that most Americans are not very interested in politics, do not know much about it, and therefore depend on shortcuts to make sense of it.²² Party ID, then, should remain a helpful tool. And among people for whom partisanship is a strong group attachment, more information would probably not weaken their partisan feelings.

In fact, indicators of partisanship *have* rebounded since the 1970s. In particular, strong partisanship has made a comeback (see Figure 6.2). The proportion of strong party identifiers in 2016 slightly exceeded what it had been in the 1950s, which was considered an era of strong party ID. Among those who vote, the decline in party ID has been largely reversed.²³ In fact, the proportion of voters who consider themselves partisans, and the consistency between partisanship and vote choice, have recently been the highest in more than 20 years. The main changes between the 1950s and today have been a decrease in the proportion of weak partisans and a big increase in the numbers of independent "leaners," those who call themselves independents but then acknowledge, when probed by poll takers, that they lean toward one party. It is the increase in "leaners" that is typically used to support the contention that Americans have become more independent politically. Researchers disagree on whether these "leaners" are really "closet partisans," but most find that leaners vote and think much more like partisans than they do like independents.²⁴ A main difference between leaners and other partisans is that the former are not as strongly polarized in their attitudes toward the two parties.²⁵

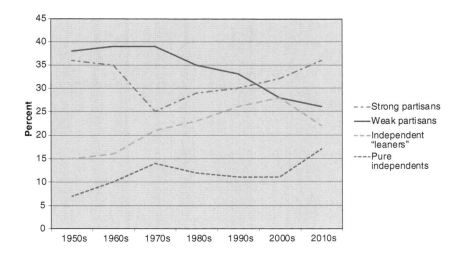

FIGURE 6.2 Change in Strength of Party ID, 1950s–2010s

Note: This is a "folded" party ID scale in which Democrats and Republicans in each category are combined (i.e., the category "strong partisans" includes strong Democrats and strong Republicans).

Source: Calculated from American National Election Studies, University of Michigan; data made available through the Inter-University Consortium for Political and Social Research.

Recent Changes in the Direction of Party ID

As partisanship revived in the 1980s and 1990s, the Democratic edge in party ID began to shrink. The increase in partisanship, then, seemed at first to benefit Republicans. But the parties' fortunes have varied a lot since then. Another measure of people's feelings toward the parties is the public approval ratings of the two parties. As you can see in Figure 6.3, the Democrats and the Republicans have exchanged places several times during the past two decades in their effort to win public support. The Republican Party's approval levels soared and then dropped during the presidency of Democrat Bill Clinton. After the September 11, 2001 terrorist attacks, Republican standing rose, only to sink dramatically during Republican president George W. Bush's second term. The decline continued during the presidency of Democrat Barack Obama. Although polls showed that most respondents felt the Republican Party had strong principles, majorities also described it as "too extreme," "inflexible," and "out of touch with the American people."[26]

The Democratic Party has risen and fallen in public opinion as well. Its approval ratings rose during Bill Clinton's second term, but in the early 2000s, the party's standing was a mirror image of President Bush's popularity; Democratic approval ratings dropped early in the Bush presidency, when the president did better in the polls, and then rose as Bush's approval ratings declined. The Democrats' image took a major hit in

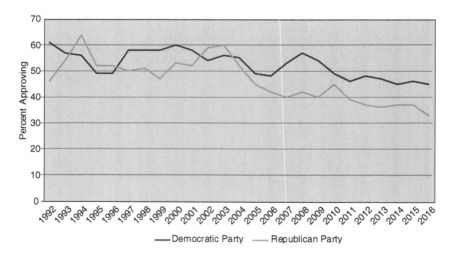

FIGURE 6.3 Public (Dis)approval of the Parties since 1992

Note: Data points are the percentages who say that "your overall opinion of [the party] is very favorable [or] mostly favorable," as opposed to "mostly unfavorable," "very unfavorable," or "can't rate." Multiple data points in a given year are averaged.

Source: Pew Research Center for the People & the Press, www.pewresearch.org/data-trend/political-attitudes/democratic-party-favorability/ and www.pewresearch.org/data-trend/political-attitudes/republican-party-favorability/ (accessed June 21, 2016).

2009 and 2010 when the economic recovery from the Great Recession moved at a snail's pace and controversy arose over the Obama administration's stimulus program and health-care reform. Democratic approval ratings have improved only slightly since then, but Democrats hold more positive feelings toward their party and its leaders than Republicans do about theirs.[27]

What accounts for these shifts in the parties' fortunes? The sharper differentiation between Democratic and Republican stands on issues (see Chapter 15) can lead to big changes in policy when the party in power changes. Voters often recognize what they oppose more easily than what they favor. When a Republican-led government cuts back on government services and regulations, many voters find that they miss the lost services. When Democrats put new government programs in place, many voters are irritated by the greater reach of government into their lives. Big policy change tends to produce a strong backlash.[28] The more recent slump in the Republican Party's favorability seems also to be related to grassroots Republicans' increasing frustration with the performance of their party's congressional majority and, among some Republicans, conflicting feelings about the party's nomination of Donald Trump.[29]

Longer-term demographic trends are likely to help the Democrats.[30] The share of the electorate who are married, white Christians—the core supporters of the Republican Party—has declined in recent years. The fastest-growing groups in the adult population are Latino Americans and young people who came of age politically during the Obama years. Both groups leaned heavily Democratic in the 2010s. But their continued enthusiasm for the Democrats depends heavily on the two parties' candidates and issue stances. If Republicans were to recruit more Latino American candidates, that might dampen the Democrats' appeal to Latino and Hispanic voters. On the other hand, if major Republican figures continue to take stands on immigration, abortion, and LGBTQ rights that are unpalatable to many Latinos and young people, their Democratic leanings are likely to strengthen, as is their motivation to register and vote. That may well happen, because those stands resonate with the Republican base in the South and among conservative Christians. No matter which party is favored at any given time, however, party remains an influential attachment, and the earlier discussion of party decline is at an end.

Partisanship and Intense Negative Feelings

The data you've seen so far paint a mixed picture. Partisanship has made a comeback, yet both parties' public approval ratings are clearly less positive now than they were two decades ago. Why would people become more attached to parties they like less? The answer reflects partisans' growing hostility toward the *opposition* party.[31]

Recently, people's party ID has become more and more characterized by anger, fear, and even hatred toward the other party and its supporters. In many cases, party identifiers' disgust with the other party's policies is stronger than their agreement with their own party's stands. Not only do most partisans hold very unfavorable views of the opposition party, one poll (discussed in Chapter 1) found that a remarkable 45 percent of Republican identifiers saw the Democratic Party's policies as "so misguided that they threaten the nation's well-being," and 41 percent of Democrats felt the same about Republican policies. The figures were even higher among those who contributed money to campaigns—a level of animosity that has increased greatly in the past 20 years.[32] Partisanship, as the beginning of this chapter showed, has always had an emotional component. But among many Americans, party ID is now driven more by negative feelings toward the other side than by positive feelings toward their own. This became especially obvious in 2016 when a majority of Donald Trump supporters, and at times a majority of Hillary Clinton supporters, said their choice was driven mainly driven by disgust with the other party's candidate rather than by enthusiasm for their own party's presidential candidate.

Party Identification and Political Views

Party loyalties help to condition the way most Americans feel about policies and candidates,[33] even more than is the case in many other democracies.[34] The polarization of American politics (see Chapter 15) seems to strengthen the impact of partisanship on people's attitudes.[35] Republicans are normally much more critical of big government than Democrats are, very much more hostile toward former President Obama, and more favorable to the idea that traditional values should be universally followed.[36] As you'll see in Chapter 7, Democrats are much more liberal than Republicans on issues such as abortion, the environment, gun control, civil rights, and government involvement in the economy and health care. Although both sets of partisans regard the economy and jobs as their highest priorities, Democrats put higher priority than Republicans on improving the educational system, reducing health-care costs, and protecting the environment. Republicans are more concerned with reducing the budget deficit, defending against terrorism, reducing illegal immigration, and strengthening the military.[37] Party ID even seems to guide perceptions of the strength and progress of the economy. In 2015, for instance, Democratic identifiers were about twice as likely as Republicans to rate economic conditions positively, though both groups were presumably viewing the same economy.[38]

Figure 6.4 shows that feelings about the federal government can change markedly, consistent with party ID, when partisan control of the government changes. In 2006, during the big slide in Republican President Bush's approval ratings, fully 57 percent of Democratic identifiers agreed that the federal government "poses an immediate threat to the rights and freedoms of ordinary citizens," as did only 21 percent of Republicans. In sharp contrast, just before the 2010 elections, with Democrat Obama in the White

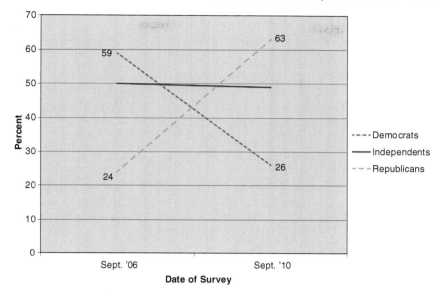

FIGURE 6.4 Changing Feelings about the Federal Government, by Party ID, 2006 and 2010

Note: Data points are the percentages of each group who say "yes" to the question, "Do you think the federal government poses an immediate threat to the rights and freedoms of ordinary citizens, or not?"

Source: Gallup Poll at www.gallup.com/poll/185720/half-continue-say-gov-i8mmediate-threat.aspx (accessed June 21, 2016).

House and Democrats in control of Congress, the number of Republicans feeling threatened by the federal government had tripled, whereas the number of worried Democrats dropped by more than half. During that time, "pure" independents' sense of threat had hardly changed at all.[39]

For an even more dramatic example, consider the controversial 2000 election, when the Supreme Court stopped the recount of votes in some Florida counties and decided the presidential election in favor of Bush. In a poll taken two months before the election, 70 percent of Democratic identifiers had said that they approved of the Supreme Court's job performance, and only 18 percent disapproved. A month after the Court's verdict on the presidential race, just 42 percent of Democrats now said they approved of the way the Court was handling its job, and 50 percent said they disapproved. Conversely, approval of the Court among Republicans rose from 60 percent in August 2000 to 80 percent in January 2001.[40] A similar (but less marked) shift occurred when the Court narrowly upheld most of the Democratic Affordable Care Act health reform law in 2012. This party polarization of attitudes toward government reduces the chance to find middle ground and heightens the stakes in campaign rhetoric.

Party Identification and Voting

The most important effect of party attachments is their influence on voting behavior. Even though partisans have to fight their way through long ballots and the culture's traditional distrust of strong parties, party identifiers tend to support their party fairly faithfully. Where partisanship is weak, as in new democracies where party ID is still developing, voting choices are more likely to be unstable and changeable.[41]

Party Voting

During the past half-century, party identifiers have voted for their party's candidates most of the time. (The data can be found in Tables A.3 and A.4 and Figures A.1 and A.2 in the Online Appendix.) A majority in each category of partisanship has voted for their party's presidential candidate in every year, except for weak Democrats in 1972 and independent Democrats in 1980 (both GOP landslide years). As with party ID, party voting declined somewhat during the late 1960s and early 1970s. But recent studies show that the overall impact of party ID on voting behavior has been on the upswing since the mid-1970s[42] and continued to increase in the 2000s. (Republicans' support for their party's candidate dropped in 1992 because a minority of Republicans voted for independent candidate Ross Perot.) The polarization of the major parties in recent years has probably helped some voters to clarify their political attachments and to heighten their sense of loyalty to a party and its candidates. The most faithful are the strong partisans. In the last four presidential elections, at least 94 percent of strong Democrats supported their party's candidate. Strong Republicans have been just as loyal; only once in 50 years has their support for the GOP presidential candidate dipped below 90 percent.

These patterns appear in congressional elections as well. A majority within each group of partisans has voted for their party's congressional candidates in each election, and strong partisans have been the most consistent party voters. In 2016 House races, more than 90 percent of partisans voted for the congressional candidate of their party.[43] We find similar results in voting at the state and local levels. **Straight-ticket voting**—voting for one party's candidates only—declined among all partisan groups during the 1960s and 1970s, but the stronger an individual's party ID, the more likely he or she was to vote a straight ticket.[44] And as with other indicators of party influence, the decline has reversed. The 2016 elections were the first time every state voting for a Democrat for Senate also voted Democratic for president, and the same consistency was true for Republicans: an impressive level of straight-ticket voting.

Party Versus Candidates and Issues

The level of party voting varies over time because individuals' voting decisions are affected by the give-and-take of two sets of forces: the strength of their party ID (if they have one) and the power of the **short-term forces** operating in a given election, such as the attractiveness of the candidates and issues in that campaign. Usually these two sets of forces incline the voter in the same direction; as we have seen, a party ID encourages an individual to see the party's candidates and issue stands in a favorable light.

At times, however, an especially attractive candidate or a particularly compelling issue—an economic disaster or the threat of terrorism—may lead a voter to desert one or more of his or her party's candidates. Although some voters split their tickets in order to create a moderate or divided government,[45] it is more common for voters to defect from their party ID because they are attracted to a well-known candidate running a well-funded campaign, most often an incumbent of the other party.[46] Typically, those with the weakest party ID or the most ambivalent attitudes about the parties—for example, those who have at least some positive feelings about both parties[47]—are the most likely to defect.

Partisanship as a Two-Way Street

Which is more important in influencing people's votes: party ID, candidate characteristics, or current issues? One challenge for political scientists in answering this question is that these three forces are strongly interrelated. The early studies of party ID in the 1950s assumed that party "came first" in the causal ordering—that it affected people's feelings about candidates and issues but was not in turn influenced by them. These early studies did not have good measures of how close the voter felt to the candidates on issues.

Since then, with the use of better measures, researchers have shown that there are reciprocal relationships among these three influences. Just as an individual's party loyalty influences the way he or she views politics, feelings about candidates and issues can affect the individual's party ID. In particular, reactions to a president's management of the economy (so-called **retrospective evaluations,** in that they refer to past actions rather than hopes for the future) can feed back on party loyalties and weaken or change them. In this way, it is possible to see partisanship as a kind of running tally of party-related evaluations.[48] Even if party ID is usually stable enough to withstand an individual's disappointment in a particular party candidate or in the party's position on an issue or two, an accumulation of these negative experiences, especially on an issue important to him or her, can weaken or change an individual's partisanship.[49] That is what happened over several decades to the long-standing Democratic loyalties of many conservative white southerners, when Democratic presidents and legislators became increasingly committed to civil rights for black Americans and liberal positions on social issues such as abortion. Many analysts are watching to see whether the Democratic loyalties of blue-collar white men are further weakened by Hillary Clinton's candidacy and whether the declining Republican ID of college-educated women is eroded by the candidacy of Donald Trump.

In the short run, then, issues and the candidates in a particular election can have a major impact on the outcome. But party ID has continuing power to influence voters' choices and to affect their feelings about issues and candidates as well.[50] So whether we want to explain the general trends of American voting behavior or the choices of voters in a particular election, party ID plays a prominent role.

TABLE 6.1 Political Involvement of Partisans and Independents, 2016 (in percent)

	Democrats		Independents			Republicans	
	Strong	Weak	Closer to Dems	Closer to Neither	Closer to Reps	Weak	Strong
Likely to vote*	85	65	88	64	83	93	94
Registered to vote	78	66	72	56	76	90	89
Interested in politics some or most of the time	82	59	72	69	80	78	89
Worn a campaign button, posted a yard sign	38	10	14	11	17	16	28
Gave money to a candidate in last 12 months	29	12	17	12	16	10	23
Likely to attend a political meeting*	28	15	17	13	14	14	24
Joined a protest or rally in last four years	20	11	9	12	4	10	18
Likely to distribute political/social information*	19	7	8	11	10	9	17

Note: * Figures are the percentage of respondents who say they are "very likely" or "extremely likely" to participate in each of these ways.

Source: 2016 American National Election Study Pilot Survey; data made available by the Inter-University Consortium for Political and Social Research.

Party Identification and Political Activity

Another important effect of party ID is that individuals who consider themselves Democrats and Republicans are more involved in political life than are those who call themselves independents. Partisanship is emotionally engaging; it gives partisans a stake in the outcome of political events. Therefore, the strongest partisans are the most likely to vote, pay attention to politics, and become politically active. In 2016, as in previous years, strong Democrats and Republicans were more likely than weak identifiers or independents to attend political meetings and discuss political questions with others and to be registered to vote (Table 6.1).[51] The only peculiarity in this table is that the "pure" independents (those labeled "closer to neither") are a little more politically interested in 2016 than usual, probably because independent Democrat Bernie Sanders attracted a lot of support from independents in his run for the Democratic presidential nomination against Hillary Clinton, close to the time this poll was taken.

Party Identification and Party Differences

Strong party identifiers see a greater contrast between the Republican and Democratic Parties' policies than do weak identifiers and independents (see Figure 6.5). As we have seen, they are more polarized in their evaluations of

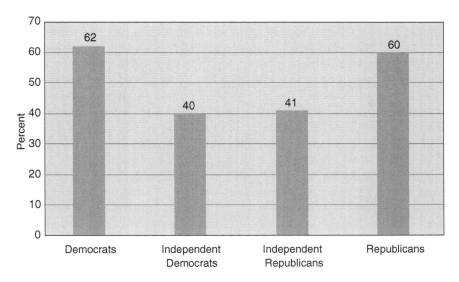

FIGURE 6.5 Percent Saying the Two Parties' Policies Are "Very Different," 2016

Note: Bars are the percentage of respondents in each category responding "very different" to the question, "How different are the policy positions of the Republican and Democratic Parties?"

Source: Pew Research Center, "Partisanship and Political Animosity in 2016," June 22, 2016, at www.people-press.org/2016/06/22/partisanship-and-political-animosity-in-2016/ (accessed June 23, 2016).

the two parties' candidates as well as of the parties' ability to govern for the benefit of the nation. In the mind of the strong partisan, in short, the parties are clearly defined and very different from one another on the important dimensions of politics.

A stronger party ID, by itself, is not enough to account for greater political activism and sharper party images. Other factors, such as higher socioeconomic status (SES), can also promote political activity. The relatively greater involvement of partisans (and, in most years, of Republicans) comes in part from their generally higher SES as well as from their more ideological commitment to politics.[52] Even so, party ID has a major impact on people's political attitudes.

The Myth of the Independent

Independence is a cherished value in politics as well as in other areas of American life. In contemporary elections, however, it has become increasingly rare. The age-old notion of the independent—the thoughtful citizen who votes for the candidate or the issues, not the party—has given way to the reality of almost universal partisanship, even among those who prefer to call themselves independents.

Attitudinal Independents

The definition of "independent" used so far in this chapter is someone who tells a poll taker that he or she does not identify with a political party. Studies show that these independents tend to split their tickets more often than other voters do and wait longer in the campaign to decide how to vote. In those ways, they would seem to fit the myth of the thoughtful, deliberative citizen. But they fall short of the mythical picture of the independent in most other ways. In 2016, independents stayed home from the polls at a higher rate than did party identifiers and, as you saw in Table 6.1, scored lower than partisans on several other indicators of political involvement.

When pollsters ask these independents a follow-up question, however, they hear a different story. Those who say they do not consider themselves a Democrat or a Republican are then asked if they *lean toward* either major party. In fact, two-thirds of these "independents" report that they do. Evidence suggests that these independent leaners are often more politically involved (see Table 6.1) and sometimes even more partisan in voting than weak partisans are (see Figures A.1 and A.2 in the Online Appendix). This suggests that independent leaners are really "closet partisans" who call themselves independents mainly because "independence" is an admired quality.[53] It is only in comparison with strong partisans that these leaners fall short.

The remaining respondents are classified as "pure" independents. But this highly valued independent vote turns out not to be so valuable. First, it's small; only about 10 percent of survey respondents are "pure" independents. Second, it's largely apolitical; pure independents are less informed, on average, than are other Americans.[54] And finally, most pure independents don't vote. Few campaigns can succeed, then, by putting major emphasis on mobilizing independents.

Behavioral Independents

We can also define independents in terms of their behavior. In his final work, the unparalleled researcher V. O. Key, Jr. explored various definitions of political independence.[55] Concerned about the picture of the American voter that was emerging from research in the 1950s and 1960s, showing an electorate much more driven by deeply ingrained party loyalties than by an understanding of major political issues, Key looked for evidence of rational behavior among voters. He focused in particular on "party switchers"— those who supported different parties in two consecutive presidential elections—rather than on the self-described independents. In practice, party switchers came much closer to the flattering myth of the independent than did the self-styled independents. These party switchers, Key found, expressed at least as much political interest as did the "stand-patters" (those who voted for the same party in both elections). Above all, the switchers showed an issue-related rationality that fit the mythical picture of the independent. They agreed on policy issues with the stand-patters toward whose party they had shifted, and they disagreed with the policies of the party from which they had defected.

It is harder to find true party switchers today. The percentage of voters choosing candidates of one party in one election and the other party in the next has never been lower; even among the pure independents who actually vote, most stick with the same party over time.[56] As the distinctions between the two major parties have clarified, the battle lines have hardened and become more emotionally fraught.

Are Independents a Likely Source of Support for Minor-Party Candidates?

One possible role remains for pure independents. Because they have the weakest ties to the two major parties, they could be more open to the charms of minor-party and independent candidates than other citizens are.[57] That has happened on occasion. One of the biggest stories of the 1992 presidential election was the unprecedented showing of independent candidate Ross Perot. A very rich man, Perot spent millions on a campaign criticizing the two major parties as irresponsible and corrupt. Unlike most independents, Perot flourished rather than faded as the campaign came to an end. He finished with almost 20 million votes, 19 percent of those cast.

On Election Day, Perot did draw many of his votes from pure independents and to a lesser extent from independent leaners.[58] Fully 37 percent of pure independents said they voted for Perot, compared with only 4 percent of strong Democrats and 11 percent of strong Republicans. The same was true of Perot's third-party candidacy in 1996, although the percentages decreased by more than half. In the end, however, there were not enough independents and disgruntled partisans to make a majority for Perot. It would be difficult for any independent or minor-party candidate to construct a winning coalition from a group as diverse as independent voters, who have little in common other than their dislike of the major parties, and who are much less likely to vote than partisans are. Such a candidate can serve as a "spoiler," however. Ralph Nader got enough votes as the Green Parties candidate in 2000, most of them from independents, to give the election to Bush, and many wondered whether the small proportion of votes for Libertarian presidential candidate Gary Johnson in 2016 would tip the election to Trump or Clinton.

In the close party competition that has characterized recent elections, even a small percentage of voters have the power to determine the winner. A major difference between the election results in 2008 and 2010, for instance, was that pure independents, who favored Democratic U.S. House candidates in 2008, were more likely to vote for Republicans in 2010. Yet in 2012, Barack Obama won the presidential election while losing the independent vote. Independents' support for Republican Mitt Romney wasn't enough to erase Obama's advantage among the much larger group of Democrats.

Change in the Impact of Party ID

Party ID, then, is a psychological commitment that is often strong enough to guide other political beliefs and behavior. Strong partisans tend to see issues and candidates through "party-tinted" glasses. They are more likely to vote for their party's candidates and to be politically active than other citizens are. Yet partisanship functions in a very different context now than it did a century ago.

A More Candidate-Centered Politics

Although the great majority of Americans still hold a party ID or "lean toward" the Democrats or the Republicans, several major changes have affected the parties' influence on citizens. Early in the 1900s, states began adopting the direct primary, in which voters had to choose candidates without the useful guidance of a party label. Partisanship remains a helpful shortcut in general elections but does not distinguish one candidate from another in a party's primary. New campaign and fund-raising technologies developed that were harder for party organizations to monopolize.

Candidates with enough money could use television, direct mail, and now the Internet to reach voters directly, over the parties' heads.

During the turbulent years of the 1960s and 1970s, as we have seen, the number of self-identified independents grew, and the impact of party ID on people's voting choices declined. Candidates found it helpful to downplay their party label, running instead as individual entrepreneurs. Now, even though party loyalties have regained much of their influence, candidates still tend to downplay their partisanship as a means of attracting voter support. In addition, other elements of American politics—new and traditional media, organized interests, campaign consultants, candidates' characteristics, issues, and current events—have important effects on campaigns. The consequence is that most elections have become less party centered and more candidate centered (see Chapter 11).[59]

The weakness of candidate-centered elections is that they make it more difficult for voters to hold government responsible. Voters may be able to hold a single candidate accountable for his or her campaign promises, but a typical election includes scores of candidates. Most citizens are too busy to gather the information necessary to evaluate each candidate as an individual. When elections focus on individual candidates, rather than on teams of candidates in which each team stands for an identifiable set of policy proposals, elections may ask more of voters than they are willing to give.

The Continuing Significance of Party

Yet even in an era when candidates seem to have so many resources with which to maintain their independence from their parties, party ID has gained strength as a force in American politics. More now than in the early days of survey research, when party ID was regarded as the "unmoved mover"[60] of voting behavior, voters see candidates, issues, and elections in partisan terms and vote accordingly. Partisanship has taken on a more emotional character for millions of Americans whose political interest and information are otherwise low. The elections of the 2000s and 2010s have mobilized strong partisans to an exceptional degree. Party-dominated contests are still very possible, even in a candidate-centered political world. The story continues in the next chapter, where we look more closely at the changes in the two major parties' supporting coalitions over time.

Notes

1 Classics in this field are David Easton and Jack Dennis, *Children in the Political System* (New York: McGraw-Hill, 1969) and Fred I. Greenstein, *Children and Politics* (New Haven, CT: Yale University Press, 1965).

2 Party identification is developing in newer democracies such as Russia and the Ukraine as well, even in the face of overwhelmingly negative attitudes toward political parties. See Ted Brader and Joshua A. Tucker, "The Emergence of Mass

Partisanship in Russia, 1993–1996," *American Journal of Political Science* 45 (2001): 69–83.

3 Donald Green, Bradley Palmquist, and Eric Schickler, *Partisan Hearts and Minds* (New Haven, CT: Yale University Press, 2002). See also Lilliana Mason, "'I Disrespectfully Agree'" *American Journal of Political Science* 59 (2015): 128–145.

4 For a summary of these approaches, see Green, Palmquist, and Schickler, *Partisan Hearts and Minds*, Chapter 5 and Thomas M. Carsey and Geoffrey C. Layman, "Changing Sides or Changing Minds?" *American Journal of Political Science* 50 (2006): 464–477.

5 Alternative forms of measurement have been suggested by John R. Petrocik, "An Analysis of the Intransitivities in the Index of Party Identification," *Political Methodology* 1 (1974): 31–47; and Herbert F. Weisberg, "A Multidimensional Conceptualization of Party Identification," *Political Behavior* 2 (1980): 33–60. See also Green, Palmquist, and Schickler, *Partisan Hearts and Minds*, Chapter 2.

6 Jeremy Zilber, *Why Mommy Is a Democrat* (Madison, WI: Jeremy Zilber, 2006); and David W. Hedrick, *The Liberal Clause* (Camas, WA: Freedoms Answer, 2010).

7 Paul Allen Beck and M. Kent Jennings, "Family Traditions, Political Periods, and the Development of Partisan Orientations," *Journal of Politics* 53 (1991): 742–763.

8 Paul Allen Beck, Russell J. Dalton, Steven Greene, and Robert Huckfeldt, "The Social Calculus of Voting," *American Political Science Review* 96 (2002): 57–73.

9 Richard G. Niemi and M. Kent Jennings, "Issues and Inheritance in the Formation of Party Identification," *American Journal of Political Science* 35 (1991): 970–988.

10 Green, Palmquist, and Schickler, *Partisan Hearts and Minds*, pp. 7–8.

11 Duane F. Alwin and Jon A. Krosnick, "Aging, Cohorts, and the Stability of Sociopolitical Orientations over the Life Cycle," *American Journal of Sociology* 97 (1991): 185–187.

12 Pew Research Center, "Partisanship and Political Animosity in 2016," June 22, 2016, at www.people-press.org/2016/06/22/partisanship-and-political-animosity-in-2016/ (accessed June 23, 2016).

13 See William Clagett, "Partisan Acquisition vs. Partisan Intensity," *American Journal of Political Science* 25 (1981): 193–214.

14 John R. Alford, Peter K. Hatemi, John R. Hibbing, Nicholas G. Martin, and Lindon J. Eaves, "The Politics of Mate Choice," *Journal of Politics* 73 (2011): 362–379. See also David E. Broockman and Timothy J. Ryan, "Preaching to the Choir," *American Journal of Political Science* 60 (2016): 1093–1107.

15 Logan Dancey and Paul Goren, "Party Identification, Issue Attitudes, and the Dynamics of Political Debate," *American Journal of Political Science* 54 (2010): 686–699.

16 James E. Campbell, "Sources of the New Deal Realignment," *Western Political Quarterly* 38 (1985): 357–376; and Warren E. Miller, "Generational Changes and Party Identification," *Political Behavior* 14 (1992): 333–352.

17 The Online Appendix can be found at www.routledge.com/9781138683686. The seminal report of studies of partisanship is Angus Campbell, Philip E. Converse, Warren E. Miller, and Donald E. Stokes, *The American Voter* (New York: Wiley, 1960).

18 See Luke Keele and Jennifer Wolak, "Value Conflict and Volatility in Party Identification," *British Journal of Political Science* 36 (2006): 671–690.

19 Philip E. Converse and Gregory B. Markus, "Plus ça change …: The New CPS Election Study Panel," *American Political Science Review* 73 (1979): 32–49. See also Paul Goren, "Party Identification and Core Political Values," *American Journal of Political Science* 49 (2005): 881–896.

20 Russell Dalton, "The Decline of Party Identification," in Russell J. Dalton and Martin P. Wattenberg, eds., *Parties without Partisans* (Oxford: Oxford University Press, 2000), pp. 19–36. On split-ticket voting, see Barry C. Burden and David C. Kimball, *Why Americans Split Their Tickets* (Ann Arbor, MI: University of Michigan Press, 2002).

21 Martin P. Wattenberg, *The Decline of American Political Parties, 1952–1994* (Cambridge, MA.: Harvard University Press, 1996), p. ix.

22 See James H. Kuklinski, Paul J. Quirk, Jennifer Jerit, and Robert F. Rich, "The Political Environment and Citizen Competence," *American Journal of Political Science* 45 (2001): 410–424.

23 Jeffrey M. Stonecash, "Changing American Political Parties," in Stonecash, ed., *New Directions in American Political Parties* (New York: Routledge, 2010), pp. 4–5.

24 See John R. Petrocik, "Measuring Party Support: Leaners Are Not Independents," *Electoral Studies* 28 (2009): 562–572. Russell J. Dalton presents a differing view in *The Apartisan American* (Washington, DC: CQ Press, 2012).

25 Pew Research Center, "Partisanship and Political Animosity in 2016."

26 For example, see Pew Research Center for the People & the Press, "GOP Seen as Principled, But Out of Touch and Too Extreme," February 26, 2013, at www.people-press.org/2013/02/26/gop-seen-as-principled (accessed June 21, 2016).

27 Pew Research Center, "Partisanship and Political Animosity in 2016."

28 See James A. Stimson, *Tides of Consent* (New York: Cambridge University Press, 2004), p. 81.

29 Samantha Smith, "24% of Americans Now View Both GOP and Democratic Party Unfavorably," Pew Research Center, August 21, 2015, at www.pewresearch.org/fact-tank/2015/08/21/24-of-americans-now-view-both-gop-and-democratic-party-unfavorably/ (accessed June 21, 2016).

30 David Madland and Ruy Teixeira, "New Progressive America: The Millennial Generation," May 13, 2009, at www.americanprogress.org/issues/progressive-movement/report/2009/05/13/6133/new-progressive-america-the-millennial-generation/ (accessed June 21, 2016).

31 See Leonie Huddy, Lilliana Mason, and Lene Aaroe, "Expressive Partisanship," *American Political Science Review* 109 (2015): 1–17, and Shanto Iyengar and Sean J. Westwood, "Fear and Loathing Across Party Lines," *American Journal of Political Science* 59 (2015): 690–707.

32 Data from Pew Research Center, "Partisanship and Political Animosity in 2016."

33 See, for example, Alan S. Gerber, Gregory A. Huber, and Ebonya Washington, "Party Affiliation, Partisanship, and Political Beliefs," *American Political Science Review* 104 (2010): 720–744, and Michael W. Wagner, "Think of It This Way," Ph.D. dissertation, Indiana University, 2006.

34 Caitlin Milazzo, James Adams, and Jane Green, "Are Voter Decision Rules Endogenous to Parties' Policy Strategies?" *Journal of Politics* 74 (2012): 262–276.

35 James N. Druckman, Erik Peterson, and Rune Slothuus, "How Elite Partisan Polarization Affects Public Opinion Formation," *American Political Science Review* 107 (2013): 57–79.

36 For instance, see Frank Newport, "Role of U.S. Gov't Remains Key Source of Party Differences," Gallup poll, October 6, 2015, at www.gallup.com/poll/186 032/role-gov-remains-key-source-party-differences.aspx (accessed September 7, 2016).

37 See, for example, Jens Manuel Krogstad, "On Views of Immigrants, Americans Largely Split Along Party Lines," Pew Research Center, September 30, 2015, at www.pewresearch.org/fact-tank/2015/09/30/on-views-of-immigrants-americans-largely-split-along-party-lines/ (accessed September 7, 2016).

38 Pew Research Center, "Negative Views of New Congress Cross Party Lines," May 21, 2015, at www.people-press.org/2015/05/21/negative-views-of-new-Congress-cross-party-lines (accessed June 21, 2016).

39 Jeffrey M. Jones, "Republicans, Democrats Shift on Whether Gov't Is a Threat," October 18, 2010, at www.gallup.com/poll/143717/Republicans-Democrats-Shift-Whether-Gov-Threat.aspx (accessed June 21, 2016). It may be that people's feelings about Bush and Obama are driving these shifts rather than feelings about government more generally; I thank Julia Azari for this point.

40 Poll data are from Green, Palmquist, and Schickler, *Partisan Hearts and Minds*, p. 127. They see these poll results, however, as evidence that the two groups of partisans are using different standards of evaluation rather than as an indicator of perceptual bias.

41 Andy Baker, Barry Ames, and Lucio R. Renno, "Social Context and Campaign Volatility in New Democracies," *American Journal of Political Science* 50 (2006): 382–399.

42 See, for example, Larry M. Bartels, "Partisanship and Voting Behavior, 1952–1996," *American Journal of Political Science* 44 (2000): 35–50.

43 2016 exit poll at www.cnn.com/election/results/exit-polls/national/house.

44 Paul Allen Beck, Lawrence Baum, Aage R. Clausen, and Charles E. Smith, Jr., "Patterns and Sources of Ticket Splitting in Subpresidential Voting," *American Political Science Review* 86 (1992): 916–928.

45 Kyle L. Saunders, Alan I. Abramowitz, and Jonathan Williamson, "A New Kind of Balancing Act," *Political Research Quarterly* 58 (2005): 69–78.

46 Barry C. Burden and David C. Kimball, "A New Approach to the Study of Ticket-Splitting," *American Political Science Review* 92 (1998): 533–544.

47 Scott Basinger and Howard Lavine, "Ambivalence, Information, and Electoral Choice," *American Political Science Review* 99 (2005): 169–184.

48 See Morris P. Fiorina, *Retrospective Voting in American National Elections* (New Haven, CT: Yale University Press, 1981); and Michael B. MacKuen, Robert S. Erikson, and James A. Stimson, "Macropartisanship," *American Political Science Review* 83 (1989): 1125–1142.

49 And on which the individual sees differences between the parties; see Carsey and Layman, "Changing Sides or Changing Minds?"

50 See Paul R. Abramson, John H. Aldrich, and David W. Rohde, *Change and Continuity in the 2008 and 2010 Elections* (Washington, DC: CQ Press, 2012), Chapter 8.

51 These figures are much higher than those presented in Chapter 8 because respondents to the American National Election studies often overreport their levels of voter turnout.

52 Kay Lehman Schlozman, Sidney Verba, and Henry E. Brady, *The Unheavenly Chorus* (Princeton, NJ: Princeton University Press, 2012), Chapter 9.

53 Samara Klar and Yanna Krupnikov. *Independent Politics* (Cambridge: Cambridge University Press, 2016).

54 David B. Magleby, Candice J. Nelson, and Mark C. Westlye, "The Myth of the Independent Voter Revisited," in Paul M. Sniderman and Benjamin Highton, eds., *Facing the Challenge of Democracy* (Princeton, NJ: Princeton University Press, 2011), pp. 238–263.

55 V. O. Key, Jr. (with Milton C. Cummings), *The Responsible Electorate* (Cambridge, MA: Harvard University Press, 1966).

56 Corwin D. Smidt, "Polarization and the Decline of the American Floating Voter," *American Journal of Political Science* 60 (2016): doi: 10.1111/ajps.12218.

57 Todd Donovan, "A Goal for Reform," *PS: Political Science and Politics* 40 (2007): 683.

58 See Paul R. Abramson, John H. Aldrich, and David W. Rohde, *Change and Continuity in the 1992 Elections* (Washington, DC: CQ Press, 1995), p. 245.

59 See Martin P. Wattenberg, *The Rise of Candidate-Centered Politics* (Cambridge, MA: Harvard University Press, 1991).

60 This seems to be true in many other democracies as well; see Richard Johnston, "Party Identification: Unmoved Mover or Sum of Preferences?" *Annual Review of Political Science* 9 (2006): 329–351.

CHAPTER 7

Party Coalitions and Party Change

You can tell the American parties apart simply by referring to the types of groups that support them. If, for example, you were to read that a presidential candidate (say, Donald Trump) is a businessman whose supporters tend to be white males, whereas his opponent is a woman (say, Hillary Clinton) who has been endorsed by civil rights groups and labor unions, you would probably guess that the businessman is a Republican and the female candidate is a Democrat. (And you'd be right.) Small business owners, Mormons, and evangelical white Protestants lean heavily toward the Republican Party in their loyalties. Other groups, such as women, union members, and black Americans, are much more likely to consider themselves Democrats. These patterns remain even after the unusual 2016 race.

Why is this important in understanding party politics? The social, economic, or other groups most inclined to favor a party's candidates at a particular time make up what is called that party's **coalition**. Groups may align with a party for many reasons, but once a group has become linked with a party's coalition, its interests influence the stands the party takes on at least some issues and the strategies it follows in campaigns.

The differences between the two parties' coalitions are also a helpful clue as to which issues dominate the nation's politics at that time. The facts that African Americans have identified overwhelmingly as Democrats in recent decades and that southern whites are now largely Republican remind us that racial issues continue to be powerful in American elections.[1] At various points in U.S. history, regional conflicts, ethnic and religious divisions, disputes between agriculture and industry, and differences in social class have also helped distinguish the two parties' coalitions, as they have in other Western democracies.

Party change occurs in many forms, including shifts in party control of the federal government[2] and organizational changes producing "service parties"[3] (see Chapters 3 and 4) and more candidate-centered campaigns (see Chapter 11). Yet party researchers have lavished the most attention on coalitional changes. In much of this literature, great and enduring changes in the parties' coalitions have been called **party realignments**.[4] The concept of realignment is controversial, as you'll see later in the chapter. But no matter how we characterize them, changes in patterns of group support for the Democrats and the Republicans have made a major difference in American politics and policies over time and make a fascinating story.

In this chapter, then, we will look at party change with special attention to the parties' supporting coalitions. We'll examine the development of the parties' current coalitions: from what races, regions, educational backgrounds, and other social groups do these supporters come, what attracts them to one party rather than the other, and why that matters. Finally, we will consider how best to characterize the changes in the parties' coalitions since the New Deal.

The American Party Systems

The United States has experienced at least six different electoral eras or **party systems**. (See Table 7.1 for a summary of each party system.) Although some common themes run through all of these eras, each has had a distinctive pattern of group support for the parties. Each party system can also be distinguished by the kinds of issue concerns that dominated it and the types of public policies the government put into effect. In Chapter 1, we looked at party history to learn about the interrelationships among the three parts of the party. Now let us get a different take on these events, from the perspective of changes in social group support for the parties.

The First Party System

The initial American party system (from about 1801 to 1828)[5] emerged out of a serious conflict between opposing groups in George Washington's administration: How much power should the national government exercise relative to that of the states? As Chapter 1 noted, the Federalists, led by Alexander Hamilton, wanted a strong national government that would work closely with business and industry to build the nation's economy. A national bank would centralize the states' banking systems. This plan would benefit business owners and wealthier citizens, who were concentrated in New England; these groups became the core support for the Federalists.

Farmers and the less well-off, living in the southern and mid-Atlantic states, suspected that the Federalists' proposals would hurt them financially; farmers would pay taxes but businesses and speculators would reap more of the benefits. So they supported Thomas Jefferson and James Madison's demand for states' rights, limits on the national government's power, and a more egalitarian vision of the new democracy. So did southern slave owners; states' rights would protect them against northern abolitionists. The less well-off may have had little in common with southern plantation owners other than their preference for states' rights, but that was enough; the Jeffersonian coalition expanded, and the Democratic-Republicans, as they

TABLE 7.1 Years of Partisan Control of Congress and the Presidency, 1801–2016

	House		Senate		President	
	D-R	Opp.	D-R	Opp.	D-R	Opp.
First party system						
(1801–1828)	26	2	26	2	28	0
	Dem.	*Opp.*	*Dem.*	*Opp.*	*Dem.*	*Opp.*
Second party system						
(1829–1860)	24	8	28	4	24	8
	Dem.	*Rep.*	*Dem.*	*Rep.*	*Dem.*	*Rep.*
Third party system						
(1861–1876)	2	14	0	16	0	16
(1877–1896)	14	6	4	16	8	12
Fourth party system						
(1897–1932)	10	26	6	30	8	28
Fifth party system						
(1933–1968)	32	4	32	4	28	8
Sixth party system						
(1969–1980)	12	0	12	0	4	8
(1981–2016)	18	18	17	19	16	20
(1969–2016)	30	18	29	19	20	28

Note: Entries for the first party system are Democratic-Republicans and their opponents; for the second party system, Democrats and their opponents (first Whigs and then Republicans); and for subsequent party systems, Democrats and Republicans. In 2001, Republicans were in the majority in the Senate for the first five months and Democrats for the last seven, so the Senate is counted as being under Democratic control.

came to be called, gained the presidency in 1800. The Federalists slowly slipped into a fatal decline, and the supporters of Jefferson and Madison then dominated politics for more than two decades.

The Second Party System

The next party system (from approximately 1829 to 1860) developed when the one-party rule of the Democratic-Republicans could not contain all the conflicts generated by a rapidly changing nation. The party split into two factions on the major issues of the period: not just the national government's economic powers but also how the Union should expand. One faction continued the Jeffersonian tradition of opposition to a strong national government. It included the farmers of the South and the western frontier, as well as the addition of many urban workers and their political bosses. Led by Andrew Jackson, it would later call itself the Democratic Party or, at times, "the Democracy." The other, a more elitist and eastern commercial faction represented by John Quincy Adams, referred to itself as the National Republicans and was eventually absorbed into the Whig Party.[6]

This second party system was just as class based as the first. Wealthier voters (except those in the South) supported the Whigs, and the less privileged identified as Democrats. The Democrats dominated, growing as the franchise was extended to more and more Americans, and the party system became much more mass based. Democratic rule was interrupted only twice, both times by the election of Whig war heroes to the presidency. As the issues of this period grew more disruptive, however, the Whigs began to fracture, especially over the issue of slavery, and several minor parties were formed.

The Third Party System

One of these new parties, the antislavery Republicans, quickly gained support. Founded in 1854, it replaced the seriously divided Whigs within just two years as the main opposition to the Democrats. The bitter conflict of the Civil War ensured that the new third party system (1861 to 1896) would have the most clearly defined coalitions of any party system before or since. War and Reconstruction divided the nation roughly along geographic lines. The South became a Democratic bastion once all white southern males were permitted to return to the polls in 1876, and the Northeast and Midwest remained a fairly reliable base for Republicans.[7]

The regional division was so clear that the Democratic Party's only real strongholds in the North were in the cities controlled by Democratic machines (for example, New York City's Tammany Hall) and areas settled by southerners (such as Kentucky, Missouri, and the southern portions of Ohio, Indiana, and Illinois). In the South, GOP support came only from blacks (because Republican President Abraham Lincoln had freed the slaves in the Confederate states) and people from mountain areas originally opposed to the southern states' secession. By 1876, there was close party competition in presidential voting and in the House of Representatives as these regional forces balanced one another. Competition was so intense that this period contained two of the four elections in American history in which the winner of the popular vote for president lost the vote in the Electoral College.

American industries grew during this time, especially in the Northeast and then in the Midwest. Republicans dominated the areas where these new businesses were expanding, and the GOP leadership, which had long been identified with "moral Puritanism and emerging industrial capitalism,"[8] worked to support the new industries with protective tariffs (taxes) on imported goods, a railroad system that could haul products from coast to coast, efforts to develop the frontier, and high taxes to pay for these programs. In contrast, the Democrats represented groups that had been passed over by economic expansion and who were deeply suspicious of capitalism, such as farmers and the working class, as well as the white South. Economic issues, and especially attitudes toward the growth of huge industrial monopolies, were thus closely linked with the regional divisions between the parties.

The Fourth Party System

The powerful imprint of the Civil War continued to shape southern politics for the next century, while economic conflict dominated politics elsewhere. After the economic panic of 1893 and a series of farm and rural protests, tensions within the Democratic Party between poor whites and the more conservative party leaders erupted into a fight over the party's leadership. The less wealthy, more egalitarian wing won, nominated populist William Jennings Bryan as the Democratic presidential candidate in 1896, and reformed the party's issue stances. Bryan lost, and Republicans then dominated national politics until 1932, disrupted only by their own internal split in 1912.

This period (from approximately 1897 to 1932) thus reflected both regional and economic conflicts. It pitted the eastern business community, which was heavily Republican, against the Democratic-dominated South, with the Midwest in contention. Southern Democrats, out from under the heavy hand of Reconstruction, were able to reinstitute racially discriminatory laws and to keep blacks from voting in the southern states. The waves of immigrants into an increasingly urban America swelled the ranks of both parties, although Catholic immigrants, especially from Europe, tended to be mobilized by the Democratic Party.

The Fifth Party System

The shock of the Great Depression of 1929 and the subsequent election of Democrat Franklin Roosevelt prompted the fifth, or New Deal, party system (from approximately 1932 to 1968). During the 1930s, as a means of pulling the nation out of economic ruin, Roosevelt pushed Congress to enact several large-scale social welfare programs. These Roosevelt "New Deal" programs— Social Security, wages and hours laws, and protection for labor unions—again strengthened the Democrats' image as the party of the disadvantaged. Even groups such as blacks, long allied with the Republicans, were lured to the Democratic banner; their socioeconomic needs were powerful enough to keep both blacks and southern whites as wary allies in the Roosevelt coalition. So by 1936, the new Democratic majority party had become a grand **New Deal** coalition of the less privileged and minorities—lower-income people, industrial workers (especially union members), poor farmers, Catholics, Jews, blacks—plus the South, where Democratic loyalty was deeply ingrained among whites. The costs of the New Deal and the impact of its programs heightened the stakes of the conflict between higher- and lower-income groups and between business and labor.

The Sixth Party System

The New Deal's policies had a profound impact on the parties' supporting coalitions. Once World War II brought an end to the Depression in the United States, some groups that had benefited from government assistance under Roosevelt moved up into the growing middle class. In return for this economic gain, however, they found themselves paying higher taxes to support those who still needed the assistance. That led many people to reevaluate the costs and benefits of the welfare state in their own lives. At the same time, the issue of race, which had been held in check by Roosevelt's deft maneuvering, was pushed to the top of both parties' agendas by activists hoping to change their parties' stands.

As black Americans migrated to the North in the late 1940s, liberal northern Democrats pressed their party to deliver on the long-delayed promise of civil rights for blacks.[9] When Democratic administrations responded and used federal power to end the racial segregation of schools and public accommodations such as restaurants and hotels, some conservative white southern Democrats—especially those holding conservative views about race[10]—felt betrayed by their national party. They found an alternative in 1964 when Republican presidential candidate Barry Goldwater proclaimed his opposition to the Civil Rights Act. Goldwater, the candidate of the party's newly triumphant conservative wing, believed that Republicans needed a new bloc of supporters to become the majority party. Rather than trying to regain blacks' votes, Goldwater contended, it made more sense to persuade the larger population of southern whites to switch parties by showing them that the Republican Party represented their views better than the Democrats did.[11] He argued that the Republican commitment to smaller government and states' rights required it to oppose federal government efforts to force integration on reluctant state governments. Both national parties, then, had markedly changed their positions on civil rights, due to the combination of group pressure and the lure of new voter support. The Democrats moved from an acceptance of segregation in the South to a commitment to use government as the means to secure rights for black Americans. The Republicans reacted against the big-government programs of the New Deal with a stand in favor of states' rights, even at the cost of the party's traditional pro-civil rights stand.[12]

These changes in the parties' positions led to a steady reformation of their constituencies.[13] Southern whites responded by moving slowly in the direction of Republican partisanship. The same forces caused blacks to shift rapidly toward the Democrats. When the Voting Rights Act restored southern blacks' right to vote, their overwhelmingly Democratic voting patterns led the national Democratic Party to become even more liberal on race and related issues. A further push came from legislative redistricting in 1992, in which legislatures were asked to draw majority-minority districts (see Chapter 8), and which led to the defeat of a number of longtime conservative southern Democrats.[14]

Table 7.2 shows shifts between the 1950s and the most recent decade in the representation of various groups within the Democratic and Republican Parties in the electorate. Look first at the dramatic changes with regard to race. Blacks were only 6 percent of the Democratic Party in the electorate, on average, between 1952 and 1960; at this time, of course, very few southern blacks were permitted to vote. During 2004–2012, on average,

TABLE 7.2 Change in the Parties' Coalitions, from the 1950s to the 2010s

	Democratic Voters (%)		Republican Voters (%)	
	1952–1960	2004–2012	1952–1960	2004–2012
Blacks	6	24	3	2
Latinos, Asian Americans, and Native Americans	1	13	0	7
Southern whites	24	16	8	33
Northern whites	69	49	89	59
Upper income	40	28	46	40
Middle income	30	31	26	31
Lower income	31	33	28	22
Protestant (Other Christian)	61	47	83	60
Catholic	31	22	14	21
Jewish	6		2	
Other Religion— includes Jewish		4		2
Not Religious	2	26	2	15
Married	82	49	79	68
Unmarried	18	51	21	32

Note: Entries are the proportion of all Democratic or Republican Party identifiers, among those who say they voted, who belong to the group named in the first column.

Source: American National Election Studies data for 1952–1960, calculated by Alan Abramowitz and excerpted with kind permission from Abramowitz, *Voice of the People* (New York: McGraw-Hill, 2004), p. 87, and for 2004–2012, calculated by Benjamin Toll.

blacks constituted 24 percent of all Democrats. Latinos, Asian Americans, and Native Americans added another 13 percent, totaling more than a third of Democratic voters. The change was especially profound in the South; by 2000, blacks made up a majority (52 percent) of the Democratic voters in the Deep South states of Alabama, Georgia, Louisiana, Mississippi, and South Carolina.[15]

At the same time, southern whites, who were a quarter of all Democratic partisans in the 1950s, dropped to just 16 percent in the 2000s (and this probably exaggerates Democratic strength in the South, because change in people's party ID often lags behind change in their voting behavior). Surveys show that in 1956, 87 percent of white southerners called themselves Democrats, but in 2000 only 24 percent did so.[16] In the 2010s Democrats gained strength in the coastal South, due in part to an increasing black population and in-migration to these states from other areas. But elsewhere in the South, few Democrats were elected to the U.S. House and Senate, and all represented majority-black districts. The Democratic Party's loss was the Republican Party's gain. Southern whites had increased from a mere 8 percent in the 1950s to a third of the current Republican Party in the electorate. Consistent with the change in the national parties' stands, it was the conservatives among these southern whites who moved first to a Republican identification.

This change was part of a larger shift in the parties' regional bases. In the mid-1950s, as you can see in the upper part of Figure 7.1, almost half of all Democrats in the U.S. House were southerners. By 2016, the drop in Democratic support among white southerners had left the party's House contingent much more regionally balanced. Republicans in the House, on the other hand, have moved from one regional base to another. In 1954, the great majority of Republican House members were from the Midwest and Northeast, and a substantial number of northeastern Republicans were liberals and moderates. But the Republican platform changes that drew conservative southern support made it harder for the party to appeal to liberals and moderates in New England and the Midwest. So the Northeast is predominantly Democratic now; in fact, in the 2012 elections not a single Republican U.S. House member was elected from New England. In contrast, almost half of all House Republicans now represent the South, where in 2016 every state legislature was Republican-controlled. As Seth Masket writes, emphasizing the profound shift in southern partisanship, "Today, southern states are largely off-limits to Democrats, and no amount of spending or strategizing is about to change that."[17]

In sum, the current Democratic Party in the electorate differs from the New Deal coalition in several important ways. Although it continues to include blacks and Latinos, lower-income whites, and young people, the Democrats have lost a portion of white union members and Catholics and most white southerners. On the other hand, the party has gained support among liberals, Northeast and West Coast residents, unmarried people,

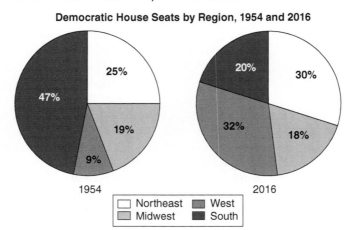

Democratic House Seats by Region, 1954 and 2016

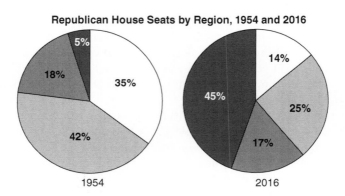

Republican House Seats by Region, 1954 and 2016

FIGURE 7.1 Democratic and Republican House Seats by Region, 1954 and 2016

Note: Percentages do not always add up to 100 percent due to rounding error.

Sources: CQ Weekly, April 20, 2009, for 1954 data; 2016 data calculated from www.house. gov and www.senate.gov.

gays, and those who don't consider themselves religious (see Table 7.3). Although the Republican coalition is still heavily white, Christian, and married, its Protestant base has shifted from mainline denominations to evangelical churches. Religiously observant whites have become the largest single group of Republican supporters,[18] and the party now has a southern base. Republicans have also gained more support from Catholics, men, rural or exurban people, and those who define themselves as conservatives.

It is clear from this brief tour of party history that the effects of socioeconomic, racial, and regional divisions have waxed and waned, but all have played a major role in shaping the parties' coalitions over time. Let us take a closer look at these relationships, before asking how changes in these coalitions affect the nature of American political debate.

TABLE 7.3 The Current Democratic and Republican Party Coalitions

	% Democratic/ Lean Democratic	% Republican/ Lean Republican	Ratio
Democratic-Inclined Groups			
Income under $30,000	54	31	1.7 to 1 D
Income $30,000–74,999	48	41	1.2 to 1 D
High school or less education	47	37	1.3 to 1 D
Some college	47	42	1.1 to 1 D
College degree but no post-grad	49	42	1.2 to 1 D
Post-graduate degree	57	35	1.6 to 1 D
African Americans	80	11	7.3 to 1 D
Asians	65	23	2.8 to 1 D
Urban	57	31	1.8 to 1 D
Ages 18–33	51	35	1.5 to 1 D
Religiously unaffiliated	61	25	2.4 to 1 D
Jews	61	31	2.0 to 1 D
Catholics	48	40	1.2 to 1 D
Hispanic/Latinos	56	26	2.2 to 1 D
Unmarried women	57	29	2.0 to 1 D
Women	52	36	1.4 to 1 D
Men	44	43	1.02 to 1

TABLE 7.3 continued

	% Democratic/ Lean Democratic	% Republican/ Lean Republican	Ratio
Republican-Inclined Groups			
Income $150,000+	45	47	1.04 to 1 R
Income $75,000–150,000	44	48	1.1 to 1 R
White men, some college or less	33	56	1.7 to 1 R
White southerners	34	55	1.6 to 1 R
Whites	40	49	1.2 to 1 R
Rural	39	47	1.2 to 1 R
Ages 69–86	43	47	1.1 to 1 R
Mormons	22	70	3.2 to 1 R
White evangelical Protestants	22	68	3.1 to 1 R
White mainline Protestants	40	48	1.2 to 1 R
Married men	38	51	1.3 to 1 R

Note: Latino/Hispanics can include people of any race; whites and blacks are non-Latino/Hispanic only. Data include 25,010 respondents during 2014.

Source: Pew Research Center surveys, "A Deep Dive Into Party Affiliation," April 7, 2015, at www.people-press.org/2015/04/07/2014-party-identification-detailed-tables/ (accessed April 22, 2016).

The Social Bases of Party Coalitions

Socioeconomic Status Divisions

James Madison noted, with characteristic perception, that economic differences are the most common source of factions.[19] The footprints of socioeconomic status (SES) conflict are scattered throughout American history, just as they are in most other democracies.[20] Social and economic status differences underlay the battle between the wealthy, aristocratic Federalists and the often less privileged Democratic-Republicans. These differences were even sharper between the Jacksonian Democrats and the Whigs a few decades later, and again during the fourth and fifth party systems. The connection between SES and partisanship weakened during the 1960s and 1970s but strengthened again beginning with the Reagan years in the 1980s.

SES is still closely related to people's partisanship, as you can see in Table 7.3, though the relationship has changed in some interesting ways. Lower-income voters have become more consistently Democratic in the past two decades as income inequality has increased.[21] Several forces help sustain the relationship between lower SES and Democratic partisanship, including differences between the parties' stands on issues of special concern to lower-income people (such as government-insured health care and social services) and the very high Democratic identification among blacks, who are predominantly lower income.[22] In 2008 and 2012, Barack Obama won a greater percentage of low- and lower-middle-income voters (with incomes up to $50,000) than had other recent Democratic presidential candidates.

Those with very limited education (high school or less) are almost as likely to call themselves Democrats as lower-income people are. Yet as Table 7.3 shows, Democratic strength is greatest not only among the least educated but also among those with a postgraduate education. At the time of the New Deal Democratic coalition, only the well-to-do were able to go to college. As a larger proportion of Americans from a wider variety of backgrounds has attended college more recently, voters with at least a college degree have become less Republican. In fact, Donald Trump ran poorly in 2016 among voters with a college or postgraduate degree. He did much better among those who didn't finish college (and especially those in that group who were older, white males).

So although higher income has a positive relationship with Republican identification, education has a curvilinear relationship: Democrats are prevalent among the least- and the most-educated, but less likely to be found in between (those with some college experience but no college degree). Similarly, upper-income people are no longer as distinctively Republican as they used to be—perhaps because this group now contains a larger proportion of professionals, such as teachers and health-care specialists, many of whom are concerned with quality-of-life issues such as the environment and women's rights. The identification of many professionals with the Democratic Party is reflected in the support Democratic candidates receive from teachers' unions and trial lawyers.[23]

These relationships between SES and partisanship aren't ironclad, of course. Trump's candidacy divided Republicans by education to a greater extent than had previous Republican presidential candidates. His support among less- and moderately educated whites was closely related to his call for a wall to keep out illegal immigrants and to ban Muslims from entering the U.S. Issues involving race and traditional morality have often related differently to people's partisanship than their positions on economic policies do.[24] This divide between college-educated and less-educated Republicans has become more pronounced in recent years, with less-educated Republicans expressing more negative attitudes toward big business and the fairness of the U.S. economic system, and more positive attitudes toward government social services that benefit people like themselves.[25]

Other groups also locate themselves in the "wrong" party from an SES point of view. For example, white fundamentalist Protestants have voted largely Republican in recent years even though their average income is closer to that of the typical Democrat than to the average Republican, and Asian Americans, with one of the highest average income levels of demographic groups, vote dominantly Democratic. As a result, the parties do not usually promote explicitly class-based appeals. Voting behavior in the U.S. tends to be less polarized by income than in several other democracies, including the United Kingdom.[26]

Race

The most striking demographic impact on party ID—and the most dramatic change—involves race.[27] The Republican Party was founded in the 1850s to oppose slavery. For almost a century it remained associated with racial equality in the minds of both black and white Americans. But when the New Deal's social welfare programs began to help lift blacks and other disadvantaged groups out of poverty, the parties' images began to change. As noted earlier, blacks' increasing presence within the Democratic Party encouraged civil rights groups to press for a national Democratic stance in favor of racial desegregation. Especially after Democratic Congresses and presidents passed civil rights laws in the 1960s and Republican leaders reversed the party's previous stands on race, black Americans became increasingly Democratic.

Since 1964, blacks have identified as Democrats in overwhelming numbers, regardless of their income, urban or rural residence, or other characteristics. Look at the stark difference in Table 7.3: Democratic identifiers outnumber Republicans by a full 69 percentage points among blacks. And although whites are not as dominantly Republican as blacks are Democratic, no Democratic presidential candidate has won a majority of whites' votes in almost 50 years. Racial differences in partisanship were especially clear during the two presidential elections in which Barack Obama was a candidate.

Interestingly, black Americans have remained staunchly Democratic even though blacks tend to be more conservative than non-black Democrats on issues such as same-sex marriage and abortion.[28] The vital importance of civil rights and the economy to black Americans has outweighed the impact of these other issues. There's good reason for this: Research shows that the economic position of racial and ethnic minorities improves when Democrats hold the White House and Congress.[29]

Attitudes toward race and race-based policies also correlated even more closely with partisanship during the Obama presidency. Donald Trump's campaign in 2016, making more explicit appeals to racial resentment than previous Republican candidates (for instance, calling Mexican immigrants "criminals" and "rapists"), primed racial attitudes among some voters. As a consequence, racial resentment better predicted Republicans' votes in 2016 than in other recent presidential elections.

Regional Divisions

Historically, where we live has divided Americans almost as much as SES. Different sections of the country have often had differing political interests. When a political party has championed these distinct interests, it has sometimes united large numbers of voters who may disagree about other issues.

The most enduring regional (more properly called "sectional") conflict in American party history was the one-party Democratic control of the South. Well before the Civil War, white southerners shared an interest in slavery and an agricultural system geared to export markets. The searing experience of that war and the Reconstruction that followed made the South into the "Solid South" and delivered it to the Democrats for most of the next century. The 11 states of the former Confederacy cast virtually all their electoral votes for Democratic presidential candidates in every election from 1880 through 1924. Although the party's nomination of a Catholic presidential candidate in 1928 worried many Protestant southerners, the New Deal economic programs and the South's relative poverty kept it allied with the Democratic Party from 1932 through 1944.

As we have seen, however, the civil rights movement was the opening wedge in the slow process that separated the South from its Democratic loyalties. The Democratic dominance of the South persisted to some degree as late as the 1990s, thanks to the overwhelming Democratic partisanship of southern blacks. But southern white voters are now predominantly Republican. In fact, in 2015, Republicans held every U.S. Senate seat, every governorship, and every state legislature in the former Confederacy except Virginia and Florida, and the last remaining white Democrat in the U.S.

House from a Deep South state was defeated for reelection. All the remaining House Democrats from the Deep South were African American.[30]

At times, the party system has also reflected the competition between the East, which used to dominate the nation's economy, and the South and West. In the first years of the American republic, the Federalists held on to an ever-narrowing base of eastern financial interests, while the Democratic-Republicans expanded westward with the new settlers. Northeasterners remained largely Republican—though moderate Republican—until recent decades, when the party's platform began to shift away from their policy stands.

The Mountain West has sometimes acted as a unified bloc in national politics on concerns that these states share, such as protecting western coal deposits and ranchers against federal environmental laws. But as these states become more urban and suburban, there has been some movement back toward the Democrats. Colorado in particular has swung from Republican control to close party competition.

Urban vs. Rural

For much of party history, Democrats won national elections by combining their strength in big cities with an overwhelming Democratic vote in both the urban and rural South. Since the decimation of rural, white southern support for Democrats, the party has become predominantly urban; Table 7.3 shows that Democrats outnumber Republicans among urban residents by a ratio of 1.8 to 1. The downside is that because big cities are now so overwhelmingly Democratic, big-city Democrats tend to win their elections by large, wasteful margins—as much as 85 percent of the vote—though they need only a little more than 50 percent. Because of these wasteful majorities in urban areas, it is not unusual for Democrats to get the most votes nationwide for the U.S. House of Representatives but to win a minority of the actual House seats. If the concentration of Democratic votes in large cities were spread more evenly across the country, then Democrats might win more House seats, rather than elect fewer Democrats by lopsided margins.[31] The Democratic Party's powerful urban base also leads the national party to take more straightforwardly cosmopolitan stands on issues such as gay people's rights. This can undercut the electoral chances of the more moderate Democrats who used to be elected from non-urban districts. Republican supporters, in contrast, are more evenly distributed around the nation and outnumber Democrats in rural areas.

Population shifts in particular areas can make a big difference in partisanship. Hurricane Katrina destroyed large sections of New Orleans in 2005, dispersing large numbers of heavily Democratic New Orleanians into other states and contributing to subsequent Republican gains in Louisiana. The severe economic decline in Puerto Rico since 2010 has led to the relocation of tens of thousands of largely Democratic Puerto Ricans to Florida, a swing state.

Age

Democrats usually have more support among young adults than Republicans do, especially in recent years (see Figure 7.2). Although the Democratic advantage in party ID appears in all but the oldest age groups, the party now has its greatest advantage among those who are college-aged and the smallest among those over 50. As younger people have become more Democratic, the oldest group of voters has become more Republican.

These trends typically reflect the state of the nation at the time when each generation moves into young adulthood. When the economy is strong and the incumbent president is popular, young adults will come into the electorate favoring the president's party; this affiliation tends to stay with these people as they age. Those currently in their 50s reached adulthood at the time of the Ronald Reagan presidency, when Republican identification was on the rise.[32] People who came of age during President Bush's second term, when the Great Recession started and Bush's popularity crashed, are now more likely to identify as Democrats. Those who turned 18 later in Obama's first term, when his approval ratings declined, have been slightly less Democratic. The stronger Democratic lean of young adults during the past decade also reflects the fact that young adults now are more racially and ethnically diverse than were past generations of young adults. But because their turnout drops markedly in midterm congressional races, young voters are a less important influence on those elections.

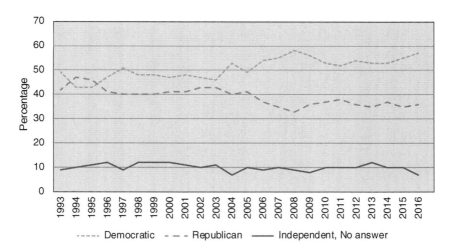

FIGURE 7.2 Young People's Partisanship since 1993

Note: Data points are the percentages of people aged 18–29 who identify themselves as Democrats, Republicans, and "pure" independents. Independent "leaners" are included with the party toward which they lean.

Source: Data derived from Gallup polls through 2013 and Pew Research Center for 2016.

Religion and Religious Commitment

There have always been religious differences between the American party coalitions, as there are in many other democracies. But the nature of the religious difference has changed in recent years. In the mid-1900s, Catholics and Jews were among the most loyal supporters of the Democratic Party, and white Protestants tended to support Republicans.

Now, the party difference rests more on the strength and type of people's commitment to religion, regardless of denomination. Those who are religiously unaffiliated, or secular, increasingly identify as Democrats and are a growing portion of the population. Jews are almost as Democratic, and Catholics still lean toward Democratic ID. In contrast, although white evangelicals split evenly between the two parties as recently as the late 1980s, they have since become a big part of the Republican base. Among white evangelicals, Republicans outnumber Democrats by more than 3 to 1. More generally, in 2014, 56 percent of Republicans called themselves religious conservatives, compared with only 13 percent of Democrats.[33] In their voting choices in 2016, about 80 percent of white evangelicals, comprising about a quarter of the electorate, reported that they voted for Republican candidates. This link is now so strong that most Americans see evangelical Christians as a largely Republican constituency.[34]

These changes reflect (and have encouraged) the Republican Party's movement since 1980 to a stand against abortion and gay people's rights and to the emphasis of many Republican leaders on traditional values and social conservatism. Most recently, Republican state legislators have promoted legislation to protect what they define as religious rights against extensions of civil rights protection to lesbian, gay, bisexual, and transgender persons. These laws, called "religious freedom restoration acts," would permit businesses and individuals to refuse to provide services to people in cases the provider feels would violate his or her religious beliefs (for instance, against homosexuality).[35] In contrast, Democrats (and Americans more generally) have become increasingly secular.

Ethnicity

Hispanic or Latino Americans are growing in numbers much faster than other ethnic groups in the U.S., but their voting power is increasing less quickly. A large proportion of Latino Americans are too young to vote yet, and even older Latinos turn out to vote less than non-Latino whites do. In 2012, for instance, 64 percent of non-Latino white eligible voters cast ballots, compared with only 48 percent of Latino Americans. The power of the Latino vote is limited further by the fact that about half of Latino Americans live in California and Texas, neither of which has been competitive in recent presidential elections. But because the Latino population has increased by 15 to 20 percentage points in several swing states just since

2012, and Latinos have surpassed non-Latino blacks as the nation's largest minority group, both parties have worked to attract Latino voter support.

Most Latino voters lean Democratic. Earlier in the 2000s, national Republican leaders hoped to erode this Democratic edge. In 2004, President Bush's proposal to give temporary legal status to undocumented (largely Mexican and Central American) workers met with some success among Latinos, as did the party's advertising in Spanish-language media. In 2012, when Republicans won only 27 percent of the Latino vote, a Republican National Committee report strongly urged the party to expand its outreach to Latinos. In fact, the Republican percentage of the Latino vote grew to 36 percent in 2014. But then came the 2016 nomination race, in which Republican presidential candidates, led by Donald Trump, vied with one another to be seen as the toughest opponents of illegal immigration and offended many Latino-Americans in the process.[36]

Gender

For more than three decades, women have supported Democrats to a greater extent than men have. Hillary Clinton's selection as the first major-party female candidate for president in 2016 produced the greatest gender difference in voting in recent years, but in 2014, even without a woman presidential candidate on the ballot, women voted for Democratic House candidates by 51 to 47 percent, while men favored Republicans by 57 to 41 percent.[37] The gender gap extends to members of Congress; in 2016, nine in ten House Republicans were white males, whereas only a minority of House Democrats were white men. Republicans controlled all House committee chair positions in 2016, and 20 of the 21 chairs were male.

Why should gender be related to partisanship? Men's and women's attitudes differ on some major issues. On average, women express greater support for social programs and less support for defense spending than men do. These differences correspond with the two parties' issue agendas; the Democratic Party emphasizes health care, education, and other social programs, whereas the Republicans put a priority on tax cuts and military strength. People's attitudes toward gender equality and abortion, in particular, have become more closely correlated with their party identification during the past three decades, and when these and other "women's issues" are stressed by candidates, a gender gap is more likely to appear.[38] The national parties also project some lifestyle differences that may affect men's and women's partisanship. In a recent YouGov poll, 47 percent of Republicans thought that a married woman should take her husband's last name, compared with only 18 percent of Democrats.[39]

Although women's political preferences have shifted leftward in many Western democracies,[40] the gender gap in American politics has evolved differently. During the 1980s and 1990s, both men and women became more Republican, but men did so at a faster pace and to a greater degree.[41]

After 2000, women returned to the Democratic Party more quickly than men did. Black women and single women have become particularly distinctive Democratic constituencies. While Democrats outnumber Republicans 1.4 to 1 among all women, the ratio rises to 2 to 1 among single women. According to the exit poll in 2016, 64 percent of single women (comprising more than one in five voters) supported Democratic House candidates, compared with only 49 percent of married women.[42] Single women, especially single mothers, are more economically insecure on average than married women are, and are probably more likely to see government social programs as an ally.[43]

The Central Role of Issues in the Group–Party Linkage

As this discussion of the gender gap suggests, there is a close relationship between the alignment of social groups with parties and the parties' stands on issues. A group's presence in a party coalition indicates that many of the group's members—white evangelical Christians, for instance—have some shared reactions to major issues and candidates, which have led them to one party rather than the other. To keep their support, the party is likely to express solidarity with the group's concerns, to speak its language, and to feature some of the group's leaders in its conventions and campaigns.

But demography isn't destiny. This relationship between social groups and parties' stands can change over time. As was the case with racial issues, a party may adapt its stands on issues to attract new sources of support, or a group may realize that the other party is becoming more sensitive to its concerns.[44] Consider, for example, that until the 1980s, there was no relationship between the abortion issue and party ID; both Democratic and Republican identifiers were split on the issue.[45] But as pro-choice activists had gained strength in Democratic ranks and convinced party leaders to support abortion rights, many pro-life Democrats, including white evangelical Christians and southerners, felt alienated from their national party. Some pro-life Democrats saw an opportunity to be heard within the Republican Party and were welcomed as a new source of Republican support. As they became a larger proportion of the voters in Republican primaries, they encouraged their new party's candidates to take stronger pro-life stands. Republican Party leaders and activists responded to these new Republican enthusiasts by incorporating stands against abortion and same-sex marriage into their platform and faith-based initiatives into their rhetoric.

As a result, abortion is now a partisan issue; Republicans tend to be pro-life and Democrats pro-choice. This issue shows a clear evolution in the relationship between the parties' issue stands and their coalitional bases. On other issues, such as attitudes toward labor unions, both parties' stands and coalitions have been very stable for many decades.

TABLE 7.4 Issue Attitudes and Party Identification, 2016

	Strong D	Weak D	Lean D	Inde.	Lean R	Weak R	Strong R	D minus R*	# Cases
A. Government spending to help people pay for health insurance									
More	36%	17	11	18	5	6	7	46	649
Same	11%	10	6	23	16	13	22	−24	226
Less	2%	5	4	24	19	23	23	−54	269
B. Should the minimum wage be ….									
Raised	33%	18	11	19	3	7	8	44	640
Kept the Same	10%	7	5	21	19	17	20	−34	382
Lowered	23%	0	4	19	28	7	18	−26	30
Eliminated	0	4	3	28	20	21	23	−57	91
C. Should employers be required to pay men and women the same amount for the same work?									
Yes	25	15	10	18	10	10	12	18	870
Neutral	16	6	2	32	12	16	17	−21	170
No	12	5	4	25	17	16	21	−33	105
D. Should U.S. send ground troops to fight Islamic militants?									
Favor	18%	10	5	16	15	14	22	−18	513
Neutral	23%	16	10	25	5	9	12	23	212
Oppose	28%	15	11	24	8	9	5	32	419

TABLE 7.4 continued

E. Ideological self-identification

Liberal	48%	19	18	8	3	1	3	78	348
Moderate	18%	14	8	38	6	11	5	18	355
Conservative	7%	6	1	16	21	19	30	−56	437

Note: Totals add up to approximately 100 percent reading across (with slight variations due to rounding).

* D minus R is the party difference calculated by subtracting the percentage of strong, weak, and leaning Republicans from the percentage of strong, weak, and leaning Democrats. Negative numbers indicate a Republican advantage in the group.

Source: 2016 American National Election Pilot Study; data made available by the Inter-University Consortium for Political and Social Research.

Clearer Differences Between the Two Parties' Coalitions on Issues

As you can see in Table 7.4, the two parties in the electorate now differ clearly from one another in their attitudes toward major issues. These party differences in attitudes closely track the issue preferences of key groups in the parties' coalitions. Begin, for example, with section A: attitudes toward government spending to help people get health insurance. At the top left of the table, you can see that 36 percent of the people who want government to spend more on helping people pay for health insurance are strong Democrats, whereas (following across that line) only 7 percent are strong Republicans. On the right side of the table, you can see in the "Dem. minus Rep." column that Democrats greatly outnumber Republicans among those who want government to provide this service.

Democrats are also much more favorable than are Republicans to raising the minimum wage (section B). Blacks, lower-income people, those with only a high school education, and those in blue-collar or unskilled jobs—all important groups in the Democratic coalition—are especially likely to favor government protection of their economic rights. The recipients of a higher minimum wage tend to be lower SES people, whose Democratic leanings can be seen in Table 7.3.

People also differ markedly by party on issues such as equal pay for equal work and defense spending (see Table 7.4, Sections C and D). In recent years, Democrats have been much more likely than Republicans to support requiring businesses to pay women and men the same wage for doing the same job. Recall from Table 7.3 the tendency of women—and especially single women, who are often heads of families—to identify as Democrats. And there is a truly striking party difference between those who call themselves liberals and those who identify themselves as conservatives (Table 7.4, Section E). As one pollster put it, "We have two massive, colliding forces ... One [the Republican coalition] is rural, Christian, religiously conservative, with guns at home. ... And we have a second America [the Democratic coalition] that is socially tolerant, pro-choice, secular, living in New England and the Pacific coast, and in affluent suburbs."[46] Party divisions have accurately been termed "culture wars."[47]

In short, there is a close but evolving relationship between the stands a party takes and the groups that form the party's core support. Parties take positions on issues to maintain the support of the groups in their existing coalition. Sometimes party leaders use issue positions to draw members of other social groups to the party, as Republicans did with white southerners since the 1960s. At times, it is the group that tries to put its concerns on the party's agenda, as was the case with the abortion issue. As these newer groups become a larger force within the party coalition, the party's leadership will try to firm up their support with additional commitments on their issues. In recent years, this process has led to a growing division on issues between the two parties' coalitions. The result is that even if most voters have not become more ideologically extreme, political debate has become more clearly divided by party, as voters have sorted themselves into the party that is closer to their views on issues.[48]

From Democratic Majority to Close Competition

The party system has changed in other important ways since the New Deal as well. The party organizations do not expect to anoint candidates now, run their campaigns, or hand out patronage jobs. Rather, the party organizations work primarily to help fund and support campaigns that are run by candidates and their paid consultants. And the relationship between party ID and election results has changed. Until 1952, the elections of the New Deal party system had usually been **maintaining elections**, in which the presidential candidate of the majority party—the party with the most identifiers—normally won. Since 1952, most national elections have been **deviating elections**—those in which short-term forces such as candidate characteristics or issues are powerful enough to cause the defeat of the majority party's candidate. Racial issues have figured prominently in this change.

Another major change has been the gradual wearing away of Democratic dominance in party identification. In the 1950s and early 1960s, many more Americans called themselves Democrats than Republicans or independents. The Democratic edge began to erode after 1964, but Republicans were not immediately able to capitalize on the Democrats' losses. The proportion of "pure independent" identifiers increased, and there was a steady stream of independent and third-party candidates.[49] These changes in partisanship struck many scholars as resembling a **dealignment**, or a decline in party loyalties.

Yet as we have seen, even as both parties were losing adherents nationally, signs of the coming change were apparent in the South. The movement toward Republican partisanship in southern states began to accelerate in the late 1960s, and Republican candidates reaped the fruits. In 1960, there had been no Republican candidate on the general election ballot in almost two-thirds of southern U.S. House districts. The only real competition was in the Democratic primary. By 1968, the number of these one-party House races had been cut by half.[50]

Party change speeded up again during the 1980s. For the first time in 50 years, young voters were more likely to call themselves Republicans than Democrats.[51] Two powerful reasons were President Reagan's popularity and the increased efforts of evangelical Christian groups to promote Republican affiliation. Republicans gained a majority in the U.S. Senate in 1980 that lasted six years, and in 1994, the GOP won control of both houses of Congress for the first time in 40 years. Republicans were now competing effectively with the Democrats in statewide races in the South. In 1994, there was a Republican majority among the region's Congress members and governors for the first time since Reconstruction. The George W. Bush administration worked to reinforce this hoped-for Republican majority by attracting more Latino, Catholic, and black votes and by working with evangelical preachers to promote voter turnout among conservative Christians.[52] But the Republican efforts were only partly successful; currently, the two parties are relatively balanced in strength, with Democrats most competitive for the presidency and the Senate, and Republicans dominating in the House and in state governments (see Chapters 2 and 8).

How Can We Characterize These Changes: Realignment, Dealignment, or What?

A number of researchers have argued that these changes can best be called a **party realignment**—a significant and enduring change in the patterns of group support for the parties, usually (but not always) leading to a new majority party. We have certainly seen the big changes in group support for the parties; the Republican coalition has become more southern, more evangelical, and more conservative, and a Democratic Party that used to draw much of its strength from the white South now depends to a much greater extent on the votes of blacks, liberals, and secularists.

These coalitional changes have affected the parties' policy stands. A Democratic Party that now draws a substantial minority of its followers from among blacks is likely to take different stands from a Democratic Party that used to depend heavily on conservative white southerners. Southern whites have provided the critical mass for the Republicans to adopt more socially conservative positions today, not only on civil rights but also on health care, abortion, women's rights, aid for big cities, and support for private schools. Chapter 15 shows these changes in the two parties' platforms. Further, as the policy preferences of blacks, southern whites, and evangelical Christians have become more consistent with their partisanship, each party has become more homogeneous internally, and more distinct from the other party on issues, than had been the case in many decades; the Democratic Party's identifiers in 2016 are much more consistently liberal than was the Democratic Party in the electorate in the 1970s, and Republican identifiers are even more homogeneously conservative.

Issue Positions Can Combine and Then Re-Combine

This evolving relationship suggests that over time, different sets of issues will "go together" in a party's coalition. During the third party system, the Republican coalition was characterized by strong support for business as well as a powerful federal government, which could meet business' needs (see pages 151–2). By the fifth party system, as the Democratic-led federal government had become more inclined to tax and regulate business in order to provide social services, the Republican bundle of beliefs was shifting to a combination of pro-business and states' rights stands. Similarly, in the current (sixth) party system, Donald Trump attracted support from many mainstream Republicans as well as people without college degrees, who felt threatened by foreign trade and illegal immigration.[53] These combinations and re-combinations of beliefs and characteristics happen when a party seeks to gain new groups of supporters loosened from their traditional partisanship by environmental change or by a candidate who speaks the language of a group recently added to the party's coalition.

Problems with the Idea of Realignment

There are both practical and theoretical reasons why other scholars are reluctant to use the *R* word (realignment) to describe these changes. In practical terms, although Republican strength has increased, Democrats still hold the edge among party identifiers. And in a theoretical sense, the idea of realignment is difficult to apply with any precision. How much change has to occur in the parties' coalitions in order to call it a realignment? As political scientist David Mayhew points out, there are no clear standards for sorting elections into periods of realignment as opposed to nonrealigning periods.[54] Many prefer to use the concept of "issue evolutions" to discuss the variety of ways in which issues have affected partisanship over time.[55]

Although the changes in southern whites' and blacks' party ID are highly significant, the parties retain their New Deal character in several ways. The Democrats remain the party of minority racial and religious groups, though the minorities have changed. As Catholics have entered the mainstream of economic and political life, they have divided more evenly between the two parties, but the Democrats still represent the majority of lower-income, black, Latino, LGBT, and nonreligious people. And even if the movement of blacks and white southerners has been dramatic enough to propel the United States into a new party system, when did that system begin? Was it during the 1960s, when southern blacks regained the right to vote and the civil rights movement shook the South? Was it in the 1980s, when southern partisan change accelerated and Ronald Reagan attracted many new voters to the Republicans? Was it in the early 1990s, when Congress finally came under Republican control? Or does it encompass all of these periods in a constantly evolving (so-called secular) change?

The debate will continue as to whether the concept of realignment is a valuable tool in understanding change in the party system. Perhaps a more useful approach is to recognize that there are many different kinds of party changes and that we have seen all of them to at least some degree in the past 50 years. The evidence for party organizational change, as presented in

Chapters 3 and 4, is convincing. There is little doubt that the Democratic dominance of the New Deal party system gave way to a greater balance in national party strength. And whether we call it a realignment or not, there has been enough change in the two parties' coalitions to produce a palpable shift in campaign and congressional debate. When Democrats support same-sex marriage and Republicans agree with the pope on abortion, we know that there is a broader agenda in national politics than simply the economic conflicts of the 1930s and 1940s.

As we approach the third decade of the 2000s, then, the American electorate is composed of two groups of partisans of roughly comparable size. The group of Democrats includes liberals, lower-income people, some highly educated professionals, and racial and ethnic minorities. Although it has shrunk a bit in recent decades, the Democratic coalition has the potential for growth, especially among Latino or Hispanic Americans. The group of Republicans is dominated by conservatives, southerners, and churchgoers. It is increasingly whiter and older. And there is a third group that could truly be termed "dealigned," in that it feels no lasting party loyalties and usually stays out of political activity.[56] Because of the demonstrated ability of both major parties to bounce back from defeat, it is also an electorate capable of producing mercurial election results. The trajectory of American politics, then, has the potential for rapid change.

Notes

1 See Edward G. Carmines and James A. Stimson, *Issue Evolution* (Princeton, NJ: Princeton University Press, 1989).

2 See, for example, Larry M. Bartels, *Unequal Democracy* (Princeton, NJ: Princeton University Press, 2008).

3 See John H. Aldrich, *Why Parties? A Second Look* (Chicago: University of Chicago Press, 2011), pp. 281–287.

4 See V. O. Key, Jr., "A Theory of Critical Elections," *Journal of Politics* 17 (1955): 3–18; and Walter Dean Burnham, *Critical Elections and the Mainsprings of American Politics* (New York: Norton, 1970).

5 These events typically unfold over a period of time, but for convenience, the beginning of each party system is located in the year in which the new majority party coalition first took office.

6 Michael Holt, *The Rise and Fall of the American Whig Party* (New York: Oxford University Press, 2003).

7 The third party system actually contained two distinct periods. From the end of the Civil War in 1865 through 1876, Democratic voting strength in the South was held in check by the occupying Union army and various Reconstruction policies and laws. So to reflect the true party balance during this time, it is helpful to differentiate between 1861–1876 and the 1877–1896 period.

8 A. James Reichley, *The Life of the Parties* (Lanham, MD: Rowman & Littlefield, 2000), p. 104.

9 See Hans Noel, "The Coalition Merchants," *Journal of Politics* 74 (2012): 156–173. For a more public opinion-driven argument, see Eric Schickler, "New Deal Liberalism and Racial Liberalism in the Mass Public, 1937–1968," *Perspectives on Politics* 11 (2013): 75–98.

10 Ilyana Kuziemko and Ebonya Washington, "Why did the Democrats Lose the South?" National Bureau of Economic Research Working Paper 21703, November 2015, at www.nber.org/papers/w21703 (accessed June 21, 2016).

11 See David Karol, *Party Position Change in American Politics* (Cambridge: Cambridge University Press, 2009), p. 112.

12 Nicholas A. Valentino and David O. Sears, "Old Times There Are Not Forgotten," *American Journal of Political Science* 49 (2005): 673.

13 Jeffrey M. Stonecash, *Political Parties Matter* (Boulder, CO: Lynne Rienner, 2006), Chapter 4.

14 Seth C. McKee, *Republican Ascendancy* (Boulder, CO: Westview Press, 2010).

15 Merle Black, "The Transformation of the Southern Democratic Party," *Journal of Politics* 66 (2004): 1001–1017.

16 Valentino and Sears, "Old Times There Are Not Forgotten," p. 676. See also Earl Black and Merle Black, *Divided America* (New York: Simon & Schuster, 2007), pp. 32–39 and 74–91.

17 Seth Masket, "How Doomed Are the Democrats?" *Pacific Standard blog,* November 9, 2015, at www.psmag.com/politics-and-law/how-doomed-are-the-democrats (accessed June 21, 2016).

18 John R. Petrocik, "Party Coalitions in the American Public," in John C. Green and Daniel J. Coffey, *The State of the Parties*, 5th ed. (Lanham, MD: Rowman & Littlefield, 2007), p. 285.

19 James Madison, *The Federalist No. 10*, November 22, 1787.

20 See Jeffrey M. Stonecash, "Class in American Politics," in Stonecash, ed., *New Directions in American Political Parties* (New York: Routledge, 2010), pp. 110–125.

21 See Jeffrey M. Stonecash, *Class and Party in American Politics* (Boulder, CO: Westview Press, 2000), pp. 13 and 139, and Chapter 4, and Jonathan Knuckey, "The Survival of the Democratic Party Outside the South," *Party Politics* 21 (2015): 539–552.

22 Paul R. Abramson, John H. Aldrich, and David W. Rohde, *Change and Continuity in the 2008 and 2010 Elections* (Washington, DC: CQ Press, 2011), pp. 203–204.

23 On the change in upper-income people's attitudes toward the Republican Party, see Mark D. Brewer, *Party Images in the American Electorate* (New York: Routledge, 2009), pp. 25–26.

24 Gary Miller and Norman Schofield, "The Transformation of the Republican and Democratic Party Coalitions in the U.S.," *Perspectives on Politics* 6 (2008): 433–450.

25 Samantha Smith and Carroll Doherty, "A Divide Between College, Non-College Republicans," Pew Research Center, March 1, 2016.

26 See Donald C. Baumer and Howard J. Gold, *Parties, Polarization, and Democracy in the U.S.* (Boulder, CO: Paradigm, 2010), pp. 164–165.

27 See Paul R. Abramson, John H. Aldrich, Brad T. Gomez, and David W. Rohde, *Change and Continuity in the 2012 and 2014 Elections* (Los Angeles: Sage/CQ Press, 2015), p. 122.

28 Frank Newport, "Blacks as Conservative as Republicans on Some Moral Issues," Gallup Poll, December 3, 2008, at www.gallup.com/poll/112807/Blacks-Conservative-Republicans-Some-Moral-Issues.aspx (accessed June 21, 2016).

29 Zoltan Hajnal and Jeremy D. Horowitz, "Racial Winners and Losers in American Party Politics," *Perspectives on Politics* 12 (2014): 100–118.

30 Campbell Robertson and Richard Fausset, "Swamped in a Red Surge, Southern Democrats Contemplate Their Rebuilding Plans," *New York Times*, November 6, 2014, p. A1. See also Ismail K. White, Cheryl N. Laird, and Troy D. Allen, "Selling Out?" *American Political Science Review* 108 (2014): 783–800.

31 See, for example, Nate Cohn, "Why Democrats Can't Win," *New York Times*, September 7, 2014, p. SR1.

32 See Frank Newport, "Party Identification Varies Widely Across the Age Spectrum," Gallup poll, July 10, 2014, at www.gallup.com/poll/172439/party-identification-varies-across-age-spectrum.aspx (accessed June 21, 2016).

33 E. J. Dionne, Jr., William A. Galston, Korin Davis, and Ross Tilchin, "Faith in Equality," Brookings Institution report, April 24, 2014.

34 See David E. Campbell, John C. Green, and Geoffrey C. Layman, "The Party Faithful," *American Journal of Political Science* 55 (2011): 42–58.

35 On religion in American campaigns, see Christopher Weber and Matthew Thornton, "Courting Christians," *Journal of Politics* 74 (2012): 400–413.

36 This was also the result of anti-immigrant ballot propositions sponsored by California Republicans in the 1990s and in other states since then; see Shaun Bowler, Stephen P. Nicholson, and Gary M. Segura, "Earthquakes and Aftershocks," *American Journal of Political Science* 50 (2006): 146–157.

37 Exit poll results at www.cnn.com/election/2014/results/race/house#exit-polls (accessed June 21, 2016).

38 Kira Sanbonmatsu, *Democrats, Republicans, and the Politics of Women's Place* (Ann Arbor, MI: University of Michigan Press, 2002), Chapter 3; see also Christina Wolbrecht, *The Politics of Women's Rights* (Princeton, NJ: Princeton University Press, 2000); and Brian Schaffner, "Priming Gender," *American Journal of Political Science* 49 (2005): 803–817.

39 Peter Moore, "Women Don't Need to Take Their Husbands' Last Name," *Front Page*, October 20, 2014, at https://today.yougov.com/news/2014/10/20/last-names/ (accessed June 21, 2016).

40 See Torben Iversen and Frances Rosenbluth, "The Political Economy of Gender," *American Journal of Political Science* 50 (2006): 1–19.

41 Janet M. Box-Steffensmeier, Suzanna De Boef, and Tse-Min Lin, "The Dynamics of the Partisan Gender Gap," *American Political Science Review* 98 (2004): 515–528; and Karen M. Kaufman and John R. Petrocik, "The Changing Politics of American Men," *American Journal of Political Science* 43 (1999): 864–887.

42 2016 exit poll at www.cnn.com/election/results/exit-polls/national/president (accessed November 10, 2016).

43 On marriage, parenthood, and political attitudes, see Laurel Elder and Steven Greene, *The Politics of Parenthood* (Albany, NY: SUNY Press, 2012).

44 Mark D. Brewer and Jeffrey M. Stonecash, *Dynamics of American Political Parties* (Cambridge: Cambridge University Press, 2009), Chapter 11.

45 Greg D. Adams, "Abortion: Evidence of an Issue Evolution," *American Journal of Political Science* 41 (1997): 718–737.

46 Quoted in Thomas B. Edsall, "Political Party Is No Longer Dictated By Class Status," *Washington Post*, November 9, 2000, p. A37.

47 See Geoffrey C. Layman, *The Great Divide* (New York: Columbia University Press, 2001).

48 Matthew Levendusky, *The Partisan Sort* (Chicago: University of Chicago Press, 2009).

49 Martin P. Wattenberg, *The Decline of American Political Parties 1952–96* (Cambridge, MA: Harvard University Press, 1998).

50 Donald Green, Bradley Palmquist, and Eric Schickler, *Partisan Hearts and Minds* (New Haven, CT: Yale University Press, 2002), pp. 141 and 158.

51 Helmut Norpoth, "Under Way and Here to Stay: Party Realignment in the 1980s?" *Public Opinion Quarterly* 51 (1987): 376–391; and Warren E. Miller, "Party Identification, Realignment, and Party Voting," *American Political Science Review* 85 (1991): 557–570.

52 Alan Cooperman and Thomas B. Edsall, "Evangelicals Say They Led Charge for the GOP," *Washington Post,* November 8, 2004, p. A1.

53 Lilliana Mason and Nicholas Davis, "Trump Attracts Poor Voters with Multiple Republican Social Identities," *Vox*, March 10, 2016, at www.vox.com/mischiefs-of-faction/2016/3/9/11186314/trump-voters-identities (accessed June 21, 2016). See also David Karol, *Party Position Change in American Politics* (Cambridge: Cambridge University Press, 2009).

54 David R. Mayhew, *Electoral Realignments* (New Haven, CT: Yale University Press, 2002); see also Carmines and Stimson, *Issue Evolution*; Byron E. Shafer, ed., *The End of Realignment?* (Madison, WI: University of Wisconsin Press, 1991); and Samuel Merrill III, Bernard Grofman, and Thomas L. Brunell, "Cycles in American National Electoral Politics, 1854–2006," *American Political Science Review* 102 (2008): 1–17.

55 Carmines and Stimson, *Issue Evolution*.

56 See Paul Allen Beck, "A Tale of Two Electorates," in John C. Green and Rick Farmer, eds., *The State of the Parties*, 4th ed. (Lanham, MD: Rowman & Littlefield, 2003), pp. 38–53.

CHAPTER 8

Parties and
Voter Turnout

In American politics, elections are decided by those who choose *not* to vote as well as those who do. Unusually large voter turnouts among young people, blacks, and Latino Americans helped propel Barack Obama to victories in 2008 and 2012. When young people and blacks stayed home from the polls in larger numbers in 2016, Hillary Clinton and many other Democrats lost. So the Democratic and Republican Parties try not only to affect voters' preferences but also to mobilize those who favor their candidates and, if possible, discourage their opponents from going to the polls.

Parties try to shape voter turnout in three ways. First, each party has worked hard over time to get its likely supporters the *right* to vote. The early Jeffersonians and then the Democrats fought to expand voting rights to include renters and other non-property owners—groups that would naturally favor their candidates rather than the Federalists or Whigs.

Second, once its supporters have the right to vote, the party can promote policies that make voting *easier and more accessible* to them (and less accessible to its opponents). Parties have been doing this since the United States began.[1] Laws governing the ease of voting may seem nonpartisan, but they often have partisan effects in practice. State laws requiring voters to show a photo ID, for instance, cause controversy because they may increase the burden on some types of people more than on others. Drivers' licenses are the most common form of photo ID, but people who can't afford a car or who are unable to drive because of physical disabilities—groups that tend to support Democratic candidates—have to make more effort to get the required ID. Similarly, local governments' decisions to site early voting centers in some parts of the community rather than others affect the ease with which different types of people can vote.

Finally, party organizations and their candidates can strive to bring more of their supporters to the polls in a particular election. This *voter mobilization* has become a key focus in competitive elections. The shifts in blacks' and Latinos' turnout between 2012 and 2014, for instance, resulted in part from differences in the effectiveness of the Republicans' and the Democrats' get-out-the-vote (GOTV) drives.

As we examine these party efforts, we need to consider their impact on American democracy. Voter turnout in the United States is relatively low. Turnout in the intense 2016 presidential race was just 59 percent of eligible voters, well below the voting rates of almost every other industrialized democracy. We need to ask why voter turnout in American elections is so limited, and what responsibility the parties bear for these low turnouts.

Elections: The Rules Affect the Results

The rules in politics, as in everything else, are never neutral. Each rule of the electoral process—such as who is eligible to vote or when elections can be held—affects different parties and candidates differently.[2] For example, if polling places close at 6:00 P.M. (as they do in Indiana and Kentucky), making it hard for office and factory workers to get to the polls on time, then the Democratic Party may lose a disproportionate number of votes. If a state makes it easy to vote by mail, then any local party organized enough to distribute mail-in ballots to its supporters will benefit.

Because election rules have partisan consequences, there will be partisan debates about whether to adopt them. The U.S., unlike almost every other democracy, has no national list of eligible voters. The voter rolls are maintained by counties and towns and their partisan elected officials. For much of U.S. history, the debate leaned toward expanding voting rights to more Americans. Since 2000, at a time of very close national elections, state legislatures have considered a variety of ways to limit that expansion.

Expansion of the Right to Vote

White male citizens were given the right to vote earlier in the United States than in any other democracy. In the early 1800s, prompted by the Jeffersonians (who expected to benefit from the change), the states gradually repealed the property, income, and taxpaying qualifications for voting by which they had so severely constrained male suffrage.[3] By 1860, no states required property holding, and only four required substantial taxpaying as a condition for voting. But that didn't stop some northeastern patricians from trying to take voting rights away from workers and immigrants in the 1870s, in order to weaken support for the urban party "machines."[4]

Women did not win the right to vote in all states until much later. The Nineteenth Amendment, forbidding states to deny the right to vote based on gender, was finally approved in 1920 after a decades-long struggle. The most recent change, the constitutional amendment lowering the voting age to 18 for all elections, was ratified by the states in 1971.

The history of black Americans' voting rights is more complex—a story of both human rights and partisanship. Some New England states granted suffrage to blacks before the Civil War. The Fifteenth Amendment, adopted after that war with support from the Republican administration, declared that no state could abridge the right to vote on account of race. (Most blacks supported Republicans, who had championed the emancipation of slaves.) But the federal government soon turned its attention to other matters, and Democratic-run southern states worked effectively to keep blacks from voting, as we will see. By the early 1900s, black turnout in the South had dropped to negligible levels. It remained that way in most southern states until the 1960s, when the Democratic Party, then the majority in Congress, changed its stance on civil rights, and federal authorities began to enforce new voting rights laws in the states.

Rules Affecting Access to Voting Rights

The Progressive movement in the late 1800s and early 1900s promoted several changes in election rules. Progressives claimed that these changes were intended to democratize American politics, but they were also designed to weaken the political party "machines" of the time.

The Secret Ballot

American elections did not always use secret ballots. In fact, not until the late 1800s was the secret ballot used throughout the nation. In the early 1800s, in many areas, voters simply told the election officials which candidates they preferred. Gradually, this "oral vote" was replaced by ballots printed by the parties or candidates. The voter brought the ballot of a particular party to the polling place and put it in the ballot box. The ballots of different parties differed in color and appearance, so observers could tell how an individual had voted. That was how the party machine wanted it; if party leaders had done a favor for someone in exchange for a vote, they wanted to be sure they had gotten their money's worth.

To discourage vote buying and to weaken the party machines, Progressives pushed for a new secret ballot system, which came into widespread use in the 1890s. These ballots were printed by the government and marked by the voter in private. Because the ballot is administered and paid for by the government, this reform involved the government in running elections, which opened the door to government regulation of the parties. It also made it easier for voters to split their tickets—to vote for the candidates of more than one party on the same ballot.[5]

The Progressives did not succeed in doing away with the **long ballot**, however, in which each state's voters are asked to elect large numbers of state and local officials who would be appointed in other democracies. To cast a meaningful vote on each of 60 or 70 state and local offices, citizens would need to spend a lot of time gathering information, a task most citizens do not find fascinating. That drives down voter turnout. People who do vote may cast ballots for some offices but not others. This "roll-off" can reduce the vote for minor offices and referenda by 20 or 30 percent compared with offices at the top of the ballot.[6] Voter fatigue caused by the long ballot leads people to use various shortcuts to make their choices. Party identification is the most common shortcut—an outcome the Progressives would certainly have hated.

Citizenship

Prior to 1894 at least 12 states permitted noncitizens to vote,[7] although some required the individual to have applied for American citizenship. Since the 1920s, all states have required that voters be U.S. citizens. This is the biggest legal barrier to voting; millions of adults, most of them in California, Florida, Texas, and Illinois, work and may even pay taxes but cannot vote until they are "naturalized" as citizens, a process that can take years to complete. Given their average income levels and ethnicity, these noncitizen residents would be more likely to vote Democratic than Republican.

Residence

For most of American history, states could require citizens to live in a state and locality for a certain amount of time before being allowed to vote there. Southern states had the longest residence requirements (to keep migrant farm workers from voting). In 1970, Congress limited states' residence requirements to a maximum of 30 days for voting in presidential elections. Since then, almost half of the states have dropped residence requirements altogether. Even so, many Americans move frequently, and those who have moved recently are much less likely to vote.[8]

Registration

Another major obstacle to voting is the registration requirement—the rule in most states that citizens must register in advance in order to vote in an election. During much of the 1800s, voters needed only to show up on Election Day to cast a ballot. Progressive reformers in the late 1800s urged states to require advance registration in order to limit voter fraud by party bosses. That increased the motivation needed to vote because it doubled the effort involved: one trip to register and a second trip to vote. These registration requirements helped to reduce the high turnout levels of that time.[9] In many other democracies—and in Oregon since 2015—the government produces the voter list, taking the burden for registering off the individual voter.

The Special Case of Voting Rights for Black Americans

Soon after blacks had been granted the right to vote by constitutional amendments in the 1860s, these new voters—one-third of the South's population—elected some African American candidates to Congress and state legislatures. The newly elected black Republicans advocated for reforms such as state-funded public schools. (Remember that changing who has the right to vote can also result in changed government policies.) Southern Democrats, who had lost their hold on power, responded with violence and, eventually, laws and administrative rulings that kept blacks from voting. So just 15 years after the Confederacy lost the Civil War, white southerners had deprived black citizens of their newly achieved voice in elections.

The Long Struggle for Voting Rights

Blacks remained largely disenfranchised for almost a century after the 1880s. During this time, southern states would devise a way to disenfranchise blacks, the Supreme Court would strike it down as unconstitutional, and the states would find another. One example was the "white primary." The Republican Party barely existed in the South at this time, so the candidate who won the Democratic primary was assured of winning the general election. Faced with the threat of blacks voting in the Democratic primary, some states declared the party to be a private club open only to whites, so blacks could not cast a primary ballot. It took 21 years of lawsuits and five Supreme Court cases to end this practice.[10]

In addition, most southern states required payment of a poll tax in order to vote—just one or two dollars, but often demanded well before an election, with the stipulation that the taxpayer keep a receipt and present it weeks later at the polling place. And local election officials in some states used tests to decide who was "literate" enough to vote. These laws were intentionally directed at the poor and uneducated black population.

Southern lawmakers also designed endless delays and other technicalities to prevent blacks from registering to vote. Observers reported:

> Separate [registration] tables would be assigned to whites and Negroes [then the customary term for African Americans]. If a line of Negroes were waiting for the Negro table, a white might go ahead of them, use the empty white table, and leave. In Anniston, Alabama, a report said the white table was larger, and Negroes were not allowed in the room when a white was using it …. In one north Florida county, the registrar … simply sat with his legs stretched out across the doorway. Negroes didn't break through them.[11]

Those who kept trying were often faced with economic reprisal (the loss of a job or a home) and physical violence. It is not surprising, in this relentlessly hostile environment, that only 5 percent of voting-age blacks were registered in the 11 southern states as late as 1940, when the U.S. celebrated its 164th birthday.[12]

Because courts found it difficult to counter these extra-legal hurdles, reformers turned to Congress and the executive branch. The federal Voting Rights Act of 1965, extended in 1982 and 2006, authorized the U.S. Justice Department to seek injunctions against anyone who prevented blacks from voting. When the Justice Department could convince a federal court that a "pattern or practice" of discrimination existed in a district, the court could send federal registrars there to register voters. It could also supervise voting procedures in states and counties where less than 50 percent of potential voters had gone to the polls in the most recent presidential election.[13]

This unprecedented federal intervention in state elections, combined with the civil rights movement's efforts to mobilize black voters, enabled the black electorate to grow enormously in the South (see Figure 8.1). By the 1990s, black registration finally reached a level close to that of white southerners, and remains so today. In the process, the conflicts between these new black voters and southern whites ate away at the Democratic Party from within and caused dramatic changes in the two parties' supporting coalitions (see Chapter 7).

From Voting Rights to Representation

Even after blacks gained voting rights, some states kept trying to dilute the impact of black votes. The federal government responded with a new twist on an old practice. Every ten years, after the U.S. Census, state legislatures

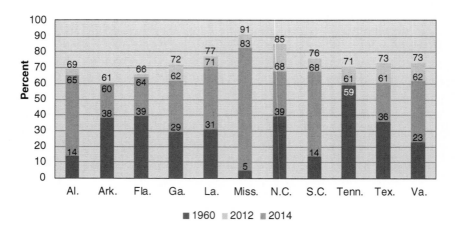

FIGURE 8.1 Black Voter Registration in the South, 1960 and 2012–2014

Note: Bars show the number of blacks in each year who were registered to vote, as a percentage of the voting-age citizen population. Note that registration levels drop in congressional election years for blacks (as shown in the 2014 levels, compared with 2012) and whites as well.

Source: U.S. Census Bureau, Table 4B at www.census.gov/hhes/www/socdemo/voting/publications/p20/2014/tables.html (accessed June 22, 2016).

must redraw the boundaries of congressional and state legislative districts so that these districts remain equal in population size. This **legislative redistricting**, ordered by the Supreme Court in the 1960s to stop state legislatures from overrepresenting rural areas and underrepresenting bigger cities,[14] has been used by resourceful politicians for short-term political gain. **Gerrymandering**—drawing district lines to maximize one's own party's strength and disadvantage the other party— is prevalent and is usually permitted by the courts.[15] For years, in the case of black Americans, it was common for legislators to draw legislative district lines that divided black voters among several districts, so as to weaken their voting strength, or to pack black voters into a few districts so that pro-civil rights candidates won these districts by large, wasteful majorities.

After the 1990 census, the first Bush administration pressed southern states to redraw congressional district lines so as to create some districts with a majority of black or Latino voters, called **"majority-minority" districts**. The argument was that these districts would usually elect minority legislators to Congress and thus improve the representation of minority citizens. Many of these districts were created by an interesting alliance of black and Latino Democrats with white Republicans. This did increase the number of congressional seats held by black Americans. And it appeared to increase turnout among registered blacks living in black-majority districts.[16]

Another effect of these majority-minority districts, however, was to elect more Republicans to Congress from the South—one reason why Republicans supported their creation. Because the districts are fashioned by packing as many (heavily Democratic) black voters into a district as possible, and thus creating safe Democratic districts, the neighboring districts are left with a higher proportion of whites and Republicans. According to one estimate, "for every overwhelmingly black Democratic district created, there is a good chance of creating two or more districts that are overwhelmingly white and Republican."[17] The majority-minority districts are largely in Democratic-majority urban areas and in some geographic regions of the South. The result is to heighten party polarization, with increasing numbers of safe Democratic and safe Republican districts.

In turn, Democratic state legislatures try to pack the GOP vote into as few districts as possible, in order to elect more Democratic representatives. The Supreme Court has rejected the most flagrantly engineered of these majority-minority districts, but has ruled that race can be an element in redrawing district lines, as long as it is not the controlling factor.[18]

Getting Blacks' Votes Counted

Achieving fair representation for black Americans is limited by the fact that about 13 percent of black males have lost voting rights because they have had felony convictions. Mandatory sentences for drug use appear to target drugs used more often by blacks, and almost all states deny felons the right to vote, at least while they are behind bars and, in most states, through the individual's parole. Almost 4 million Americans of all races are estimated to have lost their right to vote because of a felony conviction.[19] Predicting from their SES and race, most of these people would probably vote Democratic. In addition, several states have recently passed laws restricting the activities of groups that register new voters. These laws seemed to be aimed at minority voters, who are twice as likely to register through groups' registration drives as whites are. So, although black turnout rates are much higher now than they were in the mid-1900s, more subtle challenges to blacks' voting rights remain.

Efforts to Liberalize Voting Rules

Registration requirements and other "costs" imposed on voting are associated with lower turnout.[20] Yet reforms intended to reduce the costs of voting don't always increase turnout.

Election Day Registration

North Dakota does not require its citizens to register at all, and 12 other states have passed laws to allow citizens to register and vote on the same day, known as **Election Day Registration (EDR)** or **Same Day Registration**. These states tend to have higher turnout rates,[21] because citizens can cast a ballot even if they do not get interested enough to take part until the last, most engaging days of the campaign. A new California law automatically registers eligible residents when they get a new or renewed driver's license, unless they refuse. But these laws remain controversial, and in most states, prospective voters must still take the initiative to find out where and when to register, make the effort to do so, and then re-register whenever they move or fail to vote for a number of years. Experts have estimated that millions of eligible people, many of whom are less educated, lower income, or residentially mobile, tried but were unable to vote in recent elections because of registration problems.[22]

"Motor Voter" Laws

Another effort to ease restrictive registration rules was the so-called **Motor Voter law** (1993), which required the states to let citizens register to vote at driver's license bureaus, by mail, and through agencies that give out federal benefits. Voter registration surged in many areas as a result. Some opponents of "motor voter" feared that it would result in increased numbers of low-income, Democratic votes on Election Day. Most studies have shown, however, that although stricter registration rules are linked with lower voter turnout, reforms to ease these rules, including "motor voter," do not always increase turnout. Those who register at these alternate sites are less likely to vote than are other registrants.[23]

Voting by Mail, Early, and No-Excuse Absentee Voting

To increase the convenience of voting, about two-thirds of the states in 2016 allowed some form of early voting in person or no-excuse absentee voting, in which an individual can request an absentee ballot without having to explain why. In Oregon, Washington State, Colorado, and most precincts in California, all voting is now conducted by mail. As a result, more than 37 percent of American voters cast their ballots prior to Election Day in 2016. Early and no-excuse absentee voting tends to produce only a modest increase in turnout, however.

Early voting does redistribute the votes over a longer period; presidential voting in some states begins as early as late September. Thus, early voting can be a boon for local election officials, because it helps identify problems with voting systems, which can then be addressed before the bulk of voters arrive. But it poses challenges for parties and candidates. The traditional plan of building a campaign toward a big finish on Election Day doesn't work very well if large numbers of voters cast their ballots in October. To take advantage of early and no-excuse absentee voting, party organizations must be prepared to explain these options to their likely supporters and to mobilize early voters. The traditional GOTV drive, which used to take place during the weekend before Election Day, has now become at least six weeks long. On the other hand, candidates then have the benefit of access to "running lists" telling who has requested absentee ballots and who has submitted them or voted early—though not, of course, how each individual voted.

The Voter ID Controversy

Recently, these efforts to liberalize the requirements for voter participation have provoked a backlash. In 2013 a Supreme Court decision spurred several states, especially in the South, to place added burdens on would-be voters. The decision, *Shelby County v. Holder*, invalidated a key part of the Voting Rights Act. It absolved states with a history of racial discrimination in elections from having to get approval from the U.S. Attorney General or a federal district court before making any changes in their voting laws and practices. States responded with a variety of restrictive changes; in 2016, 17 states put new voting restrictions into effect.

Voter ID Laws

In a remarkably short time, many states passed and most others are considering laws requiring voters to show a state or federal government-issued photo ID card at the polls.[24] As of 2016, 33 states required voters to show some kind of ID at the polls. (A non-voter-ID alternative used by other states is to compare the voter's signature or other details with the signature or information already on file.[25])

These laws have been highly controversial. Proponents, usually Republicans,[26] contend that the laws are needed to limit vote fraud. Democratic opponents counter with evidence that vote fraud at the polls is extremely rare—in fact, one study showed that reports of voter impersonation are about as common as reports of alien abductions[27]—and that the more common cases of fraudulent absentee ballots are not covered by most voter ID laws. In particular, these laws seem to target disadvantaged groups. For instance, researchers find that voter ID requirements are more likely to be passed in states where minority turnout increased since the previous presidential election.[28] Despite the widespread impression that IDs are required everywhere, opponents point out that disproportionate numbers of poor, minority, and disabled people—who vote predominantly Democratic—are less likely to have driver's licenses and passports and therefore might lose their chance to vote, though they are otherwise eligible.

Congress has heard evidence that these rules are often applied arbitrarily. Blacks are more likely to be asked by election officials to show identification than whites are, regardless of the state's voter ID laws.[29] And in several states whose legislatures gained Republican majorities in 2010 and 2014, bills were introduced to prevent college students from using university IDs to satisfy voter ID requirements or to make it harder for students to vote in their college towns at all.[30] Some recent federal court rulings have struck down voter ID laws in North Carolina, Texas, and Wisconsin on the ground that these laws are discriminatory.[31] They cite cases such as Alabama's which, after passing a stricter voter ID requirement in 2015, closed 31 driver's license offices, most of them in rural and black-majority areas,[32] thereby making it harder for their residents to apply for an alternative state ID.

Proof of Citizenship

Arizona and Kansas require all voters to bring documents to the polls proving that they are American citizens (usually, an original birth certificate, naturalization papers, or a passport). Other states are debating similar laws. Supporters of these laws say they are needed to curb voting by non-citizens. Others claim that, as with voter ID laws, poor, disabled, and minority citizens have a harder time obtaining the required documents and could therefore have their access to the ballot taken away improperly.

State legislatures and counties often vote on other bills that would make it easier or harder to vote. These include laws allowing people to vote at malls and supermarkets, creating more or fewer precinct polling places,[33] and requiring or prohibiting the mailing of absentee ballot requests to all registered voters. In general, Democrats have been more favorable to these changes than Republicans have. It is often assumed (though not often proved) that less educated and lower-income people, who tend to identify as Democrats, would be more likely to cast a ballot if voting were less costly in time and effort.

Voter Intimidation

In some instances parties, candidates, and other groups have relied on the more straightforward techniques of voter intimidation that have stained American political history. One time-honored technique has been to station police cars near some polling places and warn prospective voters (falsely) that they could be arrested for unpaid parking tickets or child support if they cast a ballot. Another is for employers to pressure their employees to vote for certain candidates. Democrats were especially concerned about voter intimidation in 2016 when Donald Trump urged his supporters to "patrol" urban polling places and challenge voters who looked ineligible to them. An uptick in these incidents has led both parties to recruit large numbers of lawyers as poll watchers in recent elections.

Voting Systems: Are Votes Counted Fairly?

Once people have gotten to the polls, we assume that their choice of candidates will be registered accurately. That isn't always the case. Most Americans would probably be surprised to learn that U.S. elections are not highly ranked relative to those of other industrialized democracies on a wide range of criteria, from inaccurate voter lists to confusion over new voter ID requirements.[34] Some types of voting machines (such as punch card systems and electronic voting systems without a paper trail) are especially problematic.[35] Confusing ballot layouts can lead to trouble. The so-called butterfly ballot used in Palm Beach County, Florida, in 2000, led many voters to cast their ballot for a different candidate than they had intended. This was an especially worrisome issue in Florida, which tipped that year's national presidential race to George W. Bush by a margin of only 537 votes. Prospective voters in some areas—particularly large cities—continue to face lines at the polling place so long that would-be voters may give up in frustration.[36]

Why does this happen? Because elections are run by localities, voters in one county, even one polling place, may be treated differently from voters in another. Voters cast ballots at almost 700,000 voting machines in about 186,000 voting precincts across the nation. The precincts are tended by about a million poll workers who are typically poorly paid, lightly trained, partisan volunteers, supervised by local election officials often elected on partisan ballots.[37] Voter registration systems are still usually paper-based, resulting in recording errors, out-of-date information, and other inaccuracies.

In particular, counties differ in their ability to pay for the most reliable (and costly) voting systems. The result is that error-prone systems are more likely to be found in poorer and minority-dominated counties, which tend to vote Democratic. The U.S. Commission on Civil Rights reported in 2001 that although it found no evidence of a systematic effort to disenfranchise blacks, they were ten times more likely than whites to have their ballots undercounted or rejected because they lived in districts with less reliable voting systems.[38]

After media coverage of the problems with the 2000 vote, Congress passed the 2002 Help America Vote Act (HAVA) offering $3 billion to help states upgrade their voting systems, set minimum federal standards, and create computerized statewide voter registration rolls. Many counties used the money to buy electronic—touch-screen or direct-recording electronic (DRE)—voting machines. In 2006, over 80 percent of all voters used some form of e-voting, more than a third of them for the first time.

That produced new challenges. The e-voting systems raised issues familiar to anyone who has used a college computer lab: computer crashes, altered programming codes, and the possibility of hacking and rigged machines. The first cyberattack against an online election system was discovered in

Democracy on the Cheap: Is Every Vote Counted?

After almost two decades of concern about voting machines, problems remain:

- In 2016, hackers the FBI identified as Russian tried to steal voter registration rolls in Arizona and successfully breached voter data in Illinois, raising concern about the security of state voter lists just before the presidential election.
- In 2014, voters in Virginia Beach, Virginia, observed that when they selected one candidate, the machine would register their selection for a different candidate. Videos of this "vote flipping" went viral.
- In Palm Beach County, Florida, a voter arrived at the polls only to be told that she couldn't vote because she was dead. She begged to differ. She was given a provisional ballot which, poll workers said, would be counted later if she could prove to election officials that she was alive.
- The Washington DC Board of Elections and Ethics asked computer experts to probe an Internet-based voting system in 2010 to look for flaws. Within 48 hours, the experts had hacked and taken control of the site, including making it play the University of Michigan fight song each time a vote was cast.

As one expert put it, "We'd never tolerate this level of errors with an ATM. The problem is that we continue to do democracy on the cheap."

Sources: "Voting Equipment in the United States," 2014, at www.verifiedvoting.org (accessed June 22, 2016); Lawrence Norden and Christopher Famighetti, "America's Voting Machines at Risk," Brennan Center for Justice, NYU School of Law, 2015; Fernanda Santos, "In Arizona, Voters Demand: Why the Lines?" *New York Times*, March 25, 2016, p. A13.

2012, when a Miami-Dade County election website got 2,500 "phantom requests" for absentee ballots from a computer program.[39] If it had gone undetected, those votes could have been cast by the hacker. A Florida newspaper found that voters in counties using touch-screen machines were six times more likely to have their vote go unrecorded as were voters in counties using optical-scan devices, like those often used to grade multiple-choice exams.[40] Another issue was that HAVA granted the right to cast a "provisional" ballot to anyone whose eligibility to vote was challenged by an election official. But Congress set no uniform national standards as to which of these provisional ballots should be counted, which produced concerns about partisan and unequal treatment.

Studies show that at least a million registered voters have been prevented from casting their ballots in presidential elections because of administrative glitches: their names were accidentally purged from or not recorded properly on the registration rolls or they didn't bring the proper identification to the polls (see box "Democracy on the Cheap: Is Every Vote Counted?" on page 188). Solving many of these problems requires money. Even though accurate and reliable voting systems are vital to a democracy, cash-starved counties may decide not to devote the necessary resources to elections, which take place at most only once or twice a year, when they face daily demands to fund other crucial services, such as law enforcement, garbage collection, and road repair.

The Low Turnout in American Elections

In addition to enfranchising their supporters and passing laws making it easier for them to get to the polls, parties can also try to shape the electorate by mobilizing voters in a particular election. Judging from the relatively low turnout rates in American elections, it would seem that the two major parties are not doing this very effectively. Although turnout rates were higher in the late 1800s,[41] voter turnout in presidential elections never exceeded 60 percent between the 1970s and 2000.[42] Presidential turnout reached a recent high of 62 percent in the 2008 elections but dropped to 59 percent in 2016 (see Figure 8.2).[43]

By contrast, voters in Germany and Sweden regularly turn out at rates of 80 percent or more, and voter turnout in the most recent Swedish national elections in 2014 topped 83 percent. In the 2014 U.S. midterm election, turnout was only 36 percent, the lowest midterm voting rate in 70 years.

American voter turnout ought to have risen dramatically since the mid-1900s.[44] Educational levels have increased substantially, and higher education is linked with higher voter turnout. Liberalized registration, residence, and early voting rules have made it easier to cast a ballot. Of course, some types of people do vote at much higher rates than 60 percent, which gives their preferences greater weight in election results. After considering the reasons for the overall low turnout rates, this chapter will

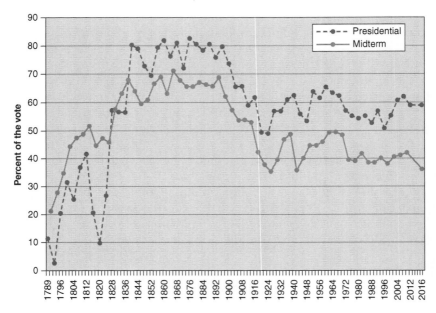

FIGURE 8.2 Turnout in American Elections, 1790–2016

Note: These are the percentages voting for president and for the office with the highest vote in midterm elections, calculated as described in Note 42 to this chapter. Data are from Walter Dean Burnham, "The Turnout Problem," in A. James Reichley, ed., Elections American Style (Washington, DC: Brookings Institution, 1987), pp. 113–114, updated for presidential elections since 1984 using http://elections.gmu.edu/voter_turnout.htm. Midterm data since 1986 come from Curtis Gans, Director of the Center for the Study of the American Electorate.

explore which groups are best represented at the polls and whether party efforts help make the electorate more representative of all citizens.

Social Group Differences in Turnout

We can think about the decision to vote in terms of its costs and benefits to the individual. Each of us pays some costs for voting, not in cash but in time, energy, and attention. What we get in return may seem minimal; the influence of a single vote in most elections is usually small. From that perspective, it may be remarkable that anyone votes at all.[45] A variety of economic and social forces, from citizens' levels of education to their social connections, affect the way individuals weigh the costs and benefits of voting. That in turn affects the parties' ability to mobilize different types of people.

Education

The biggest difference between voters and nonvoters is their level of education. Less educated Americans, who tend to identify as Democrats, are much less likely to vote[46] (see Figure 8.3, Section A). Because of the close relationships between education and income, financially insecure people also vote in lower proportions. More education helps people understand the political system and find the information they need to make political choices. More educated people are more likely to feel that they ought to vote, to gain satisfaction from voting, and to have the experience with meeting deadlines and filling out forms that will be necessary to register and vote.[47]

This relationship between education and voting sounds so obvious that we would expect to see it everywhere. Yet the relationship is weaker in many other democracies, where labor parties and other groups work to bring less-educated and lower-income people to the polls. In some nations, then, party mobilization drives can compensate for the dampening effect of lower educational levels on voter turnout.[48]

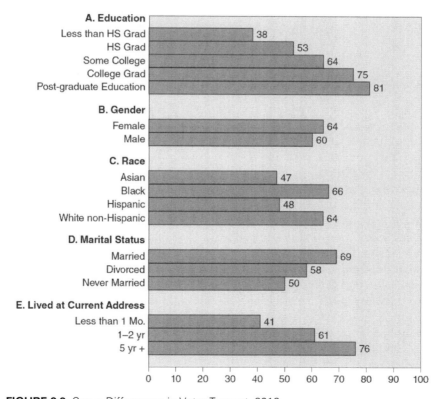

FIGURE 8.3 Group Differences in Voter Turnout, 2012

Note: Bars show the percentage of each group who reported having voted in the 2012 presidential election.

Source: U.S. Census Bureau data. Voting turnout data for 2016 will not be available until late 2017, when they will be posted in the online appendix to this book.

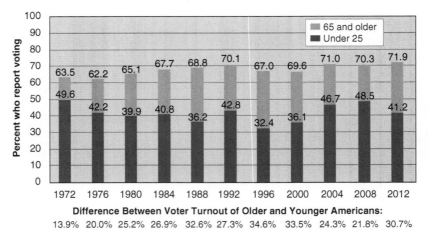

FIGURE 8.4 Voter Turnout of Younger and Older Americans, 1972–2012

Source: U.S. Census Bureau data. Turnout data for the 2016 election will not be available until late 2017, when they will be posted in the online appendix to this book.

Youth

Younger Americans, now disproportionately Democratic in their party ID, are much less likely to go to the polls than are older people (see Figure 8.4). Younger people are no less likely than their elders to take part in other community activities, such as volunteer work.[49] But their interest in service has not extended to include political service. In one survey, the only occupation young people (age 26 and under) rated less attractive than being an elected official was farming.[50] The age difference is especially clear in off-year congressional races. From 2012 to 2014, for instance, turnout share among those 30 and under dropped from 19 percent to a measly 13 percent.

Why does the lower turnout of young adults matter? There are some notable differences between younger people's and older people's attitudes. Current young adults, on average, are much more tolerant of interracial dating and same-sex marriage, much more ethnically and racially diverse, and much less negative about the impact of new immigrants on American society than their elders are.[51] When large numbers of young people don't vote, candidates pay greater attention to the issues that concern those who do vote. Social Security and Medicare rank high on the campaign agenda because older people, for whom these issues are important, have higher turnout rates than younger adults do.

Gender and Race

For many decades after getting the right to vote, women voted less often than men, but women's increasing education levels and changes in women's roles have largely eliminated this gender difference (see Figure 8.3, Section B). Black Americans now vote in proportions at least as high as whites (see Figure 8.3, Section C). Latino or Hispanic and Asian Americans have the lowest turnout rates. But as you can see in Figure 8.5, recent shifts in the U.S. population have made (non-Hispanic) whites a steadily decreasing proportion of those who turn out to vote. This trend should continue; the U.S. Census Bureau reports that in 2015 a majority of American children under age 5 are black or Hispanic, and that the population as a whole should be majority-minority by 2044.[52]

Social Connectedness

People who belong to several organizations and are closely connected with friends and family are much more likely to be mobilized to vote. Contact with politically knowledgeable people increases that likelihood.[53] Voting is also more common among those who are well integrated into the community through home ownership, long-time residence, church attendance, or a job outside the home. Even being married affects the likelihood that an individual will vote (see Figure 8.3, Sections D and E).[54]

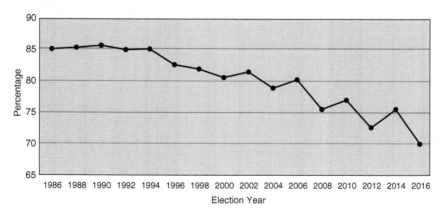

FIGURE 8.5 White (non-Hispanic) Voters as a Percentage of All Voters, 1986–2016

Source: U.S. Census Bureau data kindly provided by Michael P. McDonald at www. electproject.org/home/voter-turnout/demographics (accessed June 22, 2016).

Why Didn't You Vote?

Here's why people registered to vote said they didn't cast a ballot in 2014:

Too busy, conflicting schedule	28%
Not interested	16%
Sick or disabled	11%
Out of town	10%
I forgot	8%
Didn't like the candidates	8%
Registration problems (among registered citizens)	2%
Inconvenient polling place	2%
Transportation problems	2%
Bad weather	0.4%
Other, don't know	12%

Source: U.S. Census Bureau data, at Table 10, www.census.gov/hhes/www/socdemo/voting/publications/p20/2014/tables.html (accessed June 22, 2016).

Some forms of social connectedness have declined in recent decades. Americans are less inclined to attend religious services now and less likely to be married. These declines may counteract the effects of rising educational levels and liberalized registration rules, by weakening the social networks that stimulate voter participation.

Political Attitudes

Some civic attitudes predispose individuals to vote: feelings that government is responsive to citizens (**external political efficacy**) and can be trusted to do what is right (**trust in government**), and a sense of responsibility to take part in elections (**citizen duty**).[55] These civic attitudes have faded in recent decades. Many relatively well-informed, well-educated young people have become cynical about government and politics. More education and easier access to the vote, then, do not tempt them to become politically involved.[56] And the strength of people's partisanship also affects voting. When party ID weakened in the 1970s, turnout declined.[57]

The Impact of the Current Campaign

In addition to declines in civic attitudes and social connectedness, the characteristics of a particular election also help to explain variations in turnout.

The Excitement of the Election

Voter participation is typically highest in presidential elections and lowest in local races.[58] Presidential races are highly publicized and usually exciting. Because of the publicity, it will not take much effort for people to get information about the candidates, and because of the excitement of the race, they will probably pay more attention to the information they find. Both of these conditions reduce the costs of voting and increase its appeal.[59]

Close Competition

Hotly contested races bring voters to the polls. In addition to their excitement, competitive elections give voters more assurance that their vote will matter.[60] In fact, seeing a competitive campaign has long-term effects: It makes voters more interested and better informed about politics a year later.[61]

Party Efforts to Mobilize Voters

Party organizations must take all these forces into account when they try to get out the vote on Election Day. They know that the most effective means of mobilization is person-to-person contact.[62] Personal canvassing is especially useful in mobilizing first-time voters; most new voters say that they came to the polls because "my family or friends encouraged me to vote."[63]

Face-to-face voter mobilization had become less common in the 1900s. But during the past decade, the parties and several other groups have developed programs to increase turnout among their supporters. Civil rights groups have worked closely with the Democratic Party to bring more blacks to the polls. Organized labor mounts major GOTV drives built on union members' contacts with their friends and neighbors. Beginning in 2012, both party organizations have worked hard to inform voters about new state voter ID laws and limits on early voting. These mobilization drives seem to have helped increase turnout.[64]

Conventional wisdom says that because nonvoters tend to come from groups usually inclined to vote Democratic, such as lower-income and less-educated people, voter mobilization drives should help Democratic candidates. That is why proposals to make registering and voting easier are often assumed to benefit Democrats. It explains why organized labor spends so much money and effort on registration and GOTV campaigns.

Conventional wisdom is not always correct, however. As we have seen, close contests, dramatic conflicts, and exciting candidates can bring more people to the polls, and these conditions are not always generated by Democratic candidates. In fact, Republican presidential candidates have won most of the large-turnout elections in the past five decades.[65]

Do Party Efforts Diversify the Electorate?

Have these party mobilization drives helped to create an American electorate that more closely reflects the diversity of the American people? Or have they simply increased the representation of those already likely to vote?

Researchers find that parties and party activists tend to contact higher-income and older people more than they contact less wealthy and younger people, a tendency that has increased in recent elections.[66] College students change their addresses often, which makes it harder for party activists to find them. And both parties know that it is easier to activate those already predisposed to vote than it is to entice previous nonvoters to the polls.

As a result, most voter mobilization drives do relatively little to increase the turnout of groups that have had low voting rates over time. The most recent exception was the Obama campaign in 2008 and 2012. Its organizers set out to increase voter turnout because many of Obama's most likely supporters were a part of groups with traditionally low turnout. In addition to minority racial and ethnic groups, the campaign especially targeted young people who had recently become eligible to vote. Their work paid off. One pollster estimated that Obama won the vote of people under age 30 by a margin of about 8.3 million votes in 2008; Obama's overall margin in the popular vote was about 8 million.[67]

The Challenge to the Parties

One argument in favor of democracy is that the best decisions are made when the responsibility for decision making is most widely shared. If so, then we ought to strive for the widest possible participation in elections (see box "Which Would You Choose? We Need Every Vote ..." on page 197).[68] Yet we have seen that American voter participation lags behind that of most other democracies, and those whose voices are not heard at the polls tend to come from disadvantaged groups: young people, Asian and Latino Americans, and those with fewer economic resources and greater need for government help.

What responsibility do the parties bear for these low turnouts? Party organizations are among the main sponsors of voter mobilization drives. They have the capacity to recruit large and diverse groups of people into politics. But parties, like individuals, are self-interested; they want to stimulate turnout only among their likely supporters and to limit turnout by their likely opponents. And they find it easier to locate and contact people who have already joined the ranks of voters. In practice, then, the parties usually adjust their mobilization strategies to the electorate as it currently exists. They don't often work hard to attract new voting groups, especially the disadvantaged. The success of the Obama campaigns and the growing number of Latino and Asian Americans may change this pattern, however.

The fact that the active electorate in the U.S. is not as diverse as the nation's population probably reduces the amount of conflict in American politics and the range of political interests to which the parties must respond. Understandably, candidates and elected officials think more about the needs of those who take part in elections than those who don't. For example, studies show that members of Congress direct more federal spending to counties in their district with higher voter turnout than to those with lower turnout.[69] The cost, however, is that in the area of voter participation, the American parties have fallen short of fulfilling their democratic capabilities.

WHICH WOULD YOU CHOOSE?

We Need Every Vote …

Democracy is most vibrant when all views are heard. When as many people as possible take part in elections, government is more likely to come up with the creative solutions needed to solve problems.

Politicians pay more attention to the needs of those who vote than to those who don't. So the views and interests of the nonvoters, though real, may go unrepresented.

The most committed voters tend to be older, more educated, and more affluent than other citizens are. These people will get more than their fair share of government benefits and attention from elected officials anxious to get their votes.

It is the alienated and dissatisfied people who stay away from the polls. They can become ripe for extremist appeals. It's better to bring them into the political system where they can voice their concerns in more productive ways.

Let Sleeping Dogs Lie …

Those who are least likely to vote are also the least well informed and the least interested in government. Why should we encourage them to take part in elections? If they don't care enough or know enough to vote, shouldn't we be grateful that they stay home?

If people have the right to vote and choose not to, maybe this means they are satisfied with things as they are. If they really wanted change, they could use their votes to obtain it.

If we relax registration and residence requirements to encourage more people to vote, we're encouraging voting by people who don't care enough to register at the proper time.

American democracy has been strong enough to survive impeachments, scandals, and candidates who lose the presidency even though they won the popular vote. If it ain't broke, why fix it?

Notes

1   See John H. Aldrich, "Did Hamilton, Jefferson, and Madison 'Cause' the U.S. Government Shutdown?" *Perspectives on Politics* 13 (2015): 7–23.

2   See Pippa Norris, *Electoral Engineering* (Cambridge: Cambridge University Press, 2004).

3   The term "suffrage" means the right to vote. See Alexander Keyssar, *The Right to Vote* (Boulder, CO: Basic Books, 2009).

4   James McGregor Burns and Susan Dunn, *The Three Roosevelts* (New York: Atlantic Monthly Press, 2001), p. 23.

5   Ticket splitting at the local level did occur prior to the secret ballot; see Alan Ware, *The Democratic Party Heads North, 1877–1962* (Cambridge: Cambridge University Press, 2006), p. 21.

6   Stephen M. Nichols and Gregory A. Strizek, "Electronic Voting Machines and Ballot Roll-off," *American Politics Quarterly* 23 (1995): 300–318.

7   Paul Kleppner, *Continuity and Change in Electoral Politics, 1893–1928* (Westport, CT: Greenwood, 1987), pp. 165–166.

8   Peverill Squire, Raymond E. Wolfinger, and David P. Glass, "Residential Mobility and Voter Turnout," *American Political Science Review* 81 (1987): 45–65.

9   Walter Dean Burnham, "Theory and Voting Research," *American Political Science Review* 68 (1974): 1002–1023.

10   The Supreme Court finally ended the white primary in *Smith v. Allwright* (1944).

11   Pat Watters and Reese Cleghorn, *Climbing Jacob's Ladder* (New York: Harcourt Brace Jovanovich, 1967), pp. 122–123.

12   See V. O. Key, Jr., *Southern Politics in State and Nation* (New York: Knopf, 1949).

13   Chandler Davidson and Bernard Grofman, eds., *Quiet Revolution in the South* (Princeton, NJ: Princeton University Press, 1994).

14   The landmark Supreme Court cases are *Baker v. Carr* (1962); *Reynolds v. Sims* (1964); and *Wesberry v. Sanders* (1964).

15   The Supreme Court declined to ban partisan gerrymandering most recently in the case of *Vieth v. Jubelirer* (2004).

16   See Bernard L. Fraga, "Redistricting and the Causal Impact of Race on Voter Turnout," *Journal of Politics* 78 (2016): 19–34.

17   Thomas B. Edsall, "Parties Play Voting Rights Role Reversal," *Washington Post*, February 25, 2001, p. A1. See also Kevin A. Hill, "Does the Creation of Majority Black Districts Aid Republicans?" *Journal of Politics* 57 (1995): 384–401.

18   The cases are *Miller v. Johnson* (1995) and *Easley v. Cromartie* (2001), respectively. On majority-minority districts, see David T. Canon, *Race, Redistricting, and Representation* (Chicago: University of Chicago Press, 1999).

19   See Paul R. Abramson, John H. Aldrich, Brad T. Gomez, and David W. Rohde, *Change and Continuity in the 2012 Elections* (Los Angeles: Sage, 2015), pp. 88–89.

20   See Robert L. Dudley and Alan R. Gitelson, *American Elections: The Rules Matter* (New York: Longman, 2002), pp. 7–15.

21 See Benjamin Highton and Raymond E. Wolfinger, "Estimating the Effects of the National Voter Registration Act of 1993," *Political Behavior* 20 (1998): 79–104.

22 Nathaniel Persily, testimony before the U.S. Senate Committee on Rules and Administration, March 11, 2009.

23 Raymond E. Wolfinger and Jonathan Hoffman, "Registering and Voting with Motor Voter," *PS: Political Science and Politics* 34 (2001): 85–92; and Michael D. Martinez and David Hill, "Did Motor Voter Work?" *American Politics Quarterly* 27 (1999): 296–315.

24 See the symposium "Voter Identification," *PS: Political Science & Politics* 42 (2009): 81–130. The case is *Crawford v. Marion County Election Board* (2008).

25 On states' voting requirements, see Wendy Underhill, "Voter Identification Requirements/Voter ID Laws," National Conference of State Legislatures, January 4, 2016, at ncsl.org.

26 Keith G. Bentele and Erin E. O'Brien, "Jim Crow 2.0? Why States Consider and Adopt Restrictive Voter Access Policies," *Perspectives on Politics* 11 (2013): 1088–1116.

27 John Alquist, Kenneth Mayer, and Simon Jackman, "Alien Abduction and Voter Impersonation in the 2012 US General Election," *Election Law Journal* 13 (#4, 2014): 460–475.

28 See Bentele and O'Brien, "Jim Crow 2.0?"

29 Lonna Rae Atkeson, Lisa Ann Bryant, Thad E. Hall, Kyle Saunders, and Michael Alvarez, "A New Barrier to Participation," *Electoral Studies* 29 (2010): 66–73, and Ariel R. White, Noah L. Nathan, and Julie K. Faller, "What Do I Need to Vote?" *American Political Science Review* 109 (2015): 129–142.

30 Matt Apuzzo, "Students Joining Battle to Upend Laws on Voter ID," *New York Times*, July 6, 2014, p. A1. In 2011, the Texas legislature, for example, voted that licenses to carry concealed handguns, but not student university ID cards, are a valid form of voter ID.

31 The U.S. Government Accountability Office reported ("Elections: Issues Related to State Voter Identification Laws," October 8, 2014, at www.gao.gov/products/GAO-14-634, accessed June 22, 2016) that new voter ID laws in Tennessee and Kansas caused decreases in turnout, especially among blacks and young people.

32 Vanessa Williams, "Congressional Democrats Launch Campaign to Rally Public Support for Voting Rights Protections," *Washington Post*, November 4, 2015, p. A1.

33 Henry E. Brady and John E. McNulty, "Turning Out to Vote," *American Political Science Review* 105 (2011): 115–134.

34 On the problems with American elections, see Pippa Norris, *Why Elections Fail* (New York: Cambridge University Press, 2015).

35 See Justin Buchler, Matthew Jarvis, and John E. McNulty, "Punch Card Technology and the Racial Gap in Residual Votes," *Perspectives on Politics* 2 (2004): 517–524.

36 See Fernanda Santos, "In Arizona, Voters Demand: Why the Lines?" *New York Times*, March 25, 2016, p. A13.

37 David C. Kimball and Martha Kropf, "The Street-Level Bureaucrats of Elections," *Review of Policy Research* 23 (2006): 1257–1268.

38 See Michael Tomz and Robert P. Van Houweling, "How Does Voting Equipment Affect the Racial Gap in Voided Ballots?" *American Journal of Political Science* 47 (2003): 46–60.

39 Gil Aegerter, "Cyberattack on Florida Election Is First Known Case in US, Experts Say," NBC News, March 18, 2013, at http://openchannel.nbcnews. com/_news/2013/03/18/17314818-cyberattack-on-florida-election-is-first-known-case-in-us-experts-say?lite (accessed June 22, 2016).

40 Abby Goodnough, "Lost Record of Vote in '02 Florida Race Raises '04 Concern," *New York Times*, July 28, 2004, p. 1.

41 Walter Dean Burnham, "The Changing Shape of the American Political Universe," *American Political Science Review* 59 (1965): 7–28.

42 Because of the difficulties in estimating American turnout, many "official" turnout figures *underestimate* it. The percentages here and in Figure 8.2 correct for this underestimation. Their denominator is an effort to estimate the *eligible* population: the voting-age population minus the number of noncitizens living in the United States. The numerator of the turnout fraction is the number of voters who cast a vote for president or for the office with the highest vote in midterm elections. See Walter Dean Burnham, "The Turnout Problem," in A. James Reichley, ed., *Elections American Style* (Washington, DC: Brookings, 1987), pp. 97–133; and Michael McDonald, "United States Elections Project," at www. electproject.org/home/voter-turnout/voter-turnout-data (accessed June 22, 2016).

43 Unless otherwise indicated, turnout figures are those of Michael McDonald (see note 42).

44 Richard A. Brody, "The Puzzle of Participation in America," in Anthony King, ed., *The New American Political System* (Washington, DC: American Enterprise Institute, 1978), pp. 287–324.

45 See John H. Aldrich, "Rational Choice and Turnout," *American Journal of Political Science* 37 (1993): 246–278.

46 Rachel Milstein Sondheimer and Donald P. Green, "Using Experiments to Estimate the Effects of Education on Voter Turnout," *American Journal of Political Science* 54 (2010): 174–189; and Robert A. Jackson, "Clarifying the Relationship between Education and Turnout," *American Politics Quarterly* 23 (1995): 279–299.

47 See Rebecca B. Morton, *Analyzing Elections* (New York: Norton, 2006), pp. 53–55.

48 See Sidney Verba, Norman H. Nie, and Jae-On Kim, *Participation and Political Equality* (Cambridge: Cambridge University Press, 1978).

49 Cliff Zukin, Scott Keeter, Molly Andolina, Krista Jenkins, and Michael X. Delli Carpini, *A New Engagement?* (Oxford: Oxford University Press, 2006).

50 Karl T. Kurz, Alan Rosenthal, and Cliff Zukin, "Citizenship: A Challenge for All Generations," 2003, at www.ncsl.org/Portals/1/documents/public/trust/citizenship.pdf (accessed June 22, 2016).

51 Pew Research Center, "Partisan Polarization Surges in Bush, Obama Years," June 4, 2012, at www.people-press.org/2012/06/04/partisan-polarization-surges-in-bush-obama-years (accessed June 22, 2016).

52 D'Vera Cohn, "It's Official: Minority Babies Are the Majority Among the Nation's Infants, But Only Just," Pew Research Center, June 23, 2016, at www.

pewresearch.org/fact-tank/2016/06/23/its-official-minority-babies-are-the-majority-among-the-nations-infants-but-only-just (accessed June 23, 2016).

53 Scott D. McClurg, "The Electoral Relevance of Political Talk," *American Journal of Political Science* 50 (2006): 737–754.

54 Nancy Burns, Kay Lehman Schlozman, and Sidney Verba, "The Public Consequences of Private Inequality," *American Political Science Review* 91 (1997): 373–389.

55 See Steven J. Rosenstone and John Mark Hansen, *Mobilization, Participation, and Democracy in America* (New York: Longman, 2003), pp. 141–156.

56 Lyn Ragsdale and Jerrold G. Rusk, "Who Are Nonvoters?" *American Journal of Political Science* 37 (1993): 721–746.

57 Paul R. Abramson, John H. Aldrich, and David W. Rohde, *Change and Continuity in the 2004 and 2006 Elections* (Washington, DC: CQ Press, 2007), p. 97.

58 Robert A. Jackson, "The Mobilization of U.S. State Electorates in the 1988 and 1990 Elections," *Journal of Politics* 59 (1997): 520–537.

59 See Danny Hayes and Jennifer L. Lawless, "As Local News Goes, So Does Citizen Engagement," *Journal of Politics* 77 (2015): 447–462.

60 Cindy D. Kam and Stephen M. Utych, "Close Elections and Cognitive Engagement," *Journal of Politics* 73 (2011): 1251–1266.

61 Heather K. Evans, Michael J. Ensley, and Edward G. Carmines, "The Enduring Effects of Competitive Elections," *Journal of Elections, Public Opinion and Parties* 24 (2014): 455–472.

62 See Donald P. Green and Alan S. Gerber, *Get Out the Vote!* (Washington, DC: Brookings Institution, 2004); and Kevin Arceneaux and David W. Nickerson, "Who Is Mobilized to Vote?" *American Journal of Political Science* 53 (2009): 1–16.

63 Thomas Patterson, press release from the Vanishing Voter Project, John F. Kennedy School of Government, Harvard University, November 11, 2004.

64 See Jan E. Leighley and Jonathan Nagler, "Unions, Voter Turnout, and Class Bias in the U.S. Electorate," *Journal of Politics* 69 (2007): 430–441.

65 Jack Citrin, Eric Schickler, and John Sides, "What If Everyone Voted?" *American Journal of Political Science* 47 (2003): 75–90.

66 Ryan D. Enos, Anthony Fowler, and Lynn Vavreck, "Increasing Inequality," *Journal of Politics* 76 (2014), and David W. Nickerson, "Do Voter Registration Drives Increase Participation?" *Journal of Politics* 77 (2015): 88–101; but see Paul A. Beck and Erik Heidemann, "The Ground Game from the Voter's Perspective," in John C. Green, Daniel J. Coffey, and David B. Cohen, eds., *The State of the Parties*, 7th ed. (Lanham, MD: Rowman & Littlefield, 2014), pp. 251–269.

67 Adriel Bettelheim, "Youth's Long-Term Role in Politics," *CQ Weekly*, November 10, 2008, p. 2973.

68 APSA Task Force Report, "American Democracy in an Age of Rising Inequality," *Perspectives on Politics* 2 (2004): 658.

69 Paul S. Martin, "Voting's Rewards," *American Journal of Political Science* 47 (2003): 110–127. More broadly, see William W. Franko, Nathan J. Kelly, and Christopher Witko, "Class Bias in Voter Turnout, Representation, and Income Inequality," *Perspectives on Politics* 14 (2016): 351–368.

PART FOUR

Parties, Nominations, and Elections

Even though the party organization, party candidates, and their party identifiers don't always march to the same drummer, it seems likely that they will try to pull together at election time, because they can all benefit by doing so. When candidates run more effective campaigns, they improve not only their own ability to attract money and other resources but also that of their party organization. When candidates are elected, their party's activists and identifiers are more likely to see action on the issues that draw them to the party. When a party's identifiers feel enthusiastic about its candidates, they may be more inclined to contribute to the party organization and to bring their friends to the polls to support the whole party slate.

All this cooperation does not come easily, however. Almost every aspect of elections can pit the needs of one part of the party against those of another. When primaries are used to select a party's candidates, at times party voters will choose a nominee who is regarded as a disaster by party leaders. Only a month after Republican voters selected Donald Trump as their presidential candidate in 2016, for instance, some Republican consultants advised vulnerable Senate candidates to improve their chances by telling voters that because Trump was destined to lose, voters should elect a Republican Senate to balance the incoming Democratic president! Candidates want to choose which issues they will emphasize; these choices affect the image of the party as a whole, even when the party's leaders and activists do not share these preferences. Once in office, the party's candidates may feel the need to ignore or downplay some questions that are "hot button" issues to party activists. Efforts by the party organization to raise money will compete with its candidates' own fund-raising.

In addition to this competition within each party, the parties also compete on the larger electoral stage. Groups such as super PACs, labor unions, religious lobbies, insurance companies, and other corporations involve themselves in campaigns, sometimes very aggressively, to achieve their political goals. Democratic Party leaders, for example, will probably compete as well as cooperate with environmental, women's rights, and civil rights groups, and unions representing trial lawyers and government

203

employees for the attention of a Democratic candidate. This competition and cooperation is guided by a set of rules, ranging from laws to standard practices. These rules include the widespread use of primary elections, laws governing campaign fund-raising, big shifts in the media environment, and rapid advances in the micro-targeting technology used to reach specific types of voters.

The first two chapters in this section focus on parties' involvement in nominating candidates. Chapter 9 explores the nomination process in general, and Chapter 10 considers the fascinating and unusual practices with which the American major parties select their presidential candidates. In Chapter 11, we turn to the role of parties in general elections. Chapter 12 traces the flow of money into campaigns and considers how it can both expand and limit the influence of parties on their candidates.

CHAPTER 9

How Parties Choose Candidates

In most democratic nations, party leaders or the party in government select their party's candidates. Not in the U.S. People who want their party's nomination for most American elective offices, including the presidency (see Chapter 10), must first run in a primary election (more formally known as a **direct primary**). A primary is a contest in which the party's identifiers—the party in the electorate—are invited to choose which candidates will run for office under the party's label. Then, in a later **general election**, all voters can choose between the parties' nominees for each office. Although a number of democracies have been moving toward selecting their leaders in more inclusive ways, most democratic systems don't let voters tell the party organization who its candidates will be.[1]

The extensive use of primaries has changed the American parties' relationships with their candidates. It limits party organizations' ability to hold elected officials accountable. It lengthens campaigns and increases their costs. In areas where one party dominates, the real choice of elected officials will be made in the primary. Primaries also demand a great deal of the voting public. In addition to having to vote on two different occasions to elect someone to the same public office, primaries ask citizens to forsake their reliance on party identification—the main device people use to choose candidates—because in a party primary, all the candidates share the same party ID. What led to the use of this unusual, two-step election process? How does it work, and how well does it serve the needs of voters, candidates, and parties?

How the Nomination Process Evolved

For the first 110 years of the American republic, candidates for office were nominated by party caucuses and later by party conventions. In both cases, it was the leaders and activists of the party organizations who chose the party's nominees, not the rest of the voting public.

Nominations by Caucus

In the early years, as the parties built local organizations, they held local party meetings, called caucuses, to choose candidates for county offices. Caucuses of like-minded partisans in Congress continued to nominate presidential and vice-presidential candidates. Similar party caucuses in state legislatures chose candidates for governor and other statewide offices. These caucuses were generally informal, and they did not necessarily include all the major figures of the party.[2]

Nominations by Convention

As pressure for popular democracy spread, the caucuses came to be seen as an aristocratic elite—"King Caucus"—that ignored public opinion. In 1831, a minor party called the Anti-Masons held a national convention to nominate its presidential candidate, hoping to get enough press attention to gain major party status. The Jacksonian Democrats held their own convention in time for the 1832 election. From then on, through the rest of the 1800s, conventions were the main means of nominating presidential candidates. These conventions were composed of delegates chosen by state and local party leaders, often at their own lower-level nominating conventions.

These large and chaotic conventions looked more broadly representative than the caucuses but often were not. Party leaders chose the delegates and managed the conventions. Reformers denounced the convention system as yet another form of boss rule. By the end of the 1800s, the Progressive movement led the drive for a new way of nominating candidates.[3]

Nominations by Direct Primaries

The Progressives argued that voters should be able to directly select their party's candidates for each office; party leaders (who at that time included the "bosses" of the urban party machines) should not have that power. This direct, primary (meaning "first") election reflected the Progressives' core belief that the best way to cure a democracy's ills was to prescribe larger doses of democracy. Robert M. La Follette, a Progressive leader, wrote that in a primary, "The nomination of the party will not be the result of 'compromise' or impulse, or evil design [as he felt it was in a party-run caucus/convention system] ... but the candidates of the majority, honestly and fairly nominated."[4]

Some southern states had already used primaries in local elections after the Civil War, to legitimize the nominees and settle internal disputes in their one-party Democratic systems. In the first two decades of the 1900s, all but four other states adopted primaries for at least some of their statewide nominations. This was a time when one party or the other dominated the politics of many states—the most pervasive one-party rule in American history. It might be possible to tolerate the poor choices made by conventions when voters have a real choice in the general election, but when the nominees of the dominant party had no serious competition, those shortcomings were harder to accept. So the Progressives, who fought economic monopoly with antitrust legislation, used the direct primary as a weapon against political monopoly.

Although the primary was designed to democratize the nominating process, many of its supporters hoped that it would have the further effect of crippling the political parties. Primaries would take away the party organization's most important power—the nomination of candidates—and give it instead to party voters. In fact, some states, such as Wisconsin, adopted a definition of the party electorate so broad that it included any voters who chose to vote in the party's primary.

Primaries were not the first cause of party weakness in the United States. If party leaders had been strong enough throughout the country when primaries were proposed, then they would have been able to stop the spread of this reform and keep control of the nominations themselves. But primaries did undermine the party organizations' power even further. Elected officials who were nominated by the voters in primaries were unlikely to feel as loyal to the party organization as were officials who owed their nominations to party leaders. Because of the existence of primaries, party leaders in the United States have less control over who will receive the party nomination than in most other democracies. In some states, the reforms required that even the party organization's own leaders be chosen in primaries, so the parties risked losing control over their own internal affairs.

On the other hand, as some parties in other democracies are learning, giving larger numbers of partisans a chance to select their nominee can also give the party a lot of information about who those partisans are, what they want, and where they can be found. Voters in a general election don't have to declare their party preference, but voters in most primaries do; this provides party organizations with a list of their supporters. Primaries also provide the party's workers with practical training in campaigning in advance of the general election—a valuable benefit especially for the weaker party in a nation.[5]

The Current Mix of Primaries and Conventions

Although conventions are no longer common, they are still used most visibly in the contest for the presidency as well as to nominate candidates in a few states. Because states have the legal right to design their own nominating systems, the result is a mixture of primaries and conventions for choosing candidates for state offices.

Every state now uses primaries to nominate at least some statewide officials, and most states use this method exclusively.[6] In four southern states, the party may choose to hold a convention instead of a primary, but only in Virginia has the convention option been used recently, typically when activists with more extreme views hope to win the nomination for their preferred candidate. Other states use conventions to screen candidates for the primary ballot.[7] This variety of choices reminds us again that, in spite of the national parties' growing strength, the state and local parties still make a lot of important decisions on their own.

Types of Primaries

Primaries come in many different forms, based on who is allowed to vote in them.[8] In states with so-called closed primaries, only voters who have formally declared their affiliation with a party can participate. This makes it easier for party activists and identifiers to keep their party's choice of nominees in their own hands. Voters in states with "open" primaries have more freedom to choose which party's primary they want to vote in. And in a few states, Democratic and Republican candidates for state and local offices all run on the same primary ballot, so a voter can select some candidates of each party.

Closed Primaries

Eleven states hold a fully **closed primary**, in which voters have to register as a Democrat or a Republican prior to the election.[9] When they come to vote, they receive the primary ballot of only their own party. If they want to vote in the other party's primary, they must formally change their party affiliation on the registration rolls before the primary. States with traditionally strong party organizations, such as New York and Pennsylvania, are among those that have been able to keep their primaries fully closed.

In many other states, whose primaries are often called *hybrid*, or *semiclosed* and *semiopen*, voters can change their party registration when they come to vote, or they can simply declare their party preference at the polling place. They are then given their declared party's ballot and, in a few of these states, are considered to be enrolled in that party. This allows independents and even the other party's identifiers to become "partisans for a day" and vote in a party's primary. From the point of view of the voter, these primaries are not very different from an open primary. The difference is important from the party's perspective, however, because in many semiclosed primaries there is a written record of party registration that can then be used by party organizations to target appeals to the people who claim to support them.

Open Primaries

Citizens of most of the remaining states can vote in the primary of their choice without having to state publicly which party they favor.[10] In **open primaries,** voters receive either a consolidated ballot or ballots for every party, and they select the party of their choice in the privacy of the voting booth. They can vote in only one party's primary in a given election. Many of these states have histories of Progressive strength, such as Wisconsin and Minnesota.

Blanket Primaries

The state of Washington adopted the **blanket primary** in 1935. It gives voters even greater freedom. The names of candidates from all parties appear on a single ballot in the primary, just as they do in the general election, so that in contrast to an open primary, a voter can choose a Democrat for one office and a Republican for another. Alaska's Democrats adopted the blanket primary for a time as well.

California voters approved an initiative in 1996 to hold a blanket primary. Proponents said it would bring more voters to the polls and encourage the choice of more moderate candidates.[11] Party leaders saw it differently. They claimed that the plan prevented the party's loyal supporters from choosing the candidates who best represented their views. That, they said, violated their First Amendment right to freedom of association and kept the party from offering a clear and consistent message to the voters. In 2000, the U.S. Supreme Court sided with the parties and gave the right to decide who votes in a primary, at least in California, back to the party organizations.[12]

"Top Two" Primaries In 2008, Washington moved to a type of blanket primary called a top two (or nonpartisan) system. Like a blanket primary, all candidates' names appear on the same ballot. Unlike a blanket primary, the top two vote getters for each office, regardless of party, advance to the general election. The party organization can still endorse a candidate, but if voters prefer (and they often do), they can select two Democrats, or two Republicans, to run against one another in the general election. California voters adopted a similar system two years later. The purpose of the change was to force candidates to appeal to all voters, not just to the extremes of their own party. Observers disagree on whether the top two system has succeeded in producing more moderate candidates, but it didn't increase voter participation, and elections in 2014 showed that it reduced the number of minor party candidates.

Louisiana uses a version of this system for state and local elections: If one candidate for an office wins more than 50 percent of the votes in the nonpartisan primary, he or she is elected to that office immediately. If no candidate for the office wins an outright majority in the primary, then the two top candidates (again, regardless of party) face one another in a runoff. Not surprisingly, the major parties oppose the use of a nonpartisan or top two system and prohibit states from adopting it in their presidential primaries.

When states shift from one type of primary to another, it is usually because state party leaders are trying to protect their party's interests in the nominating process under changing political conditions. In some cases, a state party has attempted to attract independent voters by switching to an open primary. In others, party leaders have urged the legislature to adopt new primary rules that would advantage candidates the party leaders favor in a particular election year. Sometimes, change has been prompted by nonparty or antiparty groups, as happened in California.

Why Does the Type of Primary Matter?

These varieties of primaries represent different answers to a long-standing debate: Is democracy better served by competition between strong and disciplined parties or by a system in which parties have relatively little power? The closed primary reflects the belief that citizens benefit from having clear choices in elections, which can best be provided by strong, internally unified parties; therefore, it makes sense for a party's candidates to be selected by that party's loyal followers. In contrast, open and blanket primaries are based on the view that rigid party loyalties can harm a democracy, so candidates should be chosen by all voters, regardless of party.

Most party organizations prefer the closed primary in which voters must register by party before the primary. It pays greater respect to the party's right to select its candidates. Prior party registration also gives the parties a bonus—published lists of their partisans. Further, the closed primary limits the greatest dangers of open and blanket primaries, at least from the perspective of party leaders: crossing over and raiding. Both terms refer to people who vote in the primary of a party that they do not generally support. They differ in the voter's intent. Voters **cross over** in order to take part in a more exciting race or to vote for a more appealing candidate in the other party. **Raiding** is a conscious effort to weaken the other party by voting for its least attractive candidates.

Crossing over is common in open primaries. Partisans rarely cross over in off-year gubernatorial primaries because that would keep them from having a voice in other state and local-level party contests. But independents and partisans are more likely to cross over in a presidential primary, especially when there is no competition in their preferred party's contest. In Vermont's 2012 presidential primary, for example, President Obama was unopposed in the Democratic primary, so as many Democrats and independents voted in the open Republican primary as Republicans did. These crossover voters often support a different candidate than the party's partisans do. In the Vermont Republican primary, libertarian Ron Paul came in second to Mitt

Romney largely because he received the plurality of votes of independents and crossover Democrats.

Candidates, then, take the type of primary into account in building their campaign strategies. Those in the mainstream of their party put a lot of their effort into closed primaries, such as New York's, where voters must be registered with that party in order to vote in its primary; candidates with a more independent stance often emphasize states with open or hybrid primaries, where independents can vote for them. In 2016, for example (see Figure 9.1), Hillary Clinton's opponent for the Democratic presidential nomination, Sen. Bernie Sanders, had more support among independents than among registered Democrats. Understandably, then, Sanders worked especially hard in open- and semiclosed primary states, such as New Hampshire, where his independent supporters could vote. Candidates outside of their party's mainstream may even encourage crossovers in these open primaries by discussing issues that appeal to the other party's voters.[13]

Organized raiding would be a bigger problem. Party leaders dread the possibility that opponents will make mischief by voting in the party's primary for the least appealing candidate. Studies of open primaries have

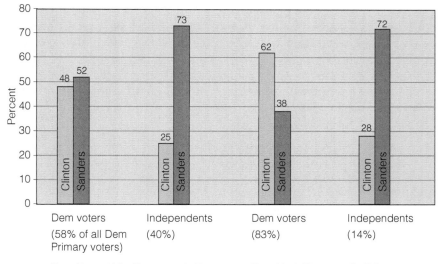

FIGURE 9.1 Voting in Open Primaries Differs from Closed Primaries: Hillary Clinton vs. Bernie Sanders, 2016

Note: Bars show the percentage of Democratic and independent voters in New Hampshire's Democratic primary, in which independents can vote, and New York's closed Democratic primary who cast a ballot for Hillary Clinton and Bernie Sanders.

* But 14 percent of the registered Democratic voters in the primary told exit pollsters that they now consider themselves independents.

Source: Exit polls at cnn.com/election/primaries/polls/ (accessed June 23, 2016).

found little evidence of raiding, however. Voters usually cross over to vote for their real preferences rather than to weaken the party in whose primary they are participating.[14]

How Candidates Qualify

States also vary in the ease with which candidates can get their names on the primary ballot and in the support required to win the nomination.

How Do Candidates Get on the Ballot?

In most states, candidates get on the primary ballot by filing a petition. State election laws specify how many signatures the petition has to contain— either a specific number or a percentage of the vote for the office in the last election.[15] States vary a lot in the difficulty of this step. Some have complicated rules requiring a lot of signatures, designed to favor party insiders. In other states, a candidate needs only to appear before the clerk of elections and pay a small fee. A few states even put presidential candidates on the ballot if they are "generally recognized" to be running.

These simple rules have consequences for the parties. The easier it is for candidates to get on the ballot, the more likely it becomes that dissident, or even crackpot, candidates will enter a race and engage the party's preferred candidates in costly primary battles. In states with easy ballot access, citizens can be treated to grudge campaigns, in which people file to oppose the sheriff who arrested them, for instance, or who simply enjoy the thought of wreaking havoc in a primary.

Runoffs: When Too Many Candidates Get on the Ballot

What if the leading candidate in a primary gets less than a majority of the votes? In most states' primaries, a plurality is enough. Almost all the southern and border states, however, hold a runoff between the top two candidates if one candidate does not win at least 40 or 50 percent of the vote. During the long period of one-party Democratic rule of the South, Democratic factionalism often produced three, four, or five serious candidates for a single office in a primary. The runoff was used to ensure a majority winner in order to present a unified face to the electorate and to ward off any challenges in the general election from blacks and other Republicans.

The southern runoff primary has long been controversial. Citing instances in which black candidates who received a plurality in the first primary lost to whites in the runoff, recent studies show that runoffs disadvantage minority groups.[16]

What Parties Don't Like About Primaries

The Progressives designed the direct primary to break the party organization's monopoly control of nominations. In important ways, it did. In the process, it challenged parties' effectiveness in elections more generally.

Difficulties in Recruiting Candidates

Candidate recruitment has never been an easy job, especially for the minority party. The direct primary makes the challenge even more difficult. If an ambitious candidate can challenge the party favorite in the dominant party's primary, he or she is less likely to consider running for office under the minority party's label. So, some argue, the minority party will find it even harder to recruit good candidates for races that it is not likely to win. Little by little, the majority party becomes the only viable road to success, and the minority party atrophies.[17]

This argument should not be taken too far. One-party politics declined after primaries became more common. And even in areas dominated by one party, the internal competition promoted by primaries can keep officeholders responsive to their constituents.[18] Nevertheless, the fact that party organizations cannot guarantee the outcome of their own primaries means that they have less to offer the candidates they are trying to recruit.

The Risk of Unappealing Nominees

Normally, only about half as many voters turn out for a primary as for a general election.[19] If this smaller group of primary voters is not representative of those who will vote later, then it may select a candidate who, because of his or her issue stands or background, may not appeal to the broader turnout in the general election. Imagine the discomfort of Democratic Party leaders in southern California, for instance, when a former official of the Ku Klux Klan captured the Democratic congressional nomination in a multicandidate primary race. In particular, some primary voters might be tempted to choose a candidate who is more extreme than the electorate as a whole, and as a result is less likely to win the general election.[20]

Another reason why primary voters might choose a weak candidate is that in a race in which all the candidates are of the same party, voters cannot use their party identification to select candidates, and many voters will not have any other relevant information available. They may choose a candidate because his or her name is familiar or may simply vote for the first name listed on the ballot (see box "Even His Mother Didn't Know He Was Running" on page 214). If a party convention chose the nominees, it is often argued, convention delegates would know the prospective candidates better, so they would not be prone to these misjudgments.

Even His Mother Didn't Know He Was Running

Robert Gray is a long-haul truck driver who lives in a small town in Mississippi. He decided to run for governor in 2015, though he cited no particular issues as having prompted him to run. He recruited a campaign staff of two, one of whom was his sister. He didn't actually campaign, because he hated to interrupt whatever people were doing. He had no money to spend on ads or canvassing or rallies or yard signs. On Election Day, he didn't get around to voting because his rig needed a lot of work. (His mother did vote for him, though she hadn't known about his candidacy until the election.)

So who won the Democratic nomination for governor? Robert Gray. He beat two other candidates. Immediately after his victory, he "gave some interviews and then set off with a truck full of sweet potatoes for a potato chip factory in Pennsylvania."

When we imagine a gubernatorial campaign, we don't usually think of people like Robert Gray. How did he manage to win his party's nomination? As the executive director of the state's Democratic Party summed it up, "He was the first name on the ballot, and he was a man." (His opponents were both female.) The governor's race was not a major priority for Mississippi Democrats, the primary campaign was very low-key, and voters had little or no information about the candidates. In such circumstances, it is not unusual for the candidate listed first on the ballot to get at least a small advantage in the vote totals. The reason is not obvious, but it may be that in the absence of relevant information, a small proportion of voters weigh more heavily the first choice they are given—an interesting challenge to the democratic process, not to mention a good indicator of the weakness of the Democratic Party in the South.

Sources: Campbell Robertson, "Chosen by Mississippi Democrats, Shy Trucker Is at a Crossroad," *New York Times*, September 8, 2015, p. A1 (from which the quote is drawn); Jonathan G. S. Koppell and Jennifer A. Steen, "The Effects of Ballot Position on Election Outcomes," *Journal of Politics* 66 (2004): 267–281.

Divisive Primaries

When parties hold primaries, their internal conflict becomes public. In some cases, activists who had campaigned for the candidate who lost the primary may sit out the general election rather than work for their party's nominee. Supporters of Hillary Clinton during the Democratic presidential primaries in 2008, indignant when she lost the nomination to Barack Obama, were less likely to vote for Obama in the general election than were those who had supported Obama in the primaries.[21] If Obama's general election race had been close, the loss of these Clinton supporters could have been decisive. The charges raised by a candidate's primary opponent are often reused by the opposition in the general election, a source of free campaign help to the other party. In 2016, some of Clinton's most hard-hitting campaign ads against Donald Trump featured attacks on Trump by his primary opponents and other Republicans. If a divisive primary is expensive, it may eat up much of the money the primary winner needs to run an effective campaign in the general election.

A divisive primary could be especially damaging if the losing candidate refuses to take "no" for an answer and runs in the general election anyway, as an independent or minor party candidate. The sore loser could draw enough support to destroy the chances of his or her primary rival. In the great majority of states, however, "sore loser" laws and simultaneous filing deadlines prevent primary losers from using this kind of end run to get on the general election ballot.

Despite these concerns, divisive primaries don't always weaken a party. Running in a competitive primary might make the winner an even stronger candidate in the general election. In 2008, the experience Obama gained in his long nomination contest with Clinton gave him the opportunity to build and test his campaign organization prior to the general election race. And at times, when an incumbent candidate has shown signs of diminishing support due to scandal or change in the district, the national party has encouraged viable challengers. Although that might provoke a divisive primary, it could also produce a party nominee who is better able to hold the seat for the party in the fall.

The large numbers of safe House races can make divisive primaries more common. When the redistricting that followed the 2000 and 2010 U.S. Census increased the numbers of safe congressional seats, several ambitious candidates saw primary elections as their best and least expensive way to win a House seat. That attracted the attention, and the lavish spending, of dozens of interest groups aiming to change the ideological orientation of Congress. The Democrats are famous for their internal disputes, but we can see just as many divisive primaries in the Republican Party: for instance, when candidates linked to the Christian Right challenge Republicans who are more moderate on social issues.[22] Other groups, including the Club for Growth, have financed primary campaigns as a way to warn other Republicans that they will face a primary opponent if they don't take the strictest possible anti-tax position.[23]

Problems in Holding Candidates Accountable

When candidates are chosen in primaries rather than by party leaders, the party loses a powerful means of holding its candidates and officeholders accountable for their actions. In England, for example, if an elected official breaks with the party on an important issue, party leaders can usually keep him or her from being renominated. If the party cannot prevent the renomination of a maverick officeholder, then it has no way of enforcing loyalty. That, of course, is just what the Progressives had hoped. Thus, primaries have these drawbacks:

- Primaries permit the nomination of candidates hostile to the party organization and leadership, opposed to the party's platform, or out of step with the public image that party leaders want to project.
- Primaries greatly increase nomination spending. The cost of a contested primary is almost always higher than that of a convention.
- Primaries extend political campaigns, already longer in the United States than in other democracies, to a degree that can try many voters' patience.

The Party Organization Fights Back

Parties are clearly aware of the threats posed by primary elections, but they are just as aware that a direct attempt to abolish primaries would fail. So party organizations have developed a range of strategies for trying to limit the damage primaries can cause. The success of these strategies varies. As we will see in Chapter 10, the presidential nomination process has often been dominated by party leaders, and some local parties have been able to influence primaries effectively. Other party organizations have neither the strength nor the will to try.

Persuading Candidates to Run (or Not to Run)

The most effective way for a party organization to control a primary is to make sure that the party's favored candidate has no opponent. Some party organizations try to mediate among prospective candidates or coax an attractive but unwilling candidate to run. If they have a strong organization, they may be able to convince less desirable candidates to stay out of the race. Even if they have little to offer or withhold, many party leaders have the opportunity to influence prospective candidates' decisions; researchers have found that almost 70 percent of nonincumbent state legislative candidates discussed their plans to run with local party leaders before announcing their candidacy.[24]

Endorsing Candidates

Some of the stronger state parties, such as those in Massachusetts and Minnesota, endorse preferred candidates before the primary, to try to affect voters' choices. Recall that in several states, at least one of the parties holds a convention to formally endorse candidates for state office. Usually, a candidate who gets a certain percentage of the convention's vote automatically gets his or her name on the primary ballot. Endorsements are sometimes accompanied by campaign money and organizational help. In some other states, including Illinois, Ohio, and Michigan, party leaders may meet informally to endorse some candidates.

Do these endorsements influence voters? The record is mixed. Formal endorsements can often discourage other candidates or well-funded interest groups from challenging the party's choice in the primary. Besides, the process of winning a formal endorsement usually involves the candidate in so many face-to-face meetings with party activists that the resulting visibility, and the resources that the endorsing party can provide, can give the endorsed candidate some vote-getting benefits.[25]

But some states' laws keep parties from endorsing candidates prior to the primary. In these cases, informal party endorsements are less effective. Only the most politically attentive voters are likely to know that the party is supporting a particular candidate, and they are the ones least in need of the guidance provided by a party endorsement.[26] And even where party endorsements have been found to add to the endorsed candidate's vote in primaries, endorsements make a difference only for some types of candidates and to some types of voters.[27]

Providing Tangible Support

If the party can't prevent a challenge to its preferred candidates, then it must find ways to make those candidates more attractive to voters. It may urge party activists to help the favored candidates circulate their nominating petitions or offer party money and expertise to these candidates. Party leaders may encourage campaign donors and talented campaign workers to support its favored candidates.[28] They may publish ads announcing the party's endorsements or print reminder cards that voters can take into the polling booth.

Although state and local parties vary in their efforts to influence primaries, recruiting candidates is probably the most frequent form of activity. Trying to clear the field for a favored candidate is less common. In most parts of the country, parties are only one of a number of groups encouraging men and women to run for office. Local business, professional, and labor groups; civic associations; ethnic, racial, and religious organizations; and other interest groups and officeholders may also be working to recruit candidates. The party organizations that seem best able to control candidate recruitment are generally those that endorse and support candidates in the primary itself.

Candidates and Voters in the Primaries

Two facts help make the primaries more manageable for the parties: Often only one candidate runs for each office in a primary, and most Americans do not vote in them. The party may be responsible for one or both of these situations. There may be no competition in a primary, for example, because of the party's skill in persuading and dissuading potential candidates. The result is that nominations can be more easily controlled by aggressive party organizations.

Many Candidates Run Without Competition

Many candidates have no opponent in their primary race. Probably the most important determinant of the competitiveness of a primary is the party's prospects for victory in the general election. There is not usually much competition for the nomination of the party likely to lose. Primaries also tend to be less competitive when an incumbent is running (unless the incumbent is already thought to be vulnerable), when parties have made preprimary endorsements, and when the state's rules make it harder to get on the ballot.[29]

The power of incumbency to discourage competition is one of the many ironies of the primary. In an election in which voters cannot rely on the party label to guide their choices, name recognition and media coverage are important influences. Incumbents are more likely to have these resources than are challengers. To dislodge an incumbent, a challenger will usually need large amounts of campaign money, but few challengers can raise large campaign budgets. By weakening party control of nominations through the direct primary, then, Progressive reformers may have unintentionally made it harder to defeat incumbents.

... And Voters Are in Short Supply

If competition is scarce in primaries, so are voters. Turnout tends to be especially low in the weaker party's primary, in primaries held separately from the state's presidential primary, and in elections in which independents and the other party's identifiers are not allowed to vote.[30] In addition to the lack of competition in many primary contests, the fact that no one is elected in a primary probably depresses turnout. A race for the nomination lacks the drama inherent in a general election that is followed by victorious candidates taking office.

Southern primaries in earlier years were the one great exception to the rule that few people vote in primaries. Because winning the Democratic nomination in a one-party area was tantamount to winning the office itself, competition and turnout in Democratic primaries were relatively high. When the Republican Party became more competitive in the South, however, the Democratic primaries lost their special standing. The result is that participation has declined in southern primaries. Republican primaries are attracting many more voters now because their candidates' prospects in the general election have greatly improved, but the GOP increase has not been big enough to offset the drop in Democratic turnout.[31]

The primary electorate is distinctive in several ways. Many primary voters are strong party identifiers and activists, which makes them more responsive to party endorsements of certain candidates. As would be expected, people who vote in primaries have higher levels of education and political interest than nonvoters do. Some recent evidence suggests that primary voters are more intense and more consistent in their views than are people who vote only in the general election, and they tend to be more hostile toward the opposition party.[32] But because primaries usually attract such a small sample of the eligible voters, they can be more easily dominated by well-financed organized interests, such as anti-tax or pro-gun groups, than can general elections.

Primary voters often make unexpected choices. Because primary campaigns don't get much media coverage, the candidates are often not well known. Thus, the voter's choice in a primary is not as well-structured or predictable as that in a general election. Many voting decisions are made right in the polling booth. It is small wonder that parties are rarely confident about primary results and pollsters find it hard to predict them accurately.

The Impact of the Direct Primary

On balance, how has the use of primary elections affected us? Has the primary democratized nominations by taking them out of the hands of party leaders and giving them to voters? Has it weakened the party organizations overall? In short, have the Progressives' hopes been realized?

Has It Made Elections More Democratic?

Many more people vote in primaries than take part in conventions or caucuses. In that sense, the process has been made more democratic. But the democratic promise of primaries is reduced by the number of unopposed candidates and the low levels of voter turnout. If voters are to have meaningful alternatives, then there must be more than one candidate for an office. If the results are to be meaningful, then people must go to the polls.

It is not surprising that turnout in primaries is low. Adopting the direct primary doubled the number of elections in the U.S. That may have given citizens more opportunities to take part in politics than they would have preferred. Because party ID can't be used as a shortcut to make voting decisions in a primary, participants have to do more work to cast an informed ballot. Would-be candidates are put off by the cost of an additional race, the difficulty of getting on the primary ballot, and the need to differentiate themselves from other candidates of their party. If widespread competition for office and extensive public participation in the nominating process were goals of the primary's architects, then they would be seriously disappointed.

In addition, as we have seen, party organization leaders can often influence the results of primaries. If only 25 percent of eligible voters go to the polls, then 13 percent will be enough to nominate a candidate. Parties count on the fact that a large part of that group will be party loyalists who care about the party leaders' recommendations. Thus, strong party organizations—those able to muster the needed voters, money, activists, and organization—can still make a difference in the outcome. But working to influence primary elections is very costly and time consuming, even for strong parties. The large number of elected offices in the United States, from senator to surveyor, forces party organizations to be selective in trying to affect primaries. Parties sometimes stand aside because picking a favorite in the primary might produce resentment. Of course, party leaders' greatest fear is that if they support one candidate in a primary and another candidate wins, they could lose all influence over the winning officeholder.

In some ways, then, the primary has been a democratizing force. In competitive districts, especially when no incumbent is running, voters have the opportunity for choice envisioned by the reformers. In all districts, the primaries place real limits on the power of party leaders. Parties, even strong ones, can no longer award a nomination to anyone they choose. Research in some other nations shows that in comparison with systems where party leaders select the candidates, primaries can help the weaker party choose a candidate with greater voter appeal.[33] And the primary gives dissenters a chance to take their case to the party's voters, so it offers them a potential veto over the party leaders' preferences. That certainly was true of Donald Trump's victory in the 2016 Republican presidential primaries, in the face of clear opposition by many Republican leaders and elected officials.

How Badly Has It Harmed the Parties?

On the other hand, is it possible to say that the direct primary has strengthened democracy in the United States if it weakens the political parties? From the risk of divisive primaries to the added campaign funding and voter mobilization they require, primaries strain party resources and create headaches for party leaders. Even though some party organizations have been able to influence primary results by making preprimary endorsements or holding conventions to nominate some candidates, the bottom line is this: When a party organization cannot choose who will carry the party label into the general election, the party has been deprived of one of its key resources.

The direct primary has redistributed power within the parties. The Progressives' goal was to shift the power to nominate candidates from the party organization to the party in the electorate, but a funny thing happened along the way. Because candidates (especially incumbents) can win the party's nomination even when they defy the party organization, the idea of party "discipline" loses credibility. Just as the direct primary undercuts the ability of the party organization to recruit candidates who share its goals and accept its discipline, it prevents the organization from disciplining partisans who already are in office. The primary, then, empowers the party's candidates and the party in government at the expense of the party organization. This sets the United States apart from many other democracies, in which the party organization has real power over the party in government.

Primaries also contribute to the decentralization of power in the American parties. As long as candidates can appeal successfully to a majority of local primary voters, they are free from the control of state or national party leaders. In all these ways, the direct primary has gone beyond changing the nominating process. It has helped to reshape the American parties.

Is the Primary Worth the Cost?

How to nominate party candidates has been a controversial question since political parties first appeared in the United States. It raises the fundamental question of what a political party is. Are parties only alliances of officeholders—the party in government? That seemed to be the prevailing definition in the early years when public officials nominated candidates in party caucuses. Should the definition be expanded to include the party's activists and organizational leaders? The change from a caucus to a convention system of nominations, in which the party organization played its greatest role, reflected this change in the definition of party.

Should we extend the idea of party well beyond the limits accepted by most other democracies and include the party's supporters in the electorate? If so, which supporters should be included—only those willing to register formally as party loyalists or anyone who wants to vote for (or against) a party candidate in a primary election? The answer has evolved over the years toward a more inclusive definition of party. Even though the Supreme Court insists that the parties' freedom of association is vital, the "party," especially in states with an open or "top two" primary and, in practice, in semiclosed or semiopen primary states, has become so permeable that its boundaries are hard to define.

The methods we use to nominate candidates have a far-reaching impact. The Jacksonians promoted the convention system in order to gain control of the party from congressional party leaders. Progressives used their preference for the direct primary as a weapon to wrest control of the party and, ultimately, the government from the party organization. Because of the importance of nominations in the political process, those who control the nominations have great influence on the political agenda and, in turn, over who gets what in the political system. The stakes in this debate, as a result, are extremely high.

Notes

1 See Jean-Benoit Pilet and William Cross, eds., *The Selection of Political Party Leaders in Contemporary Parliamentary Democracies* (New York: Routledge, 2014).

2 Stephen J. Wayne, *The Road to the White House 2008* (Belmont, CA: Wadsworth, 2008), pp. 6–8.

3 See Chapters 7 and 21 in Marjorie Randon Hershey, ed., *Guide to U.S. Political Parties* (Los Angeles: Sage, 2014).

4 Robert M. La Follette, *La Follette's Autobiography* (Madison, WI: R. M. La Follette, 1913), pp. 197–198.

5 Sasha Issenberg, "America Exports Democracy, But Not the Way You Think," *New York Times*, March 16, 2014, p. SR4.

6 Some states allow third parties to nominate their candidates through conventions.

7 See L. Sandy Maisel and Mark D. Brewer, *Parties and Elections in America*, 5th ed. (Lanham, MD: Rowman & Littlefield, 2008), pp. 204–205.

8 The National Conference of State Legislatures lists the states' various primary election systems at www.ncsl.org/research/elections-and-campaigns/primary-types.aspx (as of June 24, 2014; accessed June 23, 2016).

9 For one typology, see Thomas M. Holbrook and Raymond J. LaRaja, "Parties and Elections," in Virginia Gray, Russell L. Hanson, and Thad Kousser, eds., *Politics in the American States*, 11th ed. (Washington, DC: CQ Press, 2017), Table 3-3. Note that experts disagree on these definitions and on what should be the dividing line between an "open" and a "closed" primary.

10 A 1986 Supreme Court decision (*Tashjian v. Republican Party of Connecticut*) upheld the Connecticut party's efforts to establish an open primary. This decision affirmed the authority of the party, rather than the state, to control its own nomination process. However, many state parties would prefer a closed primary to an open one.

11 Researchers differ as to whether closed primaries are more likely to produce ideologically extreme candidates. Compare Karen M. Kaufmann, James G. Gimpel, and Adam H. Hoffman, "A Promise Fulfilled?" *Journal of Politics* 65 (2003): 457–476, with David W. Brady, Hahrie Han, and Jeremy C. Pope, "Primary Elections and Candidate Ideology," *Legislative Studies Quarterly* 32 (2007): 79–106.

12 *California Democratic Party v. Jones* (2000). On blanket primaries, see Bruce E. Cain and Elisabeth R. Gerber, eds., *Voting at the Political Fault Line* (Berkeley, CA: University of California Press, 2002).

13 Lynn Vavreck, "The Reasoning Voter Meets the Strategic Candidate," *American Politics Research* 29 (2001): 507–529.

14 Gary D. Wekkin, "Why Crossover Voters Are Not 'Mischievous' Voters," *American Politics Quarterly* 19 (1991): 229–247.

15 See the monthly newsletter *Ballot Access News* at www.ballot-access.org.

16 See, for instance, Thomas A. Reitz and Rebecca B. Morton, "Majority Requirements and Minority Representation," *NYU Annual Survey of American Law* 63 (2008): 691–725.

17 V. O. Key, Jr., *American State Politics: An Introduction* (New York: Knopf, 1956), p. 195.

18 John G. Geer and Mark E. Shere, "Party Competition and the Prisoner's Dilemma," *Journal of Politics* 54 (1992): 741–761.

19 In 2016, for example, turnout in primaries was estimated at 28 percent, according to the Pew Research Center, compared with 59 percent in the general election.

20 Andrew B. Hall, "What Happens When Extremists Win Primaries?" *American Political Science Review* 109 (2015): 18–42.

21 Priscilla L. Southwell, "The Effect of Nomination Divisiveness on the 2008 Presidential Election," *PS: Political Science & Politics* 43 (2010): 255–258. See also Marjorie Randon Hershey, "The Media: Coloring the News," in Michael Nelson, ed., *The Elections of 2008* (Washington, DC: CQ Press, 2009), pp. 128–129.

22 Paige L. Schneider, "Factionalism in the Southern Republican Party," *American Review of Politics* 19 (1998): 129–148.

23 Matt Bai, "Fight Club," *New York Times Magazine*, August 10, 2003, pp. 24–27.

24 Gary F. Moncrief, Peverill Squire, and Malcolm E. Jewell, *Who Runs for the Legislature?* (Upper Saddle River, NJ: Prentice Hall, 2001), p. 39.

25 Sarah McCally Morehouse, *The Governor as Party Leader* (Ann Arbor, MI: University of Michigan Press, 1998), pp. 22–23.

26 L. Sandy Maisel, Linda L. Fowler, Ruth S. Jones, and Walter J. Stone, "Nomination Politics," in L. Sandy Maisel, ed., *The Parties Respond* (Boulder, CO: Westview, 1994), pp. 155–156.

27 Thad Kousser, Scott Lucas, Seth Masket, and Eric McGhee, "Kingmakers or Cheerleaders?" *Political Research Quarterly* 68 (2015): 443–456. See also William C. Binning, Melanie J. Blumberg, and John C. Green, "A Report from Mahoning County," in Green, Daniel J. Coffey, and David B. Cohen, eds., *The State of the Parties*, 7th ed. (Lanham, MD: Rowman & Littlefield, 2014), pp. 323–338.

28 See Hans J. G. Hassell, "Party Control of Party Primaries," *Journal of Politics* 78 (2016): 75–87.

29 See Jay Goodliffe and David B. Magleby, "Campaign Finance in U.S. House Primary and General Elections," in Peter F. Galderisi, Marni Ezra, and Michael Lyons, eds., *Congressional Primaries and the Politics of Representation* (Lanham, MD: Rowman & Littlefield, 2001), pp. 62–76.

30 See Molly Rockett and Austin Plier, "2016 Presidential Primary Voter Turnout Analysis to Date," May 6, 2016, Fairvote, at www.fairvote.org/2016_presidential_primary_voter_turnout_analysis_to_date (accessed June 23, 2016).

31 For instance, see Chris Kromm, "Democratic Turnout Plummets in Southern Primaries," *Facing South*, March 4, 2016, at www.facingsouth.org/2016/03/2016-elections-gop-turnout-soars-democratic-turnou

32 Michael P. McDonald and Thessalia Merivaki, "Voter Turnout in Presidential Nominating Contests," *The Forum* 13, Issue 4 (February 2016): 597–622; but see Pew Research Center, "2012 Republican Primary Voters," Jan. 28, 2016, at www.people-press.org/2016/01/28/2012-republican-primary-voters-more-conservative-than-gop-general-election-voters/ (accessed June 23, 2016).

33 James Adams and Samuel Merrill III, "Candidate and Party Strategies in Two-Stage Elections Beginning with a Primary," *American Journal of Political Science* 52 (2008): 344–359.

CHAPTER 10

Choosing the Presidential Nominees

Here's the first thing you need to know about presidential nominations: No sane person would intentionally devise a nomination system like that of the American parties. As you'll soon find out, it has evolved into a very complicated process, hard to understand, easy to criticize, and occasionally vulnerable to odd results (see: Donald Trump). The process itself has not changed fundamentally since the early 1970s. But recent changes in the American political environment have made an already convoluted and decentralized nominating system even more challenging to explain and predict. Because of the big increase in media coverage (including partisan media and social media), the growth in partisan hostility, and the steep increase in free-spending super PACs, candidates who might not have been considered seriously in earlier presidential races have now been able to gain media exposure and attract other resources. In this more fluid political environment, what does it take to gain a party's presidential nomination?

The "Invisible Primary"

Most serious presidential candidates begin several years before the election to take polls, raise money, identify active supporters in the states with early contests, and compete for the services of respected consultants (see box "How a Presidential Candidate Is Chosen" on page 225). The competition heats up during the months before the first primaries and caucuses. Journalists are competing at this time as well; they each want to be the first to predict who will win the nomination. The indicators they use are the candidates' standing in polls, their fund-raising success, and the endorsements made by prominent political figures. This process of early fund-raising and jockeying for media attention and support has become so important to the eventual result that it has come to be called the **invisible primary** or the "money primary."[1] In 2015, some journalists referred to this period as the "Koch primary," when many candidates for the Republican presidential nomination sought the favor of big campaign donors linked with oil billionaires Charles and David Koch.[2]

How a Presidential Candidate Is Chosen

Step 1: Assessing Their Chances. Many people who think they might stand a chance—governors, senators, House members, people well known in another field—consider running for president. They take private polls to see how they are viewed by prospective voters. To assess their prospects of getting the resources they'd need, they contact fund-raisers and potential donors and try to get well-respected consultants to commit to their candidacy. (Donald Trump is a rare exception here, because he planned to use his own fortune to pay for most of his campaign.) They visit states with early primaries and caucuses to gain support from local officials.

Timing: Typically, several years before the presidential election.

Step 2: Entering the Race. Those who feel they have a good chance—and some who don't—set up exploratory committees to raise money for advertising and to fund their increasingly frequent trips to Iowa, New Hampshire, and other states with early delegate selection events. Then they formally declare their candidacy and work to get on every state ballot.

Timing: Typically, at least a year before the presidential election.

Step 3: Primaries and Caucuses. Voters cast a ballot in their states for the candidate they want their party to nominate for president. Most states hold primary elections for this purpose; the rest use participatory caucuses and state conventions. Delegates are chosen to represent each state and to vote in the party's national convention for the candidate(s) selected by their state's voters.

Timing: Between February and June of each presidential election year.

Step 4: National Nominating Conventions. The delegates vote in their party's convention for the presidential candidate(s) chosen by the voters in their state's primary or caucuses (Step 3). Then they vote for the winning candidate's choice of a vice presidential nominee and to adopt a party platform.

Timing: By tradition, the party that does not currently hold the presidency schedules its convention first, in July or August; the other party's convention is held soon after.

Step 5: General Election. The two major parties' candidates run against one another.
Timing: From the conventions until the first Tuesday after the first Monday in November.

Party leaders and activists and interest groups closely linked with the party are watching carefully as well. They want to determine which candidates would best serve their interests. Although party leaders have no formal power over the nominating process, they can communicate their choices to party activists by publicly endorsing particular candidates. In most recent presidential races, voters in the primaries and caucuses have nominated the consensus choice of the party's leaders and activists.[3] Especially in this early phase of the process, many partisans don't know much about the prospective candidates and welcome these recommendations. But as Trump's successful nomination race in 2016 shows, party leaders aren't always able to thwart the appeal of an outsider with exceptional resources—in particular, in Trump's case, the ability to generate near-constant media coverage.

Candidates who fall behind in funding and endorsements, and thus in media coverage, are likely to be winnowed out of the race even before most Americans have the chance to evaluate them. In contrast, those who raise more money than expected can greatly improve their chances. The candidates who survive this first testing period must then face a gauntlet of state party primaries and caucuses. Their aim is to win delegates who will vote for them at the party's national convention. This process, which continues to evolve, challenges the strategic capabilities of every presidential candidate.

The Adoption of Presidential Primaries

When the republic began, prospective presidential candidates needed to impress their colleagues in Congress, because presidential nominees were chosen by the congressional party caucuses. When the parties started nominating their presidential candidates in national conventions in the 1830s, as Chapter 1 showed, the real power in the process moved to the local and state party leaders. They chose their state's delegates to the national convention and told those delegates which presidential candidate to support. The selection was usually done in a series of party-controlled meetings, called caucuses, held first at the local level and then in statewide conventions.

At the urging of Progressives, who aimed to weaken party leaders' power, Florida passed the first presidential primary law in 1901 to let voters pick the party's candidate. Many other states followed. The parties later struck back; by 1936, only 14 states were still holding primaries to choose their delegates to the national conventions. That number had hardly changed by 1968.[4] Even in many states that held primaries, voters could take part in only a non-binding "beauty contest" to express their preferences about presidential candidates; the delegates who went to the national convention and actually chose the candidates were selected elsewhere. A fascinating story began to unfold in 1968, however, in which the national Democratic Party took control of the delegate selection process away from the state parties and gave new life to the use of presidential primaries.

Turbulence in the Democratic Party

Rioters fought with police in the streets outside the 1968 Democratic convention. The party was torn by disputes over civil rights and American involvement in the Vietnam War. When the convention nominated the party leaders' choice, Vice President Hubert Humphrey, as the Democratic presidential candidate, antiwar Democrats protested that the nomination did not fairly reflect the views of most grassroots party activists. Humphrey hadn't run in even one state primary, they complained. To try to make peace with these activists, the national party leaders agreed that the next convention's delegates would be selected in a more open and democratic manner.

The party created a reform commission chaired by liberal Senator George McGovern (and later by U.S. Representative Donald Fraser and known as the **McGovern–Fraser Commission**). It recommended, and the Democratic National Committee and the next Democratic convention approved, major changes to increase the influence of insurgent Democrats in the 1972 presidential nominating process. One of the striking elements of this story is the remarkable ease with which state Democratic Party leaders accepted rule changes that greatly reduced their power over the awarding of the party's greatest prize, the presidential nomination.[5]

In trying to comply with the complicated new McGovern–Fraser rules, many states stopped using caucus-convention systems and reinstituted primaries. The remaining caucuses were guided by strict party requirements that delegates be selected in open and well-publicized meetings. Techniques formerly used by state party organizations to control the caucuses were outlawed. In the process, not only were the delegate selection procedures democratized but also the principle was established that the national party, not the states or the state parties, has ultimate control over the rules for nominating presidential candidates.

Once the reform genie was let out of the bottle, it was hard to contain. The Democrats tinkered with their nomination rules prior to almost every election for the next 20 years. First, they used national party leverage to make the process more open and more representative of women, blacks, and young people. Then, the Democrats required the use of proportional representation, so that voter support for candidates was more faithfully represented in states' delegations. Starting in 1980, in order to bring party leaders (and their personal knowledge of candidates) back into the process, many Democratic elected and party officials were guaranteed a vote at the convention as uncommitted "superdelegates" (to be discussed later in this chapter).

The results dramatically transformed the process by which the Democrats select their presidential nominees. Many state legislatures responded to the new Democratic rules by changing state election laws to require primary elections in both parties. Thus, the Republicans became the unwilling beneficiaries of the Democratic reforms. Until recently, the Republicans preserved their tradition of giving state parties wide latitude in developing their own rules for selecting delegates. Since 2012, however, the national party organization has become more active in constraining the choices of the state party organizations.

Presidential Primaries and Caucuses Today

Each state decides whether to choose its delegates to the parties' national conventions in a primary election or a series of caucuses. Although primaries are more common, states can change their method of selection from one presidential election to the next (see Figure 10.1). When an incumbent president is running opposed for renomination, for instance, many states cancel that party's primary to save money.

A state holding a primary selects a date on which its eligible voters can go to a polling place (or cast a mail or absentee ballot) and choose who they'd

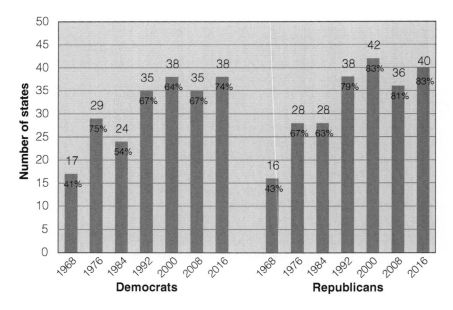

FIGURE 10.1 Change in the Number of Presidential Primaries, 1968–2016

Note: The number above each bar is the number of states that held primaries to select delegates in that year; inside the bar is the percentage of convention delegates elected in those primaries. Percentages are based on total numbers of delegates, including Democratic superdelegates and Republican unbound delegates. All 50 states plus Washington, DC, are included, but not the territories (American Samoa, Guam, Puerto Rico, Virgin Islands) or Democrats Abroad.

Sources: For 1968–1992, Michael G. Hagen and William G. Mayer, "The Modern Politics of Presidential Selection," in William G. Mayer, ed., *In Pursuit of the White House 2000* (New York: Chatham House, 2000), pp. 11 and 43–44. Figures for 2000 and 2004 were kindly provided by Mayer. Figures for 2008–2016 were calculated by the author from data provided by The Green Papers at www.thegreenpapers.com/P12/D-Alloc.phtml (accessed June 24, 2016).

Hillary Clinton and the Iowa Caucuses: Part Deux

Hillary Clinton had been the presumptive favorite for the Democratic presidential nomination throughout the 2008 "invisible primary"—until she was beaten by a first-term U.S. Senator in the Iowa caucuses, the opening event of the nomination season. The senator, Barack Obama, eventually won the party's nomination. Analysts attributed Obama's victory in Iowa to his extensive precinct-by-precinct field organizing, supported by data analytics. The Clinton caucus campaign, in contrast, was criticized as being arrogant and "entitled."

When Clinton decided to run for president again in 2016, her staff approached the Iowa caucuses very differently. She would not be out-hustled this time. With 20 field offices across Iowa months in advance of the caucuses, Clinton's campaign engaged more than a thousand volunteers not just to canvass for voter support but intensify that support by building personal relationships with likely caucus-goers. One Democratic county chairwoman said about the process: "[The Clinton staffers are] much more open and friendly ... not at all as elite as they were last time." Clinton's main opponent for the 2016 Democratic nomination, Senator Bernie Sanders, had little organization on the ground, though he had substantial support in the polls.

Yet in spite of her campaign's improvements in organizing and relating to voters, Clinton barely beat Sanders in Iowa. She won 49.9 percent of the caucus vote in 2016, which translated to 23 national convention delegates, and Sanders got 49.6 percent and 21 delegates. Why didn't Hillary 2.0's careful preparation give her a substantial victory? One reason is that people who turn out to vote in a caucus are typically more intense in their views and more ideologically consistent than is the larger turnout in primaries. So the Sanders supporters—drawn to Sanders by his consistent ideological liberalism, especially on the issue of income inequality— were more likely to take part in caucuses than Clinton's were. Clinton did much better in states holding primaries, which are more likely to attract centrists. Some candidates and types of campaigns, then, do better in caucuses than they do in primaries. Thus, a state's choice as to whether to select its national convention delegates by using caucuses or primaries can make a difference in who votes and who wins.

Sources: Philip Rucker, "On the Ground in Iowa, Clinton Tries to Fix Her 2008 Mistakes," *Washington Post*, October 27, 2015, p. A1 (from which the quote is drawn); Christopher F. Karpowitz and Jeremy C. Pope, "Who Caucuses?" *British Journal of Political Science* 45 (2015): 329–351.

like to be their party's presidential nominee. The popular vote for each candidate determines how many of the state's pledged delegates will go to the party's national convention supporting that candidate.

Other states use a longer delegate selection process that begins with precinct caucuses. In these meetings, party identifiers are invited to gather, often for an hour or more, to debate which candidate for president will best represent their party and the issues they believe in. Then they choose delegates to communicate their presidential preference to meetings at higher levels, typically at the county, congressional district, and then the state level. The state's final delegate slate for the national convention is determined at the higher-level conventions. In 2016, the first-in-the-nation Iowa caucuses, for example, began with precinct meetings in February, but Iowa's national convention delegates were not chosen until the district and state conventions in April and June.

The caucus states' activities were all but ignored by the media until 1976, when a little-known Democratic governor, Jimmy Carter, made himself a serious presidential candidate by campaigning intensively in Iowa and winning an unexpectedly large number of delegates. Since then, the Iowa caucuses have joined the New Hampshire primary as the first and most significant delegate selection events. Most media coverage of the nomination race focuses on these two states' events.[6] To dilute their impact, from 2008 through 2016 the two national parties allowed Nevada and South Carolina, states with large minority populations, to move up their delegate selection dates as well.

Candidates campaign differently in a caucus state than they do in a primary. Because the turnout at caucuses is much smaller, winning caucuses requires extensive organizing to identify and appeal to these likely caucus goers. (In contrast, media ads are better suited to reach the bigger turnout in a primary.) Caucus states played a large part in Barack Obama's successful run for president in 2008. His campaign deployed large numbers of field organizers in states holding their caucuses early in the nominating season and won most of them.[7] Bernie Sanders tried to do the same in 2016 but fell short. Some types of candidates have greater appeal to the more intense caucus-goers (see box "Hillary Clinton and the Iowa Caucuses: Part Deux" on page 229) than they do to the more representative electorate in a primary.

The Race for Delegates: Timing and Momentum

Candidates who survive the "invisible primary" know that they can create momentum by winning states whose contests are held early in the nominating process. These early wins attract more media coverage for the candidate and, in turn, more name recognition among voters. The candidate looks more and more unstoppable, so it is easier to raise money, which makes

Momentum in the Nomination Process

Each state's party organization decides how and when its voters will select their delegates to the national nominating conventions, within limits set by the national party. In 1976, only half of the states' primaries and caucuses had been held by early May. But in recent years, many states moved their primary or caucuses close to the start of the election year calendar, when they would get more media coverage, bring in more money from campaign ads, and give the state's voters more of a chance to influence the choice of the parties' nominees. The high point of this "front-loading" came in 2008, when the midpoint of the nominating season took place in early February. That dragged out the nominating process and disadvantaged the eventual nominee, who would have to endure attacks by rival candidates in his or her own party for many months. In 2012 and especially in 2016, the national parties tried to shorten the nominating season by ruling that no nomination contest could be held before early February.

Even so, the first few nominating events still received much more attention in 2016 than did later state events. The first two states to vote—Iowa and New Hampshire—are not very typical of the American population as a whole. Both states are almost entirely white, with few urban centers. In Iowa in particular, most Republican caucus voters tend to be evangelical Christians. Yet, despite their atypical characteristics, these states' voters narrowed the list of candidates other voters could consider. Six Republican candidates left the race right after Iowa and New Hampshire, and the Democratic field was reduced from three candidates to two. The early primaries and caucuses also provide momentum to at least some of their winners. Voters in later states who want to choose the strongest possible candidate for their party may take their cues from the Iowa and New Hampshire results. And later voters are exposed to the increased publicity that an early winner receives.

This curious nominating schedule, which owes its existence to tradition rather than careful planning, is often described as being biased and unrepresentative. Some reformers argue for replacing the current system with a national primary, with all states voting for their party's presidential nominee on the same day. A national primary wouldn't eliminate the role of momentum; instead, the momentum would come from the "invisible primary," advantaging the candidates who led in the polls just prior to the primary. The present sequential system, despite its flaws, does permit a lesser-known candidate to build support in Iowa and New Hampshire, which are small enough for one-on-one, "retail" voter contact.

Sources: Larry M. Bartels, *Presidential Primaries and the Dynamics of Public Choice* (Princeton, NJ: Princeton University Press, 1988) and David P. Redlawsk, Caroline J. Tolbert, and Todd Donovan, *Why Iowa?* (Chicago: University of Chicago Press, 2011), Chapter 8.

later victories more likely. This happens especially in contests when winner-take-all rules are used. Because the other candidates aren't winning any delegates, they fall further and further behind.

State legislatures also realize that holding an early primary or caucus can benefit their state. The media interest generated by an early contest brings large numbers of journalists (who spend money on food, lodging, and other needs) and campaign money into the state. The media put the state's concerns in the national spotlight. Iowa's first-in-the-nation status, for example, means that ethanol use, favored by Iowa's corn farmers, gets more notice from presidential candidates than it would receive otherwise. Thus, the nomination process became **front-loaded** in recent elections, as states moved their primaries and caucuses closer to the beginning of the nominating season (see box "Momentum in the Nomination Process" on page 231). The increase in front-loading halted by 2016, but even though the national parties required the first nominating events to take place no sooner than early February of that year, the November general election was still nine months away.

Candidates' Strategic Choices

As candidates approach these primaries and caucuses, vital decisions must be made. How much effort and money should they put into each state? Which of their issue stands and personal qualities will be most persuasive to which voters? Different types of candidates face different challenges. An early front-runner, for example, normally has to demonstrate overwhelming support in the first delegate selection events, or his or her supporters' and contributors' confidence may be so badly shaken that the candidate's chances fade. The Democrats' early front-runner in 2016, Hillary Clinton, had hoped to win big in the early primaries and caucuses and scare her competitors out of the race, but that strategy was weakened by Senator Bernie Sanders's strong showing in Iowa and clear victory in New Hampshire. Many other formal and informal "rules" structure the nominating process and affect campaigns' strategies.

The Democrats' rules differ from those of the Republicans. Recall that the Democrats' nomination reforms require the use of proportional representation (PR), so that candidates with significant support will not be shut out in any state. Since 1988, any candidates who win at least 15 percent of the vote in a state's primary or caucus get approximately the same share of the delegates as they received of the popular vote. Until 2012, the Republicans had no national rules as to how to count these votes, but most states' Republican parties used some form of a winner-take-all system: The candidate who gets the most votes in a state primary or caucus wins all or most of the state's delegates.

A winner-take-all rule produces very different results from a PR rule.[8] After Iowa and New Hampshire, Clinton regained the lead in her nomination battle with Sanders, and by the midpoint of the nominating season, she was several hundred delegates ahead. Then Sanders won seven out of the next eight primaries. Why didn't Sanders take the lead in the race overall? Because even in a state where Sanders won by 55 percent of the popular vote, the use of PR to allocate delegates meant that Clinton would still get 45 percent of the delegates. So Sanders's victories, which in a winner-take-all system would have given him a big boost in the delegate count, were not big enough under the Democrats' PR rules to let him close the gap with Clinton in delegates. They were enough, however, to draw out the nomination race until the very last states voted.[9] As one reporter noted, "the Republican who kills the buffalo gets all the meat; the Democrat has to crouch around the campfire and share it with his brethren and sistren."[10]

Rules Changes for 2012, 2016, and 2020

In 2008, Republican primary and caucus voters chose Arizona Senator John McCain as their presidential nominee. After McCain lost to Barack Obama in the general election, Republican leaders suspected that the front-loading of the nomination race had led to McCain's winning the party's nomination too quickly. To slow down the next nomination contest in 2012, the Republican National Committee (RNC) broke with its usual states' rights policy and mandated that state Republican Parties holding nomination events before April 1 must use some form of PR in allocating delegates to presidential candidates. Only states holding later nominating events could use winner-take-all rules. The use of PR in the earlier contests would help candidates other than the front-runner to stay in the race longer, and the new rule would give states a reason not to front-load their caucuses and primaries. That, Republican leaders hoped, would subject the eventual nominee to greater scrutiny from party voters and result in a stronger presidential candidate.

The change did stretch out the Republican nomination race. Challengers to the front-runner, Mitt Romney, were able to accumulate some delegates in PR states even though they were losing primaries and caucuses. New super PACs (see Chapter 12) provided the money to keep some Republican candidates in the contest even if they didn't have much public support. Romney kept having to play whack-a-mole with his competitors, and he didn't lock up enough delegates to win the nomination until late May.

After Romney lost the general election to Obama, the RNC concluded that the reformed nominating season had taken *too* long and delayed the party in uniting behind the eventual nominee. So the RNC recommended a shorter, more streamlined system for 2016. Only states with nominating events between March 1 and March 14 would have to use some form of PR rules, and the national convention was moved up to mid-July, to give the party's candidate more time to campaign for the general election.[11] But the circumstances of the 2016 campaign were very different from 2012; several

Republican leaders regretted the quick nomination victory of Donald Trump and refused to endorse him. The result was extensive discussion in 2016 about how to change the rules for 2020 to achieve the goals of various segments of the party. Party leaders often develop strategies in reaction to their most recent campaign experiences. But in the case of presidential campaigns, the long, four-year interval between campaigns allows for so many changes in the political environment that what's learned from the last election doesn't necessarily work in the next. In the immortal words of Yogi Berra, "It's tough to make predictions, especially about the future."

What Is the Party's Role?

The party organizations' interests in the nominating process are not necessarily the same as those of the presidential candidates. State and local parties want a nominee who will bring voters to the polls to support the party's candidates for state and local offices. A weak presidential candidate may hurt their chances. Party leaders also worry that a hotly contested nomination race could lead to conflict within local and state parties, which might weaken them in the general election.

Historically, some state parties protected their interests by selecting delegates uncommitted to any candidate and then casting the state's delegate votes as a bloc for a particular nominee. The ability to swing a bloc of delegates to a candidate could increase the state party's influence at the convention. But the current nominating system makes it difficult for state parties to send an uncommitted delegation. In many primary states, the candidates set up their own delegate slates, so the delegates' first loyalty is to the candidate. In caucus states, delegates committed to a candidate usually have greater appeal to caucus-goers than do uncommitted delegates. Besides, interest groups such as labor unions, environmentalists, business groups, and evangelical Christian organizations urge their activists to take part in caucuses and primaries to push for a nominee committed to their goals rather than an uncommitted slate. Hillary Clinton, for example, stressed some issues such as climate change during the nomination season, not because it was a priority for most primary voters but because it mattered a great deal to environmentalists concerned with the Democratic presidential nomination. Party leaders, then, have a harder time protecting the party's interests in a nominating process that is dominated by the candidates and their group and individual supporters.

The Democrats tried to enhance the party's role in 1980 and to a greater extent in 1984 by adding delegate seats at the national convention for elected and party officials. These **superdelegates**—all Democratic governors and members of Congress, current and former presidents and vice presidents, and all members of the Democratic National Committee—were meant to be a large, uncommitted bloc now totaling about 15 percent of all delegates, with the party's interests in mind. (See Table 10.1.)

TABLE 10.1 Who Were the "Superdelegates" in 2016?

Affiliation	Number	% of all Superdelegates
All Democratic National Committee (DNC) members*	432	61
Party enthusiasts chosen by each state's party organization		
51% male, 58% white, 23% black, 12% Hispanic American, 7% other or unknown		
All Democratic members of the U.S. House of Representatives	193	27
66% male, 59% white, 23% black, 12% Hispanic American, 6% other or unknown		
All Democratic U.S. Senators	47	7
70% male, 94% white, 2% black, 2% Hispanic American, 2% other or unknown		
All Democratic Governors	21	2
81% male, 81% white, 5% black, 5% Hispanic American, 10% other or unknown		
Distinguished party leaders	20	3
Democratic current and former presidents and vice presidents, former DNC chairs, former House and Senate Democratic leaders		
95% male, 95% white, 5% black, no Hispanic Americans or other categories		
Total Democratic Superdelegates	713	100

* Excluding the 12 DNC members who are current governors and U.S. Senate and House members, who are counted in those categories. Note that the DNC includes members from all states and Washington, DC, Puerto Rico, American Samoa, Guam, the Northern Marianas, the U.S. Virgin Islands, and Democrats Abroad.

Source: Calculated from Drew DeSilver, "Who Are the Democratic Superdelegates?" Pew Research Center, May 5, 2016, at www.pewresearch.org/fact-tank/2016/05/05/who-are-the-democratic-superdelegates/ (accessed September 7, 2016).

The closeness of the delegate count during the 2008 and 2016 Democratic contests raised concerns that the superdelegates' votes might actually decide the race. This elicited charges of "boss rule," especially by proponents of candidates who did not have majority support among superdelegates. But their suspicions were largely unfounded. All the superdelegates are either elected officials, who have a natural interest in maintaining constituent support, or party leaders, who want to choose the nominee who is most attractive to voters. For example, in 2016 although Bernie Sanders supporters feared that superdelegates were unfairly tipping the convention vote toward Clinton, the superdelegates were actually on the same side as the party's voters; Clinton had also won many more popular votes than Sanders in state primaries and caucuses. So in practice, superdelegates have not played an independent role in the nominating process as a voice for the party's interests.[12] Even so, amid continuing charges of "boss rule," the Democratic Party's rules committee voted to recommend that in 2020, about two-thirds of the superdelegates would have to vote for the candidate who won their state's primary or caucuses. Presidential candidates now owe their selection largely to their own core supporters rather than to the party organization. This limits the party organization's influence over the president once he or she is elected.

Limits on the party organization's power were especially clear in the 2016 Republican nomination race. When businessman and entertainer Donald Trump announced his candidacy for president in June 2015, most Republican leaders didn't take him seriously. But Trump was extremely effective in drawing free media coverage by saying outrageous things; in his announcement speech, for example, he disparaged Mexican immigrants. For party leaders whose official conclusion from their loss of the presidency in 2012 was that Republicans needed to appeal to Latino and Hispanic Americans, Trump's words were anathema. Even as late as March 2016, after a substantial proportion of the states' national convention delegates had been awarded, Trump's endorsements by prominent Republicans could be counted on one hand, with a few fingers to spare. Mitt Romney called Trump "a phony, a fraud," and claimed that "He's playing members of the American public for suckers."[13] The Republican Speaker of the House of Representatives held back on supporting Trump even after all of Trump's opponents had withdrawn from the race.

If Republican Party leaders didn't want Trump as their candidate, then why did he win the party's nomination? Perhaps the fact that there were 17 contenders for the nomination kept the field divided rather than letting one Republican face Trump head-on. Perhaps Republicans failed to take Trump seriously until it was too late to stop him. A more likely reason is that the RNC and the Republican Party in government do not control the party's presidential nomination process. Voters in Republican primaries and caucuses do, and in 2016, a plurality chose Trump.

Voters' Choices in Presidential Nominations

The move to primaries and participatory caucuses has increased citizen involvement in nominating a president. What determines the level of voter turnout and guides voters' choices in these contests?

Who Votes?

Turnout varies a great deal from state to state and across different years in any one state. Media attention to the early contests tends to produce higher turnouts in those states. Turnout is greater in states with a better-educated citizenry and a tradition of two-party competition—the same states where there is higher turnout in the general election. The nature of the contest matters, too. Voters are more attracted to races that are closely fought and in which the candidates spend more money and the excitement is high, all of which increase interest in the election.[14]

Are Primary and Caucus Voters Typical?

However, primaries have lower turnout than general elections do, and caucuses have lower turnout still. Are the people who turn out to vote in these events, and who therefore choose the nominees for the rest of the public, typical of other citizens? Critics of the reforms have charged that they are not and, thus, that candidates are now being selected by an unrepresentative group of citizens.

We can explore this question in several ways. When we compare presidential primary voters with nonvoters, we find that those who vote in primaries are, in fact, better educated, wealthier, and older, but then, so are general election voters. A more appropriate comparison is with party identifiers because primaries are the means by which the party electorate chooses its nominees. Using this comparison, just as is the case with primary voters more generally, voters in presidential primaries tend to be slightly older, better educated, more affluent, better integrated into their communities, somewhat more partisan and interested in politics, and less likely to be black or Hispanic. The differences are not substantial, however.[15]

Do Voters Make Informed Choices?

Another criticism of primaries is that voters do not make very well-informed decisions. Compared with voters in the general election, primary voters tend to pay less attention to the campaign and have less knowledge about the candidates. Especially in the early contests, voters are influenced by candidate momentum, as support builds for at least some candidates who have won unexpectedly or by a large margin. Candidates' personal characteristics influence voters in the primaries,[16] but issues often have only a minor impact. The result, so the argument goes, is a series of contests decided mainly on the basis of short-run, superficial considerations.[17]

Many analysts think that this is too strong an indictment. They feel that voters respond with some rationality to the challenge of having to choose among several candidates without the powerful guidance provided by party labels.[18] Although it may seem pointless to support a candidate simply because he or she has momentum, primary voters often find only minor issue differences among their party's candidates and just want to pick the candidate with the best chance of winning the presidency for their party. Momentum seems to matter especially when voters are being asked to sort through a pack of candidates about whom they know little[19] and when there is no well-known front-runner.[20] Even then, the candidates who move to the head of the pack are usually subjected to more thorough evaluation, which gives voters more reasons to support or oppose them. In short, even though primary voters often have less information about the candidates than do general election voters, the quality of their decisions may not differ very much from those in general elections.[21]

Do Primaries Produce Good Candidates?

The current primary-dominated system has produced some talented candidates and some less distinguished nominees, just as the earlier nominating system did. The older nominating system tended to favor mainstream politicians who were acceptable to the party's leaders, including some candidates who had earned their nomination through party loyalty rather than through their personal appeal or their skills at governing. Primaries are more likely to give an advantage to candidates whose names are well known to the public and those who have the support of issue activists and people with intensely held views.[22]

Compared with the earlier nominating process, the current system gives presidential candidates more opportunities to demonstrate their public support, raise more campaign money, and test their stamina and ability to cope with pressure. On the other hand, candidates' performance in the primaries may not be a good indicator of their likely competence in the White House.

The National Conventions

Once the states have chosen their delegates in primaries and caucuses, the delegates go to their party's national convention and vote for a presidential nominee. But the conventions function much differently now than they did at their origins in the 1830s.

How the Conventions Began

The national party convention is an old and respected institution, but it began, at least in part, as a power grab. In 1832, Andrew Jackson's nomination as the Democratic-Republican candidate for president was a foregone conclusion, but state political leaders wanted to keep Henry Clay, the favorite of the congressional caucus, from being nominated as vice president; they preferred Martin Van Buren. So these leaders pushed for a national convention to make the nominations. In doing so, they wrested control of the presidential selection process from congressional leaders. By the time the Republican Party emerged in 1854, the convention had become the accepted means by which major parties chose their presidential candidates. Since 1856, both major parties have held national conventions every four years.

Before the nomination reforms of the 1970s, the delegates who would select the party's nominee in the national convention were chosen by state and local party leaders, not by voters. When the first round of balloting did not produce a majority for one candidate, intense bargaining would follow among state party leaders and the remaining candidates. The leading candidates would work to hold their supporters while negotiating for the votes of state delegations that had come committed to other candidates. In recent years, however, one candidate has won a majority of delegate votes well before the convention starts, so only a single round of balloting has been necessary at every convention beginning in 1956.

This pattern was tested in 2016, when the presence of a large Republican field and questions about the electability of Donald Trump led to speculation that the Republican convention would need more than one ballot to pick a nominee. But the speculators ignored an important rule of the process. About 95 percent of the convention delegates are bound by state or party rules to vote on the first convention ballot for the candidate their state's voters told them to support. If no candidate gets a majority, then on the second ballot almost 60 percent of the delegates are freed from that commitment; they can vote for a different candidate. Some delegates, sent by their states to vote for Trump, actually preferred another candidate. If the convention had needed a second ballot, then Trump would have probably lost the nomination. But a series of Trump victories in late primaries convinced his remaining competitors to drop out of the race, and the first-ballot tradition was preserved.

What Conventions Do

By the time the delegates arrive at the convention arena, of course, the nation already knows which candidate in each party won the most delegates in the primaries and caucuses and thus is the party's nominee. But the national conventions have much more to do. They begin by taking advantage of this national media exposure to spotlight the party's most popular figures and to introduce its most exciting new candidates and office-holders. Then they roll out the convention's star in what they hope will be a rousing and persuasive blastoff for the general election campaign:

Formalizing the Presidential Nomination Conventions must bring supporters of defeated primary candidates back into the party fold. So the winning nominee will stress unifying themes and party traditions as well as the major goals he or she will stress in the general election. Films will be shown depicting his or her appealing childhood and family life and linking the candidate with the party's most widely beloved figures, both historical and current.

Approving the Vice Presidential Nominee The day after the presidential nomination is ratified, delegates vote again to select the vice presidential candidate. This, too, is ceremonial; presidential nominees choose their own running mates and conventions ratify their choice.[23] In years past, the vice presidential nominee was selected by the (usually exhausted) presidential candidate at the time of the convention. Now, presidential nominees announce their "veep" choice before the convention begins, often in order to increase their support among some groups of voters.

Approving the Platform In addition to nominating candidates, the convention's main job is to approve the party's **platform**—its statement of party positions on a wide range of issues. The platform committee often asks for public comments, online as well as in hearings, long before the convention opens. The finished platform is then presented to the convention for its approval.

Because they are approved in nominating conventions whose main purpose is to choose a presidential candidate, platforms usually reflect the candidate's views or the bargains the candidate has made to win support or preserve party harmony.[24] So a platform usually lists the policy preferences of various groups in the party's (and the candidate's) supporting coalition. Platforms are also campaign documents, intended to help the party's candidates win their races.

Yet platforms are much more than just a laundry list of promises. They often define the major differences between the parties, as the leading scholar of party platforms shows.[25] As a result, they can provoke spirited debates at the convention because many delegates care deeply about this statement of the party's beliefs on such issues as abortion, taxes, pollution, and American involvement in the world (see Chapter 15).

Launching the General Election Campaign The final business of the convention is to present the party's presidential candidate to the American public. Candidates hope that their glowing portrayal in the convention will boost their public support, known as a "convention bounce."

Many other events take place at the conventions as well. Lobbyists host lavish dinners and receptions to curry favor with elected officials. Even though conventions are partly funded by tax dollars, most of their costs are paid by big donors with an interest in federal policies—corporations (especially for the Republicans), unions (for the Democrats), and wealthy individuals.

Who Are the Delegates?

Convention delegates help to shape the public's image of the two parties. What kinds of people represent their parties at these events?

Apportioning Delegates Among the States

The national parties determine how many delegates each state can send to the convention. The two parties make these choices differently. The Republicans allocate delegates more equally among the states; the Democrats weigh more heavily the size of the state's population and its record of support for Democratic candidates.

These formulas affect the voting strength of various groups within the party coalitions, as they do in the two national committees (see Chapter 4). The GOP's decision to represent the small states more equally with the large states has advantaged its conservative wing. In contrast, by giving relatively more weight to the larger states with stronger Democratic voting traditions, the Democrats have favored the more liberal interests in their party, and in particular, urban areas with large minority populations.

How Representative Are the Delegates?

The delegates to the Democratic and Republican conventions have never been a cross-section of American citizens or even of their party's voters. White males, the well-educated, and the affluent are traditionally overrepresented in conventions. Reflecting their different coalitional bases, since the 1930s, Democratic delegations have had more labor union members and black Americans, and Republican conventions have drawn more Protestants and small business owners.

Demographics The Democrats used affirmative action plans after 1968 to increase the presence of women, blacks, and, for a brief time, young people. We can see the results in surveys of convention delegates. At recent Democratic conventions, more than a third of the delegates were people of color (compared with only about 5 percent of Republican delegates), and since 1980 the DNC has required that half of the delegates be women. The percentage of female delegates at Republican conventions has increased during this period as well, without party mandates. The DNC has urged state parties to recruit more low- and moderate-income delegates, but their lesser political involvement and the high price of attending a convention stand in the way. As a result, conventions remain meetings of the wealthy and well educated. In recent conventions, a quarter to a third of both parties' delegates said they were millionaires, and most had post-graduate education.[26]

Political Experience We might assume that delegates would be recidivists, making return appearances at convention after convention. That has not been the case. After the reforms, the percentage of convention first timers jumped to about 80 percent. Even after the Democrats began granting convention seats to politically experienced superdelegates, most of the delegates were newcomers. However, the great majority are long-time party activists. Many have been active in their party for at least 20 years, and most currently hold party office.

Issues Convention delegates tend to be more extreme in their views and more aware of issues than most other voters are. They are also, as you might expect, very polarized by party. Democratic delegates tend to be more liberal than the average Democratic voter, and many more Republican delegates call themselves "very conservative" than do other GOP voters. For instance, the overwhelming majority of Democratic delegates in recent presidential conventions have favored providing health care coverage for all Americans even if taxes go up, whereas fewer than 10 percent of Republican delegates have agreed. Most Democratic delegates have favored same-sex marriage, unrestricted abortion rights, and stricter gun control laws, while the proportion of Republican delegates holding those views is only about 5 percent. The two parties' delegates differ most from one another in their views on health-care coverage and tax cuts. Although the use of primaries and caucuses was intended to make the conventions more representative of the parties' grassroots supporters, it seems to reflect the views of party activists—not surprisingly, given that they are regular participants in delegate selection events—more than the average party identifier.

Purists or Pragmatists? One reason for the Democratic Party reforms of the 1970s was to give greater voice in the nominating process to party purists—those described in Chapter 5 as attracted to politics by issues, more insistent on internal party democracy, and less willing to compromise. That aim was successful; there were more purists in the 1972 convention than there had been in 1968. At the same time, the proportion of pragmatists— those who hold long-term commitment to the party and who are more willing to compromise on issues in order to win the general election—went down.[27] As we have seen, the Democrats later moved to reverse this trend by adding superdelegates, to bring the skills of party professionals and elected officials back into the nomination process. Research shows that both before and after the reforms, delegates remained strongly committed to the parties and their goals.[28] It may be that for both pragmatists and purists, involvement in this very public party pageant strengthens delegates' commitment to the party's aims.

Who Controls the Delegates? It would not matter how representative delegates are if they act as pawns of powerful party leaders. For most of the history of party conventions, that is exactly how the state delegations behaved. But state party leaders no longer control their state delegations. When the Democrats eliminated their long-standing unit rule in 1968, through which a majority of a state delegation could throw all the delegation's votes to one candidate, they removed a powerful instrument of leadership control. Perhaps the strongest force preventing state party leaders from controlling the conventions is the fact that the delegates in both parties now come to the conventions already committed to a candidate. That makes them unavailable for "delivery" by party leaders. If anyone controls the modern conventions, then, it is the party's prospective nominee for president, not leaders of the state parties.

How Media Cover Conventions

In addition to all these changes in the convention's delegates and power centers, media coverage of conventions has changed significantly. On one hand, conventions have been reshaped and rescheduled to meet the media's needs.[29] On the other hand, ironically, media attention to the conventions has declined sharply in recent years.

Beginning with the first televised national party conventions in 1948, TV journalists and politicians found ways to serve one another's interests. In the early days of television before the convenience of videotape, networks were desperate for content with which to fill broadcast time, so they covered the party conventions live, from beginning to end. The convention became a major story, like the Olympics, in which TV news could demonstrate its skill and provide a public service. Reporters swarmed through the convention halls, covering the strategic moves of major candidates, the actions of powerful party leaders, and the reactions of individual delegates.

For party leaders, television coverage offered a priceless opportunity to reach voters and to launch the presidential campaign with maximum impact. So they reshaped the convention into a performance intended as much for the national television audience as for the delegates. Party officials gave key speaking roles to telegenic candidates, speeded up the proceedings, and moved the most dramatic convention presentations into prime-time hours. More and more, the aim of the convention shifted from the conduct of party business to the wooing of voters.

Once the nomination reforms took effect, however, and the choice of the parties' presidential candidates was settled before the convention started, conventions lost most of their suspense. To hold viewers, media searched the conventions for new sources of excitement, such as potential conflicts. But party leaders had no interest in making their disputes public; that would interfere with the positive message they were trying to convey. As the conventions became more scripted, and therefore less exciting to the public, the major networks cut their coverage markedly. Although convention junkies still can turn to cable TV to watch the entire proceedings, coverage on ABC, CBS, and NBC decreased from about 60 hours per convention in 1952 to only four hours in 2016.

Do Conventions Still Have a Purpose?

Since the nomination reforms, then, conventions have greatly changed. They are no longer the events at which the major parties actually select their presidential nominees. That happens in the primaries and caucuses; the conventions simply ratify the results. The national conventions have lost much of their deliberative character and independence.

In another way, however, the conventions have become more significant. Because candidates must mobilize groups of activists and voters in order to win primaries and caucuses and because many of these groups are concerned with particular policies, the nomination reforms have made issues all the more important in convention politics. Many delegates arrive at the convention committed not only to a candidate but also to a cause. The pressures exerted by Christian conservatives at recent Republican conventions to preserve the party's stated opposition to same-sex marriage and abortion are a good illustration.

In spite of all these changes—or perhaps because of them—the national conventions are living symbols of the national parties. They provide an occasion for rediscovering common interests and for celebrating the party's heroes. They motivate state and local party candidates, energize party workers, and launch presidential campaigns. They may not compete with *Dancing with the Stars* for ratings, but they do remind party activists and identifiers why the party matters to them.

Should We Reform the Reforms?

The McGovern–Fraser reforms were part of a time-honored pattern in American politics: reformers trying to break up concentrations of power in the party leadership. As we have seen, however, the reforms have had many unintended effects as well. Primaries can create internal divisions in party organizations that may not heal in time for the general election. The low turnouts in many primaries and caucuses can increase the influence of well-organized groups on the ideological extremes: the right wing of the Republican Party and the left wing of the Democrats. The results of a few early contests in states not very representative of the nation have a disproportionate effect on the national outcome.[30] In most years, by the time most voters know enough about the candidates to make an informed choice, the nominees have already been chosen. And candidates must invest such an enormous amount of time, energy, and money in the nomination process that the winning candidates are bone-weary—just in time for the general election campaign to begin.

There is no going back to the old system, however. As the reformers charged, it was controlled by state and local party leaders who were often out of touch with the electorate. It kept many party voters and even party activists out of the crucial first step in picking a president. It violated the desire for a more open, democratic politics, and it did not help presidential candidates learn how to prepare for the most powerful leadership job in the world.[31]

What Could Be Done?

Criticisms of this complicated, lengthy process have prompted frequent proposals for further reform.[32] A Republican task force in 2013 recommended that the long march of primaries and caucuses be compressed into four regional events, in which all the states in a given region would all schedule their primaries or caucuses on the same day. The enormous strain on the candidates would be reduced by shortening the nomination season and holding elections on only four days. That has been tried in part; beginning in the late 1980s, most southern states have held their primaries on the same day in early March, called Super Tuesday. Their aim was to encourage Democrats to nominate moderate candidates who shared southern concerns. But a set of regional primaries doesn't solve many problems. The first region to vote, with its peculiarities and specific concerns, would disproportionately influence the nominations. Regional primaries could still lead to internal party divisions; in fact, they might heighten a sense of regional party polarization.

And as we have seen, holding a national primary in which all the states' primaries and caucuses take place on a single day poses big problems as well. It advantages the candidates with the most money and name recognition, those capable of campaigning in dozens of states at the same time. It limits the roles of the party organizations and the states in selecting presidential candidates. As is so often the case in politics, there is no "right" answer here—just a series of options, each of which favors some kinds of candidates and interests and disadvantages others.

Notes

1 Marjorie Randon Hershey, "Shedding Light on the Invisible Primary," in Larry J. Sabato, ed., *Get in the Booth! The Presidential Election of 2004* (New York: Longman, 2004), pp. 27–47.

2 Ashley Parker, "'Koch Primary' Tests Hopefuls in the G.O.P.," *New York Times*, January 21, 2015, p. A1.

3 Marty Cohen, David Karol, Hans Noel, and John Zaller, *The Party Decides* (Chicago: University of Chicago Press, 2008), especially Chapter 9.

4 See John S. Jackson III and William J. Crotty, *The Politics of Presidential Selection*, 2nd ed. (New York: Longman, 2001), Chapters 3 and 4.

5 See Larry M. Bartels, *Presidential Primaries and the Dynamics of Public Choice* (Princeton, NJ: Princeton University Press, 1988), pp. 17–21.

6 William G. Mayer and Andrew E. Busch, *The Front-Loading Problem in Presidential Nominations* (Washington, DC: Brookings Institution Press, 2004), pp. 24–25.

7 James W. Ceaser, Andrew E. Busch, and John J. Pitney, Jr., *Epic Journey* (Lanham, MD: Rowman & Littlefield, 2009), p. 22.

8 See John H. Aldrich, *Before the Convention* (Chicago: University of Chicago Press, 1980); and Paul-Henri Gurian and Audrey A. Haynes, "Campaign Strategy in Presidential Primaries," *American Journal of Political Science* 37 (1993): 335–341.

9 Proportional representation doesn't always slow down a nomination race. If one candidate gains early momentum, as has happened in most recent Democratic races, then the party can settle on a nominee quickly. But when the leading candidates are closely matched in support, PR can prolong their competition.

10 John M. Broder, "Show Me the Delegate Rules and I'll Show You the Party," *New York Times*, February 17, 2008, Week in Review, p. 1.

11 Team GOP, "The Official Guide to the 2016 Republican Nominating Process," October 8, 2015, at www.gop.com/the-official-guide-to-the-2016-republican-nominating-process/ (accessed June 24, 2016).

12 Kim Fridkin, Patrick Kenney, and Sarah Gershon, "Comparing the Views of Superdelegates and Democratic Voters in the 2008 Democratic Nomination Campaign," *Party Politics* 18 (2012): 749–770. The Republicans send a smaller number of unpledged delegates, including state party chairs, to their national convention.

13 Reported in Ed O'Keefe, "Mitt Romney Slams 'Phony' Trump," *Washington Post*, March 4, 2016, p.

14 See Barbara Norrander, "Primary Elections and Caucuses," in Marjorie Randon Hershey, ed., *Guide to U.S. Political Parties* (Los Angeles: Sage, 2014), Chapter 21.

15 Barbara Norrander, *The Imperfect Primary* (New York: Routledge, 2010), p. 63.

16 Mark J. Wattier and Raymond Tatalovich, "Gods, Generals, and the Confederate Flag," The Citadel Symposium on Southern Politics, Charleston, 2004.

17 See John G. Geer, *Nominating Presidents* (New York: Greenwood Press, 1989).

18 Samuel L. Popkin, *The Reasoning Voter* (Chicago: University of Chicago Press, 1991), Chapters 6–8.

19 Bartels, *Presidential Primaries and the Dynamics of Public Choice*, Chapter 4.

20 Paul R. Abramson, John H. Aldrich, Phil Paolino, and David W. Rohde, "'Sophisticated' Voting in the 1988 Presidential Primaries," *American Political Science Review* 86 (1992): 55–69.

21 See Walter J. Stone, Ronald B. Rapoport, and Alan I. Abramowitz, "Candidate Support in Presidential Nomination Campaigns," *Journal of Politics* 54 (1992): 1074–1097.

22 Michael G. Hagen and William G. Mayer, "The Modern Politics of Presidential Selection," in William G. Mayer, ed., *In Pursuit of the White House 2000* (New York: Chatham House, 2000), pp. 17–21.

23 See Lee Sigelman and Paul J. Wahlbeck, "The 'Veepstakes'," *American Political Science Review* 91 (1997): 855–864.

24 L. Sandy Maisel, "The Platform-Writing Process," *Political Science Quarterly* 108 (1993–1994): 671–699.

25 Gerald M. Pomper, "Party Responsibility and the Future of American Democracy," in Jeffrey E. Cohen, Richard Fleisher, and Paul Kantor, eds.,

American Political Parties: Decline or Resurgence? (Washington, DC: CQ Press, 2001), pp. 170–172.

26 These data and those cited in the rest of the chapter come from the *New York Times*/CBS News Polls of Democratic and Republican National Convention delegates.

27 See John W. Soule and Wilma E. McGrath, "A Comparative Study of Presidential Nomination Conventions," *American Journal of Political Science* 19 (1975): 501–517.

28 Geoffrey C. Layman, "Party Activists," in Hershey, ed., *Guide to U.S. Political Parties*, Chapter 16, and Kenny J. Whitby, *Strategic Decision-making in Presidential Nominations* (Albany, NY: SUNY Press, 2014). See also Priscilla L. Southwell, "A Backroom Without the Smoke?" *Party Politics* 18 (2012): 267–283.

29 Shafer, *Bifurcated Politics*, Chapter 8; and Costas Panagopoulos, ed., *Rewiring Politics* (Baton Rouge, LO: Louisiana State University Press, 2007).

30 See Emmett H. Buell, Jr., "The Changing Face of the New Hampshire Primary," in William G. Mayer, ed., *In Pursuit of the White House 2000* (New York: Chatham House, 2000), pp. 87–144.

31 Nelson W. Polsby, *The Consequences of Party Reform* (Oxford: Oxford University Press, 1983).

32 See Caroline Tolbert and Peverill Squire, eds., "Reforming the Presidential Nominating Process," *PS: Political Science and Politics* 42 (2009): 27–79.

CHAPTER 11

The General Election

Thousands of college students "felt the Bern" in the 2016 Democratic primaries, supporting Vermont Senator Bernie Sanders for the presidential nomination against Hillary Clinton. Sanders ran behind Clinton in the polls when the primary season began. Months later, he trailed in the delegate count as well. "Bern" won several states' primaries and caucuses late in the spring, but he still couldn't catch up with Clinton. The frustration of Sanders's supporters finally exploded in the Nevada caucuses in May. Sanders lashed out at Clinton and the party's leadership. Some party leaders lashed back. Sanders had become the houseguest who overstayed his welcome, they said; he needed to end his campaign and let Clinton focus on running against Republican Donald Trump. Sanders told them to mind their own business.

If his party leadership advised Sanders to stop running, then why didn't he? Because the party leaders don't run today's campaigns. The candidates and their supporters do. And candidate Sanders vowed to keep on campaigning.

This isn't the way campaigns used to work. Most campaigns were **party centered** until the mid-1900s: party leaders managed candidates' campaigns with the party's interests as their main focus, just as they do today in most other democracies. State and local party organizations provided most of the money and volunteers used by candidates. But a series of changes were undermining parties' control over campaigns. Reformers pushed for greater use of primary elections. Because it is risky for a party to take sides in a primary, candidates had to compete for their party's nomination by creating their own campaign organization, which they tended to keep after winning the primary. State and local party organizations were weakened by other reforms, ranging from civil service laws to nonpartisan elections, and their flow of volunteers dried up (see Chapter 3). Some public relations experts specialized in political consulting and provided the services—for a fee, of course—that the parties had provided for free (or at least for no monetary payment) in earlier years.

These changes freed candidates from having to depend on their parties for money, volunteers, and advice. Campaigns became more **candidate centered**, directed by the candidates and their staffs and consultants rather than by the party organizations and focusing on the candidate's needs, not the party's. But as they have throughout their long lives, the parties adjusted to these changes.[1] This chapter will look at the technologies, information sources, and means of persuasion that candidates now have, which contribute to the candidate-centered nature of most campaigns. We will also explore the conditions in which party organizations have been able to reclaim an important role in at least some campaigns.

Campaign Strategy

Designing strategy for a general election campaign[2] differs in several ways from that in a primary. Campaigning in a primary election focuses mainly on party voters, especially in states with closed primaries (see Chapter 9). In contrast, the general election audience is much larger, more diverse, and can observe the candidates for a longer time. The general election campaign is also powerfully affected by whether the candidate's party is in the majority or the minority in that district (see box "Party Campaign Strategies in 2020" on page 250).

In both primary and general election campaigns, however, one of the best ways to win office is to already hold the office you seek.[3] Incumbents normally have greater name recognition and more success in attracting (usually favorable) media coverage than do their potential opponents. Their constituent service and their paid travel to and from the district give them a substantial edge over their challengers, unless they throw it away due to scandal. Their access to power makes it easier for incumbents to raise as much campaign money as they think they need, and their experience helps them use it effectively. Also, incumbents are usually part of the majority party in the district. Because of these advantages, in both primaries and general elections, incumbents often need to do little more than stress their understanding of the district, their trustworthiness, and their commitment to widely shared values.

Challengers face a much harsher campaign environment. Especially if they have not won any other political office before, challengers do not start with an experienced organization, proven fund-raising skills, or the other incumbent advantages.[4] In the days when party organizations ran campaigns, this might not have been a problem. At a time of candidate-centered campaigns, it is. One obvious answer might be to purchase an experienced campaign organization by hiring political consultants, but most challengers do not have the money. Thus, the predictable cycle begins. The challenger lacks an existing organization and enough money to attract the interest of well-known consultants and buy media time, so he or she cannot reach many voters. Without these vital resources, a challenger will not rise in the polls or raise enough money to become better known.

Party Campaign Strategies in 2020

As the manager of a campaign in 2020, you will need to decide how much of your resources to devote to mobilizing your base—your core supporters—and how much to spend on appealing to independents. If you are running the campaign of the majority party's candidate in a congressional district, you'll win if you can turn out enough of your majority. To do that, you'll probably campaign by stressing the party's core values and the concerns of groups in its base. With more U.S. House districts "safe" for one party, this base strategy is used increasingly. If your party is in the minority or the race is competitive, then traditionally you would broaden your appeal to include independents.

Donald Trump's 2016 presidential campaign showed both the strengths and the limits of a base strategy. Trump got his strongest support from less-educated whites, especially older white men, rural people, and evangelical Christians. A base-only strategy can work only if your base is numerous enough to be within striking distance of a majority. Because social-demographic changes have left these groups a declining portion of the American population, Trump's base wouldn't have been enough to win, especially because people who have been left behind, such as the less-educated, tend to be "low propensity voters." And although he also received significant support from regular Republican voters, his claim that the election result was "rigged" left some of his supporters unconvinced that their vote would count. Fortunately for Trump, Hillary Clinton's base wasn't excited enough by their candidate to turn out. Young people and black Americans voted less in 2016 than in 2012. So although Clinton won the popular vote, she lost the Electoral College vote and, therefore, the presidency.

To add to his base, Trump tried to appeal to independents. But among people interested in politics, there are very few independents left. In 2012, Republican presidential candidate Mitt Romney began moderating his stands on abortion, taxes, and immigration once he won the party's nomination. He did so to attract independent voters, because the Republicans were the minority party. He did win most of the independent voters in the general election. But he became the first recent candidate to win the independents and lose the presidency. In these polarized times, the "center" does not consist of moderate voters. It consists largely of people who know and care little about politics and whose views on issues tend to be a grab bag of left and right. Obama used a sophisticated program of locating and targeting his base and other prospective supporters to win a majority. Although Trump's targeting operation barely existed, the Republican National Committee took over that element of his campaign.

If you are managing a 2020 presidential campaign, which approach would you take? On the Republican side, will appeals to your conservative Christian base weaken your support among the growing numbers of minority voters? If you're a Democrat, can you motivate your base to go to the polls without causing a counter-mobilization among Republican supporters? If your strategy works, you'll be hailed as a genius, and your party's candidates in 2024 will compete to hire you. If it doesn't, expect to be a frequent source of humor on social media.

No matter how resource poor they are, however, challengers can raise issues. Thus, policy issues such as abortion, health care, and taxes are more important tools for challengers than they are for incumbents.[5] Researchers find that challengers usually do better when they campaign on issues "owned" by their party, such as health care and Social Security for Democrats and national defense and taxes for Republicans.[6] But even the most powerful issues won't do a challenger much good if he or she can't attract the money or media coverage needed to publicize them.

Candidates for open seats (those where no incumbent is running) are more likely to run competitive races. Typically, people who choose to run for highly visible offices—the presidency, governorships, Senate seats—already have considerable name recognition, which increases because of the attention given to an open seat race. They can attract enough funds to pay for extensive media campaigns. Their major challenge will be to spend their money effectively and to define themselves to the voters before their opponent gets the chance to define them.

How Campaigning Has Changed

Candidates now have campaign tools that would have been the envy of campaigners decades ago. Advances in data analytics, social media, voter targeting, and fund-raising have revolutionized campaigning.

Sources of Information

Polls and Big Databases In big and competitive races, campaigns want to gather as much information as they can about each prospective voter, from issue attitudes to voting histories. Voting records, social media, and public opinion polls are the chief sources of this information.[7] The national party organizations also combine information gained from "frequent shopper" cards, other consumer databases, and the tracking of individuals' Internet browsing into massive databases on voters' attitudes, as you'll soon see.

Computers The resulting databases are mined for patterns, such as which types of voters get angry at which issues, what mobilizes them, and how they feel about the campaign. Before computers were used in campaigns, candidates relied on guesswork and the opinions of highly regarded political advisers to guide their choices. Now, big-budget campaigns can test the predicted effects of hundreds of alternative strategies on the behavior of their voter models. Campaign strategists can then create evidence-based plans for buying media time and selecting ad content. Fund-raisers can compare the amounts of money raised by different appeals. Opposition ("oppo") researchers can locate statements made by the opposing candidate on any conceivable issue. Social media marketing campaigns can be analyzed for impact and then fine-tuned.

Professional Consultants

Political consultants specialize in particular campaign services.[8] Some consultants buy media time for advertising, focusing on what programs or times of day will benefit each of their candidate clients. Others deal mainly with web-page design or canvassing or direct-mail fund-raising. Professional consultants usually work for several different campaigns at a time, but they almost always work with clients from only one party. Some consultants restrict themselves even further to one ideological grouping within the party. Although they function independently of the party organization, they normally try to keep a cooperative relationship with the party's leaders. National party committees often play a matchmaking role in bringing together consultants and candidates.

Methods of Persuasion: The Air War

Because of the large size of most state and federal election districts, candidates (and national parties as well) make extensive use of the mass media, especially television, radio, and the Internet.

Television

Television consumes most of a typical campaign's budget. In the early and inexpensive days of TV, candidates bought large chunks of time to air entire speeches to a wide audience. Now, because of TV's increased cost and voters' shorter attention spans, campaign messages are compressed into 30-second spot ads that can be run frequently.[9] Media specialists carefully target the placement of these ads. If a candidate wants to appeal to middle-aged men, for instance, then the specialist might run ads on *NCIS* and *Monday Night Football*. In midterm congressional races, where older people are a larger proportion of voters than in presidential elections, consultants reach older viewers by placing ads on *Good Morning America*, *Today*, and *CBS This Morning*. The value of broadcast advertising has been reduced by technology that can screen out campaign ads, from the "mute" button to TV Ad Blocker, but these ads remain a staple of campaigns that can afford them.

Cable TV is a cost-effective alternative to the traditional networks and works especially well in local campaigns, whose constituencies are too small to warrant buying time in major media markets. Most cable stations, such as Fox News and CBN (Christian Broadcasting Network), have more specialized "niche" audiences than do the bigger networks. This permits campaigns to target their ads to types of viewers likely to support them (called ***narrowcasting***).

Campaigns also try to get as much **free media** coverage as possible on TV and radio news and in newspapers. (Campaigners prefer to call it **earned media**.) When newscasts and print reporters cover a candidate, the information may seem more credible and "objective" than if it is conveyed through the campaign's own ads.

To get free media coverage, campaigns need to provide material that meets the media's definition of "news."[10] If "news" is that which is dramatic, controversial, and immediate, then a candidate is not likely to earn media coverage by delivering the same speech one more time. Dave Barry offers this illustration: "Let's consider two headlines. FIRST HEADLINE: 'Federal Reserve Board Ponders Reversal of Postponement of Deferral of Policy Reconsideration.' SECOND HEADLINE: 'Federal Reserve Board Caught in Motel with Underage Sheep.' Be honest, now. Which of these two stories would you read?"[11] Candidates who depend on free media need to stage campaign events that use the tamer, political equivalent of the underage sheep: dramatic confrontations, exciting settings, or meetings with well-known or telegenic people.

But free media coverage of campaigns is all too brief. Even close to Election Day, viewers are typically exposed to less than two minutes of election news during a 30-minute local newscast, most of it discussing strategy and polls, compared with four and a half minutes of paid political ads.[12] And the number of available media options now allows Americans to avoid political news altogether. The political information these news avoiders receive, then, comes entirely from campaign ads and entertainment programming.[13]

The Internet

First used by candidates in 1996, websites are now a part of every major campaign and many local races as well. Campaigns can reach their supporters directly on the Internet, thus bypassing the choices made by the broadcast media. Many websites ask visitors to register, which allows the campaign to contact them later. By loading ads online—on YouTube, for instance—campaigners can get their messages distributed nationally without paying for costly TV time.

Media buyers also place campaign ads as pop-ups on other Internet sites, or as "pre-rolls" on YouTube. Both parties buy ads on Google, so that when someone enters a search term indicating her political sympathies (for instance, "Clinton Corrupt"), a pop-up ad could appear later featuring the party or candidate closest to those views. People clicking on the ad are directed to a page where they can donate funds. By examining the "take," a consultant can measure which search terms brought the best results. Campaigns now create ads designed specifically for online use, rather than just posting made-for-TV ads on social media or other platforms. And although people under the age of 30 are most likely to be Internet users, older adults who use the Internet are increasingly likely to watch political videos and share election news online.[14]

In short, the broadcast media are an efficient way to reach large numbers of prospective voters. Their greatest strength, however—the breadth of their reach—is also one of their greatest weaknesses. (The other is their high cost.) If you were running for office, you would want to target different messages to different kinds of people so that you could speak to each individual about the issue that most concerns him or her.

Direct Contact by Mail, Text, and Twitter

Direct Mail By merging postal mail lists of people who are of special interest to a campaign, consultants can direct personalized letters to millions of people who might be inclined to respond to a particular appeal. A candidate who wants to appeal to pro-gun voters, for example, could send computer-generated letters to people on mailing lists of the National Rifle Association, donors to other pro-gun candidates, and subscribers to hunting magazines. Because these messages are designed to be read by like-minded individuals in the privacy of their homes, direct-mail appeals can be highly emotional and inflammatory, appeals that would not work as well in the broadcast media.

E-mail E-mail has the great advantage that it is cheaper than regular mail; fund-raising using e-mail and websites costs about one penny for each dollar raised, compared with about 40 cents per dollar raised by direct (postal) mail.[15] Online fund-raising remains the primary source of donations in federal campaigns and for many state and local candidates as well. The 2012 Obama campaign was a master of this; it raised about $690 million online, in part by re-contacting small donors and asking them to contribute again.[16]

Text Messaging Because postal mail misses large numbers of young people whose addresses change from year to year, campaigns increasingly use texting to contact supporters.[17] The Obama campaign led here as well. It outraised the Romney campaign substantially in contributions made by text message, using its "Quick Donate" program. In battleground states, every voter who had signed up for Obama texts got several messages on Election Day reminding him or her to vote.

Facebook Social media have become central to campaigning.[18] People were more likely to engage with the 2016 presidential campaigns on social media than on the candidates' websites. By sending a campaign message on Facebook (or through e-mail, texting, or blogs) and urging each recipient to forward it to his or her friends on social networks, a campaign can increase its reach exponentially at little or no cost, called viral marketing. In 2015 Facebook began collaborating with the marketing company Acxiom so that campaigns could upload any list of voters and match it to their Facebook accounts, thus connecting the campaign directly with those on the list. Because Facebook has a lot of specific information about each user, this interface allows candidates to fine-tune their micro-targeting.

Twitter Although Facebook has a broader audience, politically minded Twitter users are more apt to follow breaking news on the site than are similarly interested posters on Facebook. Campaigns can segment the Twitter audience according to individuals' expressed interest, just as they can on Facebook. Posts on both of these sites are substantially more negative about the candidates than is coverage in the mainstream media.[19] Both social networking sites have exploded as information sources; between 2010 and 2016, Twitter's active users had increased ten-fold to 310 million. Donald Trump in particular relied heavily on Twitter to spread his own message or to retweet those of others.

The Ground War: "Under the Radar"

One of the most effective ways to persuade voters is to talk with them one-on-one. House-to house canvassing and phone calls to selected individuals are known as the **ground war**. Canvassing has been reinvigorated in the 2000s, now that it has been married to high-tech advances in voter targeting.

Canvassing and Phone Banks

In the days of machine politics, party organizations sent their patronage workers and other activists to the homes of people who might vote for party candidates, to tell them about the party ticket. Democratic local party organizations were especially adept at door-to-door canvassing, often using labor union volunteers. These efforts declined in the late 1900s, because parties found it harder to enlist willing workers. But the recent increase in party polarization has motivated new volunteers. And the prospect of arming canvassers with extensive information about the individuals they are trying to persuade gives the ground war a new appeal. The Republicans moved first, experimenting with a canvassing program in the 2002 midterm elections. They flooded precincts in some competitive states with volunteers and paid staffers, especially during the last 72 hours of the campaign. This **72-hour project** was expensive, costing $200 million, but observers felt that it increased Republican turnout by about 3 percent over that of the last midterm election. Republicans won most of the close contests, maintained control of the House, and narrowly regained control of the Senate.[20] Thus, they greatly expanded the 72-hour project in 2004 based on the concept of **micro-targeting** or "niche marketing."

What the National Parties Probably Know About You

The two national parties know more about you than many of your friends do. For starters, both parties' national committees have probably bought or received from state election officials all the information you provided if you registered to vote. The information varies by state, but it likely includes your name, address, sex, age, whether you asked for a Republican or Democratic ballot in primary elections, whether or not you voted in previous general elections (though not *how* you voted), and in some states, your party affiliation and race. To this base of information, the national parties add your contact information, any campaign contributions you've made, and Census data about your area's demographics and voting trends. Even if you have not registered to vote, you are still likely to be in the parties' databases, minus the information gathered when people register.

The national parties may then choose to add more personalized information about you. When a party canvasser comes to your door, he or she may ask about your issue and candidate preferences and add them to your record in the party's database. Your online viewing habits can be tracked by the parties, just as they are by a variety of advertisers. By buying data from supermarkets and other merchandisers using "customer loyalty" cards, they can find out about your consumption patterns. So the parties are likely to know whether you answer e-mail and, if so, at what time of day; whether you prefer Coors or Miller beer, belong to a church, a mosque, or Hillel, and what issue angers you the most.

Why do the parties want to know all this about you? Because campaigns and party organizations can use these data to predict the chance you'll vote in a primary or general election, whether you are a likely supporter, and the types of campaign appeals to which you'll respond most positively. That lets the party determine whether to contact you, how often, and the issues most likely to trigger your support.

Micro-Targeting

If you knock on every door in a big city, you'll reach a lot of Democrats. Republican voters are not as concentrated geographically as Democrats tend to be. So Republican strategists determined in the early 2000s that they would have to use more high-tech means to locate likely Republican voters. Drawing on market research techniques developed by their business allies, the national Republicans turned to micro-targeting: using electoral and consumer data to pinpoint the interests of individuals and then delivering a message tailored to their particular concerns. Republicans collected data on millions of people's voting histories, viewing habits, magazine subscriptions, and buying preferences. They entered these data into a national Republican database called **Voter Vault**. Analysis of the data showed that people who tune in to country or religious stations, Fox News, or the Golf Channel; drive BMWs rather than Chevys, go to exercise clubs after work, drink bourbon or Coors beer, and watch college rather than pro football are more inclined to support Republicans. Although these consumer preferences may not be as predictive of political behavior as are strictly political data (such as voter registration lists in states where people register by party), they can help to flesh out a picture of each voter (see box "What the National Parties Probably Know About You" on page 256).

With these massive databases, the campaign and the Republican National Committee (RNC), in coordination with Republican state and local parties, worked to cherry-pick likely Republican voters in the 2004 election. They focused especially on seven million likely Republicans and ten million conservative-leaning independents who had not voted regularly in the past. Then they classified these targets into a series of types and determined which issues were most likely to activate voters in each type. One voter type could be approached with a personal contact or phone call dealing with same-sex marriage; another might receive an appeal about terrorism.

This Republican success in the ground war led the national Democrats to ramp up their own program beginning in 2008. Democrats quickly developed the staff; the experts with particular skill at cutting-edge data analytics tended to be social liberals, and in 2008 and 2012 they were hired in large numbers by the Obama campaign, where they transformed the ground war. In 2012, for instance, Obama's presidential campaign claims to have recruited 2.3 million volunteers and knocked on 7 million doors on one day alone.[21] The program seemed effective; one careful study found that in 2012, the two presidential candidates' canvassing, phoning, and mail appeals to voters increased turnout by 7–8 percentage points in battleground states.[22]

By 2014, Democratic groups were using smartphone technology to give canvassers extensive, up-to-date information—candidate preference, the voter's key issue—about each of the households they were hoping to convince. The Democratic Senatorial Campaign Committee created the Bannock Street Project to expand canvassing in ten states with competitive Senate races that year, fueled by 4,000 paid staffers and up to $60 million in funding. The RNC's self-examination of the 2012 presidential campaign acknowledged that the GOP had lost its edge in this area and called for Republicans to improve their micro-targeting and canvassing and cultivate a "culture of data."[23] Americans for Prosperity, a tax-exempt non-profit conservative group organized by oil billionaires David and Charles Koch, helped Republicans expand their data collection for 2014 and 2016. The RNC funded much of the effort.[24] Both national parties, then, had extensive and well-financed grassroots canvassing campaigns by 2016.

Canvassing is not a magic bullet (see box "Micro-Targeting in 2016: Trumped?" on page 258). It may not hit its intended targets.[25] Campaigns have to select their canvassers carefully; those whose characteristics do not match those of the area they're canvassing can do more harm than good.

Micro-Targeting in 2016: Trumped?

The Obama campaign put major emphasis on the ground war in 2008—the block-by-block, phone-by-phone effort to contact as many individuals as possible. It was widely hailed as the main reason for his victory. In 2012, Obama 2.0 not only beefed up these field operations but also invested extensively in technological innovations. The data analytics team of the 2012 Obama campaign, quadruple the size of that of the 2008 Obama organization, merged massive amounts of data from field staffers, fund-raisers, pollsters, state Democratic voter files, and social media information. Obama staffers and volunteers interacted with continuously updated voter information. Using the database, analysts could tailor their appeals, canvassing, and fund-raising requests to the characteristics of each recipient. The campaign had enough data to assign a "support score" from 1 to 100 to every voter in each battleground state. Mitt Romney's campaign technology proved to be much less effective.

Republicans saw the need for upgraded technology. In 2016, presidential candidate Ted Cruz answered the call. His campaign added psychological research to the usual micro-targeting data in order to pinpoint likely supporters. They also used "geo-fencing," a tool to direct tailored messages to devices within a very narrow geographic area, such as a National Rifle Association convention.

For a time, it looked as though these sophisticated ground-war techniques would prevail. Cruz narrowly beat rival Donald Trump in the 2016 Iowa Republican caucuses, and Trump acknowledged that his campaign had not invested enough in direct personal contact. But soon after, Trump piled up a steady diet of victories in primaries and caucuses using little or no micro-targeting. Instead, he rode the crest of unremitting media coverage of his anti-immigrant, provocative claims. Trump combined his showmanship skills with his instinct for the outrage felt by less-educated, older white men at marked recent demographic changes in the U.S. population. Trump's huge wave of "free media" trumped Cruz's superior ground game.

Trump continued this freewheeling campaign style through the November election, relying heavily on free media. He paid so little attention to organizational matters that his county staffer in one Colorado county was a 12-year-old boy. He delegated the get-out-the-vote mechanics to the Republican National Committee. Some strategists called it "campaign malpractice."

In contrast, his Democratic opponent in the general election, Hillary Clinton, ran a much more high-tech, data-driven race. Yet Trump won in November, leading some experts to wonder whether micro-targeting has its limits, or, as many suspected, that Donald Trump is an exception to most rules.

Sources: See Eitan Hersh, *Hacking the Electorate* (Cambridge: Cambridge University Press, 2015); and Tom Hamburger, "Cruz Campaign Credits Psychological Data and Analytics for Its Rising Success," *Washington Post*, December 14, 2015, p. A1.

But when combined with micro-targeting, the ground war is again a staple of modern campaigning.

In addition to door-to-door canvassing, many campaigns bring supporters to a central location (a *phone bank*) with telephones—often a business, union, or party or campaign headquarters, or even an empty building where volunteers can use their smartphones—to dial lists of numbers identified by the campaign's micro-targeting. Phone banking is cheaper than door-to-door contact, though usually not as persuasive. Even cheaper are virtual phone banks, where supporters anywhere in the nation go online to get a list of phone numbers and a script to read, and **robocalls,** in which volunteers or computers can direct automated phone calls to large numbers of people on a campaign's target list. Robocalls are often used to send a negative message or to do **push polling**—attack messages disguised as public opinion polls. In high-profile races, households may receive several of these calls a night as the election approaches. These techniques have limits, too: Caller ID lets people screen their calls, and the growing number of cell-phone-only individuals makes calling more costly.

Negative Campaigning

This negative campaigning is nothing new; political figures have been viciously attacked personally as well as ideologically since the U.S. began. But negative advertising seems to be on the increase recently. News media cover negative ads more than positive ads, because conflict and controversy better fit the media definition of "news." Media coverage of these negative ads then carries their message to even more people.[26] In North Carolina alone in 2014, almost 11,000 negative TV ads were aired in *one week* in a closely fought Senate race, compared with about 24 ads with a positive tone. Party independent spending, super PACs (see Chapter 12), and other outside groups were responsible for most of the negative ads. This benefits candidates, who don't have to take the blame for "going negative" because the damaging information is being aired by others.[27]

Much recent evidence suggests that negative campaigning works under some conditions. Negative ads are often particularly memorable and emotionally engaging; that can increase voter information and turnout. Attack ads probably do their worst damage to candidates who are less well known to the public—challengers, for instance—because their public images are not yet fixed. The timing of the ads matters as well. Before an individual chooses a candidate, negative ads can be informative and useful. After the individual has made his or her choice, attack ads are more likely to depress turnout, especially among people who are not strong partisans.[28] But negative ads are less effective when they emphasize an issue the candidate doesn't want to stress or when their tone is harsh enough to offend viewers.

Putting These Tools to Work

These campaign tools have been used in a variety of ways in recent elections. In addition to the innovations in ground-war techniques, the population to which campaigners have to appeal has changed in fundamental ways.

A Democratic Wave in 2008

Democrats held a strong position coming into the 2008 presidential election. Democrats took control of both houses of Congress in 2006 for the first time in 12 years, in large part because Republican President George W. Bush's public approval ratings were sinking like a stone, as was public approval of the war in Iraq. As Chapter 4 showed, the Democratic National Committee (DNC) and several other Democratic-leaning groups put heavy emphasis on matching the Republicans' micro-targeting skills. Using the DNC's upgraded VoteBuilder databank as well as data from the privately owned Catalist, the Obama campaign designed an extensive ground game. In addition to door-to-door canvassing, it contacted voters successfully through the Internet, text messaging, and other electronic tools.

Perhaps the most notable accomplishment of Obama's campaign was its ability to expand the playing field. Prior to 2008, Democratic presidential campaigns had targeted a group of reliably Democratic East and West Coast states and then aimed to pick up just enough "battleground" states (typically, Ohio, Pennsylvania, and Florida) to reach an Electoral College majority. Obama's staffers tried to create more alternative paths to victory. They put particular effort into some previously Republican states, such as Colorado and Virginia, whose demographic profile was becoming more favorable to Democratic candidates.

Even so, it wasn't an easy race for the Democrat. As a self-proclaimed "maverick" and reformer, Republican candidate John McCain was able to separate himself from the unpopular President Bush. McCain was a war hero, a longtime political presence in comparison with Obama's relative inexperience in national politics, and a personality attractive to independents. McCain's campaign sought to overcome a Democratic trend by portraying Obama as an elitist who did not "share our values," and he seemed to be succeeding shortly after the Republican convention. But the financial disaster of mid-September, and McCain's unsteady response to it, broke McCain's momentum. Blacks and Latinos, women, city dwellers, upscale suburbanites, and liberals formed the core of Obama's victory. Democratic successes were crowned by gains of 8 Senate seats and 21 in the House. Like 2006, 2008 was a Democratic wave election.

Backlash in 2010

After two back-to-back victories for the Democrats, the tide turned again. The economy was improving only slowly. Although a unified Democratic government had passed major legislation in 2009 and 2010, including health-care reform and a massive economic stimulus package, these accomplishments did not boost the party's approval ratings. Republicans charged that Obama and the Democratic Congress were trying to engineer a government takeover of health care and other parts of the economy. Extensive coverage of bargaining on the health care bill made the process look distasteful to many voters and triggered an energetic anti-Democratic protest by Tea Party activists.[29] President Obama's job approval ratings slipped below 50 percent. Thus, the two main predictors of election results—presidential approval ratings and economic indicators—pointed to major Democratic losses in 2010.

In addition, as happens in wave elections, many of the Democrats who had been elected in 2006 and 2008 had won districts and states that were normally Republican. These "exposed" incumbents were in danger when the partisan tide shifted. The national Democrats were forced to use resources to protect these vulnerable incumbents, whereas the national Republican committees were able to expand their targeting to include powerful Democratic House members and senators as well as junior members.

The Democrats suffered a monumental defeat in 2010. Although Democratic campaign spending outpaced the GOP, and Democratic candidates actually won more House votes than Republicans did (see Chapter 7), Republicans gained a House majority by winning 66 seats and losing only three—the biggest gain by either party since 1948. The GOP also gained 6 Senate seats (but not majority control) and 6 governorships, plus more than 700 state legislative seats. That gave Republicans increased control over the redistricting of state legislative and congressional seats that took place in 2011. Democratic losses were especially heavy among moderates and those who supported the health-care reform bill and the extension of President Bush's bank bailout.[30] The pattern of defeats left the Democratic congressional party more liberal, and the Republicans more conservative, than before.

A Democratic Revival in 2012

Yet the parties' voter support was still balanced enough that the Democrats were able to regain strength in 2012. It is not surprising that midterm congressional elections differ from presidential races. Turnout at midterm is normally only about two-thirds of the presidential turnout, In current politics, midterm voters are more likely to be white, older, and wealthier than the general electorate, and this was markedly true in 2010. The 2012 electorate, then, would be younger, more diverse, more weighted toward blacks and Latinos, and thus friendlier to Democrats.

The political environment differed as well. Although real incomes were only slightly higher than four years earlier and the unemployment rate remained high, the income growth rate increased in September, just in time to allay some of the economic pessimism and boost Obama's prospects of reelection.[31] And much of the public pinned the lion's share of the blame for the recession on Bush, Obama's predecessor.

But the Obama campaign knew that economic confidence was still low and the president's approval ratings remained marginal. So they began their air war very early, in May, with heavy ad spending to define Romney to a national audience before Romney had the chance to define himself. Obama ads portrayed the Republican as a super-rich, heartless corporate raider with little understanding of ordinary people's lives. Romney inadvertently confirmed the image by commenting at what he thought was a private fund-raiser that 47 percent of Americans believe they are entitled to health care, food, and housing, and that government has a responsibility to care for them, so they don't take personal responsibility for their own lives. Film of the comments went viral.

The Obama campaign emphasized its ground game as well, with an elaborate network of field offices. As the box on page 258 showed, Obama's organization relied on a massive, integrated database to mobilize occasional voters who were inclined to favor Obama and to raise unprecedented sums from small donors. Romney got more help than Obama from very well-funded outside groups, but the Republicans' post-election self-study concluded that this funding, spent mainly on TV advertising (the air war), had not brought enough of a return in votes.[32]

Obama won reelection, but most demographic groups gave him less support in 2012 than in 2008. Latino Americans were an important exception. Romney took a hard line on immigration, suggesting that undocumented immigrants "self-deport." One Republican activist complained that increasing the Republican vote among Latinos is not possible when "some Republicans talk as if they're for the deportation of your mother or your aunt."[33] Romney found himself in a difficult spot on this and other issues. Because his main primary competitors were extremely conservative, he was pushed to take far-right positions to win Republican primaries and caucuses. But that left him unable to appeal effectively in the general election campaign to Latinos and others who rejected these positions.

... And the Republican Comeback in 2014

The Democrats faced a more hostile terrain in 2014. President Obama's approval ratings were dropping. Polls showed that Republican voters were much more engaged in the campaign than were Democrats. The midterm electorate would be more receptive to Republicans. The Senate incumbents who were up for reelection had last been elected in the Democratic wave of 2008, leaving many of them "exposed." Democrats had to defend 21 Senate seats in 2014, seven of them in states won by Romney in 2012; Republicans had to defend only 15. On top of all these disadvantages, the states electing senators in 2014 tended to be smaller and more conservative than were the states comprising the other two Senate election cycles.

Republicans used their improved data analytics to tie each Democratic candidate to President Obama and to public discontent with the new Affordable Care Act (which Republicans termed "Obamacare"). Spending by both party and non-party groups reached new heights (see Chapter 12). "Dark money" groups (nonprofit, tax exempt "social welfare" organizations allowed by federal law to keep the names of their donors secret), and super PACs, both of which can accept unlimited donations from individuals, corporations, and unions, blanketed the airwaves.

Then a series of frightening news stories appeared just before the election: terrorism by the Islamic State, a major outbreak of the Ebola virus in Africa, a rush of undocumented children crossing into the U.S. from Mexico. Everything pointed to a Democratic defeat, but the outcome was even worse than Democrats feared. Republicans gained a net 13 seats in the House, for a total of 247, their biggest House majority since the 1920s. With a switch of nine Senate seats from Democratic to Republican, the Republicans now held majorities in both houses of Congress, though the Senate majority was slim.

2016: The Unprecedented Campaign

Then came the strangest nomination race in years. The Republican field was exceptionally large; 17 candidates sought to replace the retiring President Obama. The most unusual of these was real-estate mogul Donald Trump, a billionaire and reality TV star (*The Apprentice*) with a talent for attracting media attention with his bombastic comments. Trump seemed to be testing all the traditional rules of presidential campaigning. He spent very little on polls and ads until late in the campaign, relying heavily instead on the astronomical amount of free media coverage he received. He leveled no-holds-barred attacks on other candidates, as well as Latinos, Muslims, and women. His rhetoric (denigrating Democrats, minorities, Muslims, the media, even other Republicans) seemed to tap into the anger of many in the Republican base. Because of his outrageous statements and his deviations from conservative orthodoxy, analysts expected Trump's candidacy to flame out fairly quickly. It didn't.

Trump attracted about 45 percent of the vote in Republican primaries and caucuses, but that was enough, in a multi-candidate race, to lock up his party's nomination. Then his challenges began. When Trump became the presumptive nominee, many Republican big donors and super PACs pulled out of the presidential race. The RNC had earlier reached an accommodation with various outside groups that the party would focus its efforts on data

Why Did Donald Trump Win in 2016?

Very conservative Republicans argued that Donald Trump won the White House because, despite his personal foibles, he stood up for conservative values, including stopping abortion and appointing a very conservative justice to the Supreme Court. The lesson, they said, was to nominate consistent conservatives in the future.

Somewhat less conservative Republicans contended that Trump appealed to a wide range of voters because he sounded authentic and independent. A down-the-line Tea Party conservative would have alienated too many independents.

Many moderate Democrats felt that Hillary Clinton was a flawed candidate with too much baggage involving scandals; to gain greater support, the party should emphasize a broader economic message to appeal to independents and white men.

Many liberal Democrats claimed that Trump won mainly because Clinton was too closely linked with the status quo, and that Bernie Sanders, her opponent for the nomination who called himself a Democratic Socialist, would have beaten Trump by a bigger margin. Democrats, then, should stress issues such as income inequality, as Sanders did, rather than more moderate-sounding policies.

It is common for different groups to interpret (or "spin") the meaning of an election differently, in ways that support their own preferred views. Journalists, who are the targets of the spin, often become cynical about it. Jon Margolis, former national political reporter for the *Chicago Tribune*, claims that he switched to the sports beat because he said he'd never seen a sports story that read, "The Chicago Cubs defeated the St. Louis Cardinals today by a score of 2–1. The Cardinals denied it."

Sources: Margolis quoted in Ronald D. Elving, "Campaign Data Can Be Calculated Nonsense," *CQ Weekly*, August 19, 1995, p. 2602; Josh Barro, "The Crisis in the Republican Party Is Even Worse Than It Looks," *Business Insider*, May 3, 2016, at www.businessinsider.com/donald-trump-nomination-gop-crisis-2016-5 (accessed June 25, 2016), with thanks to David Karol.

collection, field operations, and digital advances, while the non-party groups would fund "independent" spending on TV ads. The biggest of these outside groups, however—those associated with the oil billionaire Koch brothers (see Chapter 12)—were unwilling to help elect Trump and instead concentrated their funds on Senate and other races. He did develop an impressive small donor base to add to his own personal funds, but not until summer.

Trump's public image was much more intensely unfavorable than that of any previous presidential candidate. It didn't help that he was frequently caught in outright lies about his businesses, his international experience, and his opponent, to the point where even conservative journalists began referring to him as a "master fabulist" and a "short-fingered vulgarian."[34]

The Democratic campaign was unprecedented as well. Former Secretary of State Hillary Clinton became the first woman to win a major party's presidential nomination, after a close race against Sen. Bernie Sanders. Under normal circumstances, this would have been a tough year for Democrats; when one party has held the White House for two terms, the other party is favored to win.

Trump's campaign, often at odds with other Republicans, was understaffed and disorganized. Clinton hammered on Trump's personal failings. In the end, however, Trump's call for "change" resonated more than Clinton's attacks on Trump's character. The intense media focus on corruption charges against Clinton, spotlighted by an eleventh-hour FBI investigation, let most Republicans overcome their qualms about their candidate; the percentage of self-identified Republicans supporting Trump was slightly higher than the percentage of Democrats voting for Clinton. And in contrast to many analysts' expectations that Trump's candidacy would reshape the Republican coalition, his levels of support from whites, black and Latino Americans, and other social-demographic groups turned out to resemble the demographic support for previous Republican candidates. So despite the peculiarities of the 2016 presidential race, party identification continued to shape people's candidate perceptions.

As always, however, the results were interpreted in different ways, depending in part on the agenda of the observer (see box "Why Did Donald Trump Win in 2016?" on page 264).

Do Campaigns Make a Difference?

Many people naturally assume that campaign events are responsible for the election's outcome, probably because campaigns attract so much media attention and massive spending. Yet careful statistical analysis shows that election results can often be predicted fairly well from conditions that existed before the campaign began, such as the incumbent's previous poll ratings, economic conditions, and the distribution of party loyalties in the district. That doesn't leave much room for campaigns to determine the outcome. Instead, it suggests that campaigns simply remind voters of these longer lasting conditions and, in this way, help move them toward a largely preordained outcome. Does this mean that the candidates' strategies are not important?

The Argument That Campaigns Matter

Candidates certainly believe that campaigns affect election results. That's why they try so hard to raise money, attend events, and avoid gaffes that might turn off some voters. Some evidence does indicate that certain types of campaigning matter. For instance, research suggests that canvassing has a small but potentially meaningful effect on both turnout and voters' choices.[35] One dramatic example occurred in 2012, when polls indicated declining enthusiasm for Obama by Latinos and young people; that was expected to translate into lower voter turnout by these groups. The Obama campaign responded by targeting Latinos and young people in their fieldwork. In fact, their turnout did not drop on Election Day. Seth Masket's calculations show that even the small difference made by Obama's field offices was enough to change the outcome in Florida, which went narrowly for Obama.[36]

Research finds that voters are activated more effectively by door-to-door canvassing than by phone contact, and both kinds of contact are more effective than mailings.[37] The quality of the contact can matter at least as much as the medium.[38] Canvassing probably makes a bigger difference in local elections than in presidential races because there are fewer alternative sources of information in local contests. Where a party canvasses actively, its vote share can increase by a few percentage points, which could be the critical margin in a close race.[39]

As would be expected, television news and advertising—and the money that pays for the ads—can also influence voters' decisions.[40] But the impact of TV ads is usually short lived.[41] Campaign debates and other events make a difference in the election result under some circumstances.[42] All these sources of campaign information, taken together, can improve citizens' knowledge, influence their choices, and increase their turnout.[43]

Some voters are more affected by campaigning than others. For instance, those with limited political interest may pick up only a little information about campaigns, but the few bits of information that break through—often, perceptions of a candidate's likeability—can have a big impact on their attitudes.[44] People whose party ID is weak and who are uneasy about their party's candidate can be especially affected by the campaign communications they receive.[45] And the emphasis placed by media[46] and campaigns[47] on different aspects of the race or the candidate can influence what the voters regard as important.

The Argument That They Don't

On the other hand, there are several reasons why campaigning may have only a limited effect. Television news, ads, and ground war activities offer viewers a wide range of conflicting messages about candidates—positive, negative, and neutral information and opinions, all mixed together. The inconsistency of these messages makes it harder for a campaign to have a single, consistent impact on viewers' minds.[48] In races for high-level offices and open seats, in most cases, both candidates have access to sophisticated campaign techniques.

The 2016 presidential race was an exception. Team Clinton out-raised, out-spent, out-organized, and out-advertised Team Trump. And, of course, Clinton won the popular vote. But the unique strength of Trump's audience appeal and media dominance seemed to compensate for the weaknesses of his non-traditional campaign.

In addition, we know that voters pay only selective attention to media and other campaign communications. People interested in politics tend to surround themselves with friends, information, and even personal experiences that support their beliefs and loyalties,[49] and they often ignore information that conflicts with their opinions. The media environment has become highly diversified in recent years, with blogs, newsletters, talk radio, and cable channels presenting a broad array of perspectives. As a result, it is not hard for people to find media outlets that reinforce their views: think of Fox News for conservatives and MSNBC for liberals. Most campaign messages, then, probably have the effect of reinforcing and activating the voter's existing political leanings, as they always have.[50] That can explain why so much campaign effort is directed at getting people out to vote—to act on whatever opinions they already hold—rather than at trying to change their voting decision.

Some Tentative Answers

Rather than asking whether campaigns matter, we should ask about the conditions under which campaigns are more likely to matter. Close elections are an obvious condition. In the information-rich environment of current politics and among the large numbers of weak partisans and independent "leaners," the potential for campaigns to shape voters' perceptions may be at least as great as it has ever been. But some forces will continue to limit the impact of campaigns: voters' tendency to pay attention to the messages with which they already agree and their ability to tune out most political messages altogether.

Candidate-Centered or Party-Centered Campaigns?

As well as affecting voters, the campaign techniques explored in this chapter have affected the balance of power in campaigns between parties and candidates. Broadcast media, which need large audiences, tend to focus on individual personalities rather than on institutions such as parties. Tools such as Internet and TV advertising are available to any candidate who can pay for them; they let candidates communicate with voters without the party's help. The technologies that have developed since the mid-1900s, in short, have helped candidates run their campaigns independently of the party organizations. If the American parties had been as strong organizationally as those in many other nations when these technologies developed, then they might have been able to monopolize the use of TV and other media for campaign purposes. But as we have seen, the American parties have always struggled to maintain their power in a political culture hostile to their functioning.

American politics has long been guided by rules that disadvantage political parties.[51] Instead of parliamentary-cabinet government or proportional representation, which would encourage voters to see contests between parties for control of government rather than contests between candidates, the U.S. government has a separation of powers, which hinders the ability of parties to act collectively. American campaign finance rules make it difficult for parties to coordinate the campaigns of several candidates. And the direct primary, as Chapter 9 shows, allows candidates to run without the party organization's approval.

Consequently, it is the candidates and their advisers, not the parties, who make the strategic decisions in most campaigns. Candidates have their own headquarters and staffers rather than using the party's facilities. Candidates maintain their own relationships with voters rather than rely on the party organization as an intermediary. Party organizations, rather than running campaigns, often work instead to strengthen the appeal of individual candidates. And they must compete with consultants, interest groups, and others for the chance to do so.

Party Influence in Competitive Campaigns

The parties, however, are fighting back. The party organizations' greatly expanded fund raising during the past four decades has let them help individual campaigns with money and other services.[52] As Chapter 4 noted, soft money enabled party organizations to pour millions of dollars into campaign ads in a few battleground states until 2003. Since then, massive party fund-raising and voter contact drives have expanded the party presence in more races, even as the presence of other groups has also expanded (see Chapter 12).

The national parties have become more visible especially in the most competitive Senate and House elections. In some cases, party organizations using independent spending have spent even more than the candidates themselves. But because independent spending does not allow the parties to coordinate their efforts with their candidates, much less to run their campaigns, party-funded ads have sometimes stressed different themes from those the campaign preferred to emphasize and, frequently, more negative messages than the campaign's own advertising.[53] Because voters rarely pay attention to the source of any particular message, candidates have gotten blamed for negativity and claims that they have not made. And in most races, the party's role is less noticeable.

The Continuing Struggle between Candidates and Party Organizations

If you value economic efficiency, an expanded party role in campaigns makes sense. Party organizations can distribute appeals for a number of candidates at the same time and register voters to help the entire ticket. Parties can buy media advertising and consultants' services for use by many candidates at cost-effective prices. Party organizations can coordinate Election Day activities for all the party's candidates, provide poll watchers to guard against voting irregularities, send cars to bring people to the polls, and check voter lists to mobilize nonvoters late in the day.

But this efficiency comes at the cost of limiting the candidates' independence. Party organizations and candidates do not always have the same goals. The party, aiming to maximize the number of races it wins, puts its scarce resources into the most competitive campaigns and spends as little as possible on the races it considers hopeless. Each candidate, in contrast, is committed above all to his or her own victory and to gaining the resources needed to achieve it, no matter how unlikely that victory may be. The party, in its drive to win every competitive race, is likely to do whatever it takes, whether through negative or positive campaigning. The candidate, in contrast, has to face the voters; a constant barrage of attack ads may give the candidate a bad image.

The result is a continuing struggle between the party organizations and the candidates—the party in government—for control of campaigns. In most elections, the candidates have won the fight. Although the parties have more to offer candidates now than they did just a few years ago, party organizations still contribute only a fairly small percentage of candidates' overall spending in most races. In contrast, European parties often provide more than half the funding for most candidates.

Why should you care? Because candidate-centered campaigning has an important impact on governing. When they control their own campaigns, winning candidates can develop personal relationships with their constituents, unconstrained by party ties. Candidates are free to form close alliances with interest groups, which enhance the ability of these groups to influence public policy. In short, candidate-centered campaigning strengthens the power of the party in government relative to that of the party organization. That leads to an important question: If strong party organizations can help to hold elected officials accountable for their actions, then how much accountability do voters get from a candidate-centered politics?

Notes

1 On the American parties' adaptation to reforms, see Seth Masket, *The Inevitable Party* (New York: Oxford University Press, 2016).

2 See Paul S. Herrnson, *Congressional Elections*, 7th ed. (Los Angeles: Sage/CQ Press, 2016); and Marjorie Randon Hershey, *Running for Office* (Chatham, NJ: Chatham House, 1984).

3 See Gary C. Jacobson, *The Politics of Congressional Elections*, 8th ed. (New York: Pearson, 2012).

4 Edward I. Sidlow, *Challenging the Incumbent* (Washington, DC: CQ Press, 2003).

5 See Herrnson, *Congressional Elections*, pp. 218–222.

6 John R. Petrocik, William L. Benoit, and Glenn J. Hansen, "Issue Ownership and Presidential Campaigning, 1952–2000," *Political Science Quarterly* 118 (2003): 599–626.

7 James A. Thurber and Candice J. Nelson, eds., *Campaign Warriors* (Washington, DC: Brookings, 2000).

8 See David A. Dulio, *For Better or Worse* (Albany, NY: SUNY Press, 2004).

9 See Darrell M. West, *Air Wars*, 6th ed. (Washington, DC: CQ Press, 2013).

10 See Doris A. Graber and Johanna Dunaway, *Mass Media and American Politics*, 9th ed. (Washington, DC: CQ Press, 2014), Chapter 4.

11 Dave Barry, "Scandal Sheep," *Boston Globe Magazine*, March 15, 1998, pp. 12–13.

12 Jeff Valenzuela, "Midwest Local TV Newscasts Devote 2.5 Times as Much Air Time to Political Ads as Election Coverage," press release, Joyce Foundation, November 21, 2006.

13 Markus Prior, "News vs. Entertainment," *American Journal of Political Science* 49 (2005): 577–592.

14 Amy Mitchell, Jeffrey Gottfried, and Katerina Eva Matsa, "Millennials and Political News," Pew Research Center, June 1, 2015, at www.journalism.org/2015/06/01/millennials-political-news/ (accessed June 26, 2016)

15 Richard J. Semiatin, *Campaigns in the 21st Century* (Boston: McGraw Hill, 2005), p. 178.

16 Joshua Green, "The Science Beyond Those Obama Campaign E-Mails," *Bloomberg BusinessWeek*, November 29, 2012, at www.businessweek.com/articles/2012-11-29/the-science-behind-those-obama-campaign-e-mails (accessed June 26, 2016).

17 Allison Dale and Aaron Strauss, "Don't Forget to Vote," *American Journal of Political Science* 53 (2009): 787–804.

18 Michael Barthel, Elisa Shearer, Jeffrey Gottfried, and Amy Mitchell, "The Evolving Role of News on Twitter and Facebook," Pew Research Center, July 14, 2015, at www.journalism.org/2015/07/14/the-evolving-role-of-news-on-twitter-and-facebook (accessed June 26, 2016).

19 See Marjorie Randon Hershey, "The Media: Different Audiences Saw Different Campaigns," in Michael E. Nelson, ed., *The Elections of 2012* (Washington, DC: CQ Press/Sage, 2013), pp. 97–118.

20 Paul R. Abramson, John H. Aldrich, and David W. Rohde, *Change and Continuity in the 2000 and 2002 Elections* (Washington, DC: CQ Press, 2003), pp. 261–262.

21 Ryan D. Enos and Eitan Hersh, "Party Activists as Campaign Advertisers," *American Political Science Review* 109 (2015): 252.

22 Ryan D. Enos and Anthony Fowler, "Aggregate Effects of Large-Scale Campaigns on Voter Turnout," unpublished paper, 2015.

23 Republican National Committee, "Growth and Opportunity Project," March 18, 2013, pp. 35 and 39, at http://growthopp.gop.com/default.aspx (accessed June 26, 2016).

24 Herrnson, *Congressional Elections*, p. 119.

25 Paul A. Beck and Erik Heidemann, "The Ground Game from the Voter's Perspective," in John C. Green, Daniel J. Coffey, and David B. Cohen, *The State of the Parties*, 7th ed. (Lanham, MD: Rowman & Littlefield), 2014, pp. 251–269.

26 John G. Geer, "The News Media and the Rise of Negativity in Presidential Campaigns," *PS: Political Science & Politics* 45 (2012): 422–427.

27 See Conor M. Dowling and Amber Wichowsky, "Attacks without Consequences?" *American Journal of Political Science* 59 (2015): 19–36.

28 Yanna Krupnikov, "When Does Negativity Demobilize?" *American Journal of Political Science* 55 (2011): 797–813.

29 Christopher F. Karpowitz, J. Quin Monson, Kelly D. Patterson, and Jeremy C. Pope, "Tea Time in America?" *PS: Political Science & Politics* 44 (2011): 303–309.

30 Calculations by Nate Silver, "Health Care, Bailout Votes May Have Hurt Democrats," *FiveThirtyEight.com*, November 16, 2010.

31 Larry Bartels, "The Economy and the Campaign," *The Monkey Cage*, January 14, 2013, at http://themonkeycage.org/blog/2013/01/14/the-economy-and-the-campaign/#more-26660 (accessed June 26, 2016).

32 RNC "Growth and Opportunity Project," p. 49.

33 Quoted in Peter Wallstein, "Republicans Face Murky Political Future in Increasingly Diverse U.S.," *Washington Post*, November 7, 2012, p. 1.

34 Jennifer Rubin, "Donald Trump, Master Fabulist," *Washington Post*, May 2, 2016, at www.washingtonpost.com/blogs/right-turn/wp/2016/05/02/Donald-trump-master-fabulist (accessed September 14, 2016).

35 See Thomas M. Holbrook and Scott D. McClurg, "The Mobilization of Core Supporters," *American Journal of Political Science* 49 (2005): 689–703, and Seth E. Masket, "Did Obama's Ground Game Matter?" *Public Opinion Quarterly* 73 (2009): 1023–1039.

36 Seth Masket, "The Ground Game in 2012," *Mischiefs of Faction*, January 31, 2013, at www.mischiefsoffaction.com/2013/01/the-ground-game-in-2012.html (accessed June 26, 2016).

37 Donald P. Green and Alan S. Gerber, *Get Out the Vote!* (Washington, DC: Brookings Institution Press, 2004), pp. 92–93.

38 David W. Nickerson, "Quality Is Job One," *American Journal of Political Science* 51 (2007): 269–282.

39 Yard signs have less effect but still can make a difference in very close races; see Donald P. Green, Jonathan S. Krasno, Alexander Coppock, Benjamin D. Farrer, Brandon Lenoir, and Joshua N. Zingher, "The Effects of Lawn Signs on Vote Outcomes," *Electoral Studies* 41 (2016): 143–150.

40 Daron R. Shaw, "The Effect of TV Ads and Candidate Appearances on Statewide Presidential Votes, 1988–96," *American Political Science Review* 93 (1999): 345–61.

41 Alan S. Gerber, James G. Gimpel, Donald P. Green, and Daron R. Shaw, "How Large and Long-lasting Are the Persuasive Effects of Televised Campaign Ads?" *American Political Science Review* 105 (2011): 135–150.

42 Daron R. Shaw, "A Study of Presidential Campaign Effects from 1952-1992," *Journal of Politics* 61 (1999): 387–422.

43 See Paul Freedman, Michael Franz, and Kenneth Goldstein, "Campaign Advertising and Democratic Citizenship," *American Journal of Political Science* 48 (2004): 723–741.

44 Matthew A. Baum, "Talking the Vote," *American Journal of Political Science* 49 (2005): 213–234.

45 Shanto Iyengar and John R. Petrocik, "'Basic Rule' Voting," in James A. Thurber, Candice J. Nelson, and David A. Dulio, eds., *Crowded Airwaves* (Washington, DC: Brookings, 2000), p. 142.

46 See Joanne M. Miller and Jon A. Krosnick, "News Media Impact on the Ingredients of Presidential Evaluations," *American Journal of Political Science* 44 (2000): 295–309.

47 David A. M. Peterson, "Campaign Learning and Vote Determinants," *American Journal of Political Science* 53 (2009): 445–460.

48 Russell J. Dalton, Paul A. Beck, and Robert Huckfeldt, "Partisan Cues and the Media," *American Political Science Review* 92 (1998): 111–126.

49 See Paul Allen Beck, "Voters' Intermediation Environments in the 1988 Presidential Contest," *Public Opinion Quarterly* 55 (1991): 371–394.

50 See Alan I. Abramowitz, "It Don't Mean a Thing If It Ain't Got That Swing," *Larry Sabato's Crystal Ball*, July 19, 2012, at www.centerforpolitics.org/crystalball/articles/it-dont-mean-a-thing-if-it-aint-got-that-swing (accessed June 26, 2016).

51 John H. Aldrich, *Why Parties? A Second Look* (Chicago: University of Chicago Press, 2011), pp. 266–269.

52 See Holbrook and McClurg, "The Mobilization of Core Supporters."

53 See Paul S. Herrnson and Diana Dwyre, "Party Issue Advocacy in Congressional Election Campaigns," in John C. Green and Daniel M. Shea, eds., *The State of the Parties*, 3rd ed. (Lanham, MD: Rowman & Littlefield, 1999), pp. 86–104.

CHAPTER 12

Financing the Campaigns

Most Americans "know" things about campaign money that are not true. The candidate with the most campaign money *doesn't* always win the election. Individuals, corporations, and labor unions *can't* give unlimited sums directly to candidates' campaigns. The cigar-chomping party bosses who chose candidates and handed them cash in the days of the political machine are about as common today as typewriters.

There are a lot of myths about political money. But the real story is at least as dramatic as the myths. Money does remain the key to mobilizing the resources needed for a viable campaign. The cost of these resources—huge databases, TV advertising, paid professional consultants, polls—has risen greatly in recent decades. Court decisions have permitted big givers to pump millions of dollars into elections (though not directly into candidates' campaign budgets). These big givers are not college students, nurses, or truck drivers; their daily lives do not reflect the experiences of the average American.[1] But their spending and that of political parties, organized interests, and many other individuals affects elections. People who run for office, especially at the federal and state levels, are not likely to be taken seriously unless they start with a big campaign budget or a proven talent for fund-raising.

For most of American history, money used in campaigns was collected and spent in secret. Candidates were not required to disclose how they raised funds, and citizens had no way to be sure who was paying for a candidate's campaign or what the givers might be getting in return. Regulations adopted in the 1970s gave us a flood of information about campaign contributions and spending. But as the result of recent court decisions, much of the money spent on campaigns since 2010 is now as hard to trace as in the days before the reforms.

Let us clarify this complicated story by first reviewing its main themes. Then the chapter will continue by explaining how campaign finance reached this dismal state.

How Much Money Is Spent on Campaigns?

Campaigns for all levels of office in the United States cost over $7 billion collectively in 2016 and $3.8 billion in the midterm elections of 2014[2]—an enormous increase over the amounts spent just two decades ago. Inflation has reduced the purchasing power of the dollar during this period, so the real, inflation-adjusted increase is not nearly as dramatic. But the growth in spending since 1996 is impressive by any standard.

Campaign spending has shot upward for many reasons. Fund raisers have become much more skilled at energizing both small and big donors. A polarized political system has heightened the stakes in elections. The Supreme Court's evisceration of campaign finance laws has permitted non-party groups to spend record sums in campaigns. So although federal regulations had slowed the arms race in campaign funding from the 1970s to the 1990s, we are back to the days when secretive giving by big contributors threatens the integrity of the electoral process and the effectiveness of the political parties.

Presidential Campaigns

The 2012 presidential race was touted as the most expensive in history (see Figure 12.1), even though there was no contest for the Democratic nomination. It looked as though this record would not last; by January 1, 2016, campaign fund-raising was already approaching $1 billion.[3] But the presidential candidates' own campaigns collectively raised and spent "only" $1.3 billion in 2015–2016. The campaign of former Secretary of State Hillary Clinton, the Democratic nominee, outraised that of Republican businessman Donald Trump by a substantial margin, though spending by the national party organizations and outside interests, in addition to Trump's remarkable ability to draw free media coverage by making controversial statements, helped to level the playing field. In part because of the unusually low public approval ratings of both candidates, their supporters spent a large proportion of their money on negative advertising.

Congressional Campaigns

The 2014 midterm elections set records (see Figure 12.2 and Figure 12.3), with about $3.8 billion in total spending, including $1.7 billion by candidates. The first hundred-million-dollar Senate races took place in 2014, including the $121 million North Carolina race between incumbent Democrat Kay Hagan and Republican Thom Tillis and the $104 million Colorado campaign in which Republican challenger Cory Gardner unseated incumbent Democrat Mark Udall. Spending on congressional races in 2016 rose even higher, to $4.3 billion, especially due to the intense efforts of Democratic-leaning groups to recapture control of the U.S. Senate and the spending by Republican backers to keep that from happening.

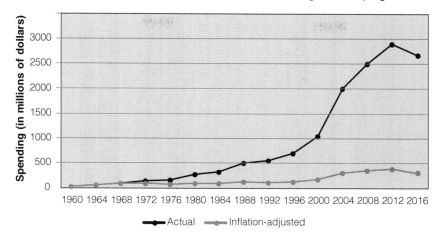

FIGURE 12.1 Total Spending by Candidates, Parties, and Groups in Presidential Elections, 1960–2016

Note: Estimates are for two-year cycles ending in the presidential election years. Inflation-adjusted figures are computed by deflating the actual expenditures by changes in the price level as measured by the Consumer Price Index yearly averages (with 1960 as the base year).

Sources: FEC data reported by the Committee for Responsive Politics. Data for 2016 are reported as of November 28, 2016. The inflation-adjusted figure is based on the Consumer Price Index produced by the U.S. Department of Labor, Bureau of Labor Statistics calculator at www.bls.gov/data/inflation_calculator.htm (accessed November 16, 2016).

One of the most striking findings in congressional races is that incumbents greatly outraise and outspend their challengers in every election year. In 2014, among House general election candidates, incumbents outraised challengers by three to one: the average incumbent House member raised about $1.4 million compared with $437,000 for the average Democratic challenger and $574,000 for the average Republican challenger.[4] In Senate contests, the average Senator collected just under $11 million ($13 million for the average incumbent Democrat, $8 million for the average Republican Senator) compared with only about $3.5 million for the average Democratic challenger and $5.9 for the average Republican. Candidates for open seats— those where no incumbent is running—raised more than the average challenger but less than the average incumbent.

Republican candidates usually hold a fund-raising edge over Democrats in congressional campaigns. The size of that advantage in a given election depends on which party has the most incumbents and, therefore, controls each house of Congress. Control of a legislative body is worth a great deal to a party, quite literally. So when Senate Republicans seemed in danger of losing their majority in 2016, Republican Senate candidates outraised Democrats by a substantial amount. In the House, the Republicans had a 1.2 to 1 advantage.[5]

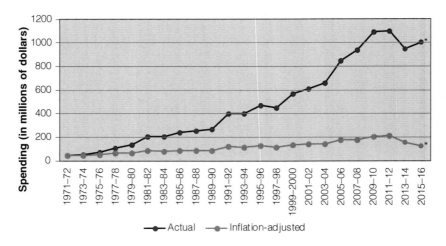

FIGURE 12.2 Total Candidate Spending in House Campaigns, 1971–1972 to 2015–2016

Source: FEC data from the Committee for Responsive Politics. *Data for 2016 are as of November 2, 2016.

Note: Inflation-adjusted figures are computed by deflating the actual expenditures by changes in the price level as measured by the Consumer Price Index yearly averages (with 1972 as the base year).

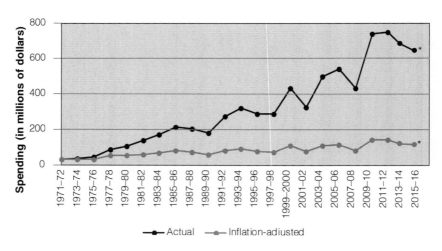

FIGURE 12.3 Total Candidate Spending in Senate Campaigns, 1971–1972 to 2015–2016

Source: FEC data from the Committee for Responsive Politics. *Data for 2016 are as of November 2, 2016.

Note: Inflation-adjusted figures are computed as in Figure 12.2.

State and Local Campaigns

Even though local governments make a major difference in people's daily lives, many local races are still relatively low-spending affairs. But the totals are increasing, with occasional eye-popping results. In 2009, for instance, Michael Bloomberg spent $100 million of his own funds to win a third term as New York City mayor. Campaigns for governor now can cost as much as U.S. Senate races; in 2014, candidates, parties, and outside groups spent more than $100 million on TV ads in the Florida gubernatorial contest alone. Most dramatic has been the increase in spending by non-party groups, including a large number who do not disclose where their money comes from. Even state Supreme Court elections have become big-spending contests. The all-time record was set in 2015 by Pennsylvania's state supreme court contests in which spending totaled just under $16 million. In these judicial races, most of the money comes from business interests and trial lawyers who have a big stake in the judges' rulings.[6]

These figures must be kept in perspective. As substantial as it is, the total cost of all U.S. campaigns is just a tenth of the money Americans spend on lottery tickets each year (see box "Campaign Spending: Too Much or Too Little?" on this page). To the extent that campaigns give us a chance to learn about the strengths and weaknesses of the people who would govern us, the amounts spent on campaign advertising could be considered a real bargain.[7] There are important questions to be asked, however, about the motivations

Campaign Spending: Too Much or Too Little?

What will $7 billion buy in the United States?

- Half the amount Americans spent on snacks, TVs, and other items for the 2015 Super Bowl.
- About 1/115th of what the U.S. spent on the war in Iraq.
- Less than one-tenth what Americans paid for lottery tickets in 2014.
- Construction of one Nimitz-class aircraft carrier (not counting operating costs).
- All the political campaigns run at all levels of government by and for all candidates in 2016.

Sources: Charles Passy, "Americans Eat 1.25 Billion Chicken Wings on Super Bowl Sunday," *Market Watch*, January 30, 2015, at www.marketwatch.com/story/americans-will-spend-over-14-billion-on-the-super-bowl-2015-01-29; Danielle Kurtzleben, "What Did the Iraq War Cost? More Than You Think," *U.S. News & World Report*, December 15, 2011, at www.usnews.com/news/articles/2011/12/15/what-did-the-iraq-war-cost-more-than-you-think; "Americans Spend More on the Lottery Than On ...," CNN Money, February 11, 2015, at http://money.cnn.com/2015/02/11/news/companies/lottery-spending/index.html; and http://wiki.answers.com/Q/How_much_does_an_aircraft_carrier_cost (all accessed June 26, 2016).

of contributors and the fund-raising disparities among candidates. And although tens of millions of people keep lotteries in business, the money that funds campaigns—and whatever influence derives from it—comes from a much smaller number of individuals.

What Is the Impact of Campaign Spending?

Money doesn't necessarily buy victory, but it rarely hurts. In the general election for president, both sides usually have enough money to reach voters with their messages, so the candidate with the largest war chest does not gain a big advantage. Money matters more in the early months of the presidential nomination race, especially in buying the early visibility that is so vital to an underdog. But even then, it is not sufficient in itself; the $150 million raised by former Florida governor Jeb Bush and his super PACs didn't bring him a single Republican primary or caucus win in 2016. And in later events, when the candidates are better known, a monetary edge may not help. In late May 2016, for example, Hillary Clinton had outraised Donald Trump by $42 million to $1.3 million, yet Clinton had only a small lead in the polls.

In congressional elections, most researchers find that money does make a difference—for challengers. The more challengers spend when they run against incumbents, the better their chances of victory. The same is not true for incumbents. Gary Jacobson found that the more incumbents spend, the worse they do in the race.[8] In 2014, for instance, Sen. Kay Hagan raised more money than any other Senate candidate ($24 million) but lost to her Republican challenger, who spent half as much. It is not that incumbent spending turns voters off, but rather that incumbents spend a lot when they face serious competition. A big budget for an incumbent, then, typically means that he or she has (or worries about getting) an unusually strong challenger.

Other researchers disagree and report that when incumbents spend more, they do get a return in terms of votes. The dispute turns on thorny questions about the proper way to estimate the impact of spending,[9] but there is general agreement on three points. First, House incumbents do not usually face a serious challenge for reelection. Second, challengers need a lot of money to have a chance of beating an incumbent. Third, incumbents may not be able to survive a strong challenger by pouring more money into their campaigns. Consider, for example, the effort by U.S. House Republican majority leader Eric Cantor to win renomination in the 2014 primary. In response to a grassroots Tea Party challenge questioning his conservative credentials and his commitment to the district, Cantor spent $5 million. His opponent, college professor David Brat, raised about $200,000—and won.[10]

For political scientists, measuring the effects of campaign spending is a complicated task. For candidates, the answer is simple: More is better—especially at the state level, where the party that spends more is more likely to win a legislative majority.[11]

A Never-Ending Story: How "Interested Money" Flows into Campaigns

It's no surprise that people and groups try to put money into campaigns. Government actions inevitably help some groups and harm others; even the most popular policy proposals (cutting taxes, for example) would cause damage to some people (by reducing the funds available to government to spend on defense or to subsidize businesses or poor people). So it makes sense that people and groups will use whatever legal methods they have available to ensure that they will be among the winners, not the losers, in government policy making. Money is primary among those methods.

Money now comes into campaigns in two different ways. First, individuals and groups can **give money to a candidate's campaign**. The campaign then decides how to spend the money it receives. Second, groups and individuals (other than candidates) can spend their own money on campaign communications and activities, usually independent of the campaign ("outside spending"; see Figure 12.4). In this case, it is the spenders, not the campaign, who choose how to spend the money. Since the early 1970s, money donated directly to a candidate's campaign has been limited by law. But outside spending—called **independent spending** or **express advocacy** and **issue ads**—is largely unregulated. As a result, outside spending has mushroomed.

The "Wild West" Days of Campaign Finance

Before the campaign finance reforms of the 1970s, American campaign finance laws were weak, inconsistent, and usually ignored. Congressional

	Who gives it?	Who gets it?	$ is spent on
Candidate's Campaign (amounts limited by law)	Individuals ⟶ Parties Traditional PACs Candidate's personal funds	The candidate's campaign	TV and Internet ads Staff salaries Field work and all other campaign activities
Outside Spending (unlimited amounts; no provable coordination with candidate)	Parties ⟶ Traditional and super PACs Nonprofits (527, 501c) Corporations, unions Other organized interests Wealthy individuals		Independent spending ads Issue ads Registering voters Promoting policies

FIGURE 12.4 How Money Flows into Federal Campaigns

Source: Created by the author. Thanks to Jennifer Victor, who refers to outside spending as the "unofficial campaign" in "The Dark Campaign Web Rises," April 1, 2015, at www.mischiefsoffaction.com/2015/04/the-dark-campaign-web-rises.html (accessed June 26, 2016).

A Billionaire's Under-Funded Campaign

Donald Trump's 2016 presidential campaign interrupted the trend toward increasing campaign spending. Trump boasted that he'd self-fund his campaign; because he had made billions in business, he assured voters, he wouldn't be beholden to any special interests.

His claim turned out to be partly accurate. Trump did pay for most of his nomination campaign, though he also accepted contributions from others. But after receiving substantial donations in early summer, his fund-raising fizzled. Republican big donors spent their money on Senate races instead. Trump stopped holding fund-raising events in October, to the disappointment of the Republican National Committee, which would have shared in the receipts.

Although he pledged to spend $100 million of his own funds on the campaign, his actual donations fell far short. So did his campaign's spending. Trump ran only a quarter as many TV ads as Hillary Clinton did. In fact, by the end of September, the Trump campaign had spent more on embroidered "Make America Great Again" hats than on either polling or direct mail advertising.

We should probably not conclude that being outspent by your opponent is the new way to win elections. But it is a useful reminder that money is not the only asset in a campaign.

and presidential candidates were allowed to take unlimited sums of money from individuals. Reformers tried periodically to regulate campaign fundraising and spending. A new episode of reform was under way in the early 1970s when the Watergate scandals broke. Corporations and wealthy individuals were found to have given large sums of money to President Nixon's reelection campaign in 1972 in return for preferential treatment ranging from tax breaks for businesses to ambassadorships for individual big givers. The revulsion caused by these fund-raising scandals led Congress to pass the most extensive federal law on the subject in U.S. history: the **Federal Election Campaign Act (FECA)** amendments of 1974. The Supreme Court invalidated some of these reforms in 1976. But the resulting legislation put limits on federal campaign contributions and set up a system of public funding for presidential campaigns, as a means of tying a candidate's fundraising more closely to his or her public support.

The FECA Reforms of the 1970s

FECA mandated significant changes in campaign finance. Here are the most notable:

Limits on Direct Contributions to Campaigns

From Individuals Among the most vivid Watergate stories were those of big contributions from wealthy, so-called "fat cat" donors who received advantages in public policy in return for their money. In response, FECA limited the amounts of money an individual could give directly to a candidate. Beginning in 1976, individuals were allowed to contribute no more than $1,000 to each candidate per election (counting primary and general as separate elections), and no more than $25,000 to all candidates combined, on the assumption that $1,000 was too small an amount, in the context of a candidate's total campaign budget, to buy big favors. These limits apply only to federal campaigns—those for president and Congress. These limited funds contributed by individuals (and by parties and PACs) under FECA's rules were called hard (or federal) money.

Once the individual contribution limit was in place, candidates found that they needed to entice many more individuals to contribute. They succeeded so well, by using regular mail and the newly developed email to raise small contributions, that even today, most of the money contributed *directly* to candidates comes from individual donors, not parties or PACs. In the 2016 elections, individuals accounted for 53 percent of the contributions to House candidates and 75 percent of the money given to Senate candidates. This expanded group of small donors is not typical of the public as a whole, however; the givers tend to be older, wealthier, male, more Republican, and more ideologically extreme than the average American voter,[12] and there is evidence that candidates listen to them more than to the average voter.[13]

From Traditional Political Action Committees (PACs) Corporations and labor unions had long been prohibited from giving money directly from their own treasuries to political candidates. So since the 1940s, labor unions had sought to make legal campaign contributions by forming political action committees, abbreviated as PACs: political groups whose sole purpose is to raise and spend money to influence elections. Because the PAC's money would be kept in a fund separate from the union's own regular revenues, union leaders figured that their PACs could contribute to federal campaigns without violating the ban on direct union contributions. At the urging of many unions, FECA confirmed the legality of PACs and the right of sponsoring organizations to pay their overhead expenses.

FECA allowed PACs to donate up to $5,000 per candidate per election, with no overall limit on the number of candidates they supported. Because candidates could get five times more money from a PAC than from an individual, PACs became an attractive source of contributions to candidates. The attraction was mutual; seeing the opportunity to contribute legally to candidates' campaigns, corporations and other groups formed thousands of PACs in the 1970s and 1980s. Corporate and trade association PACs (most of which are also business-related) soon came to dominate the PAC universe. In 2016, corporate and trade PACs provided more than 70 percent of all PAC contributions to federal candidates. The heavy hitters are in the fields of finance, real estate, health care, communications, and energy. Although labor unions are now a fairly small proportion of all PACs, and gave only 10 percent of all PAC contributions to candidates in 2016, unions still contribute millions to federal campaigns. Because unions give almost all their PAC money to Democrats, they help compensate for the usual Republican edge in business contributions (see Table 12.1). In addition, as Chapter 4 showed, members of the party in government have formed so-called "leadership PACs" from which they are expected to donate to their party's congressional campaign committee as well as to raise money for the party and its endangered candidates.

TABLE 12.1 The Biggest PAC Spenders (in Contributions to Federal Candidates), 2015–2016

		Contributions to Federal Candidates		
Rank	PAC	Total (in millions of dollars)	To Democrats (%)	To Republicans (%)
1	National Beer Wholesalers*	4.0	42	58
2	National Association of Realtors*	3.8	42	58
3	AT&T Inc.*	3.5	36	64
4	Lockheed Martin*	3.0	38	62
5	National Auto Dealers Association*	2.9	27	73
6	National Association of Insurance and Financial Advisors*	2.8	33	67
7	Honeywell International*	2.8	40	60
8	American Bankers Association*	2.7	23	77
9	Blue Cross/Blue Shield*	2.6	36	64
10	United Parcel Service	2.6	38	62

Note: * Corporate or other business-related PAC.

Source: FEC data from the Center for Responsive Politics as of November 28, 2016 at www.opensecrets.org/overview/toppacs.php?cycle=2016 (accessed December 10, 2016).

As they did when FECA was passed, traditional PACs continue to put most of their money into congressional races. In 2014, they gave a total of about $458 million to federal candidates, which was a little over 40 percent of the total interest group spending in the 2014 campaigns.[14] Because the average House candidate is less well funded than his or her Senate counterpart, PAC donations account for a higher proportion (more than a third) of House campaign budgets. Some PACs and corporate interests also donate funds to charities favored by powerful Congress members. Both parties' Hill committees connect their candidates with PACs likely to be sympathetic to their causes. PACs' aim is to gain access to elected officials: the assurance that the legislator's door will be open when the group hopes to plead its case on legislation. Thus, the great majority of PAC contributions go to incumbents. There is little advantage, after all, in getting access to a likely loser.

What PACs get in return is harder to measure. Political scientists don't find much evidence that PAC contributions affect Congress members' roll call votes,[15] although legislators who receive PAC money seem more active in congressional committees on behalf of issues that concern their PAC donors.[16] Because PACs usually give to legislators who have already voted to support that PAC's interests, it isn't clear that the PAC's money *caused* the legislator to vote that way. Their influence is greatest when they represent powerful interests in the legislator's district, when they don't conflict with his or her party's position, and when the benefit they seek is of little direct interest to anyone else (such as a small change in the tax laws giving a big break to a particular corporation).

From Party Organizations FECA treated the political party organizations as just another non-candidate group wanting to invest in campaigns, and it restricted the money parties could give to their candidates. So the American parties' role in funding campaigns is much more limited than in most other democracies, where the party organizations, not the candidates, do most of the campaign spending.

Party organizations at the state, local, and national level can give up to $5,000 to each candidate in a House race and larger amounts to Senate candidates. The parties can also spend money *in coordination with* a candidate's campaign to purchase services such as media advertising or polling for the campaign, called **coordinated spending**. This is useful to the party because party committees have more control over how the money is spent than when they make direct contributions to candidates. As of 2016, each party was permitted to spend $48,100 per House race, except in states with only one House district, where the limit was $96,100. The state party can spend the same amount or authorize the national party committee to do so. In Senate campaigns, the limit varies with the size of the state's voting-age population: from $96,100 in Delaware to $2.9 million in California.[17] But in most races, this party money still amounts to only a small fraction of the candidate's total spending.

Public Disclosure

The reformers also wanted to make campaign funding more transparent. They felt that voters could make a more informed choice if they knew who had contributed to each candidate. So FECA required that congressional and presidential candidates publicly disclose their spending and the names, addresses, and occupations of all contributors of $200 or more. The Federal Election Commission (FEC) was established to receive candidates' finance reports and make the data publicly available. In recent years, the FEC has been so dysfunctional that its commissioners deadlocked on whether to serve bagels or doughnuts at its 40th anniversary celebration,[18] but its public files, available online (https://beta.fec.gov), provide a wealth of campaign finance information.

Public Funding of Presidential Campaigns

In a final effort to remove "interested money" from elections, FECA and its amendments in the 1970s provided public funds for presidential candidates. The money comes from voluntary contributions from taxpayers, who could designate a dollar (now $3) of their tax payments to match small contributions to candidates for their party's presidential nomination and to foot most of the bill for the presidential nominees in the general election. To get the money, a candidate for a party's presidential nomination must first demonstrate broad public support by raising $5,000 in contributions of $250 or less in each of 20 states. After that, public funds match every individual contribution up to $250, as a means of encouraging small donations.[19]

The public funding treats minor party candidates differently. They receive only a fraction of that total, and then only after the election if they have received at least 5 percent of the vote. Because candidates need to pay cash for many campaign expenses, this provision of FECA adds to the difficulties faced by minor parties. Only one minor party candidate, Reform Party leader Ross Perot in 1996, has ever qualified for public funding.

Spending Limits The catch is that accepting public funds requires a candidate to abide by low spending limits in each state's primary or caucus and for the nomination and general election races as a whole. These limits have not kept up with the rising cost of presidential campaigns. And because the amount of the public funding is much lower than recent candidates have been able to raise for themselves, no recent presidential nominee has accepted those funds. Nevertheless, the availability of public money has helped some lesser-known candidates stay in the nomination race longer, which gives voters more choices.

Congress tried to include provisions in FECA limiting spending in House and Senate campaigns as well. However, the Supreme Court ruled in 1976 that restricting a candidate's spending infringed on the candidate's right to free speech. Those restrictions could be justified only if a candidate accepts public funding. Congress could apply spending limits to its own campaigns, then, only as part of a plan for subsidizing them with public money. That would mean subsidizing their challengers' campaigns as well. For congressional incumbents, who typically outspend their challengers, this was not an appealing idea.

The Loopholes That Ate the Reforms

Not long after Congress passed the FECA reforms, several groups asked the Supreme Court to overturn the law on a variety of grounds: for instance, that tax funds shouldn't subsidize campaigns, and that minor parties were treated unfairly in the reforms. In the landmark case of *Buckley v. Valeo* (1976), the Court's majority expressed a different concern. Although it agreed that Congress could limit the size of individuals' direct contributions to candidates, no such limits could be placed on a candidate's use of his or her own personal funds in a campaign (self-funding) or on outside spending: advertising that is not coordinated with a candidate's campaign.[20]

Unlimited Self-Funding by Wealthy Candidates

The Supreme Court said in *Buckley* that Congress can't limit how much federal candidates are allowed to spend of their own personal wealth on their campaigns. Why, when other donors are limited in the amount they can contribute? Because the Supreme Court has ruled that campaign finance limits exist mainly to prevent corruption, and people can't corrupt themselves. The biggest self-funders often lose, however. And because raising funds is closely related to gaining voter support, self-funders can limit their own appeal. That's what Donald Trump discovered after largely self-funding his campaign for the Republican presidential nomination in 2016; it left him without a strong base of supportive donors in his effort to raise $1 billion for the general election campaign.

Independent Spending

If you run an ad supporting a candidate or criticizing the candidate's opponent, and if you work with the candidate's campaign in doing so, then the law treats the ad as a campaign contribution, which is limited by FECA. But the Supreme Court wrote in *Buckley* that if you don't consult with the campaign about the ad, then your right to free speech allows you to spend unlimited sums on your advertising. The Court majority's reasoning was that free speech is fundamental in a democracy—more important than is limiting political corruption—and because "free" speech costs money to disseminate through TV and other media, Congress can't limit the amount that groups and individuals spend on *independent spending: ads that are run independently of a candidate's campaign*. The Court said in 1996 that political parties could also spend independently on campaign ads and, in 2003, applied this to publicly financed presidential campaigns as well.[21]

Because independent spending is unlimited, parties can use it to greatly expand their role in targeted campaigns. As a result, the national parties have put most of their campaign money into independent spending. In the 2016 elections, for instance, the parties spent more than $8 million on independent expenditures in the presidential race and $248 million on House and Senate races. Other groups spend even more; total independent spending by parties, PACs, individuals, and other groups reached $1.2 billion in 2012, $865 million in 2014,[22] and a whopping $1.7 billion in 2016. In especially competitive House races, it isn't unusual for independent spending by parties and interest groups to dwarf the advertising funded by the candidates themselves.

Independent spending poses many challenges for a democracy. Most independent spending funds negative ads. If a *candidate* launches an outrageous attack, citizens can protest by voting for his or her opponent. If a party, interest group, or individual runs an outrageous ad as an independent spender, who can be held responsible? The independent spender can't be punished at the polls; he or she isn't running for anything. And because independent spenders are not supposed to be coordinating their efforts with a candidate, is it fair to punish the candidate for the offensive ad? Thus, independent spenders are free to say whatever they wish, and neither they nor the candidate they favor can be held accountable.

Soft Money

In order to strengthen state and local party organizations, Congress amended FECA in 1979 to let them raise and spend unlimited amounts of money on party building and voter mobilization activities. This unlimited fund-raising came to be called **soft money**, and it was interpreted as extending to national party committees as well. As a result, citizens could give unlimited amounts of money to party organizations for "party building," though these same citizens' and PACs' contributions to federal candidates were strictly limited. Parties could not give this soft money directly to federal candidates, but they could pay for any nonfederal portion of a campaign effort, and the money had a tendency to migrate wherever it was needed.

In effect, then, soft money became a way for individuals and groups to launder large campaign contributions through a party organization. The parties pushed hard to get the money. In a letter made famous by a Supreme Court case, for example, then-Republican National Chair Jim Nicholson sent a draft of the party's health-care proposals to the drug company Bristol-Myers Squibb and asked for any suggested changes—and a $250,000 soft-money contribution to the RNC.[23] Fat cats had reentered the building. It was not the law's stated intention for soft money to become an end run around the FECA contribution limits, but the difficulty of monitoring the uses of these funds made it so. In most states, soft money could be raised not only from individuals and PACs but also from corporate treasuries and labor union dues—funds that could not be donated directly to federal candidates under FECA.[24]

Tremendous sums flowed through the soft-money conduit from the early 1990s until 2002, when it was banned at the federal level (see BCRA). Soft money had become so attractive a source of funding, especially for the Democrats, who did not have as many hard-money donors, that in 2002 it comprised more than half of the Democratic Party's receipts and more than one-third of the Republicans'.[25] When the 1970s reforms were passed, party organizations didn't have enough money to be big players in congressional or presidential races. But the parties have since become much more effective fund-raisers. Even after Congress prevented party committees from collecting unlimited soft money, the two parties have been able to raise more than $1 billion in each election. Their role in campaigns has grown correspondingly, especially in hard-fought races.

Issue Advocacy Ads

Issue advocacy ads (issue ads, for short) were originally defined as any political advertising that did not include the terms "elect," "vote for," "support," "oppose," or similar terms. As long as a political ad did not say these "magic words," courts held that the ad was not a campaign ad, because it did not *expressly advocate* electing a candidate. Courts again cited the vital importance of free speech in ruling that these issue ads could be aired by individuals or groups using unlimited funding, even while a campaign was in progress.

In 1996, the Democratic National Committee (DNC) argued that issue ads were actually a form of party-building and voter mobilization, so they should be able to use soft money to pay for issue ads supporting President Bill Clinton's reelection.[26] The issue ads sounded very much like campaign ads. For example, a later issue ad by Hillary Clinton's opponent in the 2000 New York Senate race featured several photogenic babies wearing New York Yankees caps, while a voice intoned, "Every one of these babies has lived in New York longer than Hillary Rodham Clinton." The ad's intent was clear. But because it did not explicitly say "vote against" Clinton or "vote for" her opponent, it was considered to be issue advocacy and thus could be funded with unlimited soft money.

From the candidate's perspective, issue ads were a mixed blessing. As with independent spenders, the issue ads run by outside groups sometimes conveyed different messages than the campaign would prefer. But they were a boon for the parties, who now had a legal way to use big donations from corporations, unions, and individuals in federal elections, and to get around FECA's spending limits for party organizations.

What Did the 1970s Reforms Accomplish?

By 2002, then, groups and parties had found some impressive loopholes in FECA, including independent spending and issue ads, paid for largely by unregulated soft money. But the limits on direct contributions to federal candidates remained.

Intended and Unintended Effects At first, the FECA reforms achieved most of their goals. They slowed the growth of campaign spending by presidential candidates for about three decades. Prior to the reforms, presidential campaign expenditures had tripled between 1960 and 1972. But real spending increased more slowly from 1972 to 2000 and actually declined in three of these eight elections. The contribution limits made small donors more valuable to candidates, which broadened the base of campaign funding. The reforms also opened much of the campaign finance process to public scrutiny.

Like all reforms, however, FECA had some worrisome, unintended effects. Most important was the growing imbalance between contributions to candidates, which are limited, and the unlimited spending that soft money, issue ads, and independent expenditures made possible. The cap of $1,000 on hard-money contributions held until 2002, although inflation had greatly eroded its value during that time. These relatively low ceilings on individual contributions made soft money and independent spending all the more attractive to parties and interest groups. Both these forms of spending raise real questions of accountability and bring back the types of money—big money from individuals and corporate and union treasuries—that FECA's sponsors had hoped to clean out of federal campaigns.

In the long run, then, the reformers' efforts failed to meet one of their major goals: reducing the influence of interested money. Currently, probably no more than 1 percent of Americans give money to any federal candidate,[27] and few give $200 or more. The other givers are groups—corporations, labor unions, and other organized interests—that want something specific from lawmakers. Whether they get what they want is not always clear, but we can assume they wouldn't be spending so much if they thought they were getting nothing in return.

Effects on the Parties For the first two decades of FECA, the prevailing view was that the reforms had harmed the party organizations. By limiting their direct contributions to presidential and congressional candidates, FECA treated the parties as no more privileged in the campaign process than were PACs or other groups. In addition, public funding of presidential campaigns went to the candidates themselves, not to the parties, as it does in most other democracies. That created more distance between the party organization and the presidential campaign.

After 1996, however, the loopholes in the reforms, including independent spending, soft money, and issue advocacy, gave the national parties the means to raise and spend much more money than ever before. Large amounts of party money went into TV and radio advertising and beefed-up voter mobilization programs. State and local parties, energized by money received from the national parties, became more involved in campaigns. Some put major effort into the labor-intensive grassroots work that was the staple of party organizations in an earlier era. Soft money allowed the parties to increase their presence in the most competitive races, and the party organizations invested some of their new riches in state and local party building.[28] However, very few of the party-funded issue ads even mentioned the party labels, so they probably did not help to strengthen the parties' ties with voters.[29]

Another Try: The Bipartisan Campaign Reform Act (BCRA)

These unintended effects—soft money in particular—created pressures for new reforms. In 2002, after another set of fund-raising scandals, Congress passed the **Bipartisan Campaign Reform Act** (known as **BCRA**, pronounced BICK-ra, or McCain-Feingold, after its sponsors).[30] BCRA banned soft-money contributions to national parties. State and local parties can still accept money from individuals, corporations, and labor unions in amounts up to $10,000 per donor per year, as well as unlimited donations for use in state elections (see Table 12.2).

BCRA also tried to shrink the issue ad loophole. If an issue ad mentioned a federal candidate but didn't engage in express advocacy (by using the "magic words" such as "vote for," "elect," and "defeat"), and if it aired within 60 days of a general election or 30 days of a primary, then it would be termed an **electioneering communication** and would be regulated. These "electioneering" ads could not be funded by corporations or unions; they had to be paid for entirely by federally regulated money or by soft money contributed only by individuals. The restriction applied only to broadcast media ads directed at targeted audiences, however, so advocacy groups could continue to use soft money for direct mail, phone banks, and voter registration during this time. Many groups did move their soft money into these activities.[31] In addition, BCRA increased the individual contribution limit to $2,000 for federal campaigns, raised the overall limit on individual contributions to candidates, parties, and other political committees combined, and let these limits rise with inflation.

Although most congressional Democrats voted for the bill, Democratic leaders worried that their party's fund-raising would be seriously undercut by BCRA. For decades, Republicans had been more successful than Democrats in raising hard money; many more of the individuals able to contribute $2,000 to a campaign identified as Republicans. Democrats had been able to narrow the fund-raising gap by attracting soft money from labor unions, which BCRA banned. Sure enough, within a year, the RNC had three times as much cash on hand as did the DNC.

TABLE 12.2 Limits on Campaign Contributions under Federal Law, 2016

	Limit on Contributions		
	Individual	Political Action Committee	State or National Party Committee
To each candidate or candidate committee per election	$2,700	$5,000*	$5,000**
To all candidates combined, per two-year cycle	$46,200	No limit	No limit
To national party committees per year	$33,400	$15,000	No limit
(NB: Joint fundraising committees, which distribute money to a party's organization and candidates, can accept up to about $800,000 from an individual during a two-year election cycle.)			
To a state or local party committee per year	$10,000	$5,000	No limit
Total per two-year election cycle to all party committees***	~$800,000	No limit	No limit

Source: Federal Election Commission, "Contribution Limits for 2015–2016 Federal Elections," at www.fec.gov/info/contriblimitschart1516.pdf (accessed June 26, 2016).

Notes: These are the limits on so-called hard-money contributions for the 2016 elections. Individual limits are indexed for inflation; PAC limits (and individual limits to PACs and state parties) are not.

* If the PAC qualifies as a "multicandidate committee" under federal law by making contributions to five or more federal candidates, the limit is $5,000. Otherwise, the committee is treated as an individual with a limit of $2,700.

** The limit is $5,000 for contributions to presidential and House candidates. The national and senatorial campaign committees can give a combined total of $46,800 to Senate candidates.

*** This limit can be augmented by individual contributions to the party's national convention.

More End Runs: 527 and 501(c) Advocacy Groups

After BCRA, then, Democrats looked for a new way to pour soft money into campaigns. They found it in a class of groups called **527s**. This odd name refers to provision 527 of the U.S. tax code, allowing certain tax-exempt groups to accept unlimited contributions and spend without limit on election advocacy—and since 2010 they can expressly call for the election or defeat of specific candidates and coordinate their activities with federal candidates or parties. They can also register voters, run get-out-the-vote drives, broadcast issue ads, send direct mail, and distribute voter guides. A small group of wealthy liberals formed several 527 groups in time for the 2004 campaign as a conduit for the soft money that would have gone to the national parties before BCRA.

Republicans had a harder time building their own network of 527s. Publicity about corporate scandals made business leaders uneasy about contributing to these groups. Then Congress required 527s to disclose their contributors and expenses. The FEC further regulated their fund-raising, treating 527s more like PACs. These groups continue to spend in elections—$250 million in 2016—but their spending has declined as a proportion of all campaign spending.

As a result, several organizations, including the U.S. Chamber of Commerce, began to funnel their independent spending through another category of groups organized as nonprofits. These tax-exempt "social welfare" groups, collectively called **501c4s**, have the advantage that they can accept unlimited donations but do not have to disclose the names of their donors publicly, as long as partisan political activity is not their "major purpose." Given that issue ads, even those referring to specific candidates, are not defined as "partisan" activities by law, there are few limits on these groups' campaign activities, as long as they do not contribute directly to candidates. Corporations in particular were attracted by this opportunity to avoid the consumer boycotts they might face if their names were publicly linked with controversial political messages. The sources of these "social welfare" groups' spending are highly concentrated. Most 501c4s are funded by very large (often million-dollar) donations from a very few individuals, and more than a third of their spending in 2014 came from 501cs formed by just two groups: $35 million from the U.S. Chamber of Commerce and $26 million from the NRA. Overall, 501c4 groups spent an estimated $336 million in the 2012 election and $450 million in 2016,[32] mainly to support Republican candidates and conservative causes. These funds, because they don't have to be publicly disclosed, are often referred to as **dark money**.

Each of these channels (see Table 12.3) is useful for certain kinds of fund-raising and spending. Thus, an organization might set up several different groups: a 501c4 to run ads with money that the givers do not want to be disclosed, a 527 for advocacy ads and ground war activities, and a PAC to give direct but limited contributions to candidates.

TABLE 12.3 Types of Non-Party Groups Allowed to Put Money into Election Campaigns

Type of Group	...donate money directly to candidates?	...accept donations?	Can the Group ... ...do independent spending?	...regulated by	...are donors anonymous?
Traditional PAC Political Action Committee	Yes	Yes—up to $5,000 per donor per election	Yes	FEC	No
Super PAC Independent Expenditure-Only Committee	No	Yes—unlimited amounts	Yes	FEC	No
527 Committee Political Organization	No	Yes—unlimited amounts	Yes	IRS	No
501c4 Social Welfare Organizations	No	Yes—unlimited	Yes, as long as campaign contributions are not the group's primary purpose	IRS	Yes

The National Parties Survived BCRA

Although BCRA deprived the national parties of unlimited soft money, the parties adapted again. They developed improved programs for attracting small contributors through the Internet. BCRA's higher limit on individual contributions let the parties raise larger donations. In addition, donors can give much bigger sums to **joint fund-raising committees**: a series of candidate and party committees linked together. The millions they have been able to raise from members of Congress (see Chapter 4) also helped the national parties survive the loss of soft money.

State and local party organizations had more difficulty adjusting to BCRA. After the ban on soft-money transfers from the national party organizations, state and local parties' fund-raising declined. State Democratic Parties suffered especially. As a result, many state parties stopped running broadcast ads for federal candidates. Most state parties found it difficult to increase their own fund-raising while complying with the complicated provisions of the new law.[33]

Bundling

Another unintended effect of BCRA was to encourage greater use of a practice called **bundling**. Although individual contributions to a campaign are limited, an individual or group can solicit large numbers of these individual donors, combine ("bundle") their contributions, deliver them to a campaign, and take credit for a much more substantial donation. When BCRA doubled the limit on individual donations, bundling became even more profitable. Groups such as the pro-choice EMILY's List and the anti-tax Club for Growth have given bundled donations totaling hundreds of thousands of dollars to a single candidate.

The Clinton campaign enthusiastically recruited bundlers in 2015–2016; by late September of 2016, they reported that 1,370 individuals had each bundled $100,000 in contributions. Trump's campaign did not release its numbers. Most of the bundlers are lawyers, lobbyists, finance executives, and developers who, like other big donors, have interests in federal policies.[34] It is clearly an end run around the contribution limits, but bundling remains legal.

Citizens United and Super PACS

The national parties survived BCRA, but BCRA did not survive the Supreme Court. The Court helped to dismantle BCRA with rulings culminating in *Citizens United v. FEC* (2010), just as it had earlier opened up huge loopholes in FECA. A narrow majority ruled in *Citizens United* that corporations and labor unions can spend as much as they'd like from their own treasuries at any time, even close to an election, on ads that expressly advocate the election or defeat of a presidential or congressional candidate.

Without this right, the majority argued, corporations' and other groups' free speech rights would be limited.

Many expected *Citizens United* to open the floodgates to massive corporate campaign spending. A vehicle for that spending quickly appeared. A federal court of appeals in *SpeechNow.org vs. FEC* (2010) stated that if a PAC confined itself to independent spending, and gave no direct contributions to candidates, then it could accept unlimited contributions from individuals. Due to *Citizens United*, these independent-expenditure-only PACs, which quickly became known as **super PACs,** could accept unlimited donations from corporate treasuries and labor unions. Super PACs can directly advocate the election or defeat of a candidate through advertising; they can also do other types of campaigning such as opposition research and voter registration.

Super PACs didn't gear up in large numbers in time for the 2010 elections. The great majority of money spent in that election came from candidates' campaigns and party organizations, not from outside groups.[35] But by 2012, over 1,200 super PACs had formed. Most of the money spent by super PACs that year came from conservative groups (see Table 12.4). This helped Republicans make up for the slight Democratic advantage in candidates' fund-raising. Super PACs were a major reason why non-party groups aired more ads in the 2012 nomination campaign than the candidates themselves did.[36] In 2016, super PACs raised $1.6 billion by early November, about 20 percent of it from just ten mega-donors[37]—a powerful statement from a set of groups that came into existence only six years earlier. They are not supposed to coordinate with candidates or parties, though most do. In fact, more than a hundred super PACs were set up in 2014 to support only one candidate each and led by the candidate's former staffers—and in one Indiana House race in 2016, the candidate's father. These super PACs, then, functioned as shadow campaign committees. Other types of super PACs are closely allied with the party organizations or with ideological or other interest groups.[38] And most of their money comes from donors who don't live in the district or state where the PAC's money is spent.[39]

By late April 2016, super PACs had raised more ($766 million) than they had in all of the 2012 election cycle. By late August 2016, outside groups had spent 47 times as much on TV ads in the North Carolina governor's race as the candidates had! As was the case with 501c4s, about half the money received by super PACs in 2016 came from a small group of wealthy people who gave $1 million or more apiece. In contrast, by about the same time, a million people had donated to Hillary Clinton's campaign, but she had raised only $161 million. Super PACs in 2016 were responsible for "an unprecedented concentration of political wealth."[40]

Like other PACs, super PACs must report who gave them money. But if individuals, groups, or corporations give to 501cs, which do not have to disclose their donors, and the 501cs in turn give the money to super PACs, the original sources of the funds can't be traced. Some groups make this very easy by setting up a super PAC and a 501c group as "sister organizations," such as the conservative group American Crossroads, a super PAC, and its 501c sister group, American Crossroads GPS. This pair spent a combined $49 million in 2014 on independent media ads and grassroots activities to support Republican candidates, much of it given by a few large donors. A reporter suggested, "In this campaign, every candidate needs his own billionaires"[41] (see box "The One Percent of the One Percent" on page 296).

TABLE 12.4 The Top Spenders Among Outside Groups (on Independent Spending and Electioneering Ads in Federal Campaigns, 2015–2016)

Rank	Group (partisan leaning)	Type of Group	Spending (in millions of dollars)
1	Priorities USA/Priorities USA Action (liberal)	Super PAC	132.4
2	Right to Rise USA (conservative)	Super PAC	86.8
3	Senate Leadership Fund (conservative)	Super PAC	85.1
4	Senate Majority PAC (liberal)	Super PAC	79.6
5	Conservative Solutions PAC (conservative)	Super PAC	55.4
6	House Majority PAC (liberal)	Super PAC	52.7
7	National Rifle Association (conservative)	501c	52.9
8	Get Our Jobs Back (conservative)	Super PAC	50.0
9	Congressional Leadership Fund (conservative)	Super PAC	39.1
10	EMILY's List (liberal)	Super PAC	33.6

Source: FEC data from the Center for Responsive Politics as of December 10, 2016, at www.opensecrets.org/outsidespending/summ.php?cycle=2016&type=p&disp=O (accessed December 10, 2016).

By 2016, a wide range of outside groups was spending large sums on ads and other campaign communications. In the season-opening Iowa and New Hampshire events, 70 percent of the ads mentioning candidates were funded by super PACs, 527s, and 501cs, and the requirement that these groups not coordinate their activities with campaigns was not enforced.

The One Percent of the One Percent

In the early months of the 2016 election cycle, just 158 families (along with companies they own or control) contributed half of all the money raised for the presidential race, mainly in the form of donations to super PACs and other outside groups, which are unlimited. These families gave an average of more than *$1 million each*, most of it to super PACs. A million dollars is more than 19 times the median income of American households. Their wealth has come mainly from financial services and oil and gas production companies. In all of the 2014 election cycle, fewer than 32,000 individuals, who comprise one percent of one percent of the total population of the U.S., collectively put $1.2 billion into federal campaigns. And that's only the contributions that were disclosed; many more gave similarly large amounts to 501c4 groups, which don't have to disclose the names of their donors. The *Citizens United* decision gave these big donors the opportunity to make their dollars felt in elections for the first time in decades.

The best-known big givers are brothers Charles and David Koch, who made their billion-dollar fortunes in the oil industry. The Kochs' ideology is libertarian—they want an end to many or most government functions—but, as practical investors, they spend their dollars to support Republicans and oppose Democrats. The Kochs developed and helped fund a network of groups, most of them nonprofits, which spent about $300 million in the 2014 elections on thousands of election ads in battleground states. The groups include Americans for Prosperity, a 501c; Freedom Partners, a 501c; Freedom Partners Action Fund, a super PAC; and the American Legislative Exchange Council (ALEC), which opposes the Affordable Care Act ("Obamacare") and climate change action. Early in 2016 the Kochs announced plans to spend almost $900 million on federal and other campaigns—in short, an amount equivalent to that spent by a presidential campaign. But the Koch brothers were disappointed by Donald Trump's issue positions and chance of victory in 2016, so they stepped out of the presidential election and put their millions into congressional and state-level races—where their dollars would go further—and into lobbying instead. Koch foundations also fund free-market economics programs at a number of universities.

Sources: Peter Olsen-Phillips, Russ Choma, Sarah Bryner, and Doug Weber, "The Political One Percent of the One Percent," Sunlight Foundation news release, April 30, 2015; Eliza Newlin Carney, "A Midterm Spending Spree by Outside Groups," *CQ Weekly*, July 14, 2014, p. 960; Center for Responsive Politics.

Will Super PACs Replace the Parties?

The massive super PAC spending raised concerns that Court decisions had given super PACs and other non-party groups a tremendous advantage over party organizations in influencing elections. If the rise of super PACs were to come at the parties' expense, the impact might be substantial. Some researchers find that parties tend to promote more moderate incumbents than many outside groups or individual donors do. If so, then a reduced role for parties might elect legislators who further polarize and gridlock state legislatures and Congress.[42]

The argument that super PACs might supplant the parties' influence rests in part on super PACs' superior ability to raise funds from big givers. Since BCRA, party organizations are no longer allowed to fund their independent spending by raising unlimited funds from individuals and groups. Instead, parties have to raise their money in limited portions from individuals and PACs. Wouldn't you rather raise $1 million from one individual, as a super PAC can, than try to persuade 1,000 people to donate $1,000 each?

However, a more recent Supreme Court decision helped correct this imbalance. In 2014, the Court in *McCutcheon vs. FEC* overturned the aggregate limits on how much a single donor could give to all federal candidates, parties, and PACs combined. Then Congress increased the amount an individual could give to a party committee under some conditions. The result was that a wealthy couple can now give more than $2 million to the national party committee of their choice in a two-year election cycle, using joint fundraising committees and donations to the party's national convention. And the *McCutcheon* decision raised speculation that the Court would remove all ceilings on donations to parties.

To this point, super PACs have not mounted a major threat to the parties' role in elections. In 2012, most of the candidates supported by super PACs lost their races. PACs pay much higher rates for media ads than candidates do, so their funds don't go as far as those contributed to candidates. Another weakness is that FEC rules don't allow super PACs to pay for campaign staff, candidate travel, or other organizational aspects of the campaign. So in 2016, two Republican candidates (governors Scott Walker of Wisconsin and Rick Perry of Texas) dropped out of the presidential nomination race even though their super PACs still had $15–20 million in funds. The money available to their super PACs, at least during the invisible primary (see Chapter 10), thus couldn't save candidates who fell short in their own fund raising and organizational expertise.

In short, super PACs are more capable of supplementing party committees' efforts than of replacing them. Because super PACs typically operate with much less overhead spending than do the RNC and DNC, they can be more nimble and flexible in supporting candidates endorsed by party committees. In 2016 super PACs were moving increasingly into opposition research, canvassing, and voter turnout in addition to funding media ads. This permits super PACs and party organizations to divide campaign tasks between them, utilizing the strengths of each type of organization. For instance, by combining with 501c groups, super PACs can avoid disclosing the sources of their funds, whereas parties cannot. If parties and super PACs are able to maintain collaborative relationships, then any expansion of super PAC fund-raising should help the party organizations by giving them additional tools to contest elections.

State Regulation and Financing

So far, the chapter has focused mainly on campaign finance for presidential and congressional races. Each state makes its own campaign finance rules for state-level offices. These state laws have gotten more attention recently by default: Because Congress has been so gridlocked by partisanship, big funders are increasingly attracted to state elections. Gaining single-party control over a state legislature and governorship allows state parties and their interest group allies to reshape state policy. Single-party control has led some state legislatures to restrict union activity or slash taxes and others to legalize marijuana. Although most states limit individuals', PACs', corporations', labor unions', and/or parties' contributions to campaigns,[43] their laws differ. State party leaders have taken advantage of these differences to move campaign money from states with more lenient laws to competitive races in other states, particularly those where party control of the legislature could flip. These creative transfers are often accomplished with the help of national groups such as the Republican State Leadership Committee and the two parties' governors' associations.[44]

In 2015, outside political groups spent millions on independent spending in a variety of governors' and state legislative races, helping to affect the agendas of those campaigns.[45] This contributed to the nationalization of state and local elections. To limit the effects of these large sums on their elections, several states and some cities (such as Portland, Oregon and New York City) have provided optional public funding for at least some types of candidates, typically covering only part of the campaign's costs.[46] But most of these programs are small and poorly funded.

Has Campaign Finance Regulation Made a Difference?

You have now read much more than you wanted to know about campaign finance reform. These reforms have had an impact. Compared with the "Wild West" period of unregulated campaign finance before FECA, citizens (and candidates' opponents) now have a much greater opportunity to learn who is giving money to whom in campaigns. Transparency is far from complete, of course, because 501c4 groups can still hide the names of their

donors, and groups running independent spending ads can still form using names ("Citizens for America") that don't tell viewers who they really are. And with the rise of 501c4 groups, the proportion of non-party groups disclosing the names of donors who paid for their political ads has dropped dramatically—and the sums spent have grown tremendously.[47]

Contributions directly to candidates are still limited and reported. But reformers have been frustrated by the ability of corporations, unions, other groups, and individuals to put much larger sums into "independent" spending on ads that look very similar to the ads run by candidates. To those who support recent Supreme Court rulings, that is the way it should be; free speech, they feel, is more important than the effort to limit corruption. Yet as a consequence, many of the reformers' aims—to limit interested money and slow the growth of campaign spending—are almost as far out of reach now as they were before FECA became law.[48] And FECA's aim of tying candidates' fund-raising more closely to their public support has been seriously frustrated by Court decisions. Super PACs can raise huge sums for candidates with little public support; all the candidate needs is a supportive billionaire or two.

Money in American Politics

Both before and after these reforms, money has played a bigger role in American elections than in those of most other democracies. The sheer size of many constituencies in the United States leads candidates to buy expensive mass media time. The large number of elected officials combined with frequent primary and general elections has produced a year-round election industry. Fund-raising occupies a great deal of the candidates' time even after they are elected, which distracts public officials from a thoughtful consideration of the public's needs and may give big contributors undue influence on public policy. Even if elected officials hold relatively safe seats, they are expected to raise a lot of money to help their more vulnerable party colleagues win reelection. And because many contributors have intense views on issues, party polarization is increased.

Campaigns don't have to be funded this way. In the United Kingdom, for instance, the active portion of election campaigns runs for only about six to seven weeks, during which all the public-service TV channels have to show the party political broadcasts.[49] Parliamentary candidates can spend no more than the equivalent of $20,000 each—about what hopeless challengers spend in the U.S. On the other hand, interested Britons have the opportunity to watch daily, and often contentious, news conferences by the parties' leaders.

The American system of campaign finance has consequences. The fact that candidates dominate the fund-raising in most American campaigns gives them greater independence from their party organizations once they take office. The parties are working hard to increase their role in the raising and spending of campaign money. Their ingenuity was sorely tested by

FECA and BCRA and now by *Citizens United*, but both parties have shown a lot of resilience in adapting to these reforms so far.

After all this experience with reforms that fall short of their mark, is there any point in continuing to try to regulate campaign finance? Many would argue that it's a useless effort, because interested money will always find its way into the pockets of power. On the other hand, although people continue to steal from others, that is not normally used as an argument for repealing laws against theft. The lifting of all campaign finance rules would lead to unrestricted influence of big money on politics, even if the big money came from other nations or drug cartels. So the struggle to contain interested money will continue.

Notes

1 Benjamin I. Page, Larry M. Bartels, and Jason Seawright, "Democracy and the Policy Preferences of Wealthy Americans," Perspectives on Politics 11 (2013): 51–73.

2 Unless otherwise noted, all figures cited in this chapter come from Federal Election Commission reports, at times (and so noted) via the Campaign Finance Institute or the Center for Responsive Politics (CRP), and in this particular case from the Center for Responsive Politics. They combine the amounts spent by candidates, parties, and interest groups. For excellent analyses of campaign finance, see Michael J. Malbin, ed., *The Election after Reform* (Lanham, MD: Rowman & Littlefield, 2006); and Paul S. Herrnson, *Congressional Elections*, 7th ed. (Los Angeles: Sage/CQ Press, 2016).

3 Data from the Center for Public Integrity, released February 1, 2016.

4 FEC data calculated by the Campaign Finance Institute at www.cfinst.org/pdf/vital/VitalStats_t2c.pdf   and   www.cfinst.org/pdf/vital/VitalStats_t5C.pdf (accessed June 26, 2016).

5 FEC data from the CRP as of November 2, 2016, at www.opensecrets.org/overview/incumbs.php?cycle=2016&party=S&type=G (accessed December 10, 2016).

6 Brennan Center for Justice, "Outside Spending Enters Pennsylvania Supreme Court Race," October 16, 2015, at www.brennancenter.org/press-release/outside-spending-enters-pennsylvania-supreme-court-race (accessed June 26, 2016). On local campaign finance, see Brian E. Adams, *Campaign Finance in Local Elections* (Boulder, CO: Lynne Rienner, 2011).

7 See John J. Coleman and Paul F. Manna, "Congressional Campaign Spending and the Quality of Democracy," *Journal of Politics* 62 (2000): 757–789.

8 Gary C. Jacobson, *The Politics of Congressional Elections*, 7th ed. (New York: Pearson-Longman, 2009), p. 45.

9 See these articles in the *American Journal of Political Science*: Donald Philip Green and Jonathan S. Krasno, "Salvation for the Spendthrift Incumbent," 32 (1988): 884–907; Gary C. Jacobson, "The Effects of Campaign Spending in House Elections," 34 (1990): 334–362; and Kenneth Benoit and Michael Marsh, "The Campaign Value of Incumbency," 52 (2008): 874–890.

10 Jonathan Martin, "House Majority Leader Upset by Tea Party Rival in Primary," *New York Times*, June 11, 2014, p. A1.

11 Andrew B. Hall, "Systemic Effects of Campaign Spending," *Political Science Research and Methods*, 4 (2016): 343–359.

12 Peter Francia, John C. Green, Paul S. Herrnson, Lynda W. Powell, and Clyde Wilcox, *The Financiers of Congressional Elections* (New York: Columbia University Press, 2003).

13 See, for example, Anne E. Baker, "Getting Short-Changed?" *Social Science Quarterly* 97 (2016): 1096–1107; Michael J. Barber, "Representing the Preferences of Donors, Partisans, and Voters in the US Senate," *Public Opinion Quarterly* 80 (2016): 225–249.

14 Herrnson, *Congressional Elections*, pp. 144–145.

15 Gregory Wawro, "A Panel Probit Analysis of Campaign Contributions and Roll-Call Votes," *American Journal of Political Science* 45 (2001): 563–579.

16 See Richard L. Hall and Frank W. Wayman, "Buying Time," *American Political Science Review* 84 (1990): 797–820, and Joshua L. Kalla and David E. Broockman, "Campaign Contributions Facilitate Access to Congressional Officials," *American Journal of Political Science* 60 (2016): 545–558.

17 FEC, "2016 Coordinated Party Expenditure Limits," at www.fec.gov/info/charts_cpe_2016.shtml (accessed September 14, 2016).

18 Rebecca Ballhaus and Brody Mullins, "Party Politics: FEC at Loggerheads on How to Celebrate Anniversary," *Wall Street Journal*, April 16, 2015, at www.wsj.com/articles/party-politics-fec-at-loggerheads-on-how-to-celebrate-anniversary-1429228827 (accessed June 26, 2016).

19 On public funding, see Michael J. Malbin, "Small Donors, Large Donors and the Internet," at www.cfinst.org/president/pdf/PresidentialWorkingPaper_April09.pdf (accessed June 26, 2016).

20 See Thomas E. Mann, "Linking Knowledge and Action," *Perspectives on Politics* 1 (2003): 69–83.

21 The cases are *Colorado Republican Federal Campaign Committee v. Federal Election Commission* (1996), known as "Colorado I," and *McConnell v. Federal Election Commission* (2003).

22 FEC data reported in Herrnson, *Congressional Elections*, p. 246.

23 From the record in *McConnell v. Federal Election Commission*, quoted in Adam Cohen, "Buying a High-Priced Upgrade on the Political Back-Scratching Circuit," *New York Times*, September 15, 2003, p. A22.

24 See Anthony Corrado, Sarah Barclay, and Heitor Gouvea, "The Parties Take the Lead," in John C. Green and Rick Farmer, eds., *The State of the Parties*, 4th ed. (Lanham, MD: Rowman & Littlefield, 2003), pp. 97–114.

25 For a different view of the partisan impact of soft money, see Raymond J. LaRaja, *Small Change* (Ann Arbor, MI: University of Michigan Press, 2008).

26 John Kenneth White and Daniel M. Shea, *New Party Politics* (Belmont, CA: Wadsworth, 2004), p. 258.

27 Michael J. Malbin, "Political Parties Under the Post-*McConnell* Bipartisan Campaign Reform Act," *Election Law Journal* 3 (2004): 183.

28 Raymond J. La Raja, "State Parties and Soft Money," in Green and Farmer, *The State of the Parties*, 4th ed., pp. 132–150.

29 Jonathan Krasno and Kenneth Goldstein, "The Facts About Television Advertising and the McCain–Feingold Bill," *PS Political Science & Politics* 35 (2002): 210.

30 Raymond J. LaRaja, "State and Local Political Parties," in Malbin, *The Election after Reform*, Chapter 4.

31 Michael M. Franz, Joel Rivlin, and Kenneth Goldstein, "Much More of the Same," in Malbin, ed., *The Election after Reform*, Chapter 7.

32 Data estimated from information provided by the Center for Responsive Politics at www.opensecrets.org/dark-money/basics (accessed December 10, 2016). Other 501(c) organizations that can raise and spend unlimited sums on political activity, though subject to legal constraints, include 501(c)3 charities, 501(c)5 labor union groups, and 501(c)6 trade associations, such as the Chamber of Commerce.

33 Joseph E. Sandler and Neil P. Reiff, "State and Local Parties Must Tread Carefully Through the Campaign Finance Minefield," *Campaigns & Elections* 25 (2004), pp. 50–51.

34 Data from the Center for Responsive Politics at www.opensecrets.org/pres12/bundlers.php (accessed June 26, 2016).

35 Michael M. Franz, "The *Citizens United* Election?" *The Forum* 8 (2010): 22.

36 Michael M. Franz, "Interest Groups in Electoral Politics: 2012 in Context," *The Forum* 10 (2012): 62–79.

37 Fredreka Schouten and Christopher Schnaars, "Super PAC Donations Surge Past $1 Billion," *USA Today*, September 21, 2016, p. A1.

38 Ibid.

39 James G. Gimpel, Frances E. Lee, and Shanna Pearson-Merkowitz, "The Check Is in the Mail," *American Journal of Political Science* 52 (2008): 373–394.

40 Matea Gold, "The New Gilded Age," *Washington Post*, April 16, 2016, p. A1. Data in this paragraph from the Center for Public Integrity.

41 Jane Mayer, "Leader of the PACs," *New Yorker*, February 8, 2012, at www.newyorker.com/online/blogs/newsdesk/2012/02/leader-of-the-pacs.html (accessed June 26, 2016).

42 Raymond J. La Raja and Brian F. Schaffner, *Campaign Finance and Political Polarization* (Ann Arbor: University of Michigan Press, 2015); Michael J. Barber, "Ideological Donors, Contribution Limits, and the Polarization of American Legislatures," *Journal of Politics* 78 (2016): 296–310.

43 See the National Conference of State Legislatures at http://www.ncsl.org/research/elections-and-campaigns/campaign-finance-an-overview.aspx (accessed June 26, 2016).

44 See Nicholas Confessore, "A National Strategy Funds State Political Monopolies," *New York Times*, January 12, 2014, p. A1.

45 Ashley Balcerzak, "Where do ads shaping state politics come from?" December 3, 2015, Center for Public Integrity press release.

46 See Michael Miller, "Gaming Arizona," *PS: Political Science and Politics* 61 (2008): 527–532. The Campaign Finance Institute has researched several types of public financing programs; see www.cfinst.org.

47 Data from the Center for Responsive Politics at www.opensecrets.org/outsidespending/disclosure.php

48 Raymond J. LaRaja, "From Bad to Worse," *The Forum* 6 (2008): Issue 1, Article 2.

49 See "Campaign Finance: United Kingdom," Library of Congress, July 1, 2015, at www.loc.gov/law/help/campaign-finance/uk.php (accessed June 26, 2016).

PART FIVE

The Party in Government

As you may recall from Chapter 1, each **party in government** includes *all the elected or appointed public officials* who see themselves as belonging to that party. They are vitally important to the party as a whole because they, not the party organization or the party electorate, have the power to vote on and then, if passed, enforce the party's proposals on college student loans, immigration, abortion, and gun rights. Without their party in government, the American parties would be very much like interest groups: lots of ideas, less ability to make them into law.

The Republican Party in government, like its Democratic counterpart, is a wide-ranging group. In addition to everyone elected to the House, the Senate, and the White House as a Republican, the Republican Party in government includes Republicans who work for federal, state, and local administrative agencies; Republican governors and state legislators; Republicans serving in local elective and appointive offices; and even judges (and Supreme Court justices) who see themselves as Republicans. In the same way, the Democratic Party in government ranges from Democratic senators to Department of Defense workers and county assessors who consider themselves to be Democrats.

These people share the same party label but they do not always share the same priorities. The design of the American political system works against a unified party in government. Because members of Congress are elected separately from the president, they do not need to act as a single Democratic or Republican "team." They represent different constituencies, so they face different pressures from their constituents as to what they, and the rest of their party, should be doing. Remember that congressional candidates are not chosen to run by their party organization; instead, they become the party's candidates by winning voter support in primary elections. The use of direct primaries combined with the separation of powers and federalism make it very difficult for members of the party in government to unite in support of a single, coherent set of policy goals. In fact, in the few cases of Congress members who represent a district that normally favors the other party, congressional party leaders may encourage them to vote against their party on an occasional bill in order to please their constituents and win reelection.

For decades, reformers have dreamed of an alternative. One is the idea of **party government**, also called **responsible parties**. Its proponents argue that American democracy would be improved if the parties were to offer clearer and fuller statements of their proposed policies, nominate candidates pledged to support those policies, and see to it that their winning candidates enact those programs. Voters would then choose not only between candidates but, more importantly, between alternative sets of policies and be assured that the winning set would be put into effect. That would greatly strengthen the parties' role, and voters, the argument goes, would be better able to hold their government accountable.

Although we do see something close to party government in several other democracies, including Britain, it is not likely to develop fully in the United States without fundamental institutional change. Because of the separation of powers, Republicans can hold a majority in Congress while a Democrat sits in the White House, or one party can dominate the House while the other controls the Senate. In fact, in the past half-century, divided party control of government has been the norm at the national level and in most states. That makes it difficult for a party to implement all its preferred policies. Instead, legislation is likely to require compromise—a process that many Americans value in theory but abhor in practice. Even at times when one party controls both Congress and the presidency, the legislative party might not always be in perfect agreement with its White House colleague, as recent (and exasperated) presidents have found. The party organization can't guarantee that all the party's candidates, selected in primary elections in differing constituencies across the nation, will run on the party's platform. And the party electorate is still connected only loosely to the party organization.

Yet the Democrats and the Republicans have been acting more like responsible parties in recent years, even without institutional reform. Congress and state legislatures now divide along party lines more than they have in decades. Partisanship has a major influence on the staffing of top executive offices and the appointment of judges. As more citizens are attracted to party work because of particular issues that concern them, the pressure builds for greater party responsibility.

The chapters in Part V address these questions of party influence in government. Chapters 13 and 14 examine the roles of the parties in the organization and operation of the legislature, the executive branch, and the courts. Chapter 15 looks at the degree to which party government can be said to exist in American politics.

CHAPTER 13

Parties in Congress and State Legislatures

When you think of Congress, the word "gridlock" probably comes to mind. To many observers, partisanship is the cause, tying Congress into knots instead of bringing the institution together to pass needed legislation.

Is this a fair indictment of party power in Congress? In the time-honored words of college professors: yes and no. Yes, it's true that Congress members now vote with their party in Congress (and their party's leadership) more regularly than they have in over a century. The parties in Congress have become more polarized on issues in the past three decades: Republicans in Congress have become more deeply and consistently conservative, and Democrats have become more consistently liberal. As a result, each party has a stronger motive to keep the other party from passing bills. Yet this would not be enough in itself to gridlock Congress; in most legislatures, the majority party would be able to pass its legislation over the minority's objections.

But Congress is not most legislatures. It was designed to put roadblocks in the path of majorities, in order to protect minority rights. One of the biggest roadblocks is the separation of powers. In a political system without a separation of powers—a parliamentary regime, such as that of Great Britain—the party that wins (or can put together a coalition of parties to win) a majority of legislative seats becomes the governing party, and its leader becomes the head of government. If a majority of legislators vote against the governing party's major policies, then either the governing cabinet must be reshuffled or the legislature must be dissolved and its members sent home to campaign for their jobs again. That provides a strong incentive for each legislative party to remain united. American legislators do not face these pressures. They can reject the proposals of a president, a governor, or even a leader of their own legislative party without toppling the government and having to face a new election.

We can see evidence of this in a dramatic confrontation in 2015, when some highly conservative House Republicans threatened to stop passage of the federal budget unless the power of their party leader, the Speaker, was reduced (because they felt he wasn't conservative enough), Planned Parenthood and "Obamacare" were defunded, and entitlement programs were cut. A Republican House member sighed, "We really don't have 218 votes [i.e., a majority] to determine a bathroom break over here on our side."[1] These conservative Republicans were part of the Tea Party-aligned "Freedom Caucus." They could reject pressure from their party leaders because, like so many other Congress members, they represent districts considered safe for their party, and active Republicans in their constituencies are highly conservative as well. Their party's base, then, rewards them for defying their party's leadership when it tries to negotiate with Democrats to pass bills.

To add to these challenges, party control of both houses has shifted frequently, so both parties have tasted majority power in recent years and hope to keep or regain it in the next election. Many Congress members are convinced that their party gains voter support by highlighting the contrasts between the parties, rather than by compromising to pass legislation. Every bill becomes a way to "send messages" to party voters.[2] Members of both parties see little point in making long-term policy concessions when they could instead take "Hell, no!" stands that please activists back home and then push for their party to win control in the next election.

So party power can't shoulder all the blame for gridlock; the design of Congress, the unusually frequent recent shifts in party control of both houses, and the greater polarization of members and activists all deserve a share. In fact, to some analysts, increased party voting doesn't reflect the power of *party* in legislative life at all. Rather, they suggest, legislators rely on their own issue preferences when they vote, and conservative legislators have sorted themselves into the Republican Party and liberals into the Democratic Party.[3] However, there is ample evidence that changes in the parties outside of Congress, organizational reforms, and party leaders themselves have expanded the legislative parties' importance.[4]

How the Parties are Organized in Congress

What are the parties in Congress? Recall from Chapter 1 that members of the first Congresses divided into two groupings reflecting their differing views on big issues and to serve their legislative needs. Now, these legislative parties coordinate ideas about public policy, set priorities, divide up the workload in moving legislation, try to get the party's bills passed, hold their leaders accountable, protect the party's reputation, and elect party candidates.[5] The congressional parties are independent of the national, state, and local party organizations but have ties to these organizations.

The members of each legislative party come together in meetings (called caucuses by the House Democrats and conferences by the Senate Democrats and both Republican parties) to select their party's leaders (see box "Party Leadership Positions in the House and Senate" on page 307). They also structure the chamber itself by nominating candidates for its presiding officer (the Speaker of the House or president pro tempore of the Senate)

Party Leadership Positions in the House and Senate

Each party creates its own leadership structure in each house of Congress; the individual leaders are elected by the entire party membership of the chamber. At the top of the hierarchy is the party leader (called the **majority** or **minority leader**, depending on whether the party controls the chamber). In the House of Representatives, the **Speaker** ranks above the majority leader as the true leader of the majority party. These party leaders have assistants called **whips**, who tell members the party's position on bills, try to convince them to vote the way the party leadership wants, and keep a head count of each bill's supporters and opponents.

Each congressional party also has several specialized leadership positions.

There is a **conference** or (among House Democrats) **caucus chair** to head the meeting of all party members. Other chairs are selected for the **Steering Committee**, which assigns party members to committees; the **Policy Committee**, which identifies the party's position on proposed legislation and sets issue priorities; the **Campaign Committee**, which provides campaign support to the party's congressional candidates; and any other committees the legislative party may create. Variations do occur; House Democrats, for example, have a single Steering and Policy Committee, and Senate Republicans have a Committee on Committees.

and approving procedures for appointing party members to congressional committees.

The majority party dominates the organization of both houses. In the House, the majority party's elected leader, the Speaker, has extensive power over the chamber's operations. The majority party leadership controls the action in committees and on the floor and chooses the chairs of all the committees. Most of each committee's members come from the majority party, by a margin that is often larger than the majority's margin in the chamber. Democrats held the House majority from the early 1950s until 1995 and again from 2007 to 2011. In the Senate, the majority leader manages floor action, to the degree that floor action can be managed in that more individualistic institution. Republicans held a Senate majority from 1981 to 1987, for most of the period from 1995 to 2007, and again beginning in 2015.

Changes in the Power of House Party Leaders

Party leaders in Congress are chosen by the votes of all members of their legislative party. Their power is, in effect, delegated to them by their party caucus (or conference), and they serve subject to its approval.[6] Party members' willingness to grant power to their congressional party leaders has changed a lot over time.

The Revolt Against "Czar" Cannon Years ago, power in the House of Representatives was highly centralized in the hands of the Speaker. In the first decade of the 1900s, powerful Speaker Joe Cannon chaired the Rules Committee, the "traffic cop" through which he could control the flow of legislation to the floor. He appointed all standing committees and their chairs, putting his chief supporters in key positions, and generally had the resources and sanctions needed to enforce party discipline.[7]

In 1910, however, dissidents within his own party combined with the minority Democrats to revolt against "Czar" Cannon. For many decades after that, Speakers were not able to muster the level of power that Cannon commanded. Instead, they had to operate in a much more decentralized House in which party discipline could be maintained only through skillful bargaining and strong personal loyalties. Successful Speakers during this era were skilled negotiators rather than commanders.[8]

After Cannon, through most of the 1900s, chairs of the standing committees that dealt with proposed legislation were selected using the **seniority rule**: The longest-serving member of the majority party on a committee automatically became its chair. Because of this rule, members of the majority party could win a chairmanship simply by being reelected to Congress many times, even if they did not support their party leadership's position on issues—in fact, even if they voted with the other party more often than with their own. That gave long-serving party members—many of them conservative southern Democrats—a base of power in Congress independent of the party leaders. Committee chairs could, and often did, use that power in a dictatorial manner.

Growing Party Coordination During the 1970s, however, the growing number of liberals in the Democratic caucus, elected in the wake of the Watergate scandals, called for limiting the committee chairs' independence. They believed that weakening the seniority rule and strengthening the party caucus would let House Democrats achieve greater policy coordination and pass more liberal policies. The House Democratic caucus first gave itself the right to vote by secret ballot on whether each committee chair would be retained. Soon after, the caucus did replace a few chairs with less senior Democrats whose views and behavior were more acceptable to liberals in the caucus.[9] The remaining committee chairs, and those who wanted to become chairs, saw that they needed to pay more attention to the views of the caucus. By reducing the chairs' autonomy, this reform expanded the power of their main competitors, the party leaders. And because the Democrats ran the House, it changed the structure of authority in the chamber as a whole.

The power to assign members to committees—a decision vital to members' careers—was moved to the new Steering and Policy Committee dominated by the Speaker. The Speaker was also allowed to choose, with the caucus's approval, the chair and other Democratic members of the Rules Committee, whose independence had formerly been a thorn in the side of the party leadership. Thus, the Speaker gained more power over other party legislators' futures and the fate of the bills they wanted to pass. The whip system, legislators responsible for informing their party colleagues about the party's stands and for finding out how many members are supporting those stands, was enlarged and made more responsive to party leaders.[10] The majority party leadership became not just a traffic cop but a major source of power and policy development.

The Gingrich Revolution

The Republican minority had no input into the Democratic procedural reforms of the 1970s and 1980s. But in 1994, Republicans won a majority of House seats for the first time in 40 years, after a campaign centered on a set of conservative policy pledges called the "Contract with America." The election of new conservative members made the House Republicans even more cohesive. Most of these newcomers had gotten campaign help from Representative Newt Gingrich, then the second-ranking Republican leader in the House, and credited him with engineering their party's unexpected takeover. They elected Gingrich Speaker and gave him unprecedented authority to push the Republican agenda.

To do so, Gingrich set aside the seniority rule entirely. The party leadership could now choose committee chairs on the basis of their commitment to bringing the party's desired bills to the floor. Each committee chair was limited to a six-year term. Why did the committee chairs agree to such a sharp reduction in their power? Republicans had only a slender majority in the House, and they faced a Democrat, Bill Clinton, in the White House. Perhaps GOP members accepted strong party discipline to have a better chance of achieving the goals of the Contract.[11] Or perhaps the change reflected the chairs' personal loyalty to Gingrich, or even fear for their political careers if they resisted. It was a major step in the expansion of party power in the House, and Gingrich became the strongest Speaker since Cannon.[12]

The result, at least initially, was a level of party discipline with which "Czar" Cannon would have felt comfortable. When the ten sections of the Contract with America came to a vote in the House, out of a possible 2,300 Republican voting decisions (ten provisions times 230 Republican House members), there were only 111 "no" votes; 95 percent of Republican votes supported the party leadership's position. More than in almost a century, the majority party disciplined itself to achieve policy goals.

... And Later Shifts in Party Control

Gingrich's aura of invincibility started to crumble in late 1995. When a standoff on the national budget between President Clinton and House Republicans led to a shutdown of the government, Gingrich and his colleagues were blamed. The Speaker was dogged by declining popularity and charges of ethics violations. House Republicans found his uneven leadership style frustrating. When the GOP lost a net of five House seats in 1998, many House Republicans demanded new leadership, and Gingrich resigned.

The Republican leadership maintained control over the selection of House committee chairs after Gingrich stepped down. When the first term-limited chairs were due to be replaced in 2001, new chairs were chosen by the leadership-dominated Republican Steering Committee, which passed over several moderate Republicans to select conservatives who were less senior.[13]

Then the Republicans gained seats in the 2002 elections, and the new Majority Leader, Tom DeLay, was nicknamed "The Hammer" for his iron-fisted use of power. The term limit on the Speaker was eliminated, seniority rules were undercut even more to move loyal leadership allies into powerful subcommittee chairs, and party leaders cracked down on Republicans who refused to follow the party's lead.[14] Democrats complained that they were being shut out of conference committees and prevented from offering amendments to bills. The Republican leadership was remarkably effective in pushing legislation through the House.

In the rapidly changing environment that has characterized Congress since DeLay resigned in 2005, the movement toward a more powerful party leadership has generally been sustained. Although the Democrats restored the practice of letting the party caucus choose committee chairs when the party won control of the House in 2007, and almost all the chairs chosen by the caucus were the most senior Democrats on their committees, incoming Speaker Nancy Pelosi imposed more party discipline on committee chairs than had previous Democratic Speakers. Chairs were now expected to support the party leadership's aims and raise a lot of money for party candidates' campaigns. And the Democratic leadership shut the minority Republicans out of the legislative process with as much zeal as the Republicans under Gingrich and DeLay had shut out the Democrats.

Republicans' outrage at the Democratic leadership's use of its power produced frequent gridlock in the House. When party control changed again in 2011, Republican Speaker John Boehner responded to demands from the new far-right Republican members by allowing a more open legislative process, with more extensive floor debate and more amendments to bills. But some new Republicans still defied Boehner's leadership, requiring him to pass legislation with the help of Democratic votes. The Republican leadership worked to keep a strong hand on House activity, reinstated the term limit for committee chairs, and increased party control over the budget process. Boehner tightened his control in 2012 with the unusual step of removing four rebellious Republican House members from desirable committee posts. He acted against dissidents again in 2015. But the Tea Party-associated House Freedom Caucus refused to fade away. Boehner resigned in frustration that year, though Rep. Paul Ryan, his successor, took advantage of the resulting leadership vacuum to protect the Speaker's powers.

Overall, the rules changes have made House members more dependent on their party leadership than they were several decades ago. If members want to pass legislation and advance in the House, they need to show considerable loyalty to their party and its leaders. To the extent that their efforts help their party gain or keep majority status in the House, members can better achieve their individual goals.[15] But this has not prevented challenges to the party leadership in the 2010s, particularly within the majority Republican ranks.

What Caused This Stronger Party Leadership?

One main reason why individual House members have been more willing to accept strong party leadership since the 1970s is that the members of each party have become more ideologically cohesive—more inclined to agree with their party colleagues on issues.[16] As discussed in Chapter 7, white southern voters were leaving the Democratic Party in increasing numbers since the 1970s, and fewer conservative southern Democrats were being elected to Congress. Democratic House members, then, became more uniformly liberal than had been the case in many decades. This process reached full flower in the mid-1990s. Because of the committee reforms, the remaining conservative southern Democrats lost their strongholds of committee power. The sharp gulf that had separated southern Democrats from northern Democrats during the mid-1900s had become an easily bridged creek. Congressional Republicans were becoming more ideologically unified as well and were energized by the conservative policy leadership coming from President Ronald Reagan in the 1980s.

When a party is ideologically cohesive, the party caucus finds it easier to agree on a unified position on legislation. The members of a cohesive party can better trust that their leaders will share and promote their policy concerns and protect their reelection interests. In addition, the two congressional parties were more at odds with one another on issues during this period than they had been for some time. So the legislators of each party became more willing to grant power to their legislative party leaders, including the power to pressure straggling legislators to fall in line, to pass the party's legislation and to keep the other party from succeeding.[17]

This account of the reasons for stronger party leadership is called **conditional party government**, or **CPG**. It stresses that as the two parties' supporting coalitions in the electorate become more polarized—the

What Makes a Strong Legislative Party Split?

The anti-government Tea Party movement claimed credit for the 2010 Republican congressional sweep. With 87 new members, the Republican Party gained a big majority in the House of Representatives. These freshmen, most of them even more conservative than the continuing House Republicans, made up more than a third of their party's conference in the House.

Once in Congress, most of the newcomers behaved like party stalwarts and supported their party almost unanimously on legislative votes. But some of the new members, with the backing of Tea Party supporters in their districts, pressed for more conservative policies including trillions of dollars of additional spending cuts, defying the leadership of their Speaker, John Boehner. Their continuing disloyalty prompted Boehner to remove four of the more rebellious freshmen from prime committee assignments in 2012, as a warning to the others. But when the Republican House majority expanded again in the 2014 midterms, defiance within the Republican conference increased. About 40 far-right House Republicans regularly undercut Boehner's authority, leading to Boehner's resignation in 2015.

Finding a new party leader proved to be tough. The ultra-conservative faction, calling itself the House Freedom Caucus (HFC), said they were willing to go so far as to shut down the government unless their party's new leader accepted their demands: major budget cuts, eliminating federal funding for Planned Parenthood, and refusing to grant amnesty to undocumented immigrants. The most broadly acceptable choice for Speaker, Rep. Paul Ryan, said he'd run—on the condition that the HFC would first agree to endorse him. The HFC held out, then caved, and an all-too-brief outbreak of sanity followed in which Congress passed a budget.

Why did the House Republicans split? The big increase in the size of the Republican House contingent also increased its diversity. Many of the new, highly conservative Republican members, reflecting the views of activists in their safe Republican districts, valued ideological purity over reelection. They were allergic to compromise and insisted on party leadership that agreed with them. Other Republican colleagues were more pragmatic and less ready to rule out compromise. According to the theory of conditional party government (see page 311), then, a vocal portion of the Republican conference did not want to grant the Speaker greater power, for fear that he would listen to party colleagues who were more willing to compromise in order to pass bills. These splits continued in 2017.

Sources: Jennifer Steinhauer, "Republican Freedom Caucus's Revolt in House Is Stoked Back Home," *New York Times*, October 20, 2015, p. A1; Jennifer Steinhauer and Emmarie Huetteman, "Ryan Is Ready to Be Speaker (On His Terms)," *New York Times*, October 21, 2015, p. A1.

identifiers of a party become more similar to one another in their preferences and more different from those of the other party—the party members representing them in Congress become more polarized as well. Then, a party's legislators will grant their congressional party leaders more power to pursue their shared policy goals.[18] Party leaders, in turn, will work hard to protect their party's "brand" so as to get more party candidates elected, because they will gain power by doing so; majority leaders can get a lot more done than minority leaders can.[19] Party leaders' staffs and resources have expanded hand in hand with their increased power.[20] Using this same logic, we can explain occasional deviations from stronger party leadership, such as the fall of Speaker Boehner. The growing division among House Republicans in the early 2010s—if not in policy beliefs, then in strategic preferences—led some Republicans to feel less trust in Boehner's leadership and thus more concern about concentrating power in the Speakership (see box "What Makes a Strong Legislative Party Split?" on page 312).

Some party leaders have been more willing than others to make use of these new sources of power. Former House Majority Leader DeLay used the congressional reforms to become a highly assertive Republican leader. A decade later, Boehner was not as comfortable with aggressive partisanship. Legislative party cohesion and party leaders' power, then, depend not only on party polarization but also on the skills and inclinations of individual party leaders.

Parties in the Senate

Clearly, the job of a House party leader is challenging, but the work of Senate party leaders is more like herding cats.[21] By the mid-1970s, Barbara Sinclair explains,[22] the U.S. Senate had moved from an institution in which committees dominated the legislative work to a much more individualistic body with a more collegial distribution of power. Increasingly, and with avid media attention, members of the Senate established themselves as national spokespersons on various policy questions. Once they had become political "stars," these senators expected to participate more fully in the Senate's work, on their way, many hoped, to greater glory and higher office.

Add to this individualistic atmosphere the unique Senate rule of the filibuster: the right of extended debate, used to talk a bill or a nomination to death if the votes are not available to defeat it in any other way. It takes 60 votes to stop a filibuster, a number that is very difficult to achieve. As a result, even the *threat* of a filibuster is enough to stop legislation. Members of the minority have been able to wrest control of the legislative agenda away from the majority by making much more frequent use of such threats, especially since 2007. The Democratic Senate majority finally limited filibusters of most presidential nominations in 2013, but other legislation can still be stopped by filibuster.

The Senate, then, developed a desperate need for a legislative traffic cop. At the same time, changes in southern politics had led to greater party polarization in the Senate, just as they had in the House. More former House members were being elected to the Senate and bringing with them their experience in that polarized institution.[23] Increasingly, then, the party leadership in the Senate tried to direct the traffic. Individual senators came to depend on their party leaders to promote the legislative party's interests. So the individualism that had developed by the 1970s was constrained by greater party polarization.

The Senate's rules make it harder for the majority to govern than is the case in the House; they do not allow as much centralization of power in the party leadership.[24] The Senate majority leader still defers to committee chairs to a greater extent than his House counterpart (the Speaker) does, and party leaders consult extensively with their party colleagues, rather than command them. But even in the Senate, party leaders now play a more important role.[25] Committee chairs were term-limited in 1996 by the Republican majority, and the Majority Leader can now name half the membership of the most valued Senate committees without needing to follow seniority.

Its increased party polarization and frequent shifts in party control since 1980 have led to such intense partisanship that gridlock and obstructionism now characterize the work of the Senate. As one senator described it, "What people want is principled bipartisanship, and what they are getting is unprincipled partisanship."[26] In 2014, under Democratic control, the Senate was one of the least productive in recent years. Republicans took back Senate control in 2015 and new Majority Leader Mitch McConnell tried to appease his most conservative members by promising a more open debate process. More legislation did get through the Senate, though much of the legislative activity was designed to showcase campaign messages rather than to fix policy.

Parties in the State Legislatures

As in Congress, the legislative parties organize the legislatures in almost every state.[27] They structure everything from the legislative leadership to its committees. The power of the legislative parties varies, however, depending in part on the legislature's rules and on the personal skills and resources of the party leaders. In a few state legislatures, daily caucuses and strong party leadership make for a party every bit as potent as in the recent U.S. House. In others, especially the traditionally one-party states, party organization is weaker than it was in Congress before the 1970s reforms.

Most state legislative party leaders have a lot of power over the day-to-day workings of the legislature. They do not usually have to defer to powerful committee chairs. The party leaders can typically choose chairs and members of powerful committees on the basis of their support for the party leader personally or for their views on issues rather than on the basis of seniority. Party leaders also exercise their influence through the party caucus. In many states with strong two-party systems, party leaders call meetings to give members information about upcoming bills, learn whether their membership is united or divided on an issue, and encourage legislators to support the party's position. Leaders in a few of these states may even try to get the caucus to hold a "binding" vote calling on all members to support the party's position on an important issue.[28]

In sum, although the parties' legislative organizations look similar across the states—their party leadership positions are fairly uniform—they differ in their behavior. Party leaders' power can vary even between the two houses of the same state legislature, as do the influence and effectiveness of the party caucus.[29]

Methods of Party Influence

How do legislative parties and their leaders exercise their power? What resources can they use to influence their members' behavior?

Carrots and Sticks

Congressional party leaders have a variety of tools to affect the behavior of their party colleagues. They rely more on incentives than on punishments because the most effective punishments are limited in their use and can backfire. The most powerful punishment would be to remove a maverick legislator from his or her seat in the House or Senate. Except in rare cases, however, party leaders do not have that power. Only the legislator's constituents can do that, and they are not likely to serve as agents of the congressional party leadership. Thus, representatives and senators can normally vote against their party's leadership, or against major bills proposed by a president of their party, without fear of losing their jobs.

Even the in-your-face disloyalty of supporting the other party's presidential candidate has not been punished consistently in Congress. Senate Democrats let Connecticut Senator Joe Lieberman keep his committee chairmanship in 2008, after he not only campaigned extensively for the Republican presidential nominee, John McCain, but also spoke for McCain at the Republican convention and ran for reelection to his own Senate seat as an independent. Democrats worried that punishing Lieberman might lead him to switch parties, which could have endangered the Democrats' Senate majority.

Perhaps the most famous example of the weakness of party penalties is the story of Phil Gramm, elected as a Democratic representative from Texas in 1978. The House Democratic leadership gave Gramm, a conservative, a seat on the prestigious House Budget Committee in return for his promise to cooperate with party leaders. But in 1983, members of the Democratic caucus were infuriated to learn that Gramm had leaked the details of secret Democratic Party meetings on the Reagan budget to Republican House members. The caucus took away Gramm's seat on the Budget Committee.

Gramm did not accept his fate quietly. He resigned from the House and then ran—as a Republican—in the special election held to replace him. His constituents reelected him to the House and later to the Senate as a Republican. In fact, he was soon back on the House Budget Committee, courtesy of the Republican leadership! As long as legislative party leaders cannot keep a party maverick from being renominated and reelected and in districts where voters are not impressed by a legislator's party loyalty, party influence will be limited. Therefore, this step is taken very rarely.[30]

In short, House and Senate party leaders have only a few punishments at their command when trying to unify their parties, and there is always the risk that punishing a legislator will cause him or her to defect or lose reelection. Instead, party leaders rely more on incentives to achieve party loyalty. They can offer or withhold desirable committee assignments and help in passing a member's bills. They can give members useful information about the status of a bill on the legislative schedule. They can make speeches and raise money for a member's reelection. The parties' congressional campaign committees, with their campaign funds and services, have helped promote party cohesion on legislation.[31] Leaders can also use their personal relationships with party colleagues to cajole them through careful listening or more hard-edged persuasion. On a House vote on school vouchers, for example, a reporter described House Republican leaders surrounding a Kentucky Republican who had opposed the leadership on this bill the week before. A senior Democrat, "Representative David R. Obey (D-WI) took to the microphone. 'Is anyone from the office of the attending physician present?' he deadpanned. 'I understand someone's arm is being broken.'" The Republican did decide to vote for the bill.[32]

Agenda Control

According to **cartel theory**,[33] another vital source of party leaders' power is their ability to control the legislative agenda. When party leaders can control which bills will come up for a vote, they can stop legislation that could divide their party's members, and they can forward bills that help the party keep its majority. In recent decades, both parties, when they held a House majority, have adopted rules that concentrate these powers of agenda control in the party leadership. Bills are normally debated under restrictive rules, set by a leadership-controlled Rules Committee, which often prevent involvement by the minority party's members. At times, legislation has been combined into "omnibus" bills so broad in scope that individual members have to rely on the party leadership to understand their content. Conference committees, which previously included representatives of both parties to iron out differences between the House and Senate versions of a bill, are now held more rarely and often exclude the minority party. Party leaders negotiate the content of legislation at points in the process that they would not have controlled several decades ago.[34]

Party Influence on Legislative Voting

When is party influence most effective? In voting on a bill, a member of Congress could be swayed by any of several forces: not only by party but also his or her beliefs about the issue at hand or pressures from the president, campaign contributors, or constituents. Yet researchers have found that the parties in Congress play an important role in members' voting, whether due to party leaders' persuasion, the majority party's agenda control, or because of the ability of a member's partisanship to structure issues and create loyalties within his or her own mind.

How Unified Is Each Legislative Party?

Several measures can be used to determine how often members vote with their party. The first, the **frequency of party** *votes*, is the proportion of roll calls on which most Democrats vote one way on a bill and most Republicans vote the other way. The second, **party unity scores** (or **party support**), is the degree to which legislators vote with their party's majority on these party votes.

Party Votes Have Become More Frequent A very demanding test of party voting would be the percentage of all legislative roll calls in which at least 90 percent of one party's members vote yes and 90 percent or more of the other party vote no. By such a strict test, party discipline appears regularly in the British House of Commons and the German Bundestag, but not as often in American legislatures. Under Czar Cannon, about a third of all roll calls in the House met this standard of party discipline. From 1921 through 1948, that dropped to only 17 percent,[35] and it declined steadily to below 10 percent in the 1950s and 1960s. During approximately the same period in the British House of Commons, this striking party division occurred on almost every roll call.

Since the late 1990s, however, there has been a notable increase in "90 percent votes" in Congress, and even in the percentage of votes on which the members of one party unanimously oppose the other party.[36] Since 2009, for example, both houses have divided almost perfectly by party on an increasing number of major issues, including federal funding of Planned Parenthood (see Figure 13.1, Case 1) and President Obama's economic stimulus program and federal budget.

The 90 percent standard is too strict, however, for a look at the American legislative experience over time. So researchers have focused on a less demanding measure: the **frequency of party votes**, or the percentage of roll

Case 1: Should the federal government cut off all funding for Planned Parenthood?

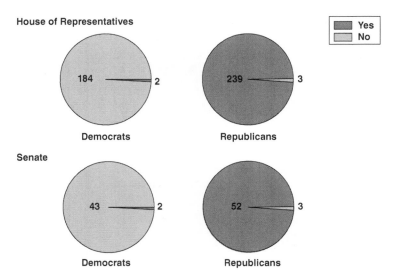

House of Representatives

| | Yes |
| | No |

184 — 2

Democrats

239 — 3

Republicans

Senate

43 — 2

Democrats

52 — 3

Republicans

Case 2: Should the federal debt limit be extended in order to pass a federal budget?

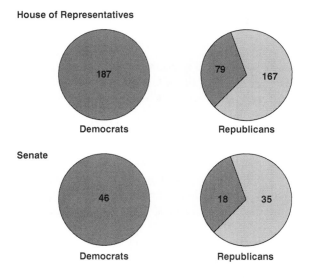

House of Representatives

187

Democrats

79 | 167

Republicans

Senate

46

Democrats

18 | 35

Republicans

FIGURE 13.1 Congressional Party Unity and Disunity, 2015–2016

Note: The figure shows the numbers of Democrats and Republicans in the Senate and House casting "yes" and "no" votes on the bills named. Senators Bernard Sanders (I-VT) and Angus King (I-ME) are counted as Democrats because they caucus with the Democrats.

Source: *CQ Weekly*, September 18, 2015 and August 3, 2015 (on defunding Planned Parenthood), and November 2, 2015 (on extending the debt limit).

calls in which the *majority* of one party opposed a majority of the other. By this measure as well, congressional party voting has greatly increased.

Let's start where senators think we should—with the Senate. During the late 1960s and early 1970s, a majority of Democrats opposed a majority of Republicans in less than 40 percent of all Senate roll call votes. The figure rose to between 50 and 65 percent during the 1990s and 2000s, under both Democratic and Republican control. Then, Obama's first term threw party voting into overdrive: after a high of 79 percent in 2010, 69 percent of the Senate votes in 2015 were party votes.

Party voting has been even more frequent in the House. In the late 1800s, party votes were common (although still far less than in the British Parliament). This was a time when the parties were competitive in most congressional districts, party leaders wielded considerable legislative authority, and Congress was a much less professionalized institution. After 1900, following the development of a more professionalized Congress,[37] the frequency of party votes decreased markedly. The start of the New Deal party system in the 1930s heightened party voting for a time, before it fell again to twentieth-century lows (of 27 percent) in 1970 and 1972.

But since the current party polarization began in the mid-1980s, party votes in the House have reached levels not seen since the New Deal. Three-quarters of House votes were party votes in 2015, just one percentage point below the recent record of 76 percent in 2011 (see Figure 13.2). Overall, since the mid-1980s, "the only line of voting cleavage of any significance in this period was partisan,"[38] and the legislative agenda has been set largely by the White House and the House party leadership.

And So Has Legislators' Party Support To what extent do legislators support their party on party votes? Beginning in the late 1930s and especially in the late 1960s and early 1970s, conservative southern Democrats often voted with Republicans in Congress to oppose civil rights bills and Democratic labor and education proposals. Their defections were tolerated by the decentralized party leadership of that time. This cross-party alliance was called the **conservative coalition**.

The reshaping of the Democratic Party's supporting coalition in the South seriously undercut the conservative coalition in the 1970s and 1980s. As noted earlier, when the Voting Rights Act brought southern blacks into the electorate, this more diverse southern Democratic constituency began to elect different types of representatives. Some conservative southern House members were defeated by moderate and liberal Democrats who could better appeal to black voters. Other conservative Democrats retired or switched parties. Most of the rest were unseated by the growing number of southern Republican House candidates. Thus, the Democratic Party in Congress lost most of its conservative wing.

The Republicans newly elected from the South beginning in the 1970s were more conservative than most of their continuing Republican colleagues.

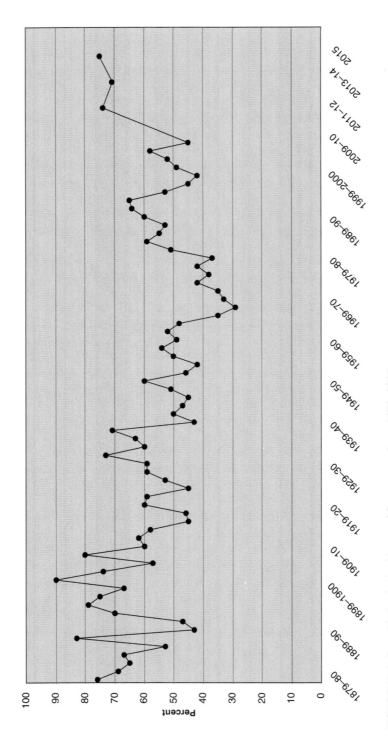

FIGURE 13.2 Party Voting in the House of Representatives, 1879–2015

Note: Entries are the percentage of roll-call votes on which a majority of one party opposed a majority of the other party. Because party voting tends to decrease in the even-numbered years, as an election approaches, the data are averaged across the two sessions of each Congress.

Source: Calculated for 1879–1974 from Jerome B. Chubb and Santa A. Traugott, "Partisan Cleavage and Cohesion in the House of Representatives, 1861–1974," *Journal of Interdisciplinary History 7* (1977): 382–383; more recent data from *CQ Weekly* in December or January issues.

Since that time, non-southern Republicans have become more conservative as well.[39] As a result, congressional Republicans—whether northern or southern—now tend to represent different types of districts than congressional Democrats do, face different pressures from party activists and organized interests, are recruited from different professions, and hold different views on big issues. As the conditional party government theory suggests, this produced a marked increase in party support, especially after Republicans won control of Congress in 1995 (see Figure 13.3). Party organizational reforms, discussed earlier in the chapter, also made it easier for congressional party leaders to unite their party.[40]

The increase in party support has not been uniform. When Democrats regained control of the House in 2007, Speaker Pelosi placed fewer demands for discipline on newly elected, moderate Democrats. The Democratic leadership needed these freshmen to be reelected in their suburban and exurban districts in order to keep its House majority, and getting reelected would require them to vote a more moderate line than the party leadership would otherwise push.[41] Many of these freshmen joined the "Blue Dog Coalition," a group of about 50 House Democrats from rural and small-town districts, typically in the South and West, who took moderate positions on issues including taxes and business concerns. As polarization spread, however, almost half of the Blue Dogs were defeated in the 2010 midterms, and only 15 were left after the 2014 elections. To protect the remaining seats, both the Senate and House Democratic leadership encouraged vulnerable Democrats to vote against Democratic bills, criticize Obama—in short, do whatever it took to get reelected in a difficult political climate.

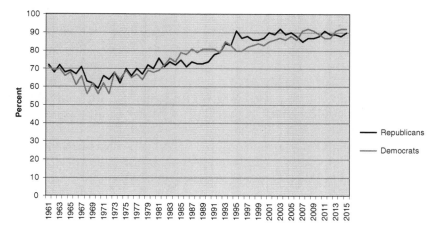

FIGURE 13.3 Average Party Unity Scores, 1961–2015

Note: Entries are the average percentages of members voting in agreement with a majority of their party on party votes—those in which a majority of one party voted against a majority of the other party. Figures for the House and Senate are averaged.

Source: Calculated from *CQ Weekly* Vote Studies, in December or January issues.

Similarly, a declining number of Republican moderates in the House (the "Tuesday Group") and a few in the Senate continue to differ from their party on social issues and sometimes on economic issues, because their constituencies differ from those of most of their GOP colleagues. And recall that the most conservative House Republicans broke with their party leadership on budget issues beginning in 2012, including voting against raising the federal debt limit in 2015 (see Figure 13.1, Case 2), reflecting the hostility toward government spending expressed by Republican activists in their districts. As long as the American parties cannot protect legislators from constituency pressures, and as long as what it means to be a Republican in New York differs from what it means to be a Republican in Mississippi, party cohesion will suffer.

These are the exceptions, however. Party support has been higher in recent years than it has been since the 1950s. In 2015, on party votes, members of the two House parties voted with their party's position 92 percent of the time. The comparable figures for the Senate were 89 percent for Republicans and 91 percent for Democrats.[42] When the Americans for Democratic Action (ADA), a liberal group, examined how often legislators voted with the ADA's position on 20 key votes, the average score for Democratic House members in 2015 was 85 percent and that for Republicans was 2 percent; 171 House Republicans earned ADA scores of zero. In the Senate, the comparable scores were 89 and 5 percent.[43]

Greater Polarization of the Congressional Parties

In short, roll-call voting shows that both the House and the Senate are more polarized by party now than they have been at any time since the late 1870s (see Figure 13.4). The center has shrunk; if all members of each chamber are arrayed along a scale from liberal to conservative, there is almost no overlap between Republicans and Democrats. In particular, since 2000 each incoming class of Republican representatives has been more conservative than those who have left.[44] In fact, in elections from 2010 through 2014, even those Republicans who won formerly Democratic districts tended to be more conservative than the continuing Republican legislators. Democrats did not follow this pattern; newly elected Democratic Congress members during this time were no more liberal than continuing Democrats.[45] This has been true of many state legislatures as well, though there is wide variation among the states.[46]

A major cause of this polarization has been the marked changes in the parties' supporting coalitions of voters. The concentration of black Americans in urban areas (Chapter 7) and the creation of majority-minority districts (Chapter 8) make these districts more consistently Democratic, while others become more consistently Republican. Partisan redistricting

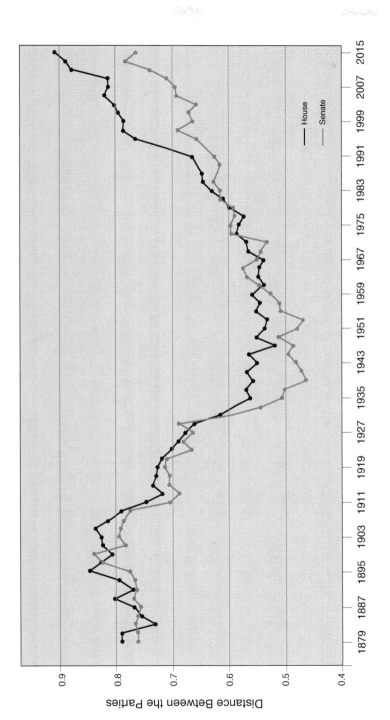

FIGURE 13.4 Party Polarization in Congress, 1879–2015

Note: Entries are the Common Space DW-NOMINATE scores comparing the polarization of the two parties in each house for each Congress. These scores rely on the scaling of roll-call votes on a liberal-conservative dimension. Higher values (closer to 1.0) mean greater ideological difference between the parties.

Source: Keith T. Poole, "New Estimates of Polarization in the 114th Congress," April 15, 2015, at https://voteviewblog.com/2015/04/15/new-estimates-of-polarization-in-the-114th-congress/ (accessed June 27, 2016). See also Clio Andris, David Lee, Marcus J. Hamilton, Mauro Martino, Christian E. Gunning, and John Armistead Selden, "The Rise of Partisanship and Super Cooperators in the U.S. House of Representatives," Plos One 10 (2015).

can encourage candidates to move to the extreme of their party's distribution, at least in the U.S. House. If a House district has been drawn to favor the incumbent's party, then (as noted in Chapter 2) the most likely source of a successful challenge is an ambitious candidate in the incumbent's party, running against him or her in a primary election. In primaries, Republican incumbents are most likely to be challenged from the right; for Democratic incumbents, from the left. This encourages House members to move toward the extreme of their party rather than toward the center. One study finds that a credible primary challenge moves a typical candidate for Congress fully 10 points along a 100-point conservative-to-liberal scale.[47]

Note that roll-call voting is only one indicator of Congress members' behavior, and the roll calls that get the greatest attention are generally those where party conflict is greatest.[48] In addition, these sharp party differences on roll call votes are not all bad. They give voters a clear choice when electing congressional candidates. But they can also produce unsettling policy changes; because the two parties are so closely balanced in strength, a relatively small shift in the political climate can lead to a change in party control of Congress. In 2009–2010, the Democrats had a large enough congressional majority to pass several landmark pieces of liberal legislation, ranging from health-care reform and overhaul of banking regulation to a repeal of the "don't ask, don't tell" rule keeping gay and lesbian personnel from serving openly in the military. After the 2010 elections, when Democrats lost control of the House to the Republicans, the agenda was transformed. Under Republican rule, and especially when 2017 brought unified Republican control, the House focused on repealing the Democratic health care and financial services reforms and on cutting taxes and spending.

What Issues Promote Party Voting?

Students of Congress and state legislatures find that three types of issues tend to prompt more frequent party votes and greater party support: those touching the interests of the legislative party as a group, those involving support of or opposition to an executive program, and those that clearly divide the party's voters.

Issues That Touch the Interests of the Legislative Parties These produce the greatest party unity. Among the best examples are the basic votes to organize the legislative chamber. In Congress, for instance, it is normally safe to predict 100 percent party unity on the vote to elect the Speaker of the House. In 2015, when Republican John Boehner lost the votes of two dozen Republican members for reelection as Speaker, it was front-page news.

The parties also tend to be highly unified on issues affecting their numerical strength and on the procedures by which the legislature is run. Votes on procedure show greater polarization than those on the final passage of laws.[49] Party discipline runs high in state legislatures on laws regulating parties and elections and the redrawing of legislative district lines, which touch the basic interests of the party as a political organization.

The Executive's Proposals Legislators often rally around their party's executive or unite against the executive of the other party. This partisanship has been mounting. In the late 1960s, on average, members of a president's party in Congress voted about 60 percent of the time for issues that he clearly designated a part of his program. In 2015, Senate Democrats supported President Obama's position 96 percent of the time, and in 2009, House Democrats' support peaked at 90 percent.

At the same time, the opposition party's support for a president's program has dropped steadily.[50] Since the 1980s, the opposition has supported the president's proposals only about one-third of the time, on average, and in 2015 House Republicans opposed Obama's proposals 89 percent of the time. The Clinton presidency is an excellent example of this party polarization. In 1998, when Clinton was impeached by the House for lying about his sexual relationship with a White House intern, the House vote to impeach and the Senate vote to acquit Clinton were close to being party-line votes. Gary Jacobson wrote, "On what everyone claimed was a conscience vote, 98 percent of Republican consciences dictated a vote to impeach the president, while 98 percent of Democratic consciences dictated the opposite."[51]

When the president's party in Congress marches in lockstep with the president's proposals, then it is important to ask whether Congress plays an independent role in the business of governing. The other party's united opposition can be a potential check on the executive, of course. But especially in the House, where even a slim majority can exercise a great deal of control, a highly partisan leadership has at times ceded congressional power to the executive branch.

Policies Central to the Party System Legislative parties are also more unified on issues that fundamentally divide the parties in the electorate—the "label-defining" issues.[52] At the time of the Civil War, the questions of slavery and Reconstruction generated the greatest cohesion within each party and the clearest divisions between the two parties. These issues were displaced by conflicts between farm and industrial interests in the 1890s. Now the parties are most internally cohesive on the role of government in the economy, including taxes and the regulation of business, and on issues such as abortion and homosexuality. In many state legislatures, for instance, an attempt to limit or expand the rights of unions will pit one unified party against another, as will environmental issues and the rights of women, gays, and minority groups. In Congress, a similar set of issues—social welfare, environmental, and tax policy—has produced the most cohesive partisan voting.

What Conditions Produce Strong Legislative Parties?

In sum, what are the conditions most likely to produce strong legislative parties?

Party Polarization and Cohesion When a party's legislators represent similar constituencies (for instance, when Republicans throughout the state or nation all get significant support from Christian conservatives and very little support from blacks), they are more likely to hold similar views, and party cohesion increases. Combined with greater distance between the two parties in the nature of their constituencies and their views on issues, this encourages legislators to accept strong party leadership in order to translate these views into policy. Legislative party strength has long flourished in California and other states where the two parties have quite different bases of support—where Democratic strength is concentrated among union members and blacks in the big cities and Republican state legislators tend to represent suburban and rural districts that are largely white and conservative.[53] This is especially true of the U.S. House, whose rules, as we have seen, permit greater control by the leadership.[54]

Greater Interparty Competition There is an interesting relationship between the competitiveness of the two parties and the degree of legislative party voting. At the level of the individual legislator, those from marginal districts, where the two parties have relatively equal shares of the electorate, are generally less likely to vote with their legislative party, and more likely to be responsive to their constituents' preferences, than are those from safer districts.[55] Two characteristics of marginal districts encourage a legislator to be highly sensitive to the constituency. First, both parties in marginal districts often have strong organizations and appealing candidates, so the opposition is a credible threat. Second, in many marginal districts, the groups that support Democrats or Republicans differ from those more typically associated with the party. When party voters in a district hold different views from the national or state party on a big issue, a representative will usually need to bend to constituency wishes in order to get reelected, even if that means opposing his or her legislative party's position.

As we've seen, party leaders may not insist on the member's party loyalty in such situations; they would rather have a legislator who will at least vote for the party's candidate for Speaker than a totally loyal legislator who is defeated for reelection because his or her constituents do not want what the national party is selling. Where constituency and party point in different directions, most legislators remember that their constituents, not their party leadership, gave them their job.

At the level of the legislature as a whole, however, close party competition can increase party voting. When the two parties in a legislature are relatively evenly balanced numerically, "the majority party must stick together to get legislation passed, and the minority party has some realistic chance of winning if it can remain cohesive."[56] Close party competition gives both parties an incentive to remain unified. In contrast, a comfortable majority can foster internal squabbles. That was true of many legislative parties in the South during the period of one-party Democratic rule. It is true today in state legislatures in which one party has a lopsided majority.

No Competing Centers of Power A legislature's standing committees can be sources of power rivaling the party leaders. This was true of Congress when seniority determined who would become a committee chair. When committee chairs are chosen on the basis of criteria other than party loyalty, then chairs owe less to their party leadership. Seniority is not used as often now in either Congress or state legislatures as a basis for appointing members to powerful positions. Moreover, other centers of power in some states— powerful business groups, labor unions, ideological groups, or other big contributors—are often closely allied with one party's leaders.

Other Needed Resources Where the party organization has more to offer a legislator, he or she will be more inclined to follow the party's lead in legislative voting. In Congress and many state legislatures, party leaders can use their power over the legislative agenda to help a member get a desired bill passed. Pork barrel projects in the member's home district can be moved up or down on the agenda by legislative party leaders to help to maintain the loyalty of their party colleagues.

Party organizations outside the legislature can also influence legislative voting if they control important resources. State parties' legislative campaign committees help fund legislative candidates in most states, and legislative party leaders' personal political action committees help in some.[57] Given the shortage of campaign funds at this level, many candidates look beyond the legislative campaign committees to the state parties themselves for campaign money and services. Many states place no ceilings on party contributions to campaigns, so parties can make substantial investments, if they can afford it. Another important resource is the party's influence on nominations. The leaders of many state parties have become more active in recruiting legislative candidates, and some may be able to convince local activists to oppose the renomination of candidates disloyal to the party (although that ability can always be undermined by primary elections).

Lesser Legislative Professionalism Congress has evolved into a highly professional legislative body. Each member controls a sizable personal staff and budget, which can help meet the member's legislative and reelection needs. Serving in Congress is a full-time job with good pay and benefits. Although state legislatures have become more professional as well, very few provide ordinary members with levels of support that even approach those in the Congress. Staff and budgets are usually minimal. Most state legislators are lucky to have as much as a private office and a personal secretary. Many state legislatures meet for only part of the year and pay so little that most members must hold other jobs. With such limited personal resources, legislators in most states welcome party leaders' help in performing their legislative tasks. When a state legislator depends on the party leadership for needed resources, he or she is more likely to listen when a leader calls for party discipline.

Styles of Individual Leaders Legislative party leaders in the states, like those in the U.S. House and Senate, vary in their willingness to use the tools of strong leadership. Their leadership styles interact with the situation of their party—whether it is a powerful majority, a competitive party, or a weakened minority—to determine how effectively they function in uniting their party members and getting their bills passed.

The Power of Legislative Parties

This chapter tells a complex story. On the one hand, parties are at the very center of the legislative process. Some even view them as "legislative leviathans" that dominate Congress in order to benefit their individual members.[58] Party affiliation explains the legislative behavior of state legislators and Congress members more fully than does any other single factor. Party voting and polarization have increased in recent years in both the houses of Congress.

Yet even now, most American legislative parties are not as unified as those of most other democracies. The fragmenting institutions of American government have left their mark. Separation of powers deprives the party of an institutional need to remain internally cohesive.[59] But under some conditions, such as when the party's legislative constituencies are more alike in their preferences and more different from the other party's, legislative parties will be more unified and party voting will be common. As increasing party polarization has brought the views of legislative leaders and party voters into closer alignment, members of Congress are less likely to face a difficult choice between party and constituency (see box "Which Would You Choose? Should Your Representative Listen More Closely to the Party or to the Constituents?" on page 329). This polarization, however, has greatly increased the likelihood that the congressional parties will gridlock, unable to move legislation or agree on priorities. The beneficiary of this loss of congressional power has been the executive.

▀▀▀▀▀▀ WHICH WOULD YOU CHOOSE? ▀▀▀▀▀▀

Should Your Representative Listen More Closely to the Party or to the Constituents?

To the constituents: This sounds like a no-brainer. If we elect members of Congress, they ought to represent the interests of their constituents, right? We have a single-member district system with candidate-centered campaigns; that encourages us to focus on the qualities of individual candidates rather than on the party's platform. We vote for a candidate, and he or she goes to Washington and is then supposed to do whatever we ask. Why should the legislator listen to the party leadership?

To their party: This constituent-centered approach sounds good, but it isn't realistic. How are members of Congress supposed to know what all of their 740,000 constituents want? Isn't it better for the two major parties to offer competing answers on issues, press their legislative party members to pass these policies, and then let voters decide whether they like the results? That asks less of us as voters and probably corresponds more closely to the (minimal) time we are willing to spend on politics. Besides, by taking a longer view, the parties can look beyond local concerns to a broader national interest.

To both: As we have seen, when the various constituencies that a party's legislators represent become more similar in views and more different from those of the other party, then most legislators don't have to choose between constituents and party. At these times, members can vote with their party colleagues and also speak for the interests and voters who, in their view, sent them to the legislature. So party and constituency are not necessarily in conflict.

Notes ▀▀▀▀▀▀▀▀▀▀▀▀

1 Rep. Charlie Dent, quoted in Ashley Parker, "G.O.P. Is Divided as It Faces a Host of Budget Bills," *New York Times*, March 9, 2015, p. A1.
2 See Frances E. Lee, "Parties as Coordinators: Can Parties Unite What the Constitution Divides?" in Marjorie Randon Hershey, ed., *Guide to U.S. Political Parties* (Los Angeles: Sage, 2014), Chapter 3.
3 Keith Krehbiel, "Where's the Party?" *British Journal of Political Science* 23 (1993): 225–266.
4 Gary W. Cox and Keith T. Poole, "On Measuring Partisanship in Roll-Call Voting," *American Journal of Political Science* 46 (2002): 477–489; and Gerald C. Wright and Brian F. Schaffner, "The Influence of Party," *American Political Science Review* 96 (2002): 367–379.
5 Steven S. Smith, *Party Influence in Congress* (Cambridge: Cambridge University Press, 2007).

6 D. Roderick Kiewiet and Mathew D. McCubbins, *The Logic of Delegation* (Chicago: University of Chicago Press, 1991).

7 Even Cannon faced limits, however; see Eric D. Lawrence, Forrest Maltzman, and Paul J. Wahlbeck, "The Politics of Speaker Cannon's Committee Assignments," *American Journal of Political Science* 45 (2001): 551–562. On the history of legislative party leadership, see Bruce I. Oppenheimer, "Ebbs and Flows in the Power of Congressional Party Leaders Since 1910," in Hershey, ed., *Guide to U.S. Political Parties*, pp. 308–323.

8 Steven S. Smith and Gerald Gamm, "The Dynamics of Party Government in Congress," in Lawrence C. Dodd and Bruce I. Oppenheimer, eds., *Congress Reconsidered*, 9th ed. (Washington, DC: CQ Press, 2009), p. 149.

9 Gary W. Cox and Mathew W. McCubbins, *Legislative Leviathan*, 2nd ed. (Berkeley, CA: University of California Press, 1993), pp. 279–282.

10 On the Speaker's powers, see Jeffery A. Jenkins and Charles Stewart III, *Fighting for the Speakership* (Princeton, NJ: Princeton University Press, 2012).

11 Barbara Sinclair, *Unorthodox Lawmaking*, 2nd ed. (Washington, DC: CQ Press, 2000), pp. 103–106.

12 Bruce I. Oppenheimer, "Ebbs and Flows," in Hershey, ed., *Guide to U.S. Political Parties* (Los Angeles: Sage, 2014), Chapter 24.

13 David Rohde and John Aldrich, "Consequences of Electoral and Institutional Change," in Jeffrey M. Stonecash, ed., *New Directions in American Political Parties* (New York: Routledge, 2010), pp. 234–250.

14 Mike Allen, "GOP Leaders Tighten Their Grip on House," *Washington Post*, January 9. 2005, p. A5.

15 Marian Currinder, *Money in the House* (Boulder, CO: Westview, 2009), Chapter 2 and p. 203.

16 David W. Rohde, *Parties and Leaders in the Postreform House* (Chicago: University of Chicago Press, 1991). See also Barbara Sinclair, *Legislators, Leaders, and Lawmaking* (Baltimore, MD: Johns Hopkins University Press, 1995).

17 See, for example, William T. Bianco and Itai Sened, "Uncovering Evidence of Conditional Party Government," *American Political Science Review* 99 (2005): 361–371.

18 See John H. Aldrich, *Why Parties? A Second Look* (Chicago: University of Chicago Press, 2011), Chapter 7.

19 Rohde and Aldrich, "Consequences of Electoral and Institutional Change."

20 Daniel J. Galvin, "The Transformation of Political Institutions," *Studies in American Political Development* 26 (2012): 1–21.

21 Analyst E. J. Dionne goes further, arguing that the Democrats in the U.S. Senate are so ideologically diverse that "the cliché about herding cats does a disservice to how relatively organized felines are." Dionne, "Harry Reid vs. the Smooth Deal," *Washington Post*, March 29, 2015, p. A28.

22 Barbara Sinclair, "The New World of U.S. Senators," in Dodd and Oppenheimer, eds., *Congress Reconsidered*, pp. 1–22.

23 Sean M. Theriault and David W. Rohde, "The Gingrich Senators and Party Polarization in the U.S. Senate," *Journal of Politics* 73 (2011): 1011–1024.

24 Smith and Gamm, "The Dynamics of Party Government in Congress," pp. 141–164.

25 See Nathan W. Monroe, Jason M. Roberts, and David W. Rohde, eds., *Why Not Parties?* (Chicago: University of Chicago Press, 2008) and Peter Hanson, *Too Weak to Govern* (New York: Cambridge University Press, 2014).

26 Sen. Michael Bennet (D-CO), quoted in Steven Pearlstein, "The Can-Do Senator in a Can't-Do Congress," *Washington Post Magazine*, June 19, 2016, p. 1.

27 The main exception is Nebraska, which is officially nonpartisan.

28 Malcolm E. Jewell and Sarah M. Morehouse, *Political Parties and Elections in American States*, 4th ed. (Washington, DC: CQ Press, 2001), pp. 236–238.

29 Keith E. Hamm and Robert Harmel, "Legislative Party Development and the Speaker System," *Journal of Politics* 55 (1993): 1140–1151.

30 See Robert Harmel, Matthew Giebert, and Kenneth Janda, *American Parties in Context* (New York: Routledge, 2016), Chapter 5.

31 Paul S. Herrnson, *Congressional Elections*, 7th ed. (Los Angeles: Sage/CQ Press, 2016).

32 Juliet Eilperin, "House GOP Practices Art of One-Vote Victories," *Washington Post*, October 14, 2003, p. A1.

33 See Gary W. Cox and Mathew D. McCubbins, *Setting the Agenda* (Cambridge: Cambridge University Press, 2005) and Jeffery A. Jenkins and Charles Stewart III, *Fighting for the Speakership* (Princeton, NJ: Princeton University Press, 2013).

34 Barbara Sinclair, "Orchestrators of Unorthodox Lawmaking," *The Forum* 6 (2008), issue 3, article 4.

35 Julius Turner, *Party and Constituency*, rev. ed., Edward V. Schneier, ed. (Baltimore, MD: Johns Hopkins University Press, 1970), pp. 16–17.

36 "Party Unity Background," *CQ Weekly*, January 21, 2013, p. 137. See Jason M. Roberts and Steven S. Smith, "Procedural Contexts, Party Strategy, and Conditional Party Voting in the U.S. House of Representatives, 1971–2000," *American Journal of Political Science* 47 (2003): 305–317.

37 Nelson W. Polsby, "The Institutionalization of the United States House of Representatives," *American Political Science Review* 62 (1968): 144–168.

38 Aldrich, *Why Parties?*, p. 243.

39 Roberts and Smith, "Procedural Contexts."

40 Rohde, *Parties and Leaders in the Postreform House*, Chapter 3. See also M. V. Hood III, Quentin Kidd, and Irwin L. Morris, "Of Byrd[s] and Bumpers," *American Journal of Political Science* 43 (1999): 465–487.

41 On Pelosi's Speakership, see Kathryn Pearson and Eric Schickler, "The Transition to Democratic Leadership in a Polarized House," in Dodd and Oppenheimer, *Congress Reconsidered*, pp. 165–188.

42 "Party Unity Background," *CQ Weekly*, February 8, 2016, p. 32.

43 "2015 Congressional Voting Record," www.adaction.org/media/voting records/2015.pdf (accessed November 13, 2016).

44 Gary C. Jacobson, "Explaining the Ideological Polarization of the Congressional Parties Since the 1970s," in David W. Brady and Mathew D. McCubbins, eds., *Party, Process, and Political Change in Congress*, vol. 2 (Stanford: Stanford University Press, 2007), pp. 91–101.

45 Edward G. Carmines, "Congressional Elections and Asymmetrical Polarization: 2001–2010," *Perspectives on Politics* 9 (2011): 645–647, and John H. Aldrich, "Did Hamilton, Jefferson, and Madison 'Cause' the U.S. Government Shutdown?" *Perspectives on Politics* 13 (2015): 7–21.

46 Boris Shor, "Party Polarization in America's State Legislatures," in John C. Green, Daniel J. Coffey, and David B. Cohen, *The State of the Parties*, 7th ed. (Lanham, MD: Rowman & Littlefield, 2014), p. 127.

47 Barry Burden, "Candidate Positioning in U.S. Congressional Elections," *British Journal of Political Science* 34 (2004): 211–227.

48 See Frank R. Baumgartner, Jeffrey M. Berry, Marie Hojnacki, David C. Kimball, and Beth L. Leech, *Lobbying and Policy Change* (Chicago: University of Chicago Press, 2009), Chapter 5.

49 Stephen A. Jessee and Sean M. Theriault, "The Two Faces of Congressional Roll-Call Voting," *Party Politics* 20 (2014): 836–848.

50 Cary R. Covington, J. Mark Wrighton, and Rhonda Kinney, "A 'Presidency-Augmented' Model of Presidential Success on House Roll Call Votes," *American Journal of Political Science* 39 (November 1995): 1001–1024.

51 Gary C. Jacobson, *The Politics of Congressional Elections*, 7th ed. (New York: Pearson-Longman, 2009), p. 255.

52 C. Lawrence Evans and Claire E. Grandy, "The Whip Systems of Congress," in Dodd and Oppenheimer, 9th ed., p. 210.

53 Boris Shor and Nolan McCarty, "The Ideological Mapping of American Legislatures," *American Political Science Review* 105 (2011): 530–551.

54 Molly C. Jackman shows the influence of legislative rules on party influence in state legislatures: see "Parties, Median Legislators, and Agenda-Setting," *Journal of Politics* 76 (2014): 259–272.

55 See John D. Griffin, "Electoral Competition and Democratic Responsiveness," *Journal of Politics* 68 (2006): 911–921.

56 Jewell and Morehouse, *Political Parties and Elections*, p. 244.

57 Anthony Gierzynski, *Legislative Party Campaign Committees in the American States* (Lexington, KY: University of Kentucky Press, 1992); and Daniel M. Shea, *Transforming Democracy* (Albany, NY: SUNY Press, 1995).

58 Cox and McCubbins, *Legislative Leviathan*.

59 See Gary Cox, *The Efficient Secret* (New York: Cambridge University Press, 1987).

CHAPTER 14

The Party in the Executive and the Courts

If you believe that the courts are—or should be—free of partisanship, then consider the firestorm that arose after conservative Supreme Court Justice Antonin Scalia died in 2016. Republican Senate leaders immediately insisted that Democratic President Barack Obama should not appoint Scalia's successor; rather, the Court should take the risk of tie (4–4) votes on cases for a year until the next president (who might be a Republican) was elected. As you'll see in this chapter, Democratic senators strongly objected, citing Obama's constitutional duty to nominate a justice who would become the tie-breaking vote. If there is no partisanship in the courts, why would anyone care whether a Democratic president has the right to nominate the replacement for a conservative Supreme Court justice?

Most Americans think of courts as being nonpartisan, just as we hope for nonpartisan behavior from police officers and the people who inspect restaurant kitchens. Yet, as we see in this chapter, American judges and executives (not just presidents and governors but also the people who head and work in government agencies) are party identifiers. Many presidents and governors behave like party leaders, and although the writers of the Constitution designed an independent federal court system with lifetime appointments, hoping to protect courts from partisan controversy, it has never been possible to design judges who are free of party identification. As a result, the nominations of U.S. Supreme Court justices and most other federal judges now provoke heated partisan conflict.

In many ways, partisanship has penetrated more deeply into the executive and judicial branches in the United States than in other Western democracies. As discussed in Chapter 2, the push for popular democracy in the U.S. led to the election of public officials who would be appointed to their jobs in most other nations, such as state school superintendents and local judges. When administrators and judges are elected, partisanship can influence their elections. Even when these officials are appointed, party affiliation is often a criterion for their appointment.

If partisanship affects their selection, wouldn't it also influence the ways in which administrators and judges do their jobs? If so, does this reflect

333

party organizations' efforts to influence the behavior of executives and judges? Or is it simply that most people feel closer to one party than the other, and people who consider themselves Republicans tend to share similar attitudes toward political issues, whether they are voters, police officers, or judges, and the same is true of those who identify as Democrats?

Presidents and Governors as Party Leaders

Barack Obama began his presidency with an effort to be "post-partisan." It didn't last. When congressional Republicans refused to respond to his initiatives, he began to use more intensely partisan rhetoric to move policy by affecting public opinion.[1] Most recent presidents have also found that partisan activity is essential to their success.

Several Republican presidents, in particular,[2] have become extensively involved in party activities by helping to recruit and campaign with party candidates and raise money for the party. These efforts have strengthened the bond between presidents and the party colleagues in Congress for whom they campaign. Especially in the current polarized atmosphere in Washington, and in many state capitals and when the party division in the legislature is close, executives nurture ties with their party's legislators to get the votes needed to pass their policies.

The President as Campaigner-in-Chief

Presidents can't "govern by themselves."[3] They are much more successful in getting their initiatives passed when their co-partisans are in the majority in Congress. To help achieve that, presidents have become vitally important campaign fund-raisers for congressional candidates of their party. Although many Democratic members of Congress complained that Obama didn't hold enough fund-raisers for other party candidates during his first term, Obama became more motivated to raise party funds after he was re-elected in 2012 and faced an intransigent, Republican-controlled House.

Presidents can do a great deal more for their party organizations as well. The state or national party organization often finds itself in the difficult position of trying to convince an attractive but reluctant prospect to run for a governorship, or urging an eager candidate not to oppose a party favorite in a primary. Presidents can be very persuasive recruiters or "decruiters," especially when their public approval is high.

The President as the "Top of the Ticket"

Even when the president doesn't campaign actively for them, a president's actions and successes can affect the prospects of other party candidates.

Coattail Effects The most direct link between presidential success and party victories has been explained by the metaphor of coattails. Presidents ran "at the top of the ticket," the explanation goes, and the rest of the party ticket came into office clinging to their sturdy coattails. This coattail effect was very common in the 1800s when the parties printed their own ballots, so a voter usually had to cast a ballot for an entire party ticket.

Coattail effects declined from the end of World War II through the 1980s.[4] Members of Congress became very talented at cultivating their constituency by attending closely to its interests and providing services to individual constituents. This helped to insulate them from outside electoral forces, including presidential popularity.[5] Incumbents gained big advantages over their challengers in fund-raising, especially in House races.

However, the relationship between presidential and congressional election results has reemerged since the early 1990s, as the parties have become more polarized.[6] Coattail effects can reach into nonfederal races as well.[7]

Coattails Even Without the Coat Presidents can influence election results even when they are not on the ballot. As congressional races have become more nationalized, voters' approval of the president's job performance affects their support for candidates of the president's party in midterm congressional elections.[8] In the 2014 midterms, for instance, 33 percent of the respondents to an exit poll said their vote for Congress was meant to express opposition to the president, and 92 percent of this group voted Republican. Fewer people (19 percent) said they were voting to express support for Obama, and 93 percent of them voted Democratic.[9]

This helps explain why the president's party has almost always suffered a decline in its share of House seats in the midterm election.[10] Most presidents' public approval ratings have dropped by the midpoint of their terms, and the president's declining popularity can drag down congressional candidates of his or her party or discourage attractive party candidates from running.[11] People who disapprove of the president's performance are more likely to vote in midterm elections than those who approve, and their disapproval can lead them to vote for the other party's candidates.[12]

The 1998 and 2002 elections broke this pattern of midterm losses by the president's party. In both years, presidential popularity was either holding steady or increasing. Although President Bush had begun his first term with fairly low approval ratings, his popularity soared to almost 90 percent after the September 11 terrorist attacks and remained above 60 percent as the 2002 election approached. His 90 percent approval among Republicans, in particular, made a difference in close campaigns.[13] But the traditional pattern returned beginning in 2006. Party identifiers—both Republicans and Democrats—increasingly express strong disapproval of presidents from the other party.

In sum, whether or not they choose to act as party leaders, presidents' popularity and success can affect the likelihood that other candidates of their party will win their races. This happens especially if the candidates' advertising stresses their connection with the president and if the president campaigns actively for them. It gives presidents a potential source of influence over the legislative party colleagues they helped elect.

Party Leadership and Legislative Relations

Presidents and governors can gain legislative support for their programs in several ways. Executives can use their ability to attract media coverage, their public approval (if it is substantial), and the coattails and favors they may have provided to individual legislators. Chief executives also have legislative liaisons: staff people who work with party leaders and other members of Congress or state legislatures to encourage support for the executive's proposals. A president's "legislative shop" can make a big difference in calming an angry committee chair or providing key information to a wavering supporter. It helps that members of the executive's party know that if they make him or her look weak, they might weaken their own reelection chances. This can encourage them to rally around the president or governor on important votes, even if they would prefer to vote differently.

Following Obama's lead, some state governors have used their fund-raising clout to affect the legislature indirectly, by affecting public opinion between campaigns. Illinois Republican governor Bruce Rauner founded a super PAC (see Chapter 12) to run ads supporting his economic agenda after he was elected, and Florida's Republican governor Rick Scott created a 527 group, also able to accept unlimited donations, to criticize his opponents and advocate for his policies after his reelection.

Legislative Support for Executives

Congress members are clearly aware of the close connection between the president's popularity and their own reelection prospects. Popular support is a key resource for the chief executive in getting Congress to go along with his or her programs. That was painfully evident to President Obama, when his steady but low approval ratings undermined his ability to gain congressional consent for his initiatives (see Figure 14.1). Presidents do better when their party controls both houses of Congress; these periods of time—the early years of the Eisenhower, Kennedy and Johnson, Carter, George W. Bush, and Obama administrations—are typically the president's greatest opportunities for success on legislation. President Obama got historic levels of support from House Democrats in 2009 and 2010, when his party held a House majority. After Republicans regained control of the House in 2011, Obama's success rate plummeted, as it did in the Senate once Democrats lost control in 2014.

Even unified party control of Congress does not *guarantee* success. During the two years when President Obama had Democratic majorities in both

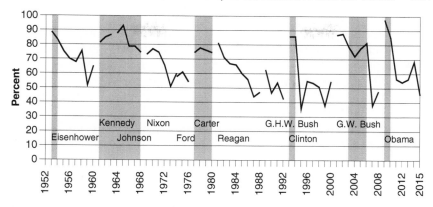

FIGURE 14.1 Presidential Success in the U.S. Congress, 1953–2015

Note: The entry for each year is the percentage of time members of both the House and the Senate voted in support of the announced position of the president. Years that are shaded are those in which the president's party controlled both houses of Congress (unified government).

Source: *CQ Weekly*, January issues.

houses, many of his most important legislative accomplishments were passed with no (or almost no) Republican votes. Republican legislators had good reason to vote "no" on the president's proposals because he was unpopular in their districts; in recent years, a huge "public approval gap" has opened between Democratic and Republican identifiers' support of the president. In Obama's case, an average of 80 percent of Democrats have approved of his job performance compared with 14 percent of Republicans—a gap of 66 percentage points.[14] As a result, the president relied heavily on Democratic legislators to get his programs passed. But those party colleagues who represent "swing" districts, in which both parties are competitive, could endanger their reelections if they vote in lockstep with the president. The bigger the president's legislative majority, the more of his party's legislators are likely to come from swing districts.

In addition, the institutional rivalries designed into a separation of powers system help to ensure that the president's party in Congress will not surrender all its powers to the co-partisan in the White House. As powerful House Democrat David Obey said in 2009, "I'm certainly willing to work with a Democratic president. But I work with him, not for him."[15]

Divided Control of Government Presidents generally get much less support, of course, when at least one house of Congress is in the hands of the opposing party, as the unshaded areas of Figure 14.1 show. Unhappily for modern presidents, divided government has been the rule during the past five decades. Almost all of the states have also experienced divided party control of the legislature and the governorship during this time.

With a divided government, executives have two main choices. They can try to negotiate successfully with at least some legislators of the other party—and in fact, some researchers find that divided government is as likely to produce significant policy change as is unified government.[16] Or they can try to brand the other party as the "party of no," the roadblock in the way of progress, hoping that voters will respond by giving the president's party a majority in the next election.

In times of both divided and unified party control, governors have some advantages over presidents in gaining support from their legislative party. In state legislatures that do not use seniority rules, governors can take an active part in selecting committee chairs and party floor leaders. Most governors have greater control over party rewards and incentives than a president does. On the other hand, governors are not as visible as presidents are, so their coattails and prestige are normally less influential than those of presidents.

Party Influence in Executive Agencies

The White House is the tip of an iceberg. Below the surface, huge and powerful, lies the rest of the executive branch. The administrators or bureaucrats who work in cabinet-level departments such as Education and Agriculture and in other agencies such as the Environmental Protection Agency (EPA) are responsible for carrying out the laws Congress passes. These executive agencies regulate vast areas of the economy—pollution, food safety, and prescription drugs, for example—under congressional mandates that require a lot of interpretation. The bureaucrats who implement these laws, then, shape policy by applying it. It is they who determine whether the milk you drank was inspected for spoilage, or how much mercury your local power plant is permitted to dump into your air.

How might partisanship (or the chief partisan in the White House) affect the people who work in these executive agencies? Do we see evidence of partisan behavior in federal agencies?

How is Presidential or Party Influence Exercised?

Partisanship can affect federal agencies because the heads of the largest agencies—cabinet-level departments such as the Department of Defense and the Department of Veterans Affairs—are appointed by the president and can be removed by the president as well. These agency heads have often had a long history of party activity. Most of President Obama's cabinet members were long-time Democratic loyalists, as was the case with his predecessors. Presidents no longer use these positions as rewards for loyal *party* service; instead, they look for loyalty to the president's *own* aims. Nevertheless, most presidential appointees have been active partisans whose values and political careers have been shaped to a significant degree by their party.

Modern presidents can make only a few thousand of these high-level political appointments, however—fewer appointive positions than some governors have—to try to gain control of an executive branch employing 2.1 million civilians. Many of these political appointees are newcomers with little time to "learn the ropes" and little hope of gaining the necessary support of the career bureaucrats who serve under them.[17] Below this top level, agency officials are less likely to have party experience. These officials are chosen primarily for their administrative skills and only secondarily for their political credentials. And most of the remaining agency employees are selected using civil service exams, not party screening procedures.

Another powerful segment of the executive branch is the large number of federal regulatory agencies such as the Food and Drug Administration (FDA). Many of these were established during the Progressive era of the late 1800s and early 1900s. The Progressives worked hard to limit party influence in these agencies, including the influence of the president. For instance, many regulatory agencies are required to be headed by commissions that include members of both parties.

These agencies, like the cabinet departments, deal with highly complex, technical issues. To decide how much mercury can be allowed in your community's air, for example, EPA staffers must be able to understand complicated scientific findings on the effects of mercury on human health and the impact of cleanup costs on the power plant's bottom line. Party loyalty does not provide this technical competence (though it may well affect an agency head's interpretation of the technical findings).

Another limit on presidential or party influence over the bureaucracy is that just as individual legislators pay attention to their constituents' needs, administrators have demanding constituencies as well. The EPA works closely with the many industries whose pollution it regulates, as well as with a variety of professional and citizen groups.[18] If the EPA's rulings in applying the Clean Air Act outrage electric power companies or big environmental groups, the EPA will be in political trouble. Presidents may try to give their agency heads protective cover at these times, but they can't always protect against the impact of a well-financed constituency group.

Changing Partisan Perspectives in the Federal Bureaucracy

In spite of these limits on party and presidential control, the federal bureaucracy does respond to partisan forces over the long run. As the federal government expanded in the 1930s, President Franklin Roosevelt drew people into the career bureaucracy who were committed to his programs.

They then resisted later efforts to weaken these programs, especially as they got promoted to more senior positions in their agencies.

Decades later, the federal bureaucracy still had a pro-Democratic slant. By 1970, Joel Aberbach and Bert Rockman found that nearly a majority of these career bureaucrats said they normally voted Democratic and only 17 percent usually voted Republican. In federal social service agencies, even the administrators who were not Democrats said that they favored liberal policies. So Republican President Richard Nixon, in office at that time, faced a federal bureaucracy that had little sympathy for his conservative agenda. His administration spent a lot of time trying to control the bureaucracy by appointing Nixon loyalists to top bureaucratic positions.[19]

By 1992, however, the bureaucratic environment had changed. Republicans had held the White House for all but four years between 1972 and 1992. When Aberbach and Rockman returned to interview career administrators in comparable positions to those they interviewed in 1970, they now found slight Republican pluralities. As older civil servants retired, a new generation, less committed to New Deal and Great Society programs, had been recruited into senior executive positions. Changes in civil service laws further allowed positions formerly reserved for career employees to be filled by political appointees who could be carefully screened by the White House. The bureaucracy was no longer as hostile to Republican initiatives.[20] The Reagan, Clinton, and George W. Bush administrations made serious efforts to put their own stamp on the federal bureaucracy, sometimes resulting in complaints of partisan bias in federal agencies' activities.[21]

In short, partisanship does influence executive branch agencies. But most presidents and governors use their party leadership role to promote their own programs and reelection, not their party's programs.[22] To the extent that the executive's goals are similar to those of his or her party, then the party's program benefits. For most American executives, however, the goals and interests of their party organization are secondary to their own policy goals and political careers.

Traces of Party in the Courts

Courts and judges are affected by party politics as well. Most American judges—even most justices of the U.S. Supreme Court—are political men and women who took office after careers that involved them in some aspect of partisan politics (see box "The Partisan Backgrounds of U.S. Supreme Court Justices" on page 341). Party conflict increasingly plays a role in the appointment and election of judges. Because of the nature of the judiciary, however, party influence can be subtle.

The Partisan Backgrounds of U.S. Supreme Court Justices

Justices Appointed by Republican Presidents

John Roberts (chief justice; appointed by G. W. Bush) served as an aide to the attorney general and as White House counsel in the Republican Reagan administration. He was the principal deputy solicitor general in the Republican G. H. W. Bush administration.

Anthony Kennedy (Reagan) was a Republican activist and campaign donor in California. He was a legal adviser to Reagan as governor. On Reagan's recommendation, Republican President Ford appointed Kennedy to the U.S. Court of Appeals, before Reagan appointed him to the Supreme Court.

Clarence Thomas (G. H. W. Bush) served on the staff of Missouri's Republican attorney general and as assistant secretary for Civil Rights and director of the Equal Employment Opportunity Commission in the Republican Reagan administration. Thomas's wife was a senior aide to former House Republican Majority Leader Dick Armey.

Samuel A. Alito, Jr. (G. W. Bush) was assistant to the solicitor general and deputy assistant to the attorney general in the Republican Reagan administration. Republican G.H.W. Bush appointed him to the U.S. Court of Appeals before G.W. Bush nominated him to the Supreme Court.

Justices Appointed by Democratic Presidents

Ruth Bader Ginsburg (Clinton) had no formal party positions or appointments prior to her nomination to the Court.

Stephen G. Breyer (Clinton) was a special assistant to the assistant attorney general under Democratic President Lyndon Johnson and special counsel and then chief counsel to the Democratic-led Senate Judiciary Committee.

Sonia Sotomayor (Obama) served as a New York County assistant district attorney, appointed by a Democratic governor. She was recommended for a federal judgeship by a Democratic senator and nominated by both a Republican (G.H.W. Bush) president and a Democratic (Clinton) president.

Elena Kagan (Obama) was appointed U.S. Solicitor General by Democratic President Obama and as domestic policy adviser by the previous Democratic president, Bill Clinton. She clerked for Democratic justices and judges and interned for two Democratic U.S. House members.

Note: As of the beginning of 2017, the Supreme Court had only eight members. President Trump would appoint the tie-breaking ninth justice.

Judicial Voting Along Party Lines

Judges appointed by Democratic presidents tend to be more liberal on issues such as civil rights and liberties, crime, labor issues, and regulation of business than are those appointed by Republican presidents.[23] An environmental research group reported that federal judges appointed by Democratic presidents were much more likely to rule in favor of environmentalists than Republican-appointed judges were.[24] U.S. District Court judges have tended to uphold redistricting plans enacted by their party more than those enacted by the opposing party.[25] And court rulings on states' voter identification laws (see Chapter 8) closely reflect whether the court's majority was nominated by Democratic or Republican officials.[26] These are the kinds of differences we would expect to find when comparing the views of Democrats and Republicans outside the courtroom.

It is not easy to distinguish the impact of judges' partisanship from other influences, including their career goals, law school training, and desire to protect their professional reputations. Judges show much less party cohesion than legislators do. Yet under some circumstances, it is clear that Democratic judges rule differently from their Republican colleagues.

What Causes Partisan Behavior on the Courts?

Very little of this apparent partisanship is due to active efforts by Democratic and Republican Party leaders to influence court decisions. That wouldn't be acceptable in most communities now. A much better explanation for the impact of party on judges' behavior is simply that judges have some discretion in applying the laws to specific cases, just as bureaucrats do. Judges, like the rest of us, have developed views on political issues and on how flexible the law should be. And among the most fundamental of those views are party identifications.

Just as the two parties reflect different sets of values, so do their identifiers, including those who become judges. Two judges might vote together on the regulation of business because of values they share about the proper role of government. Those values may have led them to identify with the same party years earlier or were developed out of experience in that party. People who want to be judges often join networks of liberal or conservative lawyers, such as the American Constitution Society (liberal) and the Federalist Society (conservative). Increasingly, these partisan values structure a judge's environment. Supreme Court justices, for instance, are now more likely to hire law clerks—lawyers who do much of the work of the Court and help shape its rulings—consistent with their partisanship: conservatives hire Republican clerks and liberals hire Democrats.[27]

When presidents and governors nominate or appoint judges, the nominees' value systems are foremost in their minds. They know that judges have flexibility in deciding some cases and that the choices they make may reflect, at least in part, the judge's own beliefs and experiences. When President Obama nominated Sonia Sotomayor to the Supreme Court, for instance, she argued that her life experience as a Latina could add to the Court's breadth of understanding, and her confirmation hearings focused intently on her background and beliefs. In most debates over judicial nominations, especially for higher courts that receive the most challenging cases, Congress members and interest groups now devote major attention to the values and attitudes of the possible nominees.

Federal Judges If you were president, you would want to nominate federal judges and Supreme Court justices who would uphold, not strike down, your policies. Prospective judges' party and ideology are among the clues you would use to predict how they would rule once in office. Thus, every American president for the past century has made at least 80 percent of his judicial appointments from within his own party. The average is higher than 90 percent.

President Reagan and both Bush administrations took special care to screen candidates for their dedication to conservative principles.[28] As a result, their appointees were even more ideologically distinctive (and more likely to have been active in party politics) than average among recent presidents—more than the Bill Clinton administration, for instance.[29] This has produced intense ideological battles between Bush-appointed conservative judges and liberal judges appointed by Democratic presidents. It has become routine for Democratic-appointed and Republican-appointed appeals court judges to attack one another's decisions in their own rulings using terms such as "unconscionable," "absurd," and "alarming."[30]

Senate action on the president's nominations to federal judgeships has become more partisan as well. Early shots were fired in the 1980s and early 1990s, when Senate Democrats and their allies waged major battles over the confirmation of two conservative nominees to the Supreme Court: Robert Bork and Clarence Thomas. (In fact, the former case gave rise to a new verb. When an intense, partisan campaign has been mustered against a nominee, he or she is said to have been "Borked.") By the end of the Bill Clinton administration, the level of partisan animosity over judicial appointments was so high that Republican Senate leaders were refusing to schedule debate on some of the president's nominees.[31] The atmosphere surrounding judicial appointments has become more and more hostile as ideological groups of various kinds use these nominations to fire up their core supporters in the public. It was Republican senators' repeated filibusters of President Obama's federal court nominees that led the Democratic Senate majority to end filibusters in such cases in 2013, except on Supreme Court nominations. This change did speed up the confirmation of some of the president's nominees to lower courts, though the Republican takeover of the Senate in 2015 put the brakes on many such Obama nominations (see box "The Battle to Replace a Supreme Court Justice" on page 344).[32]

The Battle to Replace a Supreme Court Justice

For several years, many important Supreme Court cases were decided by 5–4 votes. Five of the Court's justices had been appointed by Republican presidents and were considered conservative votes, and four were known to be liberals. Then one of the conservatives, Justice Antonin Scalia, died suddenly. Within hours a bitter partisan fight broke out. Many Republicans claimed that it was undemocratic for Democratic President Barack Obama to nominate Scalia's successor because Obama was in his last year of office. Democrats pointed out that there was no such rule or tradition, and that it was the president's constitutional responsibility to fill any Court vacancy. Republican senators vowed to keep any Obama Court nominee from getting a confirmation hearing. Democrats reminded them that without a ninth member, the Court was likely to deadlock 4–4, which would affirm lower court rulings, many of them from appeals courts regarded as liberal.

Obama named Merrick Garland, the chief judge of the United States Court of Appeals for the District of Columbia Circuit, to fill the vacancy. Judge Garland offered to meet with interested senators—a customary process—but only 14 Republican Senators agreed to see him. Activist groups spent millions on ads; conservative ads called for "letting the people decide" (i.e., waiting till after the presidential election in the hope that a Republican president would nominate a conservative to the Court), and liberal groups criticized Republican senators for failing to act on the nomination, using the hashtag #DoYourJob.

Egged on by these organized interests, the Senate confirmation process has slowed to a snail's pace. This partisan polarization of the judicial nominating process has produced extended vacancies on federal appeals courts, leading qualified candidates to withdraw their names from consideration and to backlogs in handling cases.

Sources: Carl Hulse and Mark Landler, "Senate Republicans Dig In Over Naming Next Justice," *New York Times*, February 15, 2016, p. A1; Emmarie Huetteman, "An Idle Tango of Praise and Rejection for a Court Nominee and Republicans," *New York Times*, May 10, 2016, p. A16.

State Court Judges State court judges, in contrast, are often elected rather than appointed—a practice used almost nowhere else in the world. Candidates for at least some types of judgeships must run in partisan elections in about a third of the states. Some states use a nonpartisan ballot for judges' races, though party organizations may still endorse their own candidates publicly. In these elections, candidates for judge routinely accept campaign contributions, often from lawyers and groups who will be bringing cases to their courts for a ruling. The contributors, of course, are not donating out of love for the judiciary; they have interests that they want heard.[33] These contests have become more and more costly, especially since

Citizens United (see Chapter 12). Some have been as acrimonious as nominations to the U.S. Supreme Court.

Even when judges are appointed to their posts, partisanship can still play a role. In many states, party leaders may advise on the nominations of prospective judges. A number of states have moved toward a "merit appointment" system in which nominating commissions screen prospective judges or recommend a shortlist to the governor or another official. In these cases, the appointee usually has to run in a retention election within 4–12 years of his or her appointment. Reformers hoped that these long terms and the likelihood that the appointee would be reelected (thanks to incumbency) would free judges from party pressures, or even pressures from the governor or president. But partisanship is so often already internalized in the judge's values and preferences that a long-term judgeship merely allows them to flourish.[34]

Even in these retention elections, the partisan stakes have risen in recent years. State Supreme Courts make crucial decisions on policy, and a variety of interest groups have realized that it is much cheaper to affect those policies by changing the composition of the Court than to try to change the party balance in the state legislature. In 2016, massive campaigns were waged in Wisconsin West Virginia, North Carolina, Kansas, and other states as interest groups and parties sought to influence the ideological composition of their Supreme Courts.

Many European countries choose judges differently. Someone prepares to be a judge by studying judgeship, apprenticing, and then scoring well on a special exam. In the United States, in contrast, there is no special training process for judges—no exam to take, no advanced degree in judging. Any lawyer can be a judge if he or she can win election or appointment to the job. But although the specialized training process required for judgeships in many European nations limits the impact of party organizations and partisan elections, those who become judges will still have political preferences, many of which will have been shaped by their partisanship.

The Party Within the Executive and the Judge

The best explanation for party influence on executives and judges is that, like other officeholders, executives and judges hold political beliefs, and the fact that judges and administrators have to interpret laws when applying them allows these beliefs to affect their behavior in office. Democrats usually hold different beliefs about government and the economy than Republicans do, and Democratic judges and bureaucrats, similarly, hold different views from Republican judges and bureaucrats. These party differences are reinforced by partisan aspects of the process by which presidents and governors, top executive officials, and most judges are chosen. We rarely see much evidence of direct influence by the party organization on bureaucrats and courts. The parties don't have the means to enforce party discipline in the executive or judicial branches.

Reformers have tried to take partisan considerations out of the selection process for judges and bureaucrats. When citizens suspect that partisan forces are affecting courts and administrative agencies—for instance, when judges campaigning for reelection get big campaign contributions from lawyers and groups whose lawsuits they will later decide—public confidence in courts and administrative agencies declines.[35] But there is no way to eliminate individuals' beliefs and values, including their partisanship, from their selection as administrators or judges or from their behavior in office.

Notes

1 Sidney M. Milkis, Jesse H. Rhodes, and Emily J. Charnock, "What Happened to Post-Partisanship?" *Perspectives on Politics* 10 (2012): 57–76.

2 See Daniel J. Galvin, *Presidential Party Building* (Princeton, NJ: Princeton University Press, 2010).

3 Brendan J. Doherty, "Presidential Party Fundraising in Hopes of Not Having to Govern by Himself," *The Forum* 12 (2014): 81–101.

4 James E. Campbell, "Predicting Seat Gains from Presidential Coattails," *American Journal of Political Science* 30 (1986): 164–183.

5 See Bruce Cain, John Ferejohn, and Morris Fiorina, *The Personal Vote* (Cambridge, MA: Harvard University Press, 1987).

6 See, for instance, Gary C. Jacobson, "Congress," in Michael Nelson, ed., *The Elections of 2012* (Los Angeles: Sage, 2014), pp. 156–163.

7 See Marc Meredith, "Exploiting Friends-and-Neighbors to Estimate Coattail Effects," *American Political Science Review* 107 (2013): 742–765.

8 See Gary C. Jacobson, "It's Nothing Personal," *Journal of Politics* 77 (2015): 861–873.

9 "House: Full Results," CNN Politics, December 17, 2014, at www.cnn.com/election/2014/results/race/house#exit-polls (accessed June 27, 2016).

10 The classic statement is Angus Campbell, "Surge and Decline: A Study of Electoral Change," in Campbell, Philip E. Converse, Warren E. Miller, and Donald E. Stokes, eds., *Elections and the Political Order* (New York: Wiley, 1966), pp. 40–62. See also Robert S. Erikson, "Congressional Elections in Presidential Years," *Legislative Studies Quarterly* 41 (August 2016): 551–574.

11 See James E. Campbell, "The Midterm Landslide of 2010," *The Forum* 8 (2010), issue 4, article 3.

12 Pew Research Center, "Political Polarization in the American Public," June 12, 2014, at www.people-press.org/2014/06/12/political-polarization-in-the-American-public (accessed June 27, 2016).

13 See Paul R. Abramson, John H. Aldrich, and David W. Rohde, *Change and Continuity in the 1992 Elections* (Washington, DC: CQ Press, 1994), p. 196.

14 George Gao and Samantha Smith, "Presidential Job Approval Ratings from Ike to Obama," Pew Research Center, January 12, 2016, at www.pewresearch.org/

fact-tank/2016/01/12/presidential-job-approval-ratings-from-ike-to-obama/ (accessed June 27, 2016).

15 David Baumann, "At the Top of His Game," *CQ Weekly,* May 18, 2009, pp. 1142–1143.

16 See David R. Mayhew, *Divided We Govern*, 2nd ed. (New Haven, CT: Yale University Press, 2005).

17 Hugh Heclo, *A Government of Strangers* (Washington, DC: Brookings Institution, 1977).

18 Hugh Heclo, "Issue Networks and the Executive Establishment," in Anthony King, ed., *The New American Political System* (Washington, DC: American Enterprise Institute, 1979), pp. 87–124.

19 Joel Aberbach and Bert A. Rockman, "Clashing Beliefs Within the Executive Branch," *American Political Science Review* 70 (1976): 456–468.

20 Joel D. Aberbach and Bert A. Rockman, "The Political Views of U.S. Senior Federal Executives, 1970–1992," *Journal of Politics* 57 (1995): 838–852.

21 Sanford C. Gordon, "Assessing Partisan Bias in Federal Public Corruption Prosecutions," *American Political Science Review* 103 (2009): 534–554.

22 Kenneth S. Lowande and Sidney M. Milkis, "'We Can't Wait': Barack Obama, Partisan Polarization, and the Administrative Presidency," *The Forum* 12 (2014): 3–27.

23 See Lee Epstein, William M. Landes, and Richard A. Posner, *The Behavior of Federal Judges* (Cambridge, MA: Harvard University Press, 2013).

24 Juliet Eilperin, "Environmental Group Cites Partisanship in the Judiciary," *Washington Post,* October 9, 2004, p. A2. See also Thomas J. Miles and Cass R. Sunstein, "Do Judges Make Regulatory Policy?" *University of Chicago Law Review* 73 (2006): 823–881.

25 See Randall D. Lloyd, "Separating Partisanship from Party in Judicial Research," *American Political Science Review* 89 (1995): 413–420.

26 See Robert Barnes, "Partisan Fissures Over Voter ID," *Washington Post,* December 25, 2007, p. A1.

27 Adam Liptak, "Clerks Highlight Supreme Court's Polarization," *New York Times*, September 6, 2010, p. A1.

28 Sheldon Goldman, "The Bush Imprint on the Judiciary," *Judicature* 74 (1991), 294–306.

29 Sheldon Goldman, Elliot Slotnick, Gerard Gryski, and Gary Zuk, "Clinton's Judges," *Judicature* 84 (2001): 244, 249.

30 R. Jeffrey Smith, "The Politics of the Federal Bench," *Washington Post*, December 8, 2008, p. A1.

31 See Sarah A. Binder and Forrest Maltzman, "Senatorial Delay in Confirming Federal Judges, 1947–1998," *American Journal of Political Science* 46 (2002): 190–199.

32 Christina L. Boyd, Michael S. Lynch, and Anthony Madonna, "Nuclear Fallout," *The Forum* 13, Issue 4 (February 2016): 623–641.

33 Beth Carter Easter, "Tipping the Scales of Justice," Ph.D. Dissertation, Indiana University, 2014; Melinda Gann Hall, *Attacking Judges* (Stanford, CA: Stanford University Press, 2015).

34 See Melinda Gann Hall, "State Supreme Courts in American Democracy," *American Political Science Review* 95 (2001): 315–330.

35 James L. Gibson, *Electing Judges* (Chicago: University of Chicago Press, 2012).

CHAPTER 15

The Semi-Responsible Parties

Americans have dealt with immigration problems since well before 1492. Again in 2016, fierce debates erupted over the 11 million people living in the U.S. who are not American citizens. The Republican Party in particular has been torn by the issue. Mindful of the growing numbers of Latino American voters, several Republican strategists argue that the government should let at least some illegal immigrants climb a tough path to citizenship. Some businesses such as resort hotels and big farms prefer the status quo, because undocumented immigrants are a reliable supply of cheap labor. Yet 2016 Republican presidential nominee Donald Trump, backed by large numbers of the party's grassroots activists, insisted that he would deport all 11 million and build a wall between the U.S. and Mexico.

What, then, is the party's stand on illegal immigration? Does it matter if the party's stance is unclear? In fact, it does; parties are the most effective means we have of holding elected officials collectively responsible for their actions. Because parties simplify and clarify our political choices (among other services; see Chapter 1), they make it easier for individuals to hold the awesome powers of government accountable to their preferences. If the American parties can't take clear stands on this important issue and hold their candidates accountable, then is it even possible for individuals to keep government responsive to our needs?

That the major parties are not clear enough on how they would handle big issues is only one of the many complaints people make about the parties. Some view the Democrats and Republicans as too similar in their platforms and too centrist. Many bloggers claim that both parties are controlled by moneyed special interests. Thus, they argue, government serves well-financed minorities—corporations, labor unions, single-issue groups—rather than the people.

These critics come from different perspectives, but at heart they make the same point. They both want the parties to offer clearer and more detailed stands on issues and for the winning party to put its promises to work in public policy. One possible answer is to create a system of truly "responsible parties."[1] The governing party in this system would translate a coherent

348

political philosophy into government action and would then be held responsible for the results.

To some extent, their demands have been met. The parties clearly differ now on a number of important issues. The Democratic Party is more uniformly liberal today than it was a few decades ago, and the Republicans are more consistently conservative. In fact, many Americans now think that the gulf between the parties has become *too* wide; almost half of Americans describe the Republican Party as "too extreme," and a smaller proportion say the same about the Democrats.[2] Has this party polarization made the Democrats and Republicans into "responsible" parties, and does it improve their ability to serve the needs of a democracy?

The Case for Responsible Party Government

The idea of **responsible parties,** also called **party government,** offers a vision of democracy very different from the traditional American commitment to limited government and the equally traditional American hostility to powerful political parties. Champions of party government believe that we need a strong and decisive government to solve social and economic problems. Our political institutions, they feel, may have been well suited to the limited governing of the early years of American history but do not serve us well today, when we need more vigorous government action against challenges ranging from terrorism to climate change.

Yet the public must be able to keep this strong government under control. Individuals rarely have the time, information, or desire to play an active political role or even to find out what their elected representatives are doing. Candidate-centered elections can reduce public control as well; it is much harder for voters to monitor hundreds of different candidates than to judge the performance of one governing party.

How Would Party Government (Responsible Parties) Work?

To solve these problems, party government advocates say, we should restructure the political parties and let them hold elected officials accountable.[3] The parties would take the lead in organizing the government and, in the process, reinvigorate the other institutions of popular democracy. Here's how party government would work:

- Each party would draw up a clear, detailed statement of the principles and programs it favors. It would pledge to carry out those programs if the party wins.
- The parties would nominate candidates loyal to their party's program and willing to push for it if elected.

- Each party would run a campaign that clarifies the policy differences between the two parties, so voters would grasp these differences and vote on that basis.
- Once elected, the party would hold its officeholders responsible for carrying out the party program. Voters could then determine whether they liked the results and decide whether to keep or defeat the governing party at the next election.

In this system of responsible parties, then, winning elections would not be an end in itself. The party's main focus would be on the policies it has pledged to put into effect. Nominations and elections would become no more—and no less—than a means to achieve certain public policy goals. *For this to happen, all the elected branches of government would have to be controlled by the same party at a particular time.* The party would bind the divided institutions of government into a working whole, as happens in parliamentary democracies.

What qualifies the party to play this crucial role? A prominent party scholar wrote that "the parties have claims on the loyalties of the American people superior to the claims of any other forms of political organization. ... The parties are the special form of political organization adapted to the mobilization of majorities."[4] So parties would hold a privileged position in politics compared with interest groups, their major rivals as intermediaries between citizens and government.[5]

Those who argue for party government do not always agree on the purposes they feel a strong federal government should serve. Many conservatives, once suspicious of a powerful central government, grew to like it better when conservative Presidents Reagan, Bush, and Trump used their power to urge Congress to eliminate liberal programs. Liberals frustrated by the separation of powers developed greater enthusiasm for the principle when Congress proved capable of checking some of Reagan's, Bush's, and Trump's initiatives. Party government sounds like a better idea, it seems, when your party is in charge. In any case, party government advocates feel that a government pulled together by strong parties would let citizens direct their government more effectively than they do now, and with less investment of citizens' time and effort.

The Case Against Party Government

Most American political scientists remain unconvinced of the benefits of party government. Their concerns take two forms. Many argue that party government would not produce desirable results. Others claim that it simply would not work in the American context.[6]

It Would Increase Conflict

First, the skeptics fear that the nature of party government—its dedication to providing clear alternatives on major issues—would provoke even more political conflict. Legislators, they say, would be bound to a fixed party position and would no longer be free to represent their own constituents and to negotiate mutually acceptable solutions. That would weaken the deliberative character of American legislatures.

Critics of party government also fear that a system that makes parties the main avenue of political representation could undercut the rich variety of interest groups that now exist. Without these other means of representing groups and views, the two major parties might be seriously overloaded. Minor parties would pop up, further fragmenting American politics. In short, critics fear that legislatures would be dominated by rigid, dogmatic political parties unable to resolve problems—even more than is the case today.

It Wouldn't Work in American Politics

The second major argument against responsible parties is that the idea conflicts with the American government's design. The responsible parties model eases the path to majority rule. But the American founders set up a system that limits majority rule in important ways. They divided constitutional authority among the various levels and branches of government, using the principles of separation of powers and federalism, in order to prevent tyranny. The separation of powers allows voters to give control of the executive branch to one party and the legislative branch to the other. Federalism permits different parties to dominate in different states. Equal representation of states in the U.S. Senate advantages residents of the smaller states. Any change in these and other anti-majoritarian features of the American government would require fundamental revision of the Constitution. Frances Lee also points out that the Senate's use of filibusters and other aspects of the American constitutional system require super-majorities rather than just majorities to pass policies,[7] so even a majority may not be enough to win.

American voters have made enthusiastic use of the separation of powers in recent years. Since 1950, in contrast with earlier times, we have had **divided government** most of the time, so that a president has faced at least one house of Congress controlled by the other party (see Table 15.1). State governments have often been split by party as well, though in very recent times, single-party control over a state's executive and legislative branches has become more frequent.

Divided government makes responsible party government impossible. When both Democratic-controlled and Republican-controlled parts of the government have their fingerprints on every major piece of legislation, voters find it hard to figure out which party is responsible for bad policies. Without that ability, voters can't throw out the guilty party and replace it with the opposition.

To party government advocates, divided government helps to explain why the federal government has failed to respond effectively to a number of major concerns from federal spending to climate change. The critics disagree. They argue that unified party government doesn't necessarily produce more significant legislation, that the federal government has a lot of practice in coping with shared party power,[8] and even that American voters prefer it that way.[9]

TABLE 15.1 Party Control of the Federal Government, 1951–2016

Party Control	Number of Years
Unified	24
Democrats control the presidency and both houses of Congress	18
1951–1952 (Truman), 1961–1968 (Kennedy, Johnson), 1977–1980 (Carter),	
1993–1994 (Clinton), 2009–2010 (Obama)	
Republicans control the presidency and both houses of Congress	6
1953–1954 (Eisenhower), 2003–2006 (G. W. Bush), 2017– (Trump)	
Divided	42
Democratic president, Republican House and Senate	8
1995–2000 (Clinton), 2015–2016 (Obama)	
Republican president, Democratic House and Senate	22
1955–1960 (Eisenhower), 1969–1976 (Nixon, Ford), 1987–1992 (Reagan, G. H. W. Bush), 2007–2008 (G. W. Bush)	
President's party controls one house of Congress	12
1981–1986 (Reagan), 2001–2002 (G. W. Bush)*, 2011–2014 (Obama)	

Note: The names of the presidents during these years are in parentheses.

* The Senate was Republican controlled for the first five months of 2001 until Senator James Jeffords left the Republican Party and the Democrats gained majority control.

Source: Updated from Harold W. Stanley and Richard G. Niemi, *Vital Statistics on American Politics 1999–2000* (Washington, DC: CQ Press, 2000), pp. 34–38.

The Gingrich Experiment: A Temporarily Responsible Party

Americans got at least a whiff of party responsibility starting in the mid-1990s. Spearheaded by House Republican minority leader Newt Gingrich, the great majority of Republicans running for House seats in 1994 signed a statement called a "Contract with America." It pledged that if the voters would give Republicans a House majority, they would guarantee a vote on each of ten pieces of legislation, all embodying conservative principles, within the first one hundred days of the next Congress. The statement concluded, in words that would gladden the hearts of party government advocates: "If we break this contract, throw us out. We mean it."

The Republicans did win a majority of House seats in 1994. They delivered on their promise; once in office, the new Republican leadership used its iron control of the House agenda to vote on each of the bills before the self-imposed deadline. House Republicans were more unified on these bills than they had been in decades. That, however, is when party government stalled. The Senate Republican majority had not committed itself to the Contract with America and did not feel bound to consider these bills promptly or to pass them. The House Republicans' efforts were further stymied by divided government; a Democratic president had the power to veto any legislation that made it through both houses.

What can we learn from this experiment? First, the separation of powers is a mighty roadblock in the path of responsible parties. Even the commitment of a legislative party to a set of clear and consistent principles is not enough to produce responsible party government, as long as the president and/or the other house of Congress are not willing to go along. Most voters may not have appreciated the experiment, either; although Republicans kept their House majority in the next election year, so did the Senate Republicans who had not signed the Contract with America, and the Democratic president was reelected as well.

Even when the same party controls the White House and both houses of Congress, there are obstacles to achieving party government. Because the parties' candidates are chosen by voters in primary elections, parties cannot force their candidates to be loyal to the party's program. Candidates who break with their party on important issues can still run, and win, as long as their constituents keep voting for them. Critics of the responsible parties model also claim that most American voters are not issue oriented enough to see politics only through ideological lenses, that the major parties are not centralized enough to enforce a single set of issue positions on all their officeholders, and that Americans distrust parties too much to let them try. In short, the idea of responsible parties seems to its critics to ask too much of the voters, the parties, and the institutions of American government.

Party Cohesion and Ideology

Although genuine party government is unlikely in the United States, the parties are occasionally nudged toward greater accountability. Some observers suggest that this is happening now, in the only way that would be consistent with the American system of separated powers: Each party's voters, its party in government, and its party organization have become more willing to agree voluntarily on a clear party program. But there are limits to the parties' cohesiveness on issues.

Are the American Parties Ideological?

An **ideological party** is one with clear and consistent principles on a wide range of issues, from the purpose of government to the essence of human nature. Examples include the old-style Communist parties and the Muslim fundamentalist parties that have arisen in Middle Eastern nations. The principles of an ideological party offer answers to questions such as these: What values should a government try to achieve? Who deserves to have power, and under what conditions do they forfeit that right?

Throughout their long histories, however, the American parties have tended to be more pragmatic than ideological, focusing on concrete problems rather than on the purity of their principles. Ever since their founding, each party has been a blend of its own original tradition (the egalitarian tradition of the Democrats and the Republican tradition of order and industrial capitalism) with those of other groups that associated with it because of personal ties, geographic nearness, or simple expectations of political gain.[10]

There are several reasons why the major American parties aren't ideologically "pure." Most important, there are only two of them to divide up a tremendous array of interests in American politics. In a system with several parties, a party can cater to one ideological niche in the voting public and still hope to survive. In a big and diverse two-party system, with so many different interests and people to represent, such specialized appeals can be made only by minor parties—or by a major party willing to risk self-destruction.

Do They At Least Offer Clear Choices?

Yet even though the two major parties are not as ideological as those in many other democracies, they have come to differ greatly in their stands on specific issues. This can increase voters' ability to hold them responsible. We can see these differences in the platforms they adopt every four years at their national conventions (see box "Party Differences on Major Issues" on page 355) and in the policies they pursue when they win. It would have been hard, for example, to mistake the stands taken by Donald Trump and other Republican candidates in 2016 on health care, gun rights, and women's

Party Differences on Major Issues:
The 2016 Party Platforms

Marriage Equality?

Republicans: Traditional marriage and family, based on marriage between one man and one woman, is the foundation for a free society ... (Republican platform, p. 11)

Democrats: Democrats applaud last year's decision by the Supreme Court that recognized that LGBT people—like other Americans—have the right to marry the person they love. (Democratic platform, p. 19)

Limit Abortion?

Republicans: We assert the sanctity of human life and affirm that the unborn child has a fundamental right to life which cannot be infringed. (13)

Democrats: ... every woman should have access to quality reproductive health care services, including safe and legal abortion—regardless of where she lives, how much money she makes, or how she is insured. (37)

Allow Family Planning?

Republicans: We renew our call for replacing "family planning" programs for teens with sexual risk avoidance education that sets abstinence until marriage as the responsible and respected standard of behavior. (34)

Democrats: ... quality, affordable comprehensive health care, evidence-based sex education and a full range of family planning services help reduce the number of unintended pregnancies and thereby also reduce the need for abortions. (37)

Repeal "Obamacare"?

Republicans: Any honest agenda for improving health care must start with repeal of the dishonestly named Affordable Care Act of 2010: Obamacare. (36)

Democrats: ....we are proud to be the party that passed Medicare, Medicaid, and the Affordable Care Act (ACA). (34)

Role of Religion in Public Life

Republicans: We support the public display of the Ten Commandments as a reflection of our history and our country's Judeo-Christian heritage and further affirm the rights of religious students to engage in voluntary prayer at public school events. (12)

Democrats: We support a progressive vision of religious freedom that respects pluralism and rejects the misuse of religion to discriminate. (19)

Protect Gun Rights?

Republicans: We uphold the right of individuals to keep and bear arms ... We oppose ill-conceived laws that would restrict magazine capacity or ban the sale of the most popular and common modern rifle. (12)

Democrats: ... we will expand and strengthen background checks and close dangerous loopholes in our current laws; ... and keep weapons of war—such as assault weapons and large capacity ammunition magazines (LCAMs)—off our streets. (39)

Protect Voting Rights?

Republicans: ... we support legislation to require proof of citizenship when registering to vote and secure photo ID when voting. (16)

Democrats: ... we will continue to fight against discriminatory voter identification laws, which disproportionately burden young voters, diverse communities, people of color, low-income families, people with disabilities, the elderly, and women. (24)

Immigration?

Republicans: ...we support building a wall along our southern border... (26)

Democrats: We reject attempts to impose a religious test to bar immigrants or refugees from entering the United States. (18)

Finance Student Loans?

Republicans: The federal government should not be in the business of originating student loans. (35)

Democrats: Democrats will allow those who currently have student debt to refinance their loans at the lowest rates possible. ... (31)

Public or Private Education?

Republicans: We support options for learning, including home-schooling, career and technical education, private or parochial schools, magnet schools, charter schools, online learning, and early-college high schools. (34)

Democrats: We believe that high-quality public charter schools should provide options for parents, but should not replace or destabilize traditional public schools. (34)

Fossil Fuels or Clean Energy?

Republicans: ...coal is an abundant, clean, affordable, reliable domestic energy resource. [Miners] should be protected from the Democratic Party's radical anti-coal agenda. (19)

Democrats: Democrats believe the tax code must reflect our commitment to a clean energy future by eliminating special tax breaks and subsidies for fossil fuel companies ... (27)

Limit Labor Unions?

Republicans: We support the right of states to enact Right to Work [anti-union] laws (8)

Democrats: Democrats will make it easier for workers, public and private, to exercise their right to organize and join unions. (4)

Reduce Corporate Taxes?

Republicans: [We support] lowering the corporate tax rate to be on a par with, or below, the rates of other industrial nations (p. 1)

Democrats: At a time of near-record corporate profits, slow wage growth, and rising costs, we need to offer tax relief to middle-class families—not those at the top. (13)

Preserve Affirmative Action?

Republicans: Merit and hard work should determine advancement in our society, so we reject unfair preferences, quotas, and set-asides as forms of discrimination. (9)

Democrats: The racial wealth and income gaps are the result of policies that discriminate against people of color and constrain their ability to earn income and build assets to the same extent as other Americans. (15)

Keep the Death Penalty?

Republicans: The constitutionality of the death penalty is firmly settled by its explicit mention in the Fifth Amendment. (40)

Democrats: We will abolish the death penalty, which has proven to be a cruel and unusual form of punishment. (16)

Excerpted from the parties' platforms at www.demconvention.com/wp-content/uploads/2016/07/Democratic-Party-Platform-7.21.16-no-lines.pdf and https://prod-static-ngop-pbl.s3.amazonaws.com/media/documents/DRAFT_12_FINAL[1]-ben_1468872234.pdf (accessed September 15, 2016).

---

rights for those expressed by Hillary Clinton and other Democrats. "Republicans mostly believe that the role of government is to foster greater individual economic achievement, even if it leads to more economic inequality," one perceptive analyst writes. "The Democratic philosophy is that the government should provide a safety net, even if it leads to economic inefficiency."[11] These differences, especially the Democratic commitment to fund federal social programs and the Republican desire to limit them, have animated the parties since the 1930s.

Each major party has become more unified in its stands during the past few decades as well as more different from the other party—in short, more **polarized**. A major contributor was the issue of civil rights. When racial justice became an important focus of national policy in the 1960s, national Democrats took a clear position in favor of civil rights laws and national Republicans took the opposite stance. In response, white, segregationist southerners shook off their traditional Democratic loyalty in increasing numbers and took with them into the Republican Party their more conservative views on many other issues. (This story is told more fully in Chapter 7.) This lowered the biggest barrier to unity within the Democratic Party on several issues.[12]

The Ronald Reagan presidency during the 1980s further polarized the parties. Reagan, who strongly identified with the religious, neoconservative wing of the Republican Party, demonstrated the appeal of a simple vision based on one major idea: less government. His assault on the role of government as it had developed since the New Deal gave a more ideological tone to American politics than had been seen in decades. Since then, more issue-oriented leaders have been selected in both parties,[13] and political issues—purposive incentives—have become more prominent in bringing people into party activism. As Chapter 13 showed, both congressional parties vote more cohesively on issues now than they have in decades. State parties are polarizing in a similar way,[14] especially since 2010, when several newly elected Republican governors and state legislatures have promoted major cuts in social programs and limits to collective bargaining for state employees.

But Internal Divisions Remain

These clear differences on major issues, however, do not add up to the all-encompassing political philosophies that are found in genuinely ideological parties. Consider, for instance, the interesting relationship between each party's stand on economic policy and its position on issues such as abortion and pornography. As Chapter 1 mentioned, Democrats have long stood for an activist federal government in promoting individuals' social welfare but very limited government power over individuals' decisions on abortion. Republicans generally want to loosen the federal government's grip on the economy and environmental regulation but argue for government activism in banning abortion. Nimble advocates could probably construct a rationale as to why these sets of positions are actually consistent. But in reality, these stands coexist within each party's platform because the major parties, as they always have, adjust their policy positions to attract groups of potential supporters—in this case, when Republicans found common cause with conservative Christians and Democrats reached out to pro-choice women—even at the cost of internal consistency.

In addition, because the major American parties are pragmatic and vote seeking above all, neither party has stayed completely true to the principles it articulates.[15] For instance, the Republican platform has long pledged to bring smaller government. Yet after winning control of the presidency in 2000, Republicans promoted a number of big government programs, from a huge ($500 billion) expansion of Medicare entitlements to more pork barrel spending. Their aim was to gain support from voters who value tangible economic benefits more than abstract principles. And although Democrats have long been aligned with the resource-poor, Democratic members of Congress have not been shy about backing tax breaks for businesses and wealthy interests in their districts. In addition, both parties continue to deal with internal dissent.[16]

What about party voters? Is it true, as some ideologues charge, that most Americans are committed to ideological principles and want the Democrats and Republicans to provide more clearly defined choices? Or are party voters bored with, or even put off by, the programmatic concerns of many party activists?

Ideology and the American Voter

Media reports of election results frequently use the terms "liberal" and "conservative" to describe voters' choices. The question is more complicated for political scientists, who have long debated the structure of citizens' political attitudes.

How Ideological Is the American Public?

An ideological voter, like an ideological party, would not just hold clear attitudes toward some individual issues but would also connect those attitudes into a coherent structure. However, careful study of American political attitudes raises serious doubt that most voters can be described as "ideological" or even as very consistent in their political beliefs.

Many individuals with conservative attitudes on, say, government spending may express moderate or liberal attitudes on other issues, such as gay rights or the environment.[17] People do not necessarily hold a set of fixed stands, such as an unqualified "yes" on abortion rights and a firm "no" on taxes. Rather, they might feel that taxes are a great burden *and* that they can be necessary at times. They can be pulled toward one of these views under some conditions and toward another view under other conditions. In fact, a number of survey respondents who call themselves "conservative" use the term to refer to lifestyle preferences rather than to political issues. Some of these might be considered "identity conservatives," in that their conservatism has more to do with their opposition to "political correctness," Democrats, and former President Obama than to acceptance of the conservative philosophy, and who may even express liberal views on some policies.[18] In short, most people have ambivalent attitudes toward at least some issues[19]—a sharp contrast with a more ideological thinker.

This ambivalence allows many of us to hold sets of beliefs that might drive an ideologue to drink. For instance, large numbers of survey respondents say that they want a smaller government with lower taxes *and* a government that provides more services in areas such as health care and education. That is understandable; most people would like to pay less while getting more. But it is not a likely foundation for consistent thinking.[20]

A lot of people termed "moderates" by pollsters are simply people whose views, which may sometimes be extreme, don't fit the liberal-conservative mold. Some Americans, for instance, combine a desire for more government social services with a belief that government should also uphold traditional moral values; these can be called "populists." And as you saw in Chapter 2, libertarians want less government involvement in both of these spheres.[21]

Even in elections when voters are offered clear choices, many voters tend to focus on more pragmatic considerations instead. Reagan campaigned for president in 1980 as a principled conservative, yet many voters supported him in spite of his conservative policies, rather than because of them. In fact, in both 1980 and 1984 most voters preferred the policy stands that Reagan's opponent stood for, though Reagan won both elections handily.[22] Voters' judgments turned more on their *retrospective evaluations* of presidential performance—their feelings as to whether the most recent presidency had turned out well—than on Reagan's stances on specific issues. Because many voters tend to be results oriented, parties and candidates try to stitch together winning coalitions by appealing to a range of qualities—candidates' personal characteristics, group interests, and feelings about the party in power—rather than by stressing ideological differences.

It is important to note, however, that ideology has played a bigger role in recent elections. Analysts disagree on the nature of the change. Some argue that Americans have become more extreme in their views, with fewer moderates and more conservatives and liberals.[23] Others claim that voters remain as pragmatic and nonideological as ever, but that political debate *appears* to be more ideological now because of "partisan sorting" in which most liberal Republicans have switched to the Democratic Party and most conservative Democrats have become Republicans.[24]

Partisan Sorting or Ideological Polarization?

There is no doubt that partisan sorting has taken place. We saw in Chapter 7 the remarkable degree to which conservative whites in the South and liberals in the Northeast and West have moved to the "correct" party since the 1960s. Figure 15.1 shows that Democrats are now more inclined to call themselves liberals and Republicans to consider themselves conservatives. The two parties' identifiers differ especially in their attitudes toward taxes, environmental policy, and government social services.[25] In recent polls, for instance, 68 percent of Republicans and Republican leaners said that "poor people today have it easy because they can get government benefits without doing anything in return," compared with just 28 percent of Democrats, and 59 percent of Republicans said "stricter environmental laws and regulations cost too many jobs and hurt the economy," as against 24 percent of Democrats.[26] This widening gap is due mainly to the growing conservatism of Republican identifiers.[27] The shift to the left among Democrats has been less notable, though it has grown recently.[28]

As these gaps have opened, the public images of the parties have diverged (see Figure 15.2). The Republican Party is viewed as stronger on terrorism and gun rights; the Democrats are seen as stronger on environment and education. Survey respondents rate the GOP as having firm principles but criticize it as too extreme; the Democratic Party is seen as more tolerant and more concerned about the middle class but too likely to seek governmental solutions.[29]

And partisans feel these starker differences in more personal and emotional ways. As Figure 15.3 shows, Democrats tend to see their own party's ideology as ranging from moderate to very liberal, while the plurality place the Republican Party at the most extreme (right-wing) end of the scale. Republicans return the favor; fully 45 percent of Republican respondents see the Democratic Party as the most extreme (left-wing) that it is possible to be, while rating their own party as moderate to conservative. Party identifiers dislike, even despise, the other party more than in years past.[30] This increasing emotional division strengthens the influence of party ID on individuals.[31]

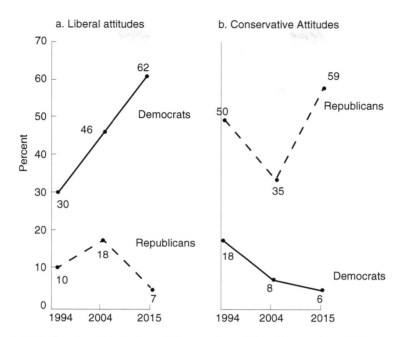

Figure 15.1 Growing Polarization of Democrats and Republicans since 1994

Note: Points are the percentages of Democratic and Republican identifiers (not including independent leaners) expressing consistently or mostly conservative attitudes, or consistently or mostly liberal attitudes, on ten Pew Research Center questions about political values.

Source: Data adapted from Samantha Smith, "5 facts about America's political independents," Pew Research Center, July 5, 2016, at www.pewresearch.org/fact-tank/2016/07/05/5-facts-about-americas-political-independents (accessed November 14, 2016).

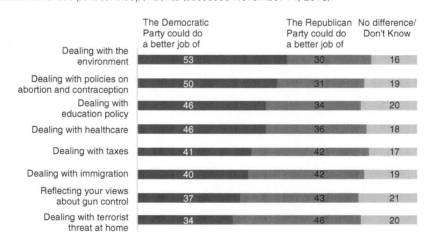

Figure 15.2 Percentage of Voters Seeing a Party Advantage on Issues, 2015–2016

Note: Rows do not always add up to 100 percent because of rounding error. Respondents who volunteered "both equally," "neither," or "don't know" were listed as "No difference, don't know."

Source: Pew Research Center data from December 8–13, 2015.

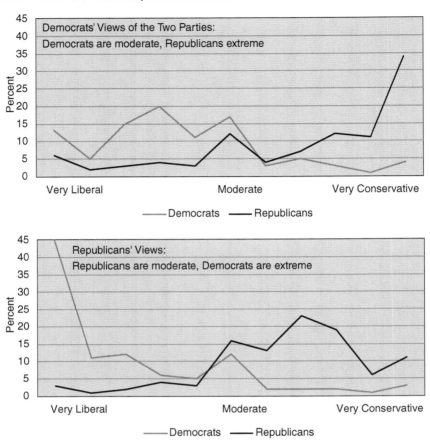

Figure 15.3 Party Identifiers See the Other Party's Ideology as More Extreme, 2016

Note: The upper part of the figure shows Democrats' views of the two parties, with the Republicans viewed as more extreme; the lower part shows Republicans' views, in which the Democrats are seen as more extreme. Identifiers include strong and weak partisans but not independent leaners.

Source: Adapted from Pew Research Center, "Partisanship and Political Animosity in 2016," June 23, 2016, at www.people-press.org/2016/06/22/partisanship-and-political-animosity-in-2016/ (accessed June 28, 2016).

Partisan sorting has been encouraged by trends in the media. The wider range of available media outlets allows partisans to choose programs and blogs that support their own beliefs and reflect their party loyalties.[32] Republicans who watch Fox News and Democrats who read the *Huffington Post* can trust that most of what they watch and read will agree with their partisan views. Even if they are exposed to more diverse sources—as can happen on social media, for instance—people are more likely to remember facts consistent with their partisanship and to resist information that challenges their preconceptions.[33]

But the change is not limited to partisan sorting. Some ideological polarization—greater extremism in people's views—seems to have occurred at about the same time. The proportion of people in the American National Election Studies calling themselves very conservative or extremely conservative, and very liberal or extremely liberal, rose markedly from the early 1970s to the present. These voters tend to be more interested and engaged in politics, so we can guess that these terms have some meaning for them. The proportion of Americans who are policy-ambivalent—who take roughly equal numbers of liberal and conservative stands on issues—has dropped from 49 percent in 1994 and 2004 to 39 percent in 2014,[34] while the share of the public that is ideologically consistent, though not large, has grown a lot in the past decade, especially among more educated people.[35] These changes improve many voters' ability to meet the demands of the responsible parties model.

In sum, Americans have become more polarized in *both* ideological and partisan terms. It is true, however, that many political activists tend to exaggerate the nature of this polarization.[36] Republicans and Democrats don't differ in their factual beliefs as much as they do in their expressive "team loyalty" toward their party.[37] The trend toward greater polarization may not last forever; people who came of age during the Obama presidency show some signs of greater moderation and liberalism, even among Republican identifiers. And a lot of Americans have managed to sit out these conflicts altogether. Paul Allen Beck refers to "two electorates—one partisan and about evenly divided, the other estranged from party politics."[38]

Differences Among Voters, Activists, and Candidates

Much of this "sorting" among voters has come in response to the increasing polarization of party leaders and party platforms.[39] The gap between Democrats and Republicans in their attitudes toward candidates and issues is much deeper among party leaders and political activists than among people who are less politically engaged.[40] For instance, there's a huge divide—almost 70 percentage points—between politically engaged Democrats and Republicans on whether government should ensure access to health care; among people who are not politically engaged, the gap is only about half as great. And fully 42 percent of politically engaged Republicans say they are angry with the federal government; that's true of only 23 percent of Republicans who are not politically engaged.[41]

This can pose a challenge for candidates and officeholders. It is not unusual for candidates to find themselves caught in between: closer to the left or right than the party's voters but not as extreme as its activists. How do candidates respond? If they try to muffle their conservative or liberal views, they risk alienating their party's activists.[42] But if they express those views candidly, more moderate voters may choose not to support them in the next election.[43] It is no wonder that many candidates prefer to remain vague when asked about issues, at least when they speak to general audiences.

These differences can aggravate the tensions among the party organization, the party in government, and the party's voters. Ideologues in both parties complain that at least some parts of the party in government are too moderate. Liberal Democrats objected to what they saw as President Obama's "sellout" on climate change and budget cuts, and Tea Party conservatives felt betrayed by some Republican House leaders' reluctance to cut federal spending to the bone, as they had allegedly promised. Bipartisan behavior in a politician seems to turn off strong partisans (who are most likely to vote), whereas weak identifiers and independents claim that they reward bipartisanship in their elected officials.[44]

The dilemma of ideology, then, is not whether the American parties can become genuinely ideological parties. That is not likely. The problem is whether the increasing ideological commitment of their activists and of many of their elected officials can be sustained without alienating their more pragmatic supporters. The parties already face a deep well of public suspicion. Much of the public feels alienated from the parties' attachment to organized interests, their affinity for negative campaigns, and their failure to keep their promises.[45] As one writer put it, moderates may become more convinced that "politics no longer speaks to them, that it has become a dialogue of the deaf, a rant of uncompromising extremes."[46]

When Is Party Government Most Likely?

Responsible parties are hard to achieve. Even the British Parliament, so often cited as a model of party government, has not always had the cohesion and the binding party discipline that a "pure" responsible party government would require.[47] Under what conditions have the American parties come closest to the ideal of responsible parties?

When There Is Strong Presidential Leadership

At times, a strong president—Ronald Reagan and George W. Bush in his first term are good examples—has been able to push Congress to enact important parts of the platform on which he ran for office. That is especially likely, of course, when the president's party controls both houses of Congress by more than a narrow margin. Party-oriented presidents can also draw voters' attention to party differences. But the result will probably be "presidential government" rather than party government; voters are likely to respond to the president's performance rather than that of the party as a whole.

In Times of Crisis

At critical times in American history, the parties have divided in ways that were, if not truly ideological, at least very policy oriented. In the 1936 presidential election, for example, the Democrats and the Republicans offered dramatically different solutions to a nation devastated by the Great Depression. The hardships of that economic collapse probably focused voter attention to an unusual degree on the possible remedies that government could provide. Combined with a campaign centered on the pros and cons of the Roosevelt program for economic change, this may well have produced something close to a mandate in the election for both the president and Congress.[48] When strong presidential leadership is combined with crisis conditions, then a degree of responsible party government might be achieved for a time.

When the Parties' Supporting Coalitions Are Reshaped

When the parties' supporting coalitions of social groups have undergone major change—sometimes called "realignments" (see Chapter 7)—American politics seems to have most closely approached the requirements for party government. At these times, the parties have divided more clearly on a single, riveting set of issues, and party leaders, activists, and voters have reached high levels of agreement with one another and major differences with the other party.

These changes in the party system typically produce a unified federal government, with one party controlling both houses of Congress, the presidency, and a judiciary that, through the president's appointment power, comes to reflect the new majority. On only five occasions in American history has one party enjoyed control of Congress and the presidency continuously for more than a decade; each time, this control was first established during a realignment. Party cohesion in Congress has been especially high at the beginning of a new party system. So it is not surprising that major bursts of comprehensive policy change followed the realignments of the parties' coalitions after the Civil War and again during the Depression.

Even at these times, it is hard to see the American parties as fully responsible. At the time of the Roosevelt New Deal as well as currently, both parties remain collections of varied interests even when they are able to unite on a few central goals.

Party Government and Popular Control

The major American parties behave more like responsible parties now than they have in a long time—perhaps ever—in the sense that each party in Congress hangs together more fully. There is a marked difference between the Republican Party organizations and activists and those of the Democrats on basic principles of public policy, both at the federal level and in increasing numbers of states. Many reformers think this is cause for celebration. When parties stand for clear principles and voters are offered clear choices in elections, they say, citizens are better able to hold government responsible for the policies it produces. That may make for a stronger and more vibrant democracy.

Yet it is not likely that the American parties and voters will ever meet all the demands of the responsible parties model. If the parties are to become more accountable, more like responsible parties in a system of party government, these differences on issues and greater organizational strength are not enough. There must be some set of basic principles that can connect different issues into a single logical structure for each party, some means by which voters and leaders are able to distill the large number of policy issues into one major dimension or a few, so that voters can easily understand and predict the party's stands.

Too many powerful forces stand in the way of achieving that much structure and coherence in the party system. Because of the separation of powers and the federal system of government, voters will always be able to divide power between the parties. No matter how much money they raise, American party organizations still won't be able to choose their own candidates; voters will make that choice in primary elections. As a result, candidates will always have some degree of independence from their party organizations. Without basic changes in the American political structure, including moving to a parliamentary system, the parties will remain semi-responsible. The consequence is that American government will remain semi-accountable to the public.

Notes

1 Committee on Political Parties of the American Political Science Association, *Toward a More Responsible Two-Party System* (New York: Rinehart, 1950).
2 CNN/ORC Poll. March 15–17, 2013, at www.pollingreport.com/dvsr.htm (accessed June 10, 2016).
3 See Austin Ranney, *The Doctrine of Responsible Party Government* (Urbana, IL: University of Illinois Press, 1964), Chapters 1 and 2.
4 E. E. Schattschneider, *Party Government* (New York: Rinehart, 1942), p. 208.
5 E. E. Schattschneider, *The Semi-Sovereign People* (New York: Holt, Rinehart, and Winston, 1960).
6 See John Kenneth White and Jerome M. Mileur, eds., *Challenges to Party Government* (Carbondale, IL: Southern Illinois University Press, 1992).
7 Frances E. Lee, "Parties as Coordinators: Can Parties Unite What the Constitution Divides?" in Marjorie Randon Hershey, ed., *Guide to U.S. Political Parties* (Los Angeles: Sage, 2014), Chapter 3.
8 John J. Coleman, "Unified Government, Divided Government, and Party Responsiveness," *American Political Science Review* 93 (1999): 821–835, and

David R. Mayhew, *Divided We Govern*, 2nd ed. (New Haven, CT: Yale University Press, 2005).

9 Richard Born, "Split-Ticket Voters, Divided Government, and Fiorina's Policy-Balancing Model," *Legislative Studies Quarterly* 19 (1994): 95–115.

10 A. James Reichley, *The Life of the Parties* (Lanham, MD: Rowman & Littlefield, 2000), Chapter 6.

11 David E. Rosenbaum, "Bush to Return to 'Ownership Society' Theme in Push for Social Security Changes," *New York Times*, January 16, 2005, p. 20.

12 Edward G. Carmines and James A. Stimson, *Issue Evolution* (Princeton, NJ: Princeton University Press, 1989); see also Geoffrey C. Layman and Thomas M. Carsey, "Party Polarization and 'Conflict Extension' in the American Electorate," *American Journal of Political Science* 46 (2002): 786–802.

13 Jason M. Roberts and Steven S. Smith, "Procedural Contexts, Party Strategy, and Conditional Party Voting in the U.S. House of Representatives, 1971–2000," *American Journal of Political Science* 47 (2003): 305–317.

14 Charles Barrilleaux, Thomas Holbrook, and Laura Langer, "Electoral Competition, Legislative Balance, and American State Welfare Policy," *American Journal of Political Science* 46 (2002): 415–427.

15 See David Karol, *Party Position Change in American Politics* (New York: Cambridge University Press, 2009).

16 Robin Kolodny, "Moderate Party Factions in the U.S. House of Representatives," in John C. Green and Daniel M. Shea, eds., *The State of the Parties*, 3rd ed. (Lanham, MD: Rowman & Littlefield, 1999), pp. 271–285.

17 The seminal study is Philip E. Converse, "The Nature of Belief Systems in Mass Publics," in David Apter, ed., *Ideology and Discontent* (New York: Free Press, 1964), pp. 206–261.

18 Christopher Ellis and James A. Stimson, *Ideology in America* (New York: Cambridge University Press, 2012).

19 John Zaller and Stanley Feldman, "A Simple Theory of the Survey Response," *American Journal of Political Science* 36 (1992): 579–616.

20 See Pew Research Center for the People & the Press, "Beyond Distrust: How Americans View Their Government," November 23, 2015, at www.people-press.org/2015/11/23/beyond-distrust-how-americans-view-their-government/ (accessed June 29, 2016).

21 See Edward G. Carmines, Michael J. Ensley, and Michael W. Wagner, "Why American Political Parties Can't Get Beyond the Left–Right Divide," in John C. Green, Daniel J. Coffey, and David B. Cohen, *The State of the Parties*, 7th ed. (Lanham, MD: Rowman & Littlefield, 2014), pp. 55–71.

22 Paul R. Abramson, John H. Aldrich, and David W. Rohde, *Change and Continuity in the 1984 Elections* (Washington, DC: CQ Press, 1986), Chapter 6.

23 Alan I. Abramowitz, *The Disappearing Center* (New Haven, CT: Yale University Press, 2009).

24 See Matthew Levendusky, *The Partisan Sort* (Chicago: University of Chicago Press, 2009), and Seth J. Hill and Chris Tausanovitch, "A Disconnect in Representation?" *Journal of Politics* 77 (2015): 1058–1075.

25 Logan Dancey, "Party Identification and Issue Attitudes," in Hershey, ed., *Guide to U.S. Political Parties*, Chapter 19.

26 Pew Research Center, "Political Polarization in the American Public," June 12, 2014, at www.people-press.org/2014/06/12/political-polarization-in-the-ameri can-public/ (accessed June 19, 2016).

27 Ibid.

28 Frank Newport, "Democrats in the U.S. Shift to the Left," Gallup Poll, June 18, 2015, at www.gallup.com/poll/183686/democrats-shift-left.aspx (accessed June 29, 2016).

29 Pew Research Center, "Democrats Have More Positive Image, But GOP Runs Even or Ahead on Key Issues," February 26, 2015, at www.people-press. org/2015/02/26/democrats-have-more-positive-image-but-gop-runs-even-or-ahead-on-key-issues (accessed June 29, 2016).

30 See Shanto Iyengar, Gaurav Sood, and Yphtach Lelkes, "Affect, Not Ideology," *Public Opinion Quarterly* 76 (2012): 405–431.

31 David C. Kimball, Bryce Summary, and Eric C. Vorst, "Political Identity and Party Polarization in the American Electorate," in Green, Coffey, and Cohen, *The State of the Parties*, 7th ed., pp. 37–54.

32 See Markus Prior, *Post-Broadcast Democracy* (New York: Cambridge University Press, 2007).

33 Jennifer Jerit and Jason Barabas, "Partisan Perceptual Bias and the Information Environment," *Journal of Politics* 74 (2012): 672–684.

34 Pew Research Center, "Political Polarization in the American Public."

35 Pew Research Center, "A Wider Ideological Gap between More and Less Educated Adults," April 26, 2016, at www.people-press.org/2016/04/26/a-wider-ideological-gap-between-more-and-less-educated-adults/ (accessed June 29, 2016).

36 See Douglas J. Ahler, "Self-Fulfilling Misperceptions of Public Polarization," *Journal of Politics* 76 (2014): 607–620.

37 John G. Bullock, Alan S. Gerber, Seth J. Hill, and Gregory A. Huber, "Partisan Bias in Factual Beliefs about Politics," *Quarterly Journal of Political Science* 10 (2015): 519–578.

38 Paul Allen Beck, "A Tale of Two Electorates," in John C. Green and Rick Farmer, eds., *The State of the Parties*, 4th ed. (Lanham, MD: Rowman & Littlefield, 2003), pp. 38–53. On the decline in polarization, see Gary C. Jacobson, "The Obama Legacy and the Future of Partisan Conflict," *The Annals* 667 (2016): 72–91.

39 Jacob S. Hacker and Paul Pierson, "Abandoning the Middle," *Perspectives on Politics* 3 (2005): 33–53.

40 For example, see Seth E. Masket and Hans Noel, "Serving Two Masters," *Political Research Quarterly* 64 (2011): 1–20. See also Kyle L. Saunders and Alan I. Abramowitz, "Ideological Realignment and Active Partisans in the American Electorate," *American Politics Research* 32 (2004): 293, and Marjorie Randon Hershey, Nathaniel Birkhead, and Beth C. Easter, "Party Activists and Political Polarization," in Mark D. Brewer and L. Sandy Maisel, eds., *The Parties Respond*, 5th ed. (Boulder, CO: Westview Press, 2013), pp. 75–102.

41 Pew Research Center, "Beyond Distrust." "Politically engaged" is defined as the 48 percent of Republicans and 34 percent of Democrats (including leaners) who say they are registered to vote, vote regularly, and follow politics most of the time.

42 See Seth E. Masket, "It Takes an Outsider," *American Journal of Political Science* 51 (2007): 482–497.

43 See Brandice Canes-Wrone, David W. Brady, and John F. Cogan, "Out of Step, Out of Office," *American Political Science Review* 96 (2002): 127–140. This can also be true of the many candidates who, according to Larry M. Bartels, are even more extreme on important issues than are their party's core supporters. See Bartels, "Failure to Converge," *The Annals* 667 (2016): 143–165.

44 Laurel Harbridge and Neil Malhotra, "Electoral Incentives and Partisan Conflict in Congress," *American Journal of Political Science* 55 (2011): 494–510.

45 John R. Hibbing and Elizabeth Theiss-Morse, "Process Preferences and American Politics," *American Political Science Review* 95 (2001): 145–153.

46 David Von Drehle, "Political Split Is Pervasive," *Washington Post*, April 25, 2004, p. A1.

47 Leon D. Epstein, "What Happened to the British Party Model?" *American Political Science Review* 74 (1980): 9–22.

48 On presidential mandates, see Julia R. Azari, *Delivering the People's Mandate* (Ithaca, NY: Cornell University Press, 2014).

CHAPTER 16

The Place of Parties in American Politics

A change in party control of government affects your life in so many ways. It helps to determine how much you'll pay in taxes and receive in benefits. It affects the ease with which you could buy a gun or have an abortion. It can say "yes" or "no" to gay couples who want to marry or to universities who want to raise your tuition. The government, and therefore the two major parties that drive it, leaves its mark on everything you do, whether you vote or not, and even whether you realize it or not.

Throughout this book you have seen big changes over time in the ways the parties organize for action, the policies they promote, and the relationships they maintain with voters and candidates. The major parties fund their campaigns much differently now from the way they used to. Hillary Clinton and Donald Trump ran for office using very different strategies and tactics from Thomas Jefferson and Abraham Lincoln. The media environment, the nature of the population, and the forms of transportation are light years distant now from what they were early in the republic's existence. But the parties have adapted to this changing landscape and remain a fundamental part of American political life.[1]

This chapter will sum up these changes in relation to a simple but important truth: Political parties are powerfully shaped not only by the people who lead and participate in them but also by the environment in which they act. They are profoundly affected by election and campaign finance rules, interest groups, citizens, legislatures, and courts, just as they influence these forces. In order to understand the changes in party power and behavior over time, we should explore the relationships between parties and their environment.

Parties and Their Environment

Political parties affect their environment in many ways. They promote public policies in response to citizens' beliefs, demands, and fears. They recruit individuals into active roles in politics and government. Through their communications and performance, parties affect public attitudes about the Democrats and Republicans and about politics more generally. Party organizations and the parties in government structure their own environment even more directly as well: They make the rules governing who will get their names on the ballot and who is allowed to cast a vote.

In turn, their environment helps to shape the parties' nature, activities, and effectiveness. Three types of environmental forces have been especially important in influencing the American parties as well as those in other Western democracies: the nature of the electorate, the nation's basic governmental institutions and rules, and the forces that affect the broader society (Table 16.1).[2]

The Nature of the Electorate

The nature and concerns of the voting population are vital influences on a party system. The societal "fault lines" that divide voters into opposing groups—race is one of the clearest and most persistent examples in American politics—help to define the parties' issue agendas. So do the social characteristics that make some groups more likely to vote than others.

TABLE 16.1 Environmental Forces Influencing the American Parties

Types of Influences	Examples
1. Nature of the electorate	Changes in the right to vote, citizens' political interest and knowledge, social characteristics of the electorate (age, race, income)
2. Political institutions and rules	
(a) Institutions	Federalism, separation of powers, single-member districts
(b) Electoral processes	Direct primary, nonpartisan elections
(c) Laws and regulations	Laws governing campaign finance, structure of party organization, voter ID laws
3. Social forces	
(a) National events and conditions	State of the economy, war, terrorism
(b) Other political intermediaries	Types of other organized interests, media, independent consultants
(c) Political culture	Attitudes toward parties and politics

Legislatures and courts have greatly expanded the right to vote in the United States. From an extremely limited suffrage—the small proportion of white male adults who owned property—it now includes the great majority of citizens over the age of 18. Political information has expanded as well. The Internet and other media have made information about politics much more accessible. More citizens have the advantage of higher education, which helps them find and understand the information. We have a lot of tools to affect politics now: primary elections, referenda, recall elections, and Internet access to public officials. Yet most people's interest in politics and their feelings of political effectiveness and trust have not increased. So at the same time as these opportunities for participation expanded, voter turnout dropped. Turnout remains lower in the U.S. than in most other industrialized democracies.

Turnout has not declined to the same degree among all groups in the population. Lower-income Americans' voting rates have declined more steeply than those with greater wealth.[3] At the same time, the income gap between the very wealthy and the rest of the population has grown larger in the United States than in most other industrialized democracies.[4] And as we saw in Chapter 8, the turnout rate of young Americans, though it rose in recent elections, is still much lower than the turnout rate of adults over 65. It is no surprise, then, that Social Security and Medicare are much more frequent campaign issues than are college loans. Those who participate are more likely to be heard.

Political Institutions and Rules

The second set of environmental influences on the parties includes the nation's basic framework of political institutions: whether the government is federal or unitary, whether it is parliamentary or has separated powers, and how its positions of power are structured. Then there are the laws that regulate the parties, ranging from the secret ballot and nonpartisan local elections to federal laws regulating campaign spending.

American political institutions differ in many ways from those of most other democracies.[5] Most democratic nations do not divide governmental powers so insistently among different branches and levels of government. Few other democracies choose most of their leaders in single-member districts with plurality rules for electing officials, or stagger the terms of different types of officials. The direct primary limits the party organization's role in selecting candidates to a degree unknown in most other democracies. American party organizations are regulated more heavily than are other nations' parties. The effect of this regulation—and in most cases its intention—is to restrict the development of the party organizations. An unintended effect is to boost the power of the party in government relative to that of the party organization.

As a result, the major American parties differ in important ways from parties in most other democracies.[6] In particular, the American parties are more decentralized; just as state and local governments have powers independent of the national government, so do state and local party organizations relative to the national party.[7] The two-party system is due in large part to the impact of American political institutions. The strength of the party in government means that the party organization's leaders have few effective tools to keep party legislators and other elected officials acting in accord with the party's stands. To survive independent of a strong party organization, candidates must raise much larger sums of money from private interests and spend much more on campaigns than do their counterparts in other democracies. With the important exceptions of the direct primary and the secret ballot, however, these rules have changed less dramatically over time than has the nature of the electorate, so they are less well able to explain changes in the parties.

Societal Forces

A third set of environmental influences refers to events in the larger society that affect politics at a particular time. Recent terrorist attacks, the relocation of American industries to Mexico and Vietnam, and changes in women's roles have powerfully affected what we talk and think about. Thus, they have become part of the parties' agendas. They affect the parties' platforms, appeals, and supporting coalitions.

These societal forces also include the number and character of organized interests in the nation, the nature and behavior of the media, and other means of representing interests. If people find alternative ways to pursue their political goals that seem more effective than the parties, they will use them. If an interest group is more vocal in opposing abortion or backing gay rights, then why should an individual try to achieve her political aims through a party? The nature of the parties at any given time, then, depends partly on the available alternatives to parties and the competition among them.

All these elements of their environment have contributed to the unique character of the American parties. Thus, as this chapter summarizes the dramatic changes that have occurred in the parties' structure, supporting coalitions, and strength during the past four decades, we will pay special attention to the effects of their environment and above all to changes in the electorate.

Party Decline in the 1960s and 1970s

A basic feature of the American parties is that the three party sectors are bound together only loosely. The party organization has not been able to involve large numbers of party identifiers in its structure and activities, nor has it been able to direct the campaigns or the policy making of the party in government. The party decline that was becoming apparent in the 1960s affected the three sectors very differently.

The Parties in the Electorate

Voters' loyalty to the parties weakened during the late 1960s and 1970s, a time of upheaval in many aspects of American life. What caused the decline? Many voters at this time, especially in the South but also in the Northeast and Mountain West, reacted to the parties' changed stances on race and other issues. These shifts undermined the strong Democratic loyalties of white southerners. Many began to think of themselves as independent "leaners" rather than as strong party identifiers. And just as the growing conservatism of the national Republican Party attracted many white southerners and some westerners, it repelled many liberal and moderate New Englanders who had long considered themselves Republicans. Overall, the early phase of this major coalitional change weakened the party loyalties of a lot of formerly strong partisans, and the parties found themselves with smaller numbers of less loyal identifiers.

Those who remained attached to a party no longer took their party's advice in elections as often as they once did. There was a surge in ticket splitting. By 1968, almost half of the respondents in national surveys said they had voted for more than one party's candidates in state or local elections, and in 1974 that figure topped out at 61 percent. The number of congressional districts selecting a presidential candidate of one party and a congressional candidate of the other party exceeded 30 percent for the first time in history in 1964 and reached 44 percent early in the next decade.[8]

In this turbulent period, some voters became more responsive to the issue-oriented candidacies of the time. The campaigns of Barry Goldwater in 1964, Eugene McCarthy and George Wallace in 1968, and George McGovern in 1972 spurred many people's awareness of political issues. As television came to be used more in campaigns, viewers were drawn to candidates' media images. The attractive faces and lively action that television screens convey evoked some of the support that party symbols once commanded.

To a greater extent than in the past, then, voters became more inclined to respond to candidates as individuals than as members of a party. Some independent candidates ran credible races for president and governor. Because candidates and issues change far more often than parties, the result was a less stable pattern of voting.

Party Organizations

The last of the great party machines were fading by the 1960s and 1970s. The famous Daley machine in Chicago was ripped apart in a series of tumultuous struggles. Party organizations could no longer depend on the patronage and preferments that once were so vital in recruiting party activists. Instead, more people were being drawn into party activism because of their commitment to particular issues. These were better-educated people, and they demanded greater participation in the party's decisions. Some of these new activists felt that standing on principle was more important than winning an election. If their party did not satisfy their ideological goals, they stood ready to leave it for other groups—candidates' campaigns and single-issue organizations— which were more narrowly targeted to meet their needs.

Other aspects of the party organization were under stress as well. As the direct primary came to dominate presidential nominations, party organizations gave up their control over nominations to whoever voted in the primary. By the time a primary season had ended, the party's presidential nominee had been determined, so its nominating convention no longer played a truly independent role. Grassroots activists took much of the party organization's own decision making away from party leaders. This was particularly true of the Democrats, who in 1972 and 1976 nominated presidential candidates well outside the mainstream of their own party.

In addition to their declining influence over nominations, by the 1960s and 1970s the party organizations had lost their central role in campaigns more generally. To run in primaries, candidates now had to build their own campaign organizations and raise their own campaign money. The knowledge and resources they once received from local party organizations could now be obtained directly from pollsters or campaign consulting firms that were, in effect, "rent-a-party" agencies. These professionals offered more sophisticated campaign skills than the party organizations could provide. The national parties began to develop greater technological expertise during the 1970s and to share their resources with state and local parties, but consultants had already established a beachhead. And campaign finance reforms gave candidates an incentive to raise nonparty money at a time when the technologies for doing so were becoming more effective.

Even in the face of new vigor in the national committees, the party organizations in the 1970s remained more decentralized than did life and politics in the United States. Voters were looking more and more to national political leaders and symbols, but the party organizations still tended to be collections of state and local activists.

The Party in Government

In the 1960s and 1970s, elected officials came to depend more than ever on direct appeals to voters. With enough money, candidates could buy media time to speak to constituents. In primary elections, and because of the increased split-ticket voting in general elections, candidates could not rely as much on party identification to generate support. Through personal style, personal appeals, and personally raised funds, they developed a "personal vote" independent of party.[9]

The personal appeals worked. Incumbents' reelection rates rose. That dissuaded attractive challengers from running. When they did, party organizations were not vigorous enough to provide challengers with the campaign resources they so desperately needed. Holding public office became more of a profession—a lifetime career—even at the state and local levels, where political professionals were once rare.

As incumbents became more secure electorally (even though many did not feel that way), members of Congress gained greater freedom from their party organizations. Legislative party leaders found it harder to convince their members to vote for the congressional party's bills. The Democratic Party in Congress was especially diverse, divided between the remaining southern conservatives and northern moderates and liberals. This made congressional Democrats reluctant to grant much power to their legislative party leaders; neither southern nor northern Democrats could trust that legislative party leaders would serve the needs of *all* members of their congressional party. Senate and House Republicans were a varied group as well. So party-line voting in Congress fell to a new low at this time. However, it was a perverse kind of freedom. Protected from the demands of party leaders, legislators were more exposed to other pressures, mainly from growing numbers of interest groups.

Without much competition from unified legislative parties, presidents and governors could exercise greater leadership. Presidents did not depend on their party organizations for much; in fact, with the help of federal campaign money after 1974, presidential candidates could run their campaigns free of obligation to the party organization at any level. By that time, however, divided government had become the norm. That undercut executives' power by permitting the opposition party to block their initiatives.

Shifting Power Centers Within the Parties

These changes had produced a major shift of power within the parties. The party organizations had lost power not only to the individual members of the party in government but also to other intermediaries, especially interest groups and the media. Party organizations and leaders became even more vulnerable to suspicions that they were run by bosses plotting in smoke-filled rooms. Visions of "boss rule" were as much alive in the 1960s and 1970s as they were in the early 1900s, even though, ironically, the party organizations no longer had the resources that could have made boss rule possible.

The result was a peculiar kind of political party. A party organization is the only sector of the party whose interests go beyond winning individual elections. It is the party organization that sustains the party when its candidates lose their races. It is the organization that links the party's officeholders and office seekers and calls them to collective action of the type that parties were created to achieve. Without it, party candidates are individual entrepreneurs seeking individual goals in a political system that requires collective decisions. The decline of the party organizations was a major force in the decline of the parties more generally.

Party Renewal Since the 1980s

This marked decline was not the end of the story, however. The American parties responded to these challenges, just as they have adapted to changing circumstances at other times. The steady decay of the parties was stopped and reversed, but some of the changes that took place in the 1960s and 1970s continue to leave their imprint even now. The parties have had to adjust to new roles in American politics.

Change in the Parties' Electoral Coalitions

The slow, steady change in the parties' supporting coalitions since the 1960s (see Chapter 7) also changed the nature of the party system. The most striking elements of this coalitional change have been the movement of white southerners into the Republican Party, which led to a dramatic decline of Democratic strength in the South (see Figure 16.1), and the growth of almost uniform Democratic identification among black Americans. Other demographic characteristics not normally associated with the party division have taken on a partisan tinge. Religious conservatives, both Catholic and

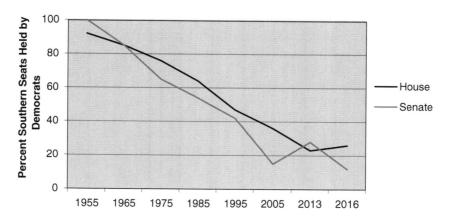

Figure 16.1 Eroding Democratic Strength in the South: U.S. House and Senate Seats, 1955–2016

Note: Data points are the percentage of U.S. senators and House members from the 13 southern states (Alabama, Arkansas, Florida, Georgia, Kentucky, Louisiana, Mississippi, North Carolina, Oklahoma, South Carolina, Tennessee, Texas, Virginia) who are Democrats.

Source: Data for 1955–1995 from *Congressional Quarterly Weekly Report*, November 12, 1994: 3231. Data for 2005, 2013, and 2016 compiled by the author from www.Senate.gov and www.House.gov (accessed June 12, 2016).

Protestant, are now a major force within the GOP. Marital status and sexual orientation have become related to partisanship; unmarried people (especially women) and gay people now identify mainly as Democrats.

These coalitional changes have transformed a Democratic-dominated political environment into one of close party competition in national politics. Republicans won both the presidency and the Senate in 1980 and gained control of both the House and Senate in 1994—the first time since 1954 that there was a Republican majority in both Houses of Congress. In the 1990s and at times in the 2000s, Republicans came closer to parity with the Democrats in both party ID and election results than they had since the 1930s. And after the 2010 midterms, Republicans won back the House, held more state legislative seats than at any point since 1929, and controlled a majority of state legislatures, even though Democrats won the presidency in 2012. Republicans won unified control of the national government in 2016.

Which Party Will Gain the Advantage?

This close party division at the national level has made election results very volatile. After their victories in 2002 and 2004, Republican candidates lost big in 2006 and 2008. Even in the South, Barack Obama won many suburban counties in North Carolina and Virginia, where educational levels are rising and high-technology jobs make up an increasing share of the economy. The ability of Democratic candidates to increase their margins among more educated and upper-income voters in all regions and to attract large majorities of the fastest-growing segments of the electorate—young people and Latinos—led to claims that the Republican Party was in serious trouble.[10]

Republicans feverishly debated what went wrong. Conservative Republicans charged that their party had sacrificed its principles (small government in particular) when it gained power and pandered to voters' desire for tangible benefits in order to win a lasting Republican majority. The declining number of moderate Republicans disagreed. Many warned that the party's hard-line stands on social issues, dear to the hearts of white evangelical Christians, were limiting the party's attractiveness to independents. They argued that to improve GOP prospects, the party would have to become more inclusive and work harder to attract more young people, Latinos, and women.

But this prescription was a hard pill for Republican activists to swallow. The steps needed to appeal to a wider audience might alienate the Republican base. Energized by the small-government enthusiasts of the Tea Party and driven by outright hostility toward President Obama, the base had dominated the 2010 and 2014 midterms, contributing to the biggest Republican House majorities in 60 years. In the period of divided party government that followed, Tea Party supporters pressed Republican congressional leaders to shun even the appearance of cooperation with Obama as a means of cementing their majority.

On the other hand, the groups forming the Republican base—married, white Christians—are shrinking as a proportion of the total electorate. The nonwhite share of the voting public, which tends to be more supportive of government social programs and services, doubled during the past two decades.[11] Unless the GOP finds issues that resonate with nonwhites and younger voters, or unless Democratic strength in these groups drops, a "base strategy" would become a risky choice.

Donald Trump's victory in 2016 gives new energy to the Republican base in the short run. Trump's winning coalition mobilized a larger proportion of whites without a college degree than have other recent Republican presidential candidates, which convinced some analysts that the Republicans could rely on socially conservative, nativist appeals indefinitely. But Trump's successes with non-college whites are new only in degree, not in kind: think of the white, working-class "Reagan Democrats" who have been a voice in the Republican Party for decades.

The longer term is less encouraging for the Republicans. The demographic changes that will make the U.S. a majority-minority nation within decades cannot be changed by the ballot box. The winners, as always, will be those who adapt. And their successes will be solidified by the continuing power of partisan identification, as demonstrated by the nine in ten identifiers who voted for the nominee of their party in 2016.

In any case, it is clear that we are now in a different party system from that of the New Deal. This sixth party system emerged differently from the New Deal party system. In contrast with the relatively quick political changes that accompanied the Depression of the 1930s, the subsequent shifts in party coalitions have developed over several decades and continue to evolve. In recent years, neither party has dominated for long. Polls show very little public enthusiasm for the major parties or, for that matter, many other aspects of American politics.

Thus, the events of the 1960s and 1970s produced an ongoing challenge to party loyalties. Large numbers of voters now rely on sources other than the parties, such as cable TV, blogs, and single-issue groups, for their political information. Sometimes these sources reinforce partisan views; in other cases, they don't.[12] Yet even with this formidable competition, parties remain important landmarks on most people's political maps. Levels of party identification rebounded beginning in the 1990s, and partisanship is now at least as strong an influence on people's voting as it was before the 1960s.[13] Split-ticket voting, especially as measured by the number of districts voting for a presidential candidate of one party and a congressional candidate of the other, hit a 50-year low in 2012.[14]

The Rise of More Cohesive Parties in Government

Well before the current revival of partisanship among voters—and one likely cause of it—the parties in government had begun a revival of their own. By the mid-1970s, the long decline in party unity in Congress had stopped and the organizational seeds had been sown for greater party strength. By the 1980s, the congressional parties were becoming more cohesive than they had been in a century. The slow, steady movement among voters from the Democratic "solid South" to a largely Republican South left both congressional parties more homogeneous, which in turn made it easier for each party to offer clear alternatives on big issues.

Demographic changes as well as redistricting caused more and more congressional districts to become safe for one party. By 2017, there were not many Congress members left representing states or districts where their party was in the minority.[15] As a result, the main threat to their reelection would come from more extreme elements within their own party rather than from the other party. Forces pushing incumbents to become more polarized—for Republicans to become more conservative and Democrats more liberal—outweighed pleas for bipartisanship and moderation. Especially "for the overwhelming majority of House Republicans, the largely white, resolutely conservative electorate that Mitt Romney relied on … is all they need to ensure reelection" to their House seats.[16] State legislative parties were also becoming more unified and polarized on issues.

Partisanship became more important in the executive branch as well. The Reagan administration came into office in 1981 as the most ideologically committed in decades. Reagan's leadership placed conservative principles at the top of the GOP's agenda and solidified the hold of his brand of conservatives on the party. The Democrats became more unified in response. By the mid-1990s, there was intense partisan conflict between a programmatically committed, Republican-led Congress and an activist Clinton White House. The battles have continued, resulting in a level of incivility and gridlock that can bring Congress to its knees. Consider one House member's recollection of a new member orientation program in which a Democratic leadership staff member suggested the importance of getting to know Republican legislators. One of the new Democrats replied, "Why would we want to do that?"[17]

The New "Service Parties"

The party organizations have revived just as dramatically. Facing an environment of candidate-centered campaigns, both parties retooled their national organizations to provide services to the party's candidates. They have used their increased funding and staffing to help state and local parties, recruit candidates, provide resources, and thus step up their role in campaigns, compared with the 1960s and 1970s.

The new service party, however, differs a great deal from the grassroots organizations of earlier years. Because its main role is to support candidates, it is not very visible to voters, nor can it always make a major impact on campaigns. In the big-spending world of campaign finance, party organizations do not bring enough money to the table to be able to dominate political campaigning. The service party is one of many forces trying to win the attention of candidates, influence elected officials, and mobilize citizens.

The party organizations, in short, are more vigorous now than they have been in years. There is a greater balance of power between the national and state and local parties now. Party organizations have adapted to new conditions by taking on a new form: the service party. However, as service parties, the party organizations are no longer as distinctive as they used to be in the sense of providing campaign resources that no other group could deliver. The main exception here is both parties' immense national databases of information on voters. But even these are not wholly under the control of the national party organizations.

Keep in mind, however, that the two major parties are not mirror images of one another. Although they have both transformed themselves into service parties and become more internally cohesive and more different from one another in their policies, they have followed different paths in doing so.[18] As Chapter 10 showed, the parties strengthened their national organizations for different reasons and in different ways. Although party polarization has led both parties in Congress to grant more power to their parties' leaders, the polarization has been asymmetric: the Republican Party in Congress has moved further to the right than the Democrats have moved to the left.[19] The Republicans in particular seem to have energized a new constituency in the 1990s and 2000s: white males without a college education who feel they have lost their status in the economy and in the community and who see government as the culprit.

The Future of Party Politics in America

These trends affect us because political parties are capable of doing important jobs for a democracy. Parties can enable political leaders to work together in achieving shared interests over time. They can provide cues that help voters make decisions on candidates and issues with relatively little effort. They can bring voters to the polls, which helps to legitimize a democracy. Perhaps most important, parties organize majorities, which are necessary for governing. Interest groups such as super PACs can effectively represent intense minorities, but there are not many alternatives to the parties for organizing lasting and predictable majorities.

A Changing Intermediary Role

Elections require voters to make large numbers of choices, even though most voters don't know much about most candidates. Parties serve as efficient guides. The value of the party label in elections is probably greatest when a mass electorate has just begun to develop and has serious need for information. As the electorate matures, its needs change. One explanation for American voters' decreased reliance on party loyalties in the 1960s and 1970s was that voters had become better educated than was the electorate in the early 1900s, and could sift through a broader range of political messages without the need for party labels as a guide.[20]

It is interesting, then, that although education levels have continued to increase since the 1960s, party identification has reasserted its influence on voters' choices. Why should partisanship help citizens who have so many other sources of information about candidates and issues? Perhaps it is *because* they are exposed to so much information. Without this simple guide, the blizzard of political messages could confuse voters rather than inform them. At the same time, the fact that the two major parties have drawn farther apart from one another on important issues lends even more value to the party labels for politically engaged citizens. Added to the heightened party competition in the 2010s and the resulting intensity of campaign messages, an individual's party tie can become more meaningful to him or her than any other political cues.

The parties face greater competition now from organized interests and the media. A century ago, someone concerned about environmental quality would probably have had to pursue his or her goals through a political party; not many groups focused specifically on energy or water pollution. Now, however, along with the growing reach of government into most aspects of private life, a huge array of organized interests has developed permitting individuals to establish a "designer link" with the political system. If someone prefers to see politics entirely from the perspective of environmental rights, or property rights, there are several groups to make that possible. There is no need to compromise or support a coalition of other groups' needs and a range of candidates, as a party loyalty would encourage.

In this fractured political world, parties take on greater significance as a means of broadening individuals' perspectives and improving their ability to hold elected officials accountable. The parties have long struggled with hostile environmental forces, from a system of separated powers that is inhospitable to strong parties to a political culture suspicious of all parties. However, as we have seen throughout this book, the parties are adaptable. They are not the intermediaries they were in 1900 or 1950, but for large numbers of Americans and for the policy-making process, the major parties remain the most important intermediaries.

The Need for Strong Parties

Although we need parties, we don't like them. We don't even like to admit that they influence us. Most of us claim that issues and candidates' personal qualities have the biggest impact on our votes. Yet it's clear that partisanship is closely related to our attitudes toward issues and candidates and is the source of much of their influence.

Democracy is unworkable without parties.[21] The United States has probably come closer to testing that principle than any other democracy; much of American local politics has been, at least officially, nonpartisan for some time. But when parties are reduced to playing a smaller role in politics, the quality of democracy can be weakened.

Consider the role strong parties can play in Congress and state legislatures. As a representative body, Congress is structured to permit legislators to give their constituents what they want: short-term, tangible benefits such as disaster relief, expanded Medicare benefits, and jobs on federal projects. Legislators facing reelection seek the Holy Grail of constituent service: a project such as a new dam or highway that provides tangible benefits to their own constituents but whose costs are paid by taxpayers all over the country. But if the individual voter and the individual legislator are motivated to pay close attention to the benefits they can get for their district, who is motivated to think about the collective cost? Very few voters support the idea of raising their own taxes in order to pay for benefits to others, or even to pay for benefits to themselves.

Strong legislative parties have an incentive to take responsibility for the collective costs.[22] Some legislative party members can gain personal career advantages by becoming leaders of their congressional party. When the party's members in Congress are elected from similar districts and hold similar views, they can afford to trust these legislative party leaders with greater power to structure the choices they will make. Members realize that although their own reelection needs are primary, they also need coordination within the legislature in order to pass bills and to help with the endless tasks of legislative life.

By using the carrots and sticks discussed in Chapter 13, legislative party leaders can induce their party colleagues to make truly national policy, not just "Christmas tree" legislation that consists of government-spending ornaments for each congressional district. By holding their legislators to this party program, legislative party leaders can create a favorable brand name for their party in elections, which voters can come to recognize and associate with their own district's candidate. In the absence of strong parties, it is difficult to imagine where this collective responsibility might come from. Without strong parties, individual members of Congress and state legislatures have every reason to behave in ways that conflict with their collective interest and that of their constituents.[23]

In a society dominated by interest groups and other intermediaries, most people would not be as well represented. Among the many links between citizens and government, only the parties have the incentive to create majorities in order to win a wide range of elections over a long period. In turn, that gives the parties, to a greater extent than interest groups or even elected officials, a reason to pay attention to those citizens who are not activists or big campaign contributors. As political scientist Walter Dean Burnham has written, parties are the only devices that can "generate countervailing collective power on behalf of the many individually powerless against the relatively few who are individually—or organizationally—powerful."[24]

It is the parties that can mobilize sheer numbers against the organized minorities that hold other political resources. The parties do so in the one political arena where sheer numbers count most heavily: elections. Because of that, parties traditionally have been the means by which newly enfranchised but otherwise powerless groups gained a foothold in American life. The old-style urban machines, for example, provided the instrument with which immigrants won control of their cities from the more established Anglo-Saxon Protestant elites.

In a less party-driven politics, well-organized minorities with critical resources—money, insider knowledge, and technological expertise—would have even greater advantages than they do now. As we have seen from research on nonpartisan elections, eliminating the party symbol often makes it tougher for citizens to hold their representatives responsible.[25] That may be one reason why voter participation has declined more sharply in recent decades among poorer and less educated Americans; they may feel less represented by a politics in which the parties are no longer preeminent,[26] even if they fail to see party change as the cause.

Finally, weakened parties would rob the political system of an effective means of governing. Without at least moderately strong parties, it is harder to mobilize majorities to pass legislation. Individual candidates, freed from party loyalties, would have to recreate majorities for every new legislative proposal. The result could be even greater gridlock, in which legislatures splinter into conflicting and intransigent groups.

It is true that the congressional parties have not distinguished themselves in resolving contentious issues recently. As Frances Lee points out, the frequent changes of party control in Congress combined with greater polarization have motivated the congressional parties to behave irresponsibly, to make points rather than to make policy.[27] But in practice, it is hard to imagine 535 House members and senators reaching any agreement at all without parties. Laws and policies could continue to be made only by shifting coalitions of elected officials, campaign contributors, and interest groups. Because these coalitions would be less permanent and less identifiable to the public, it would be much harder for citizens to hold them accountable.

How to Make the Parties Stronger

Because parties bring so much value to American democracy, some analysts have considered ways to expand the parties' role in political life. The most effective solutions—ending the separation of powers, the direct primary, and the antiparty sentiment engrained into the political culture—are not on the table, of course. But there are less dramatic ways to strengthen the parties.

One survey showed that most respondents would like the parties to be more active in helping people deal with government. Its authors propose, among other ideas, that party organizations could create "mobile units" to help citizens in areas where the U.S. (and perhaps the state) representative is from the other party. That would allow the party organization, not just members of the party in government, to perform constituent service. They note that this idea was especially attractive to respondents who described themselves as alienated from politics. By providing attractive nonpolitical benefits such as low-cost health insurance, as many interest groups do now, parties could help to build long-term loyalty among their volunteers.[28] Parties could also renew their connection with citizens by airing campaign ads promoting the party as a whole, rather than just individual candidates. These ads could strengthen the meaning of party by stressing the link between the party's stands and individuals' daily lives. And more states could join those letting taxpayers contribute to a party organization through the state tax system.

Conclusion: The Parties' Prospects

The American parties have never lacked interesting challenges. The electorate has become more and more varied. Some traditional group ties have broken down. New groups, ranging from those opposed to same-sex marriage to those favoring for-profit prisons, are tilling the ground that the major parties once owned. Most voters still identify with a party, but they also respond to candidates, issues, and national trends. The result is a more diverse, complicated politics that frustrates elected officials, party leaders, voters, and nonvoters.

The parties can't meet every political need. We can't expect the parties in government to get along if we elect candidates who are proud of their refusal to compromise. Parties find it hard to offer policy alternatives in campaigns without engaging in the conflict that many Americans find so distasteful. It is difficult for parties to unite their officeholders and office seekers on a single agenda while giving candidates the independence to choose their own appeals and meet their own districts' needs. Parties can't provide accountability to a public that wants to choose candidates individually.

Americans will continue to challenge the parties with these conflicting expectations and criticisms. The parties' distinctive character has sustained them longer than any other tool of democratic politics. For the sake of representation, effective policy making, and accountability in governance, even the most independent-minded citizens have a stake in sustaining vigorous party politics in the United States.

Notes

1 See Seth E. Masket, *The Invincible Party* (New York: Oxford University Press, 2016).
2 The classic source is Robert Harmel and Kenneth Janda, *Parties and Their Environments* (New York: Longman, 1982).
3 See Ruy A. Teixeira, *The Disappearing American Voter* (Washington, DC: Brookings Institution, 1992), Chapter 3.
4 Kay Lehman Schlozman, Sidney Verba, and Henry E. Brady, *The Unheavenly Chorus* (Princeton, NJ: Princeton University Press, 2012).
5 See Stephen K. Medvic, *Campaigns and Elections* (Boston: Wadsworth, 2010), pp. 312–314.
6 See Paul Allen Beck, "Parties in the American Political Environment," in Marjorie Randon Hershey, ed., *Guide to U.S. Political Parties* (Los Angeles: Sage, 2014), Chapter 5.
7 Robert Harmel, Matthew Giebert, and Kenneth Janda, *American Parties in Context* (New York: Routledge, 2016), Chapter 4.
8 Harold W. Stanley and Richard G. Niemi, *Vital Statistics on American Politics 1999–2000* (Washington, DC: CQ Press, 2000), pp. 44 and 133.
9 Bruce E. Cain, John Ferejohn, and Morris P. Fiorina, *The Personal Vote* (Cambridge, MA: Harvard University Press, 1987).
10 Philip A. Klinkner and Thomas Schaller, "LBJ's Revenge," *The Forum* 6 (2008), issue 4, article 9.
11 CNN exit poll at www.cnn.com/election/2012/results/race/president (accessed June 13, 2016).
12 See Robert Huckfeldt and Paul Allen Beck, "Contexts, Intermediaries, and Political Activity," in Lawrence C. Dodd and Calvin Jillson, eds., *The Dynamics of American Politics* (Boulder, CO: Westview Press, 1994), Chapter 11. On the other hand, organized interests have become more polarized by party since the Reagan years; see Jack L. Walker, Jr., *Mobilizing Interest Groups in America* (Ann Arbor, MI: University of Michigan Press, 1991), Chapter 8, and media coverage frequently refers to party; see Marjorie Randon Hershey, "If 'The Party's in Decline,' Then What's That Filling the News Columns?" in Nelson W. Polsby and Raymond E. Wolfinger, eds., *On Parties* (Berkeley, CA: Institute of Governmental Studies, 1999), pp. 257–278.
13 Larry M. Bartels, "Partisanship and Voting Behavior, 1952–1996," *American Journal of Political Science* 44 (2000): 35–50.
14 Thanks to Bruce Oppenheimer for calculating this information.
15 Alan I. Abramowitz, *The Polarized Public* (Boston: Pearson, 2013), p. 94.
16 Alex Isenstadt, "Logic of House GOP Intransigence," *Politico*, December 28, 2012, at www.politico.com/story/2012/12/the-logic-of-house-gop-intransigence-85546.html?hp=110 (accessed June 13, 2016).

17 Rep. Daniel Lipinski, "Navigating Congressional Policy Processes," in Lawrence C. Dodd and Bruce I. Oppenheimer, eds., *Congress Reconsidered*, 9th ed. (Washington, DC: CQ Press, 2009), p. 344.

18 See Daniel Galvin, *Presidential Party Building* (Princeton, NJ: Princeton University Press, 2010).

19 See Matt Grossmann and David A. Hopkins, "Ideological Republicans and Group Interest Democrats," *Perspectives on Politics* 13 (2015): 119–139.

20 See Ronald Inglehart, *Culture Shift* (Princeton, NJ: Princeton University Press, 1990), Chapters 10 and 11.

21 John H. Aldrich, *Why Parties? A Second Look* (Chicago: University of Chicago Press, 2011), p. 3; and Nancy L. Rosenblum, *On the Side of the Angels* (Princeton, NJ: Princeton University Press, 2008).

22 David R. Mayhew, *Congress: The Electoral Connection* (New Haven, CT: Yale University Press, 1974), especially pp. 141–149.

23 See Marjorie Randon Hershey, "Political Parties as Mechanisms of Social Choice," in Richard S. Katz and William Crotty, eds., *Handbook of Party Politics* (London: Sage, 2005), pp. 75–88.

24 Walter Dean Burnham, *Critical Elections and the Mainsprings of American Politics* (New York: Norton, 1970), p. 133.

25 See Gerald C. Wright and Brian F. Schaffner, "The Influence of Party," *American Political Science Review* 96 (2002): 367–379.

26 See Steven J. Rosenstone and John Mark Hansen, *Mobilization, Participation, and Democracy in America* (New York: Macmillan, 1993), Chapter 8.

27 Frances E. Lee, "Parties as Coordinators: Can Parties Unite What the Constitution Divides?," in Hershey, ed., *Guide to U.S. Political Parties*, Chapter 3.

28 Larry J. Sabato and Bruce Larson, *The Party's Just Begun* (New York: Longman, 2002), pp. 156–160.

INDEX